THE ITALIAN AMERICAN EXPERIENCE

THE ITALIAN AMERICAN EXPERIENCE

Philip di Franco

TOR

A TOM DOHERTY ASSOCIATES BOOK
NEW YORK

THE ITALIAN AMERICAN EXPERIENCE

Copyright © 1988 by RGA Publishing Group, Inc. and
J. Philip di Franco

A TOR BOOK
Published by Tom Doherty Associates, Inc.
49 West 24 Street
New York, NY 10010

Library of Congress Cataloging-in-Publication Data

Di Franco, J. Philip.
  The Italian Americans/by Philip di Franco.—1st ed.
      p.   cm.
  "TOR books."
  ISBN 0-312-93094-1
  1. Italian Americans—History. I. Title.
E184.I8D47 1988b
973'.0451—dc19   88-12172
                                                           CIP

First edition: October 1988

0 9 8 7 6 5 4 3 2 1

This book is dedicated to my beautiful family—the di Franco family from Lercara Friddi known throughout Sicily as "La Francame" in times long ago but not forgotten. . . .

To my forebears, especially my grandparents Josephine and Bartolo (who I loved so dearly) and Josephine and Anthony, who found their dreams across the sea in America. To my mother and father Josephine and Salvator, who kept those dreams alive and inspired them in their children. To my brothers Paul and Roland and my "sister" Odette, who carry those dreams now. To my son Jesse, my nephew Jean-Paul and my nieces Tamar and Gianna, who take these dreams into the future. To my brothers and sisters by "comparatico" Joshua "ZAO" Rappaport, Gunnar Louis Keel, Richard "Hap" Housman, Harold Steinberg, Michael Spirito, Philip Graziano, Diane Belmonte and Leda Sanford.

And to all those who dream dreams and are willing to pay the price to make them come true.

Acknowledgments

THERE IS *no* way this dream could have been realized without certain people who gave of themselves far beyond the call of duty. Each has given to me and I want each to know how much he or she is truly appreciated. . . .

From the beginning, Jack Artenstein, my agent, believed in this book and sold it. Tom Doherty believed in it and bought and published it. Michael Seidman was my editor. Al Dempsey carried me, like Charon the Ferryman, between Scylla and Charybdis through the treacherous waters of editing the manuscript. Lisa Aimi held my hand dearly and made the journey a success. Our copyeditor safely landed us ashore with the finished manuscript.

The creation of this book from my head to words on paper would not have been possible without Diane Hill, the "Angel" sent from heaven, who nursed the manuscript into existence through her word processor, Rick Oliver, the "Godsend," who came out of the blue to make it happen, and Judy Parks, a true friend in need, who helped write and edit many parts of it.

For their knowledge, insight and wisdom into the craziness of the Italian American experience, I thank Giovanni Cecchetti, Lucille De George, Richard Gambino, Joseph Giordano, Ron Quartararo, George Randazzo, Aileen Sirey and Lydia Tomasi. Special thanks to the late Giovanni Schiavo, truly the most dedicated chronicler of Italian American history.

In the tradition of the Renaissance, I have had patrons who as angels have saved my life more than once. For their love, support and belief in my work, I especially thank Angelo R. Mozilo and Robert J. Donato who were with me from the start. Also, Joseph J. DioGuardi, Edgar Lucidi, Ralph Di Libero, Vic Cavallaro, Paul Alongi, Richard A. Grace, Sam Perricone, Pat

Gabriele, Nick Mastroni, Rick Ricciardelli, Peter Sammartino and, especially, an *old friend* and former classmate.

I thank my dear friends Jeno Paulucci and Frank Stella for their help and assistance, and especially for their ongoing support of the Italian American community through the National Italian American Foundation. I also thank my dear Italian American friends and colleagues who have shared many crazy and memorable experiences with me working in the insane world of Italian American affairs.

Finally, I thank my own personal friends who have helped me to survive this experience through their love.

Contents

Preface

What the son forgets,
The grandson remembers.
　　　　—Saying in sociology

THE REASONS for writing this book are simple enough. The Italians and Italian Americans have contributed more to the world than any single ethnic group in history. . . yet their story has been *unknown*. Also, their story has never been told from beginning to end. This story screams to be told, from top to bottom.

In addition, the image of Italian Americans has been so tarnished by the media that the time has come to set the record straight. They have been characterized as criminals, lawless gangsters or *mafiosi* for over a century, an outrageous and frustrating state of affairs indeed. For a population of twenty or so million Italian Americans to be tainted with an image of being Mafia because of the criminal behavior of a tiny iota of a percent of Italian American mobsters is absurd and criminal in itself. To make matters worse, the prevailing romantic image of the Mafia has been perpetuated, ironically, by Italian Americans themselves in books, films, television, newspapers, magazines and the media. Nor is this a trivial matter, for the lives and careers of many an Italian American have been adversely affected by this negative stereotyping. This book seeks to present a true and positive image of who and what Italian Americans *really* are and what they have done for the world.

This book is rooted essentially in the belief that the successful achievements of Italians and Italian Americans stems from the *values* and *meanings* of a unique people's culture and civilization created over many centuries and shaped by forces of destiny unlike that of any other people.

One way to understand the importance of the contributions that have resulted from Italian values and meanings is to take away *everything* Italian from the world and see what is left. What a bare, lifeless place this would be! Another way is to tell the story of the Italians and Italian Americans, and let the values and meanings emerge intrinsically from the telling. While the former case yields an empty canvas, the latter case has yielded this book. We have provided a road map to guide you, the reader, through this odyssey by having Professor Francis X. Feminella present a picture of Italian values and meanings in his introduction following this preface. These values and meanings permeate the lives of all those I have written about in this book.

I have attempted to tell a story that hopefully will help any person of Italian heritage understand what it means to be Italian in origin, a perplexing and complex state of affairs at the least. Italian Americans of all generations have always seemed to be somewhat conflicted over their Italianness. While the first generation of Italian Americans held onto the values of their old world while struggling to survive in their new world, and while the second generation Italian Americans devoured the values of their new world while struggling to forget their old world, the destiny of the third generation Italian Americans was to rediscover the values and meanings of their rich Italian culture and heritage. The grandchildren were destined to record the history of their grandparents.

I wrote this book to *remember* that which my grandparents fought so hard to *forget,* so that my children and my children's children will *never* forget the fire, the energy and the creativity of Italians that have brought the world such great riches. My prayer is that these children will also have burn, within the smithy of their souls, the Italian passion for life and the art of living.

—Philip di Franco
July, 1988
Los Angeles, California

Foreword
Italian American Identity

Francis X. Femminella, Ph. D.
Associate Professor of Sociology and Education
State University of New York at Albany

Italian Americans have made it! This is the time of the Italians in America. Italian faces appear as American heroes on the covers of important magazines and newspapers. There are successful Italians found in every field of endeavor—from art to zymurgy; they excel in business and industry, in politics and government, in education and the media, in religion and in medicine, in science and in sports. With all this achievement, and the vast public recognition of it, one might suppose that Italian Americans know who they are.

But however surprising it may be, these questions are asked again and again by Italian Americans: "Who are we?" and "Why are we the way we are?" Italian Americans seem to have a puzzling dimension whose nature is elusive and which makes them feel that while they know they *are* Americans, they bear little resemblance to other Americans. This sense of feeling apart appears to be somewhat exaggerated in the minds of Italian Americans and, perhaps, with good reason.

Americans are a people long obsessed with the establishment of their identity. This fascination with identity has its antecedents in a number of sources, including a high mobility, the relative recentness of our founding and the duality of our heritage. Each and every American has, simultaneously, both a *domestic* and an *alien* heritage. All Americans have their origins in another nation, yet, by virtue of citizenship, through naturalization or by birth, each shares, fully and equally, the

xiii

heritage of this nation. Each participates in the governance of the nation, in the general determination of its aims and goals and in its life. These are given conditions of democracy.

It is not unusual to hear that America does not have a culture of its own. Today, the people of the United States have a little more of a sense of their uniqueness and their ways; nevertheless, as much as ever, they lack a clear sense of what it is they should be about. Small wonder, then, that Italian Americans feel the way they do, for, in fact, they are an integral part of American society. They resemble other Americans in most ways, yet differ in some ways. One particular way they are unlike other Americans is the sense they have that Italian Americans have a special mission to perform for this nation as they have become integrated into it, a mission related to the unity of the diverse peoples of the nation. Another way they differ is in the heightened, gnawing sense so many of them have that they are a disparate people.

The source of this feeling of dissimilarity is, in part, the result of interpersonal relations with the wider society, wherein Italian Americans were treated as though they were different from other Americans in ways that set them apart and posited them as an inferior people in intelligence, in moral character and in general eminence. Beyond the external press and pressure there is, additionally, an internal force which generates within many Italian Americans the belief that somehow they are essentially *not* like other Americans. This confusion engenders in the sensitive ones the questions: "Who are we?" and "Why are we the way we are?"

The first problem we have when we attempt to describe and analyze *Italian American identity* is that we tend to project our belief that the concept is relevant for the population we are dealing with. Is there such a thing as "Italian American identity" or is the construct totally without actual concrete referents. What do the words refer to? The term "identity" means different things to different people but a conventional meaning derives from the Latin origin of the term: *idem*, meaning "same." Identity may refer to the "sameness" of oneself. Freud used the term *identitaet* to refer to his connection to his heritage, to his Jewishness. Erik Erikson uses the term in a similar fashion, adding more profound embellishment to the notion, so that it becomes a powerful concept for analysis.

What comes clearly out of this is the distinction between identity as the sense, from within, of one's selfsameness, and, on the other hand, identity that comes from outside of oneself as the result of others' ascribing characteristics and qualities to us. That is, we have an understanding of who we are from within ourselves and we believe we are what others have told us we are.

We also think of ourselves as belonging to this or that group. We name ourselves with their name and so we have an identification with them. But *identification* and *identity* are not the same thing. To avoid any confusion, we define the term that Erikson uses, namely, *ego-identity*, which refers to a stage in human personal development:

> The term ego-identity points . . . to an individual's link with the unique values fostered by a unique history of his people. Yet it is also related to the cornerstone of this individual's unique development. . . . It is this identity of something in the individual's core with an essential aspect of a group's inner coherence; . . . for the young individual must learn to be most himself where he means most to others—those others, to be sure, who have come to mean most to him. The term identity expresses a mutual relation in that it connotes both a persistent sharing of some kind of essential character with others. . . . At one time then, it will appear to refer to a conscious *sense of individual identity*, at another to an unconscious striving for a *continuity of personal character;* at a third as a criterion for the silent doings of ego-synthesis; and finally, as a maintenance of an inner *solidarity* with a group's ideals and identity.

Erikson's notion of ego-identity very meaningfully bridges the gap between individual and group identifications. For each of us there is, first of all, a sense of ourselves and a concern for ourselves. This is the first and most primitive "passion" and the *first level of identification*. Next we identify with our family, immediate and, especially for Italians, extended, constituting the *second level of identification.*

In a sort of psychic sequence, we are next connected to some people who are not really our relatives at all, but whom we feel close to, whether we know them or not, bound by feelings of belonging with them, due to some mythical sense of a common fatherhood, and with whom we feel some consciousness of being one. We share a sense of "peoplehood" and this is the *third level of identification,* and referred to as our *ethnic identification.*

The *fourth level of identification* is our connection to our nation. For many, this causes confusion and paradox because they feel that loyalty to the United States implies disloyalty to one's forebears. For Italian Americans nothing could be further from the truth. There is no disloyalty first, because most "Italians" who came to North America at the turn of the century had little identification with Italy, a newly formed nation, but rather identified strongly with their villages and provinces. Secondly, Italians themselves believed that *"che paese vai, usanza che trovi!"* When in Rome, do as the Romans do!

Finally, as we piece together our loyalties to ourselves, our families, our ethnic communities and our nation, we see the futility of narrow self-centeredness and we appreciate the place we occupy and the value we derive from a world view. International identifications begin to rise. The *fifth level of identification* then, is our global identification with all human-kind.

Probably the most accurate statement that can be made about Italian Americans is that no single distinguishing trait describes Italian Americans, who are, for the most part, descendants of a village people, exhibiting extensive heterogeneity. And no set of traits depicts *all* Italian Americans. Yet, there are some qualities, not unique in and of themselves, that seem to be associated with this people. These characteristic attitudes, values and norms, together with their stylistic expression, constitute an holistic, idiosyncratic *total configuration* that might be useful for portraying Italian Americans in general. This configuration with its internal contradictions and disconti-nuities is a distinctive complex of cultural attributes—*themes*—

that sets Italian Americans apart from other Americans.

The themes are found in *individuals,* and thus it may be said that the group is within the person; and since they are group-related, they are ethnic. The themes are an aspect of ego-identity in that they are the guiding lights that direct the individual in his life choices, setting for him the standards of right and wrong, of good and bad, of beautiful and ugly, etc. Hence they are ideological. We call these *"ethnic ideological themes"* that are transmitted from generation to generation neither through genetic inheritance nor solely through socialization. Socialization is obviously the major process by which one inherits culture, but today we understand that constitutional predispositions play a role as well. These themes are long-lasting, since they are situated deep within the individual's personality, even beyond any conscious processing of them. They are *habits of life* of the immigrants, and the *habits of thought and memory* of their progeny.

Putting the following list of leit-motifs together, we see the following paragraph discussed the generalized life patterns of Italians, remembering our earlier caution that these are highly diversified and heterogeneous people and therefore defy simple characterizations. What is important is the total configuration.

Devotion to famliy and environment is united in the village mentality—*"campanilismo."* This engenders behaviors and predispositions that sometimes appear contradictory. The village people are often suspicious of one another. They are often quarrelsome, vituperative and even violent. Ashamed of their behavior, they are self-critical. They are very distrustful with respect to specific interests. But they can be infinitely generous, giving without expectation of receiving in return. Life is thought to be determined by destiny, from which one can escape only by helping others to be free. One must be independent; but in time of emergency one seeks help only in the family. Doing things individualistically is to do for the family. Women especially are found to be active and hard working, enterprising and courageous. Both men and women exhibit fidelity to a goal. They are known for their passion and for their sense of drama expressed in their mistrust and their warmth. They have a profound need to save face: *fare bella figura.* Pride, shame, success and failure, though personal, always involve family as well which demands *respetto*—respect.

They believe in the efficacy of the proverb mentioned earlier: *"che paese vai, usanza che trovi!"* ("When in Rome, do as the Romans do!) When Italians came to the United States, they tried to behave like Americans. They worked hard and tried to capture the dream of America, if not for themselves, then at least for their children. Many returned to Italy, but most did not. Of those that remained, many accepted the idea of the "melting pot," rejected their Italian heritage and attempted to present themselves as "American," that is, "Anglo." In this behavior one can read a number of the themes listed here.

This list of these themes and traits has been derived from analysis of a number of anthropological, sociological and literary studies of Italian Americans. One may ask to what extent do they now and will they in the future continue to reflect the Italian aspect of the ethnic identity of Italian Americans. From the theoretical perspective, we can expect that these ethnic ideological themes, buried deeply within the personalities of Italian Americans will be passed on to the ensuing generations, and the identity of Italian Americans, conjoining these themes and the ethnic ideological themes of other Americans will persist. Ethnic diversity without homogenization will endure in the United States.

Introduction

THE ITALIAN AMERICAN

THE ITALIAN American. The very words conjure up images of two dynamic and powerful cultures, heritages and histories—one that brought the world the Glorious Age of Rome, equality under the rule of the Law, the establishment of Christianity as a worldwide religion, the Golden Age of the Renaissance, humanism, the modern scientific method and the Great Age of Discovery, and the other that brought the world freedom, democracy, the Atomic Age, high technology and liberty and justice for all.

Italy: the touchstone of modern European culture. America: the wellspring of modern democratic ideals and self-government and the spearhead of modern Western culture.

Italy: a country whose long history and heritage, culture and civilization, values and life-styles, thinking and philosophy have significantly shaped life in the Western world. America: a *new* world, a new *kind* of world, a world based upon freedom, equality, justice, life, liberty and the pursuit of happiness—the Great Democratic Experiment.

The contributions of Italians and Italian Americans to America have been profound and remarkable, and even now they continue to shape our future. The power and energy of the Italian influence permeate every dimension of American life.

The gifts of Italians and Italian Americans encompass the arts, the sciences and the humanities; food, fashion and design; culture, technology and entertainment; politics, government and statesmanship; sports, warfare and competition; discovery, exploration and navigation; imagination, invention and innovation; thinking, philosophy and education; business, industry and finance; religion, humanism and spirituality; body, mind and soul; life itself.

Roman civilization and its heritage pervade many aspects of our lives today. The basic foundation of law in Western civilization derives from the Code of Justinian. Christianity was born and nurtured to life within the Roman Empire. The Romans conquered vast areas of the globe and brought Roman values, life-styles and culture to the farthest reaches of its dominion. To be a Roman citizen with all the equality that entailed, was an ultimate goal of most of the people at that time. The Romans raised the very concept of citizenship to its highest degree, thus forming the basis for modern participatory democracies.

The Renaissance, centered very much in central Italy, was perhaps the most dynamic creative explosion in the history of the world. It marked new peaks of human achievement in the arts, the sciences and the humanities. It found, then defined, a new way of looking at life on this planet, called humanism, perhaps the most dramatic evolutionary step in what we refer to as Western civilization. Even today, to be called a renaissance man or woman is one of the highest human accolades.

As a direct result of this phenomenal burst of creativity, imagination, innovation and new thinking came superhuman achievements in visual arts, scientific investigation and humanistic philosophy. And from this came exciting inventions, creations and discoveries, and perhaps Europe's farthest reaching contribution to modern times—the discovery of America by Christopher Columbus, and the opening up of the New World.

Led by Columbus, the children of the Renaissance came to America, and the values that they carried in their hearts, minds and souls contributed to that great experiment in self-determination—the birth of the United States.

This, then, is the story of what Italians and Italian Americans have contributed directly and indirectly to the world, to Western civilization and to American life as we know it today. This is the story of how Italians and Italian Americans not only discovered our country, but also helped form much of the philosophy and value system brought here by others.

Less well known is that from the early days of the Founding Fathers, Italian Americans have been channeling their fiery and passionate energy into the forging of this unique republic. Their creativity has contributed significantly to the progress of an ever-emerging American civilization, and their ideas, values and philosophical speculations, revolutionary in concept and expression, helped shape our nation's growth. Indeed, ever since Columbus set foot in the New World, Italians have been coming to America. While over five million immigrants came here from Italy in the late nineteenth and early twentieth centuries, the United States has had since its beginning an influential Italian American population.

Yet throughout this period Italian Americans have succeeded in integrating themselves into the American life-style while somehow simultaneously preserving the values, traditions and characteristics they inherited from a rich and splendid culture; they have been an important part of the cultural mainstream while remaining fiercely independent and wildly individualistic. Italian Americans are unique as a group, yet an absolutely integral part of American life.

However, the story of the Italian Americans and their contributions remains for the most part unknown. For example, did you know that Thomas Jefferson took certain language of the Declaration of Independence from the writings of Philip Mazzei? Did you know that John F. Kennedy claimed Italian heritage on his mother's side of the family, the Fitzgeralds, who were descended from an illustrious eleventh-century Florentine family called the Gherardini? Or that Bishop Gherardini was the confessor to Queen Isabella, and that it was he who persuaded Isabella to fund Columbus in his great "Enterprise of the Indies"? Did you know that John Cabot's real name was Giovanni Caboto? Did you know that Sebastiano Caboto, son of Giovanni, was made Pilot Major of England and

organized what became the greatest naval power in the world
—the British Navy? Did you know that the first woman Ph.D.
in the world was an Italian by the name of Elena Lucrezia
Piscopia Cornaro? Did you know that Catherine de' Medici and
her cooks created the mother cuisine of Europe when Catherine married the King of France?

Did you know that the atomic bomb, the barometer, the
electric battery, the clock, the compass, double-entry book-
keeping, the dynamo, electroplating, eyeglasses, galvanizing,
the internal combustion engine, the land mine, the lighthouse,
the musical scale, nitroglycerin, the pendulum, the piano,
porcelain, the radio, a refrigeration process, the rotary magnetic field, the telescope, the thermometer, the typewriter and
the watch were either invented by Italians or came into being
when they did and as they did because of the contributions of
Italians?

Did you know that Italians played major roles in the first
artificial insemination, the first aerial warfare, the first income
tax, the first airmail stamp, the first picture postcard, the first
opera, the first public theater, the first voting procedures, the
first pizza and the first ice cream cone?

Did you know that the Etruscans, the pre-Roman inhabitants
of Central Italy, invented the art of wiring loose teeth together
with strips of gold? Did you know that it was Leonardo
Fibonacci's work in 1202 that caused the switch from Roman
to Arabic numerals? Did you know that the doctrine of
academic freedom comes from the constitution of Bologna
University?

Did you know that the founders of modern Unitarianism
were Lelio and Fausto Socini, and that "Socinus" was a leader
of the Reformation movement? Did you know that Egidio
Colonna drafted the maritime decalogue that formed the
basis of French naval tactics? Did you know that Paolo
Acconcio was the first to stress the principle of religious
freedom? Did you know that Italian American women helped
create one of the strongest, most progressive labor unions in
the world?

Did you know that bologna, bankruptcy, cantaloupe, the
Jacuzzi, blue jeans, millinery, pants, sardines, and venetian

blinds all derive from an Italian background? Did you know that Madonna, Bruce Springsteen and Mary Lou Retton share an Italian ancestry?

And did you know that . . .

Galileo Galilei changed mankind's perception of the heavens when he lent the enormous authority of his reputation to the new theory that the earth revolves around the sun, rather than the other way.

Cristoforo Colombo changed the course of Western civilization with his discovery of the New World.

Antonio Meucci laid the foundation of the Communications Age with the contributions he made to the development of the telephone.

Guglielmo Marconi established the basis of the Media Age with his invention of the radio.

Enrico Fermi made the Nuclear Age possible when he created the world's first self-sustaining chain reaction in uranium.

Salvador Luria is on the verge of discovering the very essence of life with his Nobel-Prize winning biological research in genetic engineering.

Robert Gallo is at the forefront of research into a cure for cancer and AIDS.

Rita Levi-Montalcini, an Italian Jew, leads the research into the understanding of how cancer works in human cell structure.

Federico Faggin created a quantum leap into the Computer Age with his invention of silicon gate technology and the microprocessor.

Carlo Rubbia is close to confirming the unified field theory and to understanding the nature of matter and the big bang concept of the world's creation.

John Casani is director of the Galileo Project, sending spaceprobes to Jupiter to study the very stuff of the universe.

And finally, did you know that a game very similar to baseball seems to have been played by the Etruscans?!

Yet, the *true* story, the complete story of Italian influence throughout the history of America—a story that captures the creative spirit, the passionate pride, the deep despair, the painful prejudice, the soul-wrenching defeats as well as the soul-satisfying triumphs of daring adventurers and millions of poverty-stricken immigrants seeking a better life—is for the most part a little known story. And it is as little known to most Italian Americans as to most other Americans!

To know and to understand the Italian experience of America—from when the sons and daughters of the Renaissance, harking back to the greatness of the Roman Empire, set sail upon unknown waters to discover America and the New World, through exploration, pioneering, colonizing, religious proselytizing, and formation of missions, through the American Civil War, the mass migrations of the turn of this century, World War I, the Great Depression, World War II and up to today—is to know and understand a great deal of what it means to be an *American*.

Indeed, knowledge of this history plays an important part in what Italian Americans think about themselves and pass on to their children. As you experience this journey into the past, you will find a heritage of idealistic philosophy, creative spirit, moral courage, intellectual rigor, fiery passion, determined will, humanistic values and love of life itself.

Finally, the story of the Italian American experience is a story of success. It is the great American success story, for now, in the last years of the twentieth century, Italian Americans have come of age, and the twenty-first century may well be the century of the Italian American in America.

We hope you will find in this survey of the Italian tradition those unique meanings and values that make the Italian American experience so rich, so valuable and so important to the world. For it is within these meanings and values that the Italian American must find himself or herself.

If you are an Italian American—by birth, marriage, kinship or friendship—this is your story as well as ours, a largely *unknown* story, one that screams to be told. It is a wonderful story. I hope you enjoy reading it as much as we have enjoyed writing it.

THE ITALIAN AMERICAN EXPERIENCE

1

THE ITALIC PEOPLE

Why Columbus

THE STORY of the Italian American experience begins in 1492, when Christopher Columbus, a courageous and single-minded explorer from Genoa, set sail from Palos, Spain, in search of a new route to India. About three months later, after a lonely voyage across unknown waters, Columbus and his three bedraggled ships, the *Niña,* the *Pinta* and the *Santa María,* reached the island of San Salvador on October 12, 1492. The news of the exciting New World he had found spread like wildfire throughout all of Europe and the Old World, and Italians came.

Later in history, Italians came by the millions—first in search of political freedom and then for release from poverty, disaster, disease and death. They came by the droves in the late 1880s and early 1900s to "the land where the streets were paved with gold," only to discover, in the words of an old joke Italian Americans used to tell on themselves, that the streets not only were *not* paved with gold but weren't paved *at all,* and they, the Italian Americans, were expected to pave them! Yet Italians still came to America, for whether the streets were paved or not, they were free and in America, the land of opportunity, the promised land, the land *oltremare* (across the sea), the land of a better life.

Italians came, and they stayed. Though the demographic figure is disputed, there are now somewhere between 12 and 23 million Americans of Italian descent in the United States.

The story of Italians in America and their contributions to the quality of American life is rich and fabulous, but largely unknown. Italian Americans have shaped American life in unique and complex ways, having brought with them a culture and civilization that dates from the Etruscans, the Roman Empire, the Renaissance and the Age of Enlightenment. From this rich and varied Italian background came explorers, adventurers, artisans, missionaries, mariners, traders and enterprising fortune-seekers looking for their rainbows in the New World. The Italy these early adventures left was prosperous and dynamic.

However, the Italy that millions of Italians, mostly from southern Italy, left in the mass migrations of the late nineteenth and early twentieth centuries was a totally different country. Economic depression, pestilence—including malaria and cholera among many other diseases—crop failure, soil erosion, earthquakes, unfair taxes, exploitation by wealthy landlords, and every other conceivable catastrophe formed the background against which the immigrant Italians fled to America. This Italy was newly unified after centuries of decline, but was a disaster area.

While the blood of ancient Rome and the Renaissance may have coursed through Italian veins, centuries of upheaval, catastrophe and disaster had made nineteenth-century Italians creative, inventive and iron-willed. These Italians were true survivors and courageous fortune-seekers who looked for their salvation in the rainbows of the New World, if only just to stay alive, escape poverty and find some hope elsewhere.

Most people think that Italians discovered America, left it to the great naval powers to carve up and did not appear back in America until the late 1880s. The fact is that Italians had been coming to America ever since Columbus's day and have contributed significantly to the exploration and colonizing of America. They explored, educated and artistically enhanced America. They built schools, churches and missions. They fought in the American Revolution and the Civil War.

Let us look back now on this splendid story of the Italian American experience. It began with Christopher Columbus, but why was it an Italian from Genoa who discovered America?

Columbus's discovery occurred during the Renaissance in the 1490s and was perhaps almost an inevitable result of the great explosion of creativity at this time. Italy was then a prosperous collection of independent city-states governed by wise statesmen and magnificent princes, but it was not a unified country.

Freedom of expression, newly introduced into Renaissance Italy, had nourished cultural activities, heightened political growth and triggered economic dynamism. Reliance on *reason* as a tool of understanding meant new discoveries, inventions, explorations, a greater understanding of the world and, inevitably, more reliable knowledge. This was a fabulous era, an era of innovation, imagination and creativity, an era of change and progress, an era of widening intellectual boundaries, an era of artistic explosion never equaled to this day . . . and an era of expanded geographic horizons.

Italy was the capital of this world, the cradle of civilization.

Why? To understand why Italy was the birthplace of the Renaissance and why the Renaissance produced the Great Age of Discovery, and why an Italian from Genoa discovered America, we must go back, way back, to the beginning.

THE ITALICI

Italy has been influenced over millennia by many peoples: the Etruscans, Greeks, Romans, Byzantines, Saracens, Normans, French and Spanish. This coalescing of cultures, forces and values made for what we call the Italic people.

Anthropologists speculate that toward the end of the Ice Age, Italy was lightly populated by two main races and a whole array of groups made up what became known as the Italic people. Some of these people had been in Italy since prehistoric times. Others were descended from peoples who came from eastern and central Europe, from North Africa and the eastern Mediterranean. Some came as peaceful migratory tribes and others came later as bellicose invaders.

The Ibero-Ligurians, who had Mediterranean characteristics, generally inhabited the Italic peninsula, the continental north and the islands. From these were descended the Ligurians, the Japygiano and the Sicani. Dinaric immigrants from the Balkans settled in eastern parts of the country, and from them were descended the Veneti in the north and the Apulians and the Messapians in the south.

The Italici, or Italians, were the tribes descended from two waves of invaders from the Alpine branch of Indo-Europeans. The first wave hit Italy from the Danubian basin about four thousand years ago and brought bronze-making with them. From these were descended the Latin, Sabine, Samnite and Siculi. Between the sixteenth and thirteenth century B.C. a second wave of Alpine invaders came again from the Danubian basin, and these brought Iron Age culture with them. From these were descended the Umbrians, the Hirpini, the Lucani and the Bruttii.

Later invaders were the Celts, who first settled in Gaul (now France), and, as Gauls, occupied the Po Valley in the fifth century B.C. However, before the Gauls, Italy was overrun by newcomers, this time by sea, who brought advanced civilization, including religion, political organization, writing and highly developed economic knowledge. These were the mysterious Etruscans in the twelfth century B.C., who may have come from Asia Minor, the Greeks in the eighth century B.C., who settled in Magna Graecia, and the Carthaginians in the sixth century B.C., who came from Phoenicia. While the Carthaginians sought to expand their empire through conquest and thus maintain foreign rule, the Etruscans and the Greeks were absorbed by the indigenous culture and became native Italians. Etruscans and Greeks played vital roles in the growth and development of Italian and Roman civilization.

From these many migrations, invasions and tribal movements, two main types of Italians evolved. In the southern third of the country the Mediterranean type dominates, while in the northern two thirds, from Abruzzi north, the Alpine type prevails.

From the very beginning, Italians were never a homogenous people. Regional differences have existed from the early years of Italian history. These persist to this very day and are the source of internal factionalism both in Italy from region to region and in America between Italian immigrants from different regions. However, these very differences also make the Italian culture exciting, varied and creative. In this sense, Italy is like America.

Yet in spite of these vast regional differences, the culture, traditions and values that the Italian people share weigh more heavily than those differences; what holds Italians together is stronger than what drives them apart.

Italy has been essentially a single nation for over twenty centuries, though numerous independent states have come and gone. It was first united by the Roman state, was fragmented territorially for thirteen centuries, and was finally reunited as a modern republic around 1860. Major crises split the nation apart in the fifth, sixth, eleventh and sixteenth centuries, but somehow the country maintained its cultural homogeneity, which provided the foundation for an Italian identity. This powerful culture transcended the regional differences and accommodated variations in the individual character of Italians from all parts of Italy. Yet it is in these regional differences that the individualistic nature of Italians and Italian Americans has its roots, and these differences would be transplanted part and parcel to America in the Italian migration.

And it is this very cultural homogeneity, sweeping along with it its many currents of regional custom and tradition, that flows like a giant river from the Etruscans through ancient Rome and the Roman Empire, the Dark and Middle Ages, the Renaissance, into the Age of Discovery and across the ocean to flood the shores of America.

A ZEST FOR LIFE

In the time before Rome, an intriguing, brilliant, charming, delightful and highly humanistic people emerged in Tuscany around the ninth century B.C.; they were called the Etruscans. Whether they migrated from Asia Minor or were indigenous is not known, but they established settlements on the western peninsular coast of Italy between the Serchio and Tiber rivers. They founded such cities as Tarquinia and Cerveteri, and farther inland, Volterra and Chiusi, and then, in the upper Arno Valley, Fiesole and Arezzo, and finally in the middle Tiber Valley, Perugia. In the seventh century B.C. they moved north of the Apennines, where many were annihilated by the invading Gauls in the fifth century B.C.

The Etruscans had strong humanistic values, fervent religious attitudes and a joyful world view. All of this created an intriguing culture and a philosophy of life, rich in beautiful art, respect for family, equality of the sexes, reverence for life, high spirituality and a zest for life.

Though Etruscan settlement was centralized in Tuscany, western Umbria and Latium, Etruscan influence spread throughout the Italic peninsula all the way to the Greek territory of Magna Graecia. Etruscan art and artifacts tell us of a highly evolved people who actually civilized the Romans and whose way of life flowed through the Roman Empire into the mainstream of Western culture, becoming a seminal source of Western civilization. It comes as no surprise that the great flowering of creativity in the Renaissance blossomed in Tuscany, the land of the Etruscans, or Etruria.

The early rulers of Rome were in fact an *Etruscan* dynasty called the Tarquins. In the seventh century B.C., Rome, the "City of Seven Hills," was occupied by the Etruscans. The use of the she-wolf as a symbol of the birth of Rome is of Etruscan origin, as is the use of the eagle as a symbol of nationhood.

Unfortunately, the Etruscans were not a warrior people committed to major empire-building and had no military alliances; Etruscan citadels were therefore unable to withstand the might of Roman assaults. Thus the Etruscans, along with their amazingly creative, joyful and humanistic culture, were conquered by the Romans. Around 510 B.C. when the Romans revolted against the Etruscan kings and took control away from them, the Etruscan way of life had already blended into the Roman.

The Etruscan contributions to Roman civilization were monumental. The Etruscans taught the Romans about the construction of roads, bridges and aqueducts; about architecture, building and city planning; about mining, ore refining, iron extraction, bronze-making and goldsmithing; about decoration, painting and sculpture; about shipbuilding, navigation and merchant trading; about games, competitions and gladiatorial contests; about dancing and stage shows; about religion, worship and divinatory practices; about art and science; about education and learning; about military weapons, vehicles and tactics; about the traditional monogamous family, sex, sensuality and equal treatment of women; about the forces and mysteries of nature; and about human enjoyment, sumptuous banquets and the joy of living.

The still-used Cloaca Maxima, the sewage disposal system of Rome, was built by the Etruscans. And a wall painting in an Etruscan tomb shows various figures playing a game that looks exactly like baseball!

Much of what history has given the Romans credit for was really Etruscan. Through the spread of Roman civilization, these valuable ancient Etruscan elements became part of our present-day way of life. Granted the Roman-Italians were a breed apart and the Roman Empire ruled the known world, but so much is owed to the Etruscans for their significant contributions to Roman and Western culture that we must give them credit where credit is due. Interestingly enough, if we could transplant the Etruscans into modern times, they would fit in perfectly as New Age humanists.

THE GLORY OF ROME

Roman civilization permeates every dimension of our lives today. The twelve hundred years of Roman history from the seventh century B.C. to the disintegration of the empire in the fifth century A.D. are still alive in the values, cultures, concepts and institutions that originated then and still exist today, no matter how changed or revised.

Rome was one of many self-governing, independent, self-contained and highly diversified communities on Italian territory, along with the Etruscans in the north, the Greeks in the south and part of Sicily, and the Phoenicians in western Sicily, Sardinia and Corsica. At this time there was no concept of an Italian people. In the third and second centuries B.C., "Italy" described the boot-shaped peninsula, a geographic area that was home to about 250 communities, Rome being the strongest. By the middle of the second century B.C., Rome ruled all of southern Europe, much of western and central Europe, North Africa and parts of western Asia. In 88 B.C., most of the inhabitants of this vast area formally became Roman citizens. This same period marked the birth of the Italian nation. Rome and Italy were now one.

In addition to the early Etruscan influence, Roman culture also owes a legacy to Greece, as early Roman development was also affected by Athenian ideas. The area of Greek settlement in Italy was called Magna Graecia, "Great Greece." From this rich cultural mix flowed wealth and military power, large-scale communities, magnificent temples, theaters, palaces and buildings, and most important of all, an expansion of intellect and the establishment of democratic institutions.

According to legend, Rome was founded in 753 B.C. by Romulus and Remus, descendants of Aeneas from the royal family that ruled Troy in Asia Minor. Romulus united the many tribal groups and invented the Roman legion, the principal unit of the Roman army, thus creating an immensely powerful military organization. Numa Pompilius, his successor, was the lawgiver, and under his successors, Tullus Hostilius and Ancus Marcius, the Roman state became permanent. Tarquinius Priscus of Etruria ruled in the seventh and sixth centuries B.C., establishing the Etruscan influence on Rome. Servius Tullius, a Roman Solon, introduced a classification of citizenship for military and electoral purposes, and built the walls encircling Rome's seven hills in the sixth century.

Lucius Junius Brutus formented a revolution that instituted the Roman Republic. Early Roman government was originally ruled by an elected king aided by a council of elders, known as *seniores,* or by patricians, senators who were

heads of families known as *patres*. Like that of Greek Athens,
Rome's republic was constitutional. All officials were elected by
three different popular assemblies who also passed the laws.
There was a system of checks and balances and a division of
power. The rule of law was supreme across the Roman Empire.

Once the Romans had achieved political liberty, they had to
ensure equality, as there was an upper class of patricians and a
lower class of plebeians. By the mid-fourth century B.C., the
plebeians won equality of rights, thus strengthening the
republic and its free institutions. These republican Romans
knew somehow that in a free society, conflicts must be
resolved on the basis of equality and according to the rule of
law.

After many wars and the defeat of the Gauls in 390 B.C.,
peace was established in 334 B.C. The Roman self-governing
communities were composed of hardworking farmers who
were also exceptional soldiers. Every citizen was a soldier,
constantly in training and well disciplined. Roman armies
were composed of powerful legions of these confident warriors.

After many years of dramatic and successful campaigns,
leading victories all across Italy, the Italic peninsula had
become a confederation of about two hundred autonomous
states over which Rome ruled with supreme power. However, in each confederate state, the power of self-rule rested in
the hands of a citizens' assembly that elected its own officials
and passed laws. The Roman senate and the assemblies in
Rome handled all foreign and military matters.

By this point, political differences had faded and the
assimilation of many peoples under the unification of the
Roman Republic took place. A uniform Roman way of life
prevailed; all the inhabitants had become one people. Rome
was now a major power in the Mediterranean world, a
civilization born from ancient origins but now more advanced than any other in the then-known world.

The greatness that was Rome ran from 270 B.C. to 330 A.D.
This was truly a legendary and heroic age, a source of pride
and inspiration for all Italians. Though interrupted by wars,
conquests and expansion, this great age of Roman republican

institutions lasted over half a millennium. During this time, people cherished their liberty, equality and free form of government. They despised any form of despotism.

Though there were foreign and civil wars, there were also periods of peace, which became known as the *Pax Romana*. The Romans built a vast, complex and efficient political intrastructure to hold together the largest society of individuals ever created on earth. They made great progress in knowledgeand education, in economic and social affairs, in thought and philosophy, in morality and government, and in the transformation of society. Rome simply changed the world, and the world was better for it.

By 146 B.C. all the territories conquered by Rome became ten "dependencies," of which three—Illyria, Epirus and Greece—had special status, and seven were provinces: Sicily, Sardinia and Corsica (as one); Gallia; Cisalpina; Hither Spain; Farther Spain; Africa; and Macedonia. For two hundred years, the Roman state expanded through wars. Asia Minor and Syria, then Gaul were conquered by Julius Caesar in 58–51 B.C. Egypt, all areas south of the Danube, Mauritania (Algeria and Morocco) and Britannia (England) were annexed. With the conquest of Trajan, in 116 A.D., the Roman state had reached its maximum expansion. With a population of 60 to 120 million inhabitants, then extended two thousand miles from east to west and two thousand miles from north to south, and encompassed two million square miles.

At the end of the second century B.C., Rome faced another serious problem of inequality. Unlike the conflict between patricians and plebeians, however, these were between rich and poor, between freemen and slaves, and between citizens and subjects. Reforms were desperately needed; this brought about a major transformation of the Roman-Italian nation, which would change the world.

Two brothers, Tiberius and Gaius Gracchus, proposed reforms and formed the party of the *populares,* or democrats, who deeply cherished and dedicated themselves to republican institutions. Their proposed reforms were meant to strengthen the republic. Unfortunately, they were both killed, which precipitated riots and civil wars until the time of Caesar.

Julius Caesar, a powerful warrior, a masterful military genius, a dynamic statesman and also a gifted writer, ignited and fired the imaginations of Romans for generations to come. He revolted against the republican government as leader of the populares in 49 B.C. and ended the terrible disorder and civil strife.

Caesar then carried out some much-needed reforms by distributing money and food to the poor, checking economic inequities, giving public lands to veterans, extending the franchise, reorganizing fiscal administration, revising the senate and the judiciary, and founding settlements in the provinces. He also reformed the calendar.

Unfortunately, to achieve these badly needed reforms in a time of such turmoil, Caesar had to concentrate his power, thus bringing some loss of liberty, the very essence of past Roman success. When Caesar's ambition overtook him and he wanted to make himself king he was assassinated on the Ides of March in 44 B.C.

Octavian then assumed supreme power and with the title "Augustus" ruled wisely until 14 A.D. He established a constitution in an attempt to achieve a compromise between liberty and despotism, between republicanism and monarchism. From Octavian on, the Roman state was called the empire, and its rulers were emperors.

Octavian was succeeded by Tiberius, Caligula, Claudius, and Nero, who is famous for fiddling while Rome burned. Nerva reigned in a prosperous and peaceful era between Domitian and Trajan. The Roman Empire attained its greatest expansion under Trajan. Later came Marcus Aurelius, the stoic emperor-philosopher whose *Meditations* have inspired so many, even today. By 212 A.D., Italy and the empire were completely Romanized.

The *Pax Romana* is generally dated from 31 B.C. to 235 A.D., during which period there was quiet, order, internal peace and prosperity. The Ars Pacis, altar of peace, on the Tiber River in Rome was dedicated over two thousand years ago to celebrate this period of peace, which had such an impact on Western civilization. This was the Rome venerated by poets and statesmen, and admired by generations to come. This was the Rome whose culture and civilization reemerged with tantalizing power in the Italian and then European Renaissance. This was the Rome that Renaissance and humanist Italy tried to bring back in a rebirth of ancient culture and values.

What had Rome done that was so unique and spectacular as to encourage such universal admiration? The Romans had accomplished the first major progressive revolution in the history of mankind. They created a vast and complex state and gave peace to it. They created a society based on law and a procedure for changing the law. They defined the legal concept of the presumption of innocence. The Roman *collegia* and the *corporazioni* were the forerunners of the Dutch guilds and modern labor unions. They got all people, monarchs and individual city-states to entrust their fate to a government, not to the empire. They infused a sense of justice into the pragmatics of a given situation. They eliminated despotism. They founded a society based on liberty and equality. They created a republic in the truest sense of the word. They developed a very sophisticated concept of citizenship with moral and legal rights, obligations and responsibilities. They invented a judicial process that combined stability and flexibility, thereby making peaceful change possible. Decision-making and elections were done freely by citizens in assemblies. Judges ruled on legal matters with total freedom. Roman women enjoyed social equality and privileges unlike anywhere else at the time. The Romans built an efficient organization for running a truly worldwide nation. They set up an intricate and well-run bureaucracy to maintain order and security, handle internal administration, protect the state against external attacks and solve financial and economic problems. They provided for the religious, educational and leisure activities of their people. They cared for citizens with public welfare programs. They created public works of the highest artistic value. They were the first to define the concept of property. They set up free trade, international commerce and industry. This Roman state was truly modern, a commonwealth of nations unlike any other ancient state.

Not only had the Romans created the concept of rule by law, but they created a new kind of law by separating law from religion, and this opened a new horizon for human achievement. Religious authority gave way to approval by the citizenry. However, Rome was also the cradle of Christianity. The *Roman* Catholic Church became the most powerful religion in the world, but ironically and unwittingly, Christianity would help destroy the very empire that gave the religion its life.

The Romans believed that laws should be created according to the dictates of reason, and that government by law is the best guarantee of the citizens' security. Legal procedure was paramount. The Romans were the first to develop the concept of an individual endowed with rights and duties as person and citizen. The person is the moral individual; the citizen, the political individual. This idea is the very essence of the foundation of self-government, of government by the people. The Romans far surpassed all other groups in defining the inviolate nature of the individual and his or her personal liberty. Roman law was called *jus gentium*, the law of the people, not the law of the state; it stressed the moral and legal equality of all human beings. Romans cherished justice as a supreme value and defined it as *suum cuique tribuare*, meaning "to give each his due." From this comes a definition of what belongs rightfully to each individual and to each group and what, in a democracy, belongs to the majority and what to a minority. Romans even stressed fairness before the law to humanize and personalize the enforcement of general laws upon the individual.

Roman law, with its powerful and progressive philosophical foundation, was synthesized, compiled and codified in the sixth century by the Emperor Justinian. These laws, principles and procedures, these ideas, values and concepts have influenced the Western world ever since, and would come alive again in future governments and modern democracies. The Roman concepts of the citizen, of liberty, of equality, of justice and of government by law were basic to the British and the American Bill of Rights and also the French Declaration of Rights.

When the great humanists of the Renaissance in the four-teenth and fifteenth centuries would hark back to the Glory of Rome, it was these Roman ideas, values and culture that would captivate and inspire them.

Unfortunately, this glory was about to die.

ROME FALLS, CHRISTIANITY RISES

It took a hundred years of warfare to unify Italy under Roman power, a hundred years of warfare for Rome to assume domination of the Mediterranean, three hundred years to turn the Roman state into the empire and another three hundred years to create a Roman nation out of many different peoples. By the end of the third century A.D., after half a century of chaos, turmoil, internal unrest, external attacks, plagues, famine and invasions by the Goths, the Emperor Diocletian conquered the invading hordes and restored order to a nation on the verge of collapse. He reorganized the empire, but he also destroyed all vestiges of constitutionalism. Totali-tarianism ruled and the great Roman experiment in liberty, equality and justice begun eight hundred years before came to an end.

The collapse of the Roman Empire took about two hun-dred years and was caused by two hundred years of invasions, the downfall of republican government, which was replaced by totalitarianism, and a new way of life that was intellectual-ly dogmatic and politically authoritarian.

Also, and more significant, the people of the Roman Empire were going through a great spiritual crisis of conver-sion to Christianity. The present realities of suffering, pover-ty and cruelty were fertile soil for this new religion, Christianity, which stressed charity and love, which prom-ised redemption and resurrection, and which offered happi-ness in the afterlife that just could not be gained on earth.

In 312 A.D., the Emperor Constantine, supported by the Christians, won the battle of the Milvian Bridge outside Rome. In 313 A.D. he proclaimed equal rights for *all* reli-gions, and in 330 A.D. he moved the capital to Constantinople.

A new era had begun. Religiously Christian and politically totalitarian, these forces created a deep ideological split in the Roman nation.

Thus began the major influence on the world of Christianity, later to become Catholicism, the predominant religion of most Christians and Italians, with its birth in the Roman Empire. Catholicism would become imbued with Roman heritage, traditions, influences, values, concepts, rites, rituals and symbols. Saint Paul, one of the religion's most important personalities, was a Roman citizen, and Saint Augustine and Saint Gregory Magnus lived in and were shaped by Roman environments. And this great church would soon be called Roman Catholic.

The transition from ancient to medieval times was truly a revolutionary change from old to new beliefs. There was intellectual, economic and political decline. The territorial fragmentation of the empire began in 568 A.D. and this downward spiral would last five hundred years, until the mid-eleventh century.

By the fourth century, Germanic invaders—Vandals, Goths, Visigoths, Ostrogoths and Mishegoths—were rampaging Italy. When the Visigoths, led by Alaric, looted Rome in 410 A.D., it was like the end of the world. Roman life in Britain was obliterated, Roman Gaul was conquered by the Franks and became France, and Attila, the "scourge of God," leading the Huns, savaged the Burgundians and rushed across Europe. The Vandals captured Rome, and all of Italy was then sacked by the Huns and Vandals.

Besides invasions, poor leadership, economic decline, political chaos and military ineptitude, one essential factor perhaps more than any other contributed to the fall of Rome—the changed character of the Romans. Romans had over the years fully embraced Christianity, but this was a religion contrary to the Roman ideals of military valor; Christianity was a religion founded on love, one in which humility and charity were cherished ideals.

Thus, with a diminished will to fight, with no permanent army, with no citizen army and now with no sense of military valor, all of Italy would be taken by the invading hordes. By

476 A.D. the Roman Empire had ceased to exist and the Middle Ages had begun. Rome fell and Christianity rose.

The whole country was ravaged and plundered. Wars, famines and plagues killed the population. The country was in total ruin. Books considered heretical—that is, those written by pre-Christian authors—were destroyed. Poverty, ignorance and social unrest prevailed.

Yet somehow out of this seemingly chaotic maze of tragic events, out of this miasma of catastrophes, Italians managed to maintain a sense of unifying bond from their common use of the Latin language, from Roman law, from Roman local institutions and from a pride in the past greatness of the Roman Empire. Even the vast network of Roman roads played a unifying role. However, the most important source of unity to Italians was religion.

Roman Catholicism, the Italian version of Christianity, became the dominant force in Italy and the primary shaping force in Italian life. It was originally created in and remained under Italian influence, was centered in Rome and became richly and vividly infused with Roman elements.

Most important of all for Western civilization was the formulation of Catholic philosophical thought and theology. For most religions, beliefs are gained through subjective, intuitive processes and accepted by an act of faith, but for the Catholic religion, objective rational explanation and reasoned justification became paramount to its theologians. By combining subjective intuition with objective reasoning for the first time in the history of religion, Catholic theologians had actually created a *new kind* of religion.

Through this seemingly simple fact, Catholicism managed to save, in spite of the destruction of the savage hordes and in spite of the dissolution of the whole Roman-Italian nation, the greatest single feature of both Greek and Roman civilizations —the *conscious use of reason,* the very process of rational thinking. This may sound outlandish to our twentieth-century intellectually oriented sensibilities, but for its time, it was true. Without Catholicism, reason could have been lost in the ruins of Rome. Ironically, this saving grace for the world, which provided the foundation later for the flowering of rationalism, and thus the creation of scientific thought in modern civilization, would later cause grave crises for Catholicism and Christianity.

So Catholicism became a major force in shaping the destiny of mankind. The void left by the disintegration of the Roman Empire was filled by the church, and political power fell into the hands of church leaders, almost by default. Ecclesiastical power became linked with political power, setting the stage for serious future conflicts over the issue of separation of church and state. But, this politicization of the church and its strong centralized hierarchical structure, built over centuries, provided very pragmatic and valuable earthly solutions to the political chaos and insecurity of the times. They became permanent characteristics of Catholicism, but most of all, this very political power, organizational structure and centralized hierarchy saved Italy and its people.

The Dark Ages ran from the early fifth to the end of the eleventh century, when life flowered once again in Italy. The Italian nation now was fragmented and ravaged by more invaders—Vikings, Lombards, Franks, Germans, Magyars and Normans. In one of the greatest upheavals in history, Mohammed, prophet, statesman and warrior, united the Arab world and conquered Syria, Egypt and Libya. For a hundred years the Arabs expanded until Charles Martel defeated them in the West and Negabhata did likewise in the East.

During this dismal period of seven hundred years, in this bloody, tension-filled land of internal wars, invasions, barbaric hordes, cruelty, oppression, corruption, poverty, famine, plague, tyranny, ignorance and insecurity, the flame of the human spirit never died. Fortunately for mankind, the land of Italy still nurtured the precious seeds of human hope, the will to survive and the creative spirit and power of the Italian people. In fact, from disaster, misfortune, catastrophe and constant change came progress and a rich variety of new developments and experiences.

Out of this chaos arose the Sicilian culture, the great commonwealth of Venice, the powerful maritime city-states, the worldwide spread of Catholicism, the papal states, the Holy Roman Empire, and, finally, the birth of the second great world-influencing period of Italy—the Renaissance, the emergence of humanism and the discovery of America.

By the middle of the eleventh century, there was, miraculously, still an Italian people, though without an Italian state. Three events provided a glimmer of hope for bringing a desperately needed rebirth to Italy. First, Pope Gregory VII significantly reformed the Catholic Church and revived its strength. Second, William Bras-de-Fer, "Iron Arm," renewed efficient government in the southern peninsula and Sicily. Third, the growth of democratic communes restored liberty to the populace, a vital element for progress. These all signified the dawn of modern civilization.

The role of the Catholic Church is vital to an understanding of the progress mankind made from here on. While political unity did not exist, a unity of all Catholics within many countries did exist as a spiritual, political and cultural reality. Italian Catholicism influenced and dominated the Roman Catholic Church, which included one third of the European population and was the majority religion of a vast community of culturally advanced nations.

In the eleventh century, Pope Gregory VII's concept and vision of the papacy assumed universal scope. He fought for the supremacy of the church over the state. His reforms helped create the revolutionary upheaval of the Crusades, and affected the political and intellectual life of all Catholics, especially Italians. What Saint Gregory Magnus was to theology, Gregory VII was to the institution of the church.

While Gregory consolidated the church hierarchy and ensured the astounding continuity of the Roman Catholic Church, he also unwittingly spawned the bitter controversy over church and state—papacy versus empire—that was actually to weaken, in years to come, *both* as central authorities. However, this mutual weakening of papacy and empire gave greater liberty and power to the individual city-states and communals.

The Crusades, by their very international nature, forced Western interaction with foreign cultures, and the ensuing trade brought back to Italy knowledge that had been lost. Also during the thirteenth century, Saint Thomas Aquinas, the brilliant Catholic theologian-philosopher, succeeded in totally integrating rationalism into Catholic thought, thus creating the basis for the rise of scientific thought in the modern world, which led eventually to the Great Age of Discovery.

The papacy had reached its zenith under Pope Innocent III in 1198, but by now papal supremacy was on the wane. The church was racked with heresies and schisms, harbingers of later controversial religious upheavals. With the church no longer a vital, positive and progressive factor of Italian life, and lacking the brilliant moral and spiritual leadership of Gregory VII, the stage was set for the major split of Western Christianity in the sixteenth century and for the centuries of political chaos in Italy from the end of the Renaissance to the Risorgimento, the reunification of Italy in the 1860s.

Whatever the crises, precipitated unknowingly, which would lead to the great schism of the church after centuries of incredible power and to the political decline of Italy, Catholicism delivered the *salvation* of an Italian people in desperate need. The Catholic Church, in maintaining its own power and continuity, also saved the Italian nation.

2

ITALY DISCOVERS AMERICA

RENAISSANCE ITALY

FROM THE mid-eleventh to the mid-sixteenth century, a new Italian civilization was born whose primary centers were the large cities of Tuscany and northern Italy, the land of the Etruscans. This new Italian civilization of the later Middle Ages and the Renaissance influenced the whole world.

Popular self-government as an idea had survived in the minds of Italians proudly conscious of a great past. It was in Milan, the most important city at the time, that the commune was born. This was a basically democratic and local self-governing community organized by the populace in urban centers. The people elected city officials in assemblies called parliaments—from *parlare,* to speak. Here the citizenry discussed public matters, concerns and issues.

From these first democratic communes and later from the independent city-states grew a powerful movement of independence and emancipation—from dogmatic authoritarianism, from traditionalism, from ecclesiasticism, from despotism and from government control.

The Renaissance rekindled the flames of the glorious Roman Empire, now just flickering embers in the consciousness of the Middle Ages, and recaptured liberty in Italy. It nourished and revived an impoverished Italian people with political, economic and intellectual freedom. It encouraged personal

20

expression of body, mind and spirit. It was the source of many revolutions that would later transform Europe and all mankind. It made the genius of Italy soar to the highest reaches of human aspiration.

Out of this rediscovery of liberty, first expressed in the communes and then the independent city-states, would be born a new, expansive and modern world. The embodiment of the idea of the common will aimed at deciding as well as carrying out the common good would be the very essence of modern democratic government.

It was this liberty that gave Italians their unique way of life, that made Italian cities such stimulating centers of intellectual life, that produced guilds, the forerunners of the modern unions, that spawned large corporations, that created democratic republics, that nourished humanism and the fabulous artistic flowering of the Renaissance.

Freedom of thought and freedom of expression were the fuel that drove the dynamo of the Renaissance. From unrestricted creativity came variety, excellence, art, science, growth, progress, dynamism and vision. Life was immensely rich and fulfilling. This revolution in freedom and liberty was the most important element in creating the unique value system of Italian life henceforth.

The revival began with the rediscovery of the writings of Roman and Greek authors. The Age of Humanism began when artists, writers and thinkers began to look at man and his environment in new ways and speculated on his nature and on human life. Traditional ideas, religious or otherwise, simply did not or could not answer these questions.

This new freedom of contemplation emancipated man from the darkness of centuries and gave him free rein to be creative. This great explosion of creativity culminated in the high Renaissance. Florence became the epicenter of this powerful cultural movement and was governed by Cosimo de' Medici, and then by his grandson Lorenzo "the Magnificent" (il Magnifico), whose name would come to symbolize the age. Leon Battista Alberti, Leonardo da Vinci and Michelangelo Buonarroti came from Florence.

This was an amazing era, an era of innovation and imagination in all dimensions of life. An era in which adventurous businessmen created new enterprises, developed industries, invented banking and expanded the bounds of western commerce. It was an era of intellectual growth, revolutionary ideas, new philosophies and original thinking; an era of explosive, talented and imaginative artists freed from the bonds of conformity; an era of spiritual growth and divine inspiration. Yet it was also an era of unbearable tensions and suffering, for out of freedom and individual liberty came inner turmoil, confusion, intolerance, violence, bigoted inquisitors and lawlessness.

The greatest architects, sculptors and painters lived at this time: Bramante, da Sangallo, Laurana; Verocchio, Pollaiuolo, della Robbia; Botticelli, Lippi, Ghirlandaio, Perugino; Sansovino, Raphael, Correggio, Giorgione, Titian; Alberti, Leonardo da Vinci and Michelangelo. Such great writers as Dante Alighieri, Ariosto, Bernbo, Castiglione and Savonarola. Such great scientists as Galileo, Gioia, and Fracastoro.

The Renaissance blossomed in the fourteenth century, reached its climax in the fifteenth century and flourished well into the sixteenth century. The fourteenth century marked the transition from the Middle Ages to the Modern Age. By the end of the fourteenth century, man's total accumulation of science and exploration was very small, but the changes in the ways of thinking were already fostering new modes of thinking. Those Italians with scientific curiosity were also influenced greatly by this onrush of freedom and creativity. Humanist thinkers were discarding dogma as the source of truth in favor of using their own critical faculties for observation and experimentation, and their own experience of reality for determining truth. The use of reason became the vehicle for discovering life's *summum bonum*.

Reason and creative thinking yielded fabulous inventions and discoveries. A Roman may have invented the mechanical clock. Mondino performed autopsies, Girolamo Fracastoro founded modern medical pathology, Vannoccio Biringucci is known as the first chemist, Andrea Cesalpino described the circulation of blood, and the fallopian and eustachian tubes are named after Gabriello Fallopia and Bartolommeo Eustachio.

Eyeglasses were made at Murano near Venice. Niccolo Fontana solved the cubic equation.

Galileo, the first human to gaze upon the moon and other planets with his telescope, changed man's concept of the universe by proclaiming, at great risk to his life, that the earth travels around the sun. This he did in 1609 after, with his "optic tube," he had begun to open up to the observation of mankind the distant, magnificent and mysterious universe. The human environment expanded beyond the planet in one blink of an eye. Galileo invented the thermometer, conceived the concept of the pendulum, discovered the laws of inertia and uniform acceleration, formulated new ideas about velocity and force, laid the groundwork for Newton's theory, and was one of the earliest to develop a workable microscope, which revolutionized the biological sciences and medicine. Galileo gave birth to the modern scientific method, but unfortunately his ideas were, in his time, too revolutionary.

The universities of northern and central Italy, now rooted in a strong sense of academic freedom, became prominent centers of study, famous worldwide. The *Habita* by Emperor Frederick I, Frederick Barbarossa, served as the constitution of Bologna University in 1158 A.D., and from this document flows the doctrine of academic freedom. This new free intellectual climate influenced not just Italy but all of Europe. Copernicus, who revolutionized astronomy, and Vesalius, who revolutionized medicine, both studied in these citadels of intellectual progress, as did many other talented non-Italian as well as Italian thinkers.

Of all the great Renaissance men, Leonardo da Vinci stands above them all as *the* most gifted and brilliant artist, scientist and inventor of his time, a true genius. With Verrocchio as his teacher in Florence, he learned as a child that knowledge is born of experience. Leonardo read, observed, experienced life and capitalized on past discoveries for future speculations. He studied, he learned, he created; his mind never rested. He revolutionized science and technology, and he represented the quintessential Renaissance man.

Civilization in Italy reached the highest level ever known in the Western world during the Renaissance. Modern scientific thought was born and grew out of the Renaissance. The Renaissance signaled the end of the darkness of the Middle Ages and the dawn of modern civilization, and it ushered in the Great Age of Discovery.

It was another gifted Renaissance humanist, scientist and thinker who ignited the passionate fires of exploration and discovery. Paolo dal Pozzo Toscanelli, a brilliant thinker, turned his creative thoughts to finding one's way on the high seas and across the ocean.

COLUMBUS

In the 1490s, Italy was rich with splendid cities and men of greatness in all walks of life. It was the cultural, political and economic capital of the world. The Italian city-states were governed by wise statesmen and magnificent princes. Italy was prosperous, peaceful and heavily populated. Freedom of expression had nourished cultural progress and heightened political and economic growth.

The loss of this freedom later in the sixteenth century would doom the Renaissance, but it would also spawn one of the most meaningful developments in Western civilization—the tumultuous religious upheaval of the Reformation of Christianity, which would create political and social revolutions throughout the world. Five centuries of turbulence and great progress would end, freedom of expression would die and faith in the spiritual power of the church would come alive.

However, of supreme value to the new and higher civilization created from the Renaissance was the role reason played. The use of reason yielded discoveries, inventions, explorations and more knowledge and understanding of the world. From these came change and progress, the broadening of intellectual horizons and the expanding of geographical horizons. Man now was master of the forces of nature.

This singular aspect of Italian civilization—the use of reason —harked back to Roman civilization, which highly valued reason in the affairs of life. While Italian civilization was driven by the force of reason and the here and now, Catholic civilization was driven by the force divine revelation and the afterlife. These conflicted drives were destined to clash bitterly and mortally.

The discovery of America had its roots in the year 1245 A.D. The European world at this time was small and young, and Mediterranean Italy was the center of many thriving activities. To the west was an unknown and fearful ocean, and all around were the frightening pagan barbarians, infidel Moslems and schismatic Byzantines, all threatening Italy. Pope Innocent IV wanted to reach an accord between the Catholic commonwealth and the Mongols to destroy the Moslems. He sent Father John de Piano Carpini to find the Great Khan of the Golden Horde. When Father John reached the lower Volga, he was told the Great Khan was in Karakorum 2,500 miles away. He reached this great city in time to see Guyuk, grandson of Genghis Khan, made Great Khan in 1246, and he discovered this new world to the east.

Later, Niccolo and Maffeo Polo from Venice would also meet Kublai Khan, but it was Niccolo's son, Marco Polo, who would become the most famous explorer in the family. He would fire the imaginations of the merchants in the fourteenth and fifteenth centuries with his tales of fabulous riches, and he would inspire a certain Genoese seaman.

The same power of creative expression, intellectual curiosity and freedom of thought that had inspired the great artists, writers and thinkers of the Renaissance would also ignite the fires of passion for the great navigators, mapmakers and explorers to discover the New World. However, it was the use of reason and scientific knowledge that enabled them to fulfill their yearnings.

The tales of the Kublai Khan by Marco Polo that inspired Columbus also aroused the curiosity of Paolo dal Pozzo Toscanelli, a Florentine astronomer, astrologer, mathematician and mapmaker who dared to challenge the prevailing concepts set by Ptolemy, the Greek astronomer, mathematician and geographer, in the second century A.D. Toscanelli produced his own map showing the extension of the ocean between Europe and Asia. In truth, he produced a new concept of the world.

Since Polo had spoken of the vast eastward extent of Asia, Toscanelli conceived the idea of sailing *westward* to reach the fabled land of Kublai Khan. He outlined this bold plan in a letter to Alfonso V of Lisbon, enclosed his newly conceived map and urged a westward passage to the "noble island of Cipango," or Japan.

Christopher Columbus, a brilliant mariner, a devout Catholic and a courageous adventurer, had spent his youth in Genoa, at the time a powerful, prosperous and flourishing center famous for its shipbuilding, seafaring and mapmaking.

By 1476, Portugal had become the exploration center of Europe and the world through the gifted Prince Henry "the Navigator." The riches and rewards of taking to the high seas were obvious to everyone. Valuable cargoes of spices, ivory, gold dust and, sadly, Negro slaves were bringing fortunes to maritime powers. Christopher Columbus and his brother, Bartholomew, saw the fabulous opportunities in seafaring and started their careers by making and selling mariner's charts and maps.

Around the end of 1481, Columbus was thrilled when he heard of Toscanelli's letter and map, and he immediately wrote to obtain a copy of the map. For here was confirmation of his own intuition, that it was possible to get to the fabled Indies on a westward route. Toscanelli sent Columbus the precious chart with an encouraging letter, and the first step was taken in what became known as Columbus's great "Enterprise of the Indies."

Because by the time of the Renaissance Italy was not a unified country but a huge collection of independent city-states, Columbus had to go to powerful nations with large treasuries for funding.

Columbus first presented his "wild" proposal to King John II of Portugal in 1484. The king had his doubts, so he referred the project to a committee. These learned men rejected Columbus's proposal not, as legend has it, because they thought the world was flat but because they thought Columbus had grossly underestimated the sailing distance from Portugal west to Asia. At this time, while most scientists knew the world was round, no one had any idea, including Columbus, that there might be two vast continents between Europe and Asia. The king's experts were actually more correct in their judgment than was the zealous Columbus, who had indeed underestimated the distance to the Indies.

In 1485, after the death of his wife, Columbus left his beloved Genoa with his son, Diego, and moved to Spain. He and Bartholomew sought the support of Spain through King Ferdinand and Queen Isabella, who vacillated for years with dreary, academic and petty arguments.

They decided to approach King John II of Portugal again, but in 1488, Bartholomeu Dias found a sea route to India by rounding the Cape of Good Hope at the southern tip of Africa and this killed King John's interest in Columbus's plan. If there was a water passage open to the east to reach the Indies, why was there any need for a westward route? But the Columbus brothers persevered and hoped this discovery would stimulate a rival and competing interest in their plan. They promoted their enterprise enthusiastically in all the courts of western Europe for years.

Finally, after almost eight frustrating years of agonizing rejection, while on the verge of financial ruin and just about to leave Spain for France in despair, Columbus and his brother achieved success. Queen Isabella, in a dramatic last-minute decision, suddenly changed her mind and sent word to Columbus that Spain would indeed fund his "Enterprise of the Indies."

There is some evidence to indicate that a certain Bishop Geraldini or Gherardini was confessor to Queen Isabella and that it was he who persuaded Isabella to stake Columbus. This evidence suggests that this bishop was an ancestor to President John F. Kennedy on the Fitzgerald side of his family. If it hadn't been for this bishop, Columbus might never have discovered America.

The day of departure for Columbus and his three tiny ships, the *Niña,* the *Pinta* and the *Santa María,* was set for August 3, 1492, from Palos, and was fixed by Ferdinand and Isabella as the same day by which all Jews were to be expelled from Spain.

This horror was one of many perpetrated by the religiously intolerant Inquisition. What an irony that Christopher Columbus, who may have actually had Sephardic Jewish ancestors, set sail to discover a new world of freedom and liberty on the same waves carrying the hapless Jews out of an old world of persecution and death!

This was also the year in which the Moslems were finally defeated, ending nearly eight centuries of war that had dominated the affairs of Italy. Catholics everywhere rejoiced and exulted. Now people could turn their energies to new enterprises.

THE GREAT ENTERPRISE OF THE INDIES

At age forty-one, Columbus, having won a mighty battle on land, would now wage his war on the high seas with the *wind*. All his years of knowledge, experience and understanding of seamanship would now be singularly devoted to one purpose. He was a genius mariner and a master of the winds, but if he could not harness his considerable talent, abilities and skills to get him where he wanted to go and back, all would be for naught.

It is hard for us to imagine, here in the Atomic Age, how incredibly difficult it was for Columbus to cross uncharted seas totally dependent on the wind, for this was the Age of Sail. Fortunately for Columbus, he was blessed with that precious, mystical ingredient of any great enterprise—*luck*. The winds that blew Columbus across the Atlantic to America were so strong that Columbus's crew worried that they might not be able to return. And Columbus was gifted by the gods with weather beyond compare.

Columbus first set his course southward instead of due west from Spain, and in so doing, avoided the turbulent winds of the North Atlantic. Thus he reached the Canary Islands, where he then turned due west and luckily picked up the northeasterly trade winds, which carried him to his destiny in America—

which, of course, had *not* been his destination. At two o'clock in the morning on October 12, 1492, a man in the crow's nest of the *Pinta* shouted, *"Tierra! Tierra!"*, a shout that would reverberate for centuries around the world, and claimed the 5,000-maravedi bonus for being the first to sight land.

After a brilliantly navigated though difficult and treacherous voyage, Columbus reached the island of San Salvador in the Bahamas and planted the Castilian flag for Spain and the Christian cross for God in the New World. Not realizing that he was on America's doorstep Columbus thought he had landed at the far edge of the Indies; when he and his men were hailed by the disbelieving, wide-eyed natives, Columbus called them "Indians," and the name stuck.

Columbus was indeed a man ahead of his time, who ranks with Leonardo da Vinci as a genius. He was a cultured man, a brilliant thinker and a gifted seaman. His inquisitive and creative mind was characteristic of a true Renaissance man. Not only had he come upon a new land not known before, but he had actually discovered the best westward sea passages between Europe and North America, and he had done this with sailing ships whose only source of energy was the wind. Also, by venturing forth beyond the edge of the world into the unknown, Columbus shattered the orthodox view that beyond the Atlantic Ocean lay the edge of the Earth. In doing so, he finally faced down the fear that had sustained the belief in a flat world.

The man who changed the world died in obscure loneliness in 1506, still believing he had found some "Asiatic" islands. Little did he know there were two continents to be discovered between his destiny in America and his destination in the Indies.

This discovery would be left for another Italian. Amerigo Vespucci, born in 1454 in Florence, the seedbed of the Renaissance, had a voracious curiosity, great intellectual ambition and a brilliant mind. His family friends included Botticelli, da Vinci and Ghirlandaio, and his patron was Lorenzo the Magnificent. This pioneer of the Age of the Sea is considered the "opener of the modern mind," for it was Vespucci who realized that what Columbus had discovered was not the Indies but a New World.

Vespucci's powerful knowledge of astronomy, cosmography and cartography would push his ships to fulfill Columbus's dream of reaching Asia. By 1499, Vespucci's geographic and commercial interests drew him into the alluring quest to find a westward route to Asia.

Using Ptolemy's maps showing Catigara, described by Marco Polo as the point around which Chinese treasure poured, as the southeast tip of the Asian continent, Vespucci set sail for a passage around Catigara. This first voyage was unsuccessful, but he returned knowing Ptolemy's picture of the world was wrong and, most of all, knowing his own experience yielded more truth than theory.

On his second voyage, he not only solved the most pressing problem of navigation—that of determining latitude—but he produced the most accurate estimate of the earth's circumference in its time. In 1499 he realized South America was a continent and named its northern end "Venezuela," meaning "Little Venice" in Florentine dialect. Vespucci had started with a Ptolemaic view of the world, but his experience changed that view and taught him otherwise. Thus Vespucci broke with hallowed tradition and, based upon empirical evidence, proclaimed a *Mundus Novus*, a New World, and a fourth continent. Yet in terms of commercial enterprise, this unexpected giant land mass seemed more an obstacle than a boon, since the goal was still to find the treasures of the true Asian Indies. This new continent was simply in the way of attaining this goal.

The christening of this fourth continent is owed to a German printer, Martin Waldseemüller, who wanted to print a new edition of Ptolemy's geography. Vespucci's sensational accounts of his *Four Voyages* were more interesting than Columbus's "new route to the Indies" since they spoke of this surprising "Fourth Part of the World." Thus Waldseemüller, with a penchant for making up names, printed Vespucci's new map and named this new continent "Amerige," after its discoverer. When Waldseemüller realized his error, changed his mind and decided Columbus should be credited as the true discoverer of the New World, it was too late. His printed messages were all over Europe and could not be retrieved. Though unintentional, this may have been history's first great media hoax.

Certainly Columbus was responsible for discovering America, but it was truly Vespucci who realized, who knew, who understood, that what had been discovered was not the eastern tip of the Indies, but was in fact a New World. More important, this was representative of a new way of thinking of the world, a new mind-set, a modern mind-set. Vespucci opened up not only the New World, he opened up the modern mind. For this reason, it is perhaps more fitting for America, which means "rich in wheat" in Italian, to be named after the Renaissance man, Amerigo Vespucci. It is significant that Waldseemüller's map showed two faces at the top—Ptolemy faced east and Vespucci faced west—and to the west was the New World.

In the wake of Columbus and Vespucci came other great explorers and discoverers. When Henry VII of Great Britain entered into this new field of transatlantic discoveries, it was two Venetians, Giovanni Caboto (John Cabot) and his son, Sebastiano, who navigated for him. In 1497, Giovanni voyaged to what is now Canada and probably landed on Cape Breton, explored the coast of Nova Scotia and sighted Newfoundland. This voyage gave England legal claim to part of the continent and opened the way for the coming of America's first settlers. Thus, though the first flag implanted on the North American mainland was English, it was fixed by an Italian!

In 1498, sailing with his son, Giovanni Caboto reached Chesapeake Bay and perhaps Cape Hatteras. In 1508, Sebastiano skirted the Atlantic coast from Florida to Canada and entered the straits of New York a hundred years before Henry Hudson. Sebastiano Caboto had been pilot major of the Spanish fleet but reentered the services of England in 1548 as chief pilot. Giovanni Caboto continued to be regarded as one of the great navigators in Europe. He helped form the company of Merchant Adventurers of London, which laid the foundation of British domination of India and the whole British Empire.

This truly signified the start of Great Britain as a world empire. At the core of England's future maritime strength were Giovanni and Sebastiano Caboto, who provided the knowledge and improvements that made British naval power so eminent and great. They began an era which would bring Great Britain to world power, and would later bring economic, religious and political freedom to millions of people in America.

In 1508, Giovanni da Verrazano, from Florence, entered the St. Lawrence River, twenty-seven years *before* Jacquez Cartier. In 1524, with four ships, he sailed from France to land near North Carolina and sail north. He entered the Upper Bay of New York, the entrance to which is now called the Verrazano Narrows in his honor, then cruised along the southern coast of Long Island and discovered Block Island and Narragansett Bay. He was the first to explore the Atlantic coast in this area, to describe the Bay of New York and the White Mountains. He concluded that North America was a continent, putting to death once and for all the hope that the riches of the East were just beyond this small impediment. Thus another Italian gave France a basis for her claim to a large part of the new world. Unfortunately, for Verrazano as well as for France, he was killed, roasted and eaten by Caribbean natives in the Bahamas.

Antonio Pigafetta, an Italian adventurer from Vicenza, accompanied the great Magellan in 1519 on his voyage circumnavigating the world. His vivid eyewitness accounts of this stunning achievement were published as *Primo Viaggio Intorno al Mondo* and fascinated Europeans with vivid and exciting tales. Magellan himself was killed during this trip, during which the Pacific Ocean was first explored and named, but eighteen weary men, including Pigafetta, arrived at Seville, Spain, after having gone all around the world. Pigafetta's stories were a sensation, and within a few decades the traditional European worldview was transformed.

The concept of "island earth" as a connected land mass comprising six sevenths of the surface would be replaced by a new concept of "ocean earth" as a connected body of water comprising two thirds of the surface of the spherical planet earth. Never before in history had there been such a sudden or drastic change in man's concept of the world.

The New World was now a clear and understandable reality. Mankind's consciousness of its own earth, now based on *experience, reason* and *scientific method,* had changed dramatically, progressed significantly and made a quantum leap forward into the modern world.

The world would never again be the same.

3

NEW WORLD ITALIAN AMERICANS

The Land Of Amerigo

The news of this exciting, mysterious and exotic new world that had been discovered hit Europe like a bomb. No sooner had Columbus set foot in Spain, back from his first voyage, than Europeans, and especially Italians, began making plans to follow his course to the lands beyond the known world. Thus began a migratory wave of Italians to the "land of Amerigo."

There is a popular misperception that between the time of Columbus and the time of the mass immigration in the late 1800s there were no Italians in America. After Columbus discovered "America" and Vespucci proclaimed the New World, Italians have been coming to these new lands and contributing to the birth, growth and evolution of what would become the United States of America.

Italians have always been travelers, missionaries, seamen, adventurers and immigrants. By the time of Columbus's voyages, Italians had already explored every corner of the known world. To Italians, the discovery of America and the New World offered another exciting chance to venture out into the world in search of fortune, opportunity and experience.

Since the fall of the Roman Empire, Italians had been

34

identified regionally as Genoese, Venetians, Neopolitans or Sicilians. Italians who wished to embark for the New World had to find their way to the countries outfitting expeditions, such as Spain and England. To some extent, Italians were already living in these countries or in the port cities from which the ships sailed. Always restless and itching for new adventure, Italians enthusiastically signed up for these exciting excursions, thus inevitably and fortunately linking Italian destiny with America's.

Many Italians who had already become residents of other countries were seamen, craftsmen, merchants and skilled workers, especially in England. These Italians were actually working for trades, businesses and companies that were becoming dynamically involved with enterprises in the New World. Italy and England have always had close ties, especially since Roman Gaul included the British Isles. Italian culture had been flowing into England for hundreds of years, and now much of this culture was being shipped to America with English labels on it.

Textiles manufactured in Lombardy, Italy, were being exported to Scotland and then re-exported to the world under a British trademark; Lombard Street, the financial district of London, is named for Lombardy. An Italian Englishman Father Richard Blount, a Jesuit, assisted Lord Baltimore in founding the colony of Maryland. A Ferrar was treasurer of the Virginia Company, John Polentine was a burgess in Virginia and Edgar Allan Poe's ancestry may be traced to Italy. Many of the great English writers, Lord Byron and Shakespeare among them, got ideas and inspiration from Italy and Italian literature.

As soon as settlements were founded, Italy became a vital link in trade between America and Europe. The early English and Dutch colonists eagerly sought commercial trading relations with Italy. Italian seamen, who had worked for maritime nations for centuries, dominated the crews of ships heading for America. Henry VIII of England used these skilled seamen to help him build the strongest maritime power in the world.

Artisans from Italy were brought over to the settlements and colonies to produce wine, olive oil, silk and glass. Italian winegrowers or *vignerons,* came over along with Captain John Smith in 1610. Some of the Huguenots in South Carolina were Italian, and the Prioleans of South Carolina trace their lineage to the Doge Priuli of Venice. The Taglioferros came to Jamestown about 1637; the name Tagliaferro, usually pronounced "Tolliver" and often spelled this way today, is one of the old, revered names at the American South. These Italians lived in Virginia, the Carolinas, Pennsylvania, Maryland, New Jersey and New York. The fishing industry of New England traded briskly with Italy; traffic between America and the Mediterranean flourished. Many Italians settled in Spanish and French Louisiana, where they developed the fishing industry. They traveled from New Orleans to Missouri to engage in fur trading around St. Louis.

The most notable early pioneers were missionaries, especially Jesuits, who not only converted the unbelievers but explored the country, establishing missions in the southwestern, north central and northwestern United States.

The missionary work of Fra Marco da Nizza (usually spelled Marcos de Niza, Spanish style) ran from Panama through Nicaragua and Guatemala. In 1533, he witnessed the death of Atahualpa, the Inca ruler that Pizarro treacherously executed. In 1539 he was sent north to try to reach the fabled "Seven Cities of Cibola," but this expedition ended in disaster. However, along the way and for the first time, the interior of the United States from Mexico to Nebraska was explored.

The history of Arizona began with Fra Marco's explorations. He got as far as the Grand Canyon and what is now Kansas. Almost a century and a half later, another Italian, Father Eusebio Chino, introduced European civilization in Mexico and Arizona. A magnificent explorer, Father Chino, along with Father Gogui, accompanied Admiral Atondo in 1683 on an expedition to lower California and northern Mexico. He spent twenty-five years exploring a huge area of the Southwest. Father Chino blazed new trails and proved that lower California was actually a peninsula.

Chino was not just a successful explorer and devout missionary. Along with Father Salvaterra, he was absolutely committed to creating self-sustaining Indian communities organized according to European values. He educated and trained the Indians and established some of the early industries in the Southwest, such as stock-raising. He was the cattle king of his day. Many towns in this area trace their origins to Father Chino's missions; over thirty churches were founded by Chino, including San Xavier del Bac, the oldest mission in America.

Father Francesco Bressani was the first European to describe Niagara Falls, and he was captured by the Iroquois in 1644. Three Italian military engineers accompanied Hernando de Soto in his exploration of the Southeast from 1539 to 1543. Antonio Crisafi was governor of Three Rivers in 1703, and his brother Tomaso led the new fort at Onondaga, New York, in 1696. Gemelli-Careri traveled along the coast of California in 1698 after visiting Asia and the Philippine Islands.

Enrico Tonti, known as "Tonti, the Iron Hand," was La Salle's protégé in the late 1600s and built the first vessel to ever navigate the Great Lakes. He and La Salle were the first to follow the Mississippi River to its mouth, where La Salle took possession of it in the name of France. Tonti helped create a league of Indian tribes, that significantly influenced the economic growth of the area. For four years, this adventurous explorer helped Iberville in laying the foundations of Louisiana and Mobile.

Enrico's brother Alfonso Tonti became one of the founders of the city of Detroit and was its governor for twelve years. His wife and the wife of the French colonial governor in North America, Antoine de la Mothe Cadillac, were the first white women to settle in Detroit. Henry Tonti, Alfonso's son, was governor of Fort St. Louis, and Pierre De Lieto, Tonti's cousin, was the first white settler at the post in Chicago.

A group of Italian Protestants, the Waldensians, escaping religious persecution, came to America in 1656. These emigrants left New Netherland and moved to Delaware, where

New Castle was organized. Another group of Waldensians apparently settled on Staten Island and in 1670 built the first church of any denomination on the island.

After these early newcomers, and throughout the seventeenth and eighteenth centuries, Italians continued to cross the Atlantic and make valuable contributions to the life and culture of this new land. Italians contributed significantly to the early growth of America. They crossed the seas in search of opportunity.

Alessandro Malaspina, born in Sicily in 1754, was charged with an audacious expedition of two ships to undertake a scientific voyage around the world to rival the expeditions of Captain Cook. In 1789, he set sail from Cádiz, Spain, stopped at Montevideo, rounded Cape Horn, scooted along the Pacific shores of South America, reached Acapulco, Mexico, and headed up the California coast. He sailed by Vancouver Island, passed the mouth of the Columbia River, turned south, cruised down through the bay of San Francisco and dropped anchor in Monterey Bay. His brilliant account of the Pacific coast ranks among the foremost accomplishments of the early American experience.

In 1757, Lorenzo Ghiglino, a Genoese sea captain, piloted the first vessel flying the papal flag to America into New York harbor. Anthony Trapani, one of the first foreigners to become a naturalized citizen, was a founder of one of the first Catholic churches in America—St. Peter's on Barclay Street in New York. A man named Carrico helped found the order of the Sisters of Charity.

In 1621, a Captain Norton brought four Venetian glassmakers to Virginia for this work. When General Oglethorpe founded Georgia in 1733, one of his main purposes was to develop the area into a big silk-growing center and to experiment with vines and olive trees. Failing utterly, Oglethorpe brought a group of Piedmontese silk growers to Georgia. Paul Amatis was one of these skilled artisans who created a thriving silk industry here. In 1751 a silk factory was erected in Savannah, and another Piedmontese, Joseph Ottolenghi, was put in charge. These first successful silk enterprises would have vital and significant practical consequences for the industrial development and growth of the South.

In Virginia in 1771, a Neapolian named Fornicola became the owner of an inn at Richmond. The Marquis de Charstellux described his experience there: "Fornicola served me and my party with such magnificence and profusion that there would have been too much for twenty people." His enjoyment of a "good Italian meal" resounds today.

In New Smyrna, Florida, however, a tragedy of colonization occurred. In 1768 a Dr. Turnbull brought 1,500 emigrants from Europe, of which 110 were Italian, to colonize the area. Intolerable conditions, horrendous problems with hygiene, an infestation of malaria-carrying insects and all-but-indentured servitude combined to create one of the great tragedies of the immigrant experience. The Italians managed to survive the cruelty and hardship.

Giacomo Costantino Beltrami, a very distinguished judge from Bergamo, Italy, retired and traveled to Philadelphia in 1821 to join a military mission. He wound up in North Dakota, where he plunged into the wilderness with no knowledge of the country. A true pioneer, he paddled his birchbark canoe up the Mississippi River to Lake Julia, which he rightfully proclaimed as the true source of that mighty river.

Beltrami's picturesque descriptions of Indian life provided his good friend James Fenimore Cooper with valuable background material for his famous books. Also a friend of Lafayette and Chateaubriand, this courageous and adventurous "Italian Davy Crockett" had supreme faith in the future of America, and he proclaimed for all of Europe to hear that "the world is now in America!"

And so it was.

These adventurous Italians contributed far beyond their numbers to the new industries evolving in the new world. Along with many others who joined them, these early immigrants to America were also destined to play major roles in the artistic, economic, religious, educational, scientific, political and philosophical progress of a nation soon to be born.

LIFE, LIBERTY AND THE PURSUIT OF HAPPINESS

The American struggle for independence signaled a major victory for individual independence, liberty and equality, values Italians have cherished deeply from Roman times. The Age of Discovery and the Age of Reason clearly demonstrated the value of liberty, freedom of expression and creative thinking. Liberalism was inextricably linked with newly evolved rational processes, with positivism, with empiricism and with philosophical materialism. These all valued reason, applied the scientific method in one form or another and rejected the traditional authority of religion, revelation and the Bible. All were significantly linked to Italian thinking and philosophy.

The ideas and values, the aspirations and attitudes of the strong revolutionary storm about to sweep across the Western world had as original spokesmen, in various degrees, the Etruscans, the senators of the Roman Republic, the elected officials of the communal city-states, the humanist and Renaissance progressive thinkers, and the valiant freedom fighters of the Risorgimento to unify Italy—Camillo Benso di Cavour, Giuseppe Mazzini and Giuseppe Garibaldi.

Italians truly loved and embraced the new political formula being created by the Founding Fathers of the American Republic. This vision of a free and egalitarian society based on "life, liberty and the pursuit of happiness" was the very embodiment of Italian ideals, and Italians would actually have a hand in the birth of this new philosophy and new nation.

Filippo Mazzei, from Poggio a Caiano near Florence, came to Virginia in 1773 at the request of Thomas Jefferson and Benjamin Franklin to produce silk and cultivate vines and olives. As the friend of Jefferson, Washington, Madison, Monroe, Franklin and Lafayette, Mazzei exerted tremendous influence on the fathers of the republic, yet his heroic deeds remain unsung.

Mazzei was a dedicated believer in the equality of men and in democratic and republican ideals. He convinced Jefferson that if the struggle for independence were to be won, the people must be persuaded to reject British political institutions. They agreed that Mazzei would write about his thinkings in Italian and Jefferson would translate them. These writings also formed the basis for some of the wording of the Declaration of Independence. The following is from Mazzei's writings in Pinkney's *Virginia Gazette,* some of which he wrote under the pseudonym Furioso:

> All men are by nature created free and independent. Such equality is necessary in order to create a free government. It is necessary that all men be equal to each other in natural law. . . . a true Republican government cannot exist unless all men from the richest to the poorest are perfectly equal in their natural rights.

Mazzei helped pave the way for freedom and democracy in America with his mighty pen and with his sword as well. He and Jefferson fought together as privates against the British at Hampton under Patrick Henry. He drew up a plan for capturing the British in New York by cutting off their sea escape, a similar plan was executed at Yorktown and secured the surrender of Cornwallis. As a foreign agent for America abroad, he helped secure France's military and financial assistance. When he moved back to Europe, he wrote to Madison: "I am leaving, but my heart remains. America is my Jupiter, Virginia my Venus. . . . I do not know what will happen when I lose sight of Sandy Hook."

Yes, his heart remained and became part of the American ideal.

Another unknown hero was Francesco Vigo, born in Mondavi in 1747, who arrived in New Orleans in 1775 as a rifleman in the New Orleans militia. Vigo became a highly successful trader throughout New Orleans, Mackinac, St. Louis, Pittsburgh, Philadelphia, Detroit and Montreal, especially in furs. He was the first man to establish trade routes between the East and the western frontier.

During the American Revolution, George Rogers Clark convinced Jefferson, Henry and Madison that he could take over the territory to the rear of the thirteen colonies, or the old

Northwest Territory. At the time, Vigo was the most powerful merchant in that part of the country and a great friend of the Indians who held him in high regard. His headquarters were in St. Louis and the American cause was dear to his heart. Clark's expedition was just about to fail for total lack of supplies, food and ammunition when Vigo stepped in and bought everything needed for the troops. Without his help, the mission would have been doomed.

Again, when Fort Vincennes, under Captain Helen, was being attacked, Vigo set out at once, but was captured by the British General Hamilton, who had already won the fort. Because he was so loved by the French inhabitants, Vigo was released and immediately rushed off to Clark. Clark was resigned to defeat until Vigo arrived with his plan for a counterattack and with money to fund it. Without this successful victory, this territory would not have been won for the Colonies, and all the territory west of it, more than half the continental United States, might still be part of another country. By helping to bring about the British surrender, Vigo ultimately made possible the Louisiana Purchase and the opening of the West.

For all his valuable help, Vigo got nothing except the well-earned respect of his fellowmen. Clark's men got 149,000 acres of land in Indiana, but Vigo was not even reimbursed for his loans. He died in poverty. In 1872, thirty-six years after his death, the U.S. Supreme Court awarded $49,898.60 to Vigo's heirs.

William Paca was governor of Maryland and one of the signers of the Declaration of Independence. Captain Cosmo Medici of North Carolina received a lieutenant's commission in 1776 from the Continental Congress, appointed by Governor Caswell. Medici successfully delivered a group of British prisoners to Philadelphia, where he joined Washington's army and helped in the Battle of the Brandywine in 1777. Thousands of Italians participated in the American Revolution. Scores of Italian officers and privates are found on the rolls of American regiments.

Italian thinking, ideas and values, emanating from the Renaissance revival of a rich Roman heritage, and influenced in turn by the Age of Enlightenment and the various revolutions sweeping Europe, continued to cross the Atlantic with these early Italians. Since England and Italy were so vitally linked from Roman times, and since English thinking, ideas and values were so heavily influenced by Italian thoughts, a certain amount of "English culture" was really Italian in origin.

Just as Justinian law was the legal foundation for Western civilization, it was the humanistic philosophy of Cesare Beccaria and his treatise on *Crime and Punishments* that influenced jurisprudence around the world. The reform of the English penal laws of the nineteenth century owes much of its origin to this brilliant Italian thinker. So too does the reform of the criminal jurisprudence in America, which originated in the 1790s with William Bradford, attorney general first of Pennsylvania and then of the United States.

Bradford acknowledged the valuable and unmistakable debt Americans owed Beccaria and his thinking in a letter: "I wish the author of this book, which has been so well received in the Old Continent, to know that his efforts to extend the empire of humanity have been crowned in the New with the greatest success. . . . The honor of such a revolution in our Criminal Code must be attributed to this excellent book."

Thus Cesare Beccaria helped give impulse and inspiration to a reform movement in criminal jurisprudence that would spread across America. Beccaria also came to represent the very soul of the unification movement of Italy in the 1800s.

The Italians who came to America before the Civil War were mostly from northern Italy and were artisans, painters, musicians singers, sculptors, political exiles, seamen, merchants, priests, missionaries, traders and adventurers. They were scattered all across the country, many entering such ports as New York, New Orleans, Galveston and San Francisco.

The real founder of Buffalo, called by some the "father of Buffalo," was the Milanese Paolo Busti, who was given unlimited power to develop three million acres of land in northern New York State and Pennsylvania by the Dutch. In 1800, Busti was appointed general agent of the Holland Land Company for the sole management of this huge area.

When a young America fought against Tripoli and the

Barbary pirates, the king of the Two Sicilies and the Sicilian population assisted, entertained and feasted the Americans.

Ninety-six Italians from America joined the American forces in the War of 1812. One Sicilian, Salvatore Catalano, who in 1809 had been appointed a sailing master and had worked at the Washington Navy Yard, served as pilot of the U.S.S. *Constitution*. It was his naval skill and tact that helped Stephen Decatur succeed in destroying the *Philadelphia*, which had been captured and manned for battle against the Americans. Decatur acknowledged the debt he owed Catalano for this glorious naval victory, which echoed all around the world and brought fame to the U.S. Navy: "It would be injustice in me, were I to pass over the important services rendered by Mr. Catalano, the pilot, on whose conduct the success of the enterprise in the greatest degree depended."

Captain Joseph Zametti distinguished himself as well in this war and also served as captain in the defense of New York City and its harbor. Many Italian names appeared on the rolls of West Point, such as Pascal Vincent Bonis and Edwin R. Alberti.

Italian sailors also joined the crews of American ships going between New England and California. Giovanni Dominis, master of a ship sailing between Boston and the Pacific, brought the first cargo of salmon from the Columbia River, between Washington and Oregon, to Massachusetts, thus pioneering a whole new fishery trade. John Dominis, his son, was governor of a Hawaiian island and married Princess Lydia, who became the famous Queen Liliuokalani in 1891.

G. P. Morisini, a Venetian whose real name was Giovanni Pertegnazza, arrived on American shores in 1851 and rose to become Jay Gould's partner in the Erie Railroad. Giovanni Sartori was commissioned in 1797 as the first U.S. consul in Rome, and in 1800 he became the Pope's consul general in America. Agostino Codazzi traveled all across America and was famous for his adventurous exploration of Venezuela with Ferrari from 1816 to 1822.

In 1832, Marquis Niccolo Reggio came to Boston and established a flourishing business importing figs and raisins and exporting petroleum and its derivatives. His fierce rivalry with

Iasagi, a competitor, made Boston the top port in Near East trade.

Italian communities began to emerge in cities such as New York and Chicago. In New York, merchants and retailers, along with tailors, barbers, hairdressers and laborers, abounded. In Chicago, there were saloonkeepers, restaurateurs, fruit vendors and confectioners. Italian artisans, workers, interior decorators, cabinetmakers, bakers, carpenters, painters, stonecutters, masons and musical instrument makers were just beginning to be found in the burgeoning cities of America.

As this young nation grew, its cultural links with the Italians also grew, to the benefit of both America and the Italians.

THE FIRST AMERICAN BRAVO!

Italians have always been a creative people, whether their creativity expressed itself in the reality of simple survival or in the fabulous artistry of the High Renaissance. So it is no surprise that Italian immigrants in the early periods of America made so many contributions to America in the arts.

From the Pilgrims to the Declaration of Independence, there was hardly any art in the Crown Colonies, since the Puritans saw art as the work of the devil. In the second half of the eighteenth century, when the artistic consciousness of this new country was rising, America looked to Italy for inspiration.

The first artist to come to America was Giuseppe Ceracchi, in 1791, a gifted sculptor who had studied with the great Canova. Ceracchi created beautiful busts of distinguished Americans, such as Washington and Jefferson.

In architecture, the colonial style was really an adaptation of the Anglo-Italian style, which in turn had its roots in Rome and the Renaissance. When Thomas Jefferson built his new home on a gentle rise in Virginia, he looked to the architectural genius of the great Palladio for its design. He called it Monticello, meaning "small mountain."

A true man of the Renaissance and genius crafter of the American philosophy, Jefferson was the prime mover in bringing Italian artists to America. And it was, once again, to his dear friend, Filippo Mazzei, that Jefferson looked for help when he sought to embellish and decorate the U.S. Capitol.

Mazzei tried unsuccessfully to get Canova and instead convinced Joseph Franzoni and John Andrei to come. They produced excellent work for the U.S. Capitol. Carlo Franzoni also came; he is primarily remembered for what is now the dazzling Statuary Hall. Francesco Iardella sculpted, Antonio Capellano created bas-reliefs for the rotunda, Giuseppe Valaperti carved an eagle and Luigi Persico sculpted statues. Other sculptors were Enrico Causici, Cardeli, Francesco Vincenti, Gagliardi and Guido Butti.

Of particular note, in 1859 the gifted Costantino Brumidi, who had painted beautiful frescoes for the Vatican, settled in Washington. His work in the Capitol represents some of the best frescoes in America, including his *Apotheosis of Washington* in the rotunda and many fabulous murals in the President's Room of the Senate.

The predominance of Italian artists in America before the Civil War worked for the U.S. Government—early in the construction of the Capitol, later in the restoration of the Capitol after it was damaged in the War of 1812, and then in the building of the Capitol extension during the 1850s. Since these initial artistic efforts, Italian painters, sculptors and artisans have been enriching America with their art.

The Puritans also considered music to be sinful and frivolous, a diversion from religious worship, the only valid alternative to work. While dances, concerts and opera were enchanting the Europeans and bringing joy and zest to life, the colonists were busy passing laws prohibiting the playing of music; leisure time was devoted to prayer.

Thus, early music in America took the form of church hymns, which were permitted by the conservative Protestant church worshippers. Secular music in America was first heard in the mid-eighteenth century. After 1729 ballad operas, or pasticcios, similar to musical comedies, came into vogue, and though the words were in English, the music was composed by Italians. The first of these, *The Beggar's Opera*, was performed in New York City as early as 1750. Storace's *Doctor and Apothecary* was performed in Norfolk, Virginia, in 1796.

Although Italian musicians appeared in America around 1757 and even toured American cities before 1778, the first concert of record was presented by John Palma of Philadelphia in 1757. George Washington attended concerts by Francis Alberti from 1765 to 1767. Giovanni Gualdo, the first composer of any worthwhile music, gave some of the first legitimate concerts in America in Philadelphia. Tomaso Traetta, also in Philadelphia, set up his American Conservatorio, which was the first conservatory of music in the United States.

Thomas Jefferson again was a guiding force in bringing Italian musicians to America. He expressed his love of Italian art and music in a letter to his friend Mazzei: "If there is a gratification which I envy any people in this world, it is to your country and its music. This is the favorite passion of my soul, and fortune has cast my lot in a country where it is in a state of deplorable barbarism."

Because he was not enamored of the boring and unmelodious fife and drum music, Jefferson ordered Captain John Hall, who at the time was in Sicily fighting the war with Tripoli, to recruit Italian musicians for the first real band of the U.S. Marine Corps. Under Gaetano Caruso, fourteen Italians, mostly from Catania, came to America to lift the Marine Band to great distinction. In 1816, Venerando Pulizzi became its leader until 1827, and Joseph Lucchesi, Francis Scala and Francesco Fanciulli succeeded him.

The Italians held a virtual monopoly on secular music in America at this time. In 1836 the first band, called the Comet, toured the United States and was made up of Sicilians. The Italians literally created the American demand for orchestral music. Even Gottlieb Groupner, perhaps incorrectly called the "father of American orchestral music," owed his success to Louis Ostinelli, his conductor and first violinist. Ostinelli's daughter, Eliza, became the first Italian American opera singer and a leading prima donna.

Opera itself was an Italian art form, and the first Italian opera produced in America was Pergolesi's *La Serva Padrona* in

1790 in Baltimore. While an Italian called Traetta may have been the first to promote opera in America, Lorenzo Da Ponte, a learned and brilliant man, worked feverishly for its permanent success.

Da Ponte built the first opera house in New York on Church and Leonard streets, but this faltered and was ruined by fire in 1839. Ferdinando Palma, a wealthy restaurateur, opened another opera theater, but this too failed. Sanguiricio and Patti, father of the famous opera star Adelina, opened an opera house in 1847 on Astor Place. In 1854, the Academy of Music opened, where Adelina Patti made her debut at age sixteen. This too burned down in 1866.

Hundreds of Italian singers, opera stars and musicians came to America from the 1800s on. Though disputed, the author of the music to the hymn "America," supposedly written by Dr. John Bull, may have actually been either the famous Lulli or one Palestrina. Whoever the writer, this beautiful hymn is Italian in spirit.

These talented Italian musicians brought not just music to America, but a precious heritage and spirit that created a solid foundation for the diffusion and assimilation of Italian culture in the United States, thus enriching American life. This cultural exchange linked the traditions of the old country with the life this one.

QUEST FOR KNOWLEDGE

The quest for knowledge has always been a compelling force for Italians, along with an unquenchable thirst for learning, an insatiable curiosity and an irrepressible passion for travel, adventure and new experience. The same force that fired the Catholic theologians of the Renaissance in their philosophical commitment to the use of reason also drove the Italian missionaries and educators in America.

It is truly impossible to measure the valuable contribution of the Italian missionaries to America both in preaching the Word of God and in teaching the ways of man. The salvation of souls was always paramount with the Catholic clergy in converting the "savages" of the New World, but this also meant civilizing the person. Since Catholicism was rooted firmly in Aristotelian logic, rationalistic Thomistic theology and the use of reason in the grasping of spiritual truths, education was therefore vitally important for the purposes of spiritual conversion.

Thus, Catholic religious training was inextricably connected to worldly learning, and both were linked to an Italian value system and heritage. At the core of this uniquely Italian phenomenon was a strong humanistic and philosophical sense of mankind, a joyful zest for life, for sharing experience and for adventure, and a compelling spiritual imperative that Man *can* reach the sublime—through honest inquiry as well as through faith.

The first priest to set foot in the New World was John Bernardino Monticastri, who accompanied Columbus when he planted the Catholic cross along with the Spanish flag in American soil. The first clergymen of record in North America were Father Giulio Zarco in 1524 and Fra Marco da Nizza. Father Bressani, a Jesuit from Rome, came around 1642 and was the first European to describe Niagara Falls. In 1679, Father Gesù de Lombardi was killed by Hopi Indians in Arizona.

Many Italian priests accompanied Father Eusebio Chino in his great explorations of the American continent and his remarkable work with the Indians in the Southwest. Father Juan Maria de Salvaterra, a Visconti, founded the first mission in Lower California at Loreto and created the famous Pious Fund that made possible the Pacific coast chain of missions founded by Father Junipero Serra much later. Many of these missionaries and educators were also explorers and pioneers.

During the nineteenth century, the United States was flooded by missionary-educators, and Italian priests, especially Jesuits, could be found all across America. The vast territory from New Orleans to St. Louis was under the spiritual care of Italians. Father Cataldo is referred to as the real founder of Spokane, Washington. Italian priests labored in Alaska, and a nun, Sister Monaldi, built a hospital in Nome.

The Italian Jesuits established missions all over the South and California. Father Giuseppe Rosati, consecrated a bishop in 1824, was given charge of the New Orleans diocese, which then extended from Arkansas, Missouri and Illinois to the Rocky Mountains. Under his patronage the Jesuits founded the University of St. Louis in 1829, and Rosati helped establish St. Louis Hospital, the first of its kind. He transformed a diocese with a few log chapels into one with a cathedral, seventy-eight churches and sixty missions.

The famous Society for the Propagation of the Faith was founded by Father Angelo Inglesi in 1822. Inglesi proposed "the establishment of a great association in favor of the Catholic missions of the two worlds." Thus the principle of the universality of the church was adopted and the Old World of Europe was linked by religion with the New World of America.

Father Samuel Mazzuchelli, born into great wealth in Milan, gave it all up to devote his life to missionary work among the Indians of the Wild West in 1830. An excellent artist and architect as well, he built over thirty churches, each with a school, the first cathedral at Dubuque, Iowa, the first court-house at Galena, Illinois, and the first capitol for the State of Iowa.

From 1830 to 1860, Catholicism was attacked by members of the so-called Know Nothing movement, which spawned vicious anti-Catholic propaganda. Dr. Pise, born in Annapolis, Maryland, was ordained a priest and wrote one of the first novels about Catholicism in America. His *History of the Catholic Church* was praised by Pope Gregory XVI. This and Pise's many other works squelched the lies and accusations of the Know Nothing propaganda, and signaled a new era in the history of Catholic literature. Henry Clay had Pise appointed a chaplain of the United States Senate.

As great men of learning, former professors, bright theologians, masters of language and experts in the sciences, the immigrant Jesuits were welcome indeed to transplant their creative ideas to the fertile soil of this new country.

Father Giovanni Grassi made Georgetown the first great Catholic University in the United States in 1812. Father De Andreis founded St. Mary's College and Seminary near St.

Louis in 1818, the first institute of learning west of the Mississippi. Father Angelo Secchi, perhaps the most famous astronomer of his day, and Father Benedict Sestini, a famous scientist, came to the College of the Sacred Heart, the leading Jesuit scholasticate in North America, which was founded by Father Angelo M. Paresce and Cardinal Camillo Mazzella. Father Sestini was highly respected for his *Catalogue of Star Colors,* which is still used today, and he founded the *Messenger of the Sacred Heart.* Father Secchi's study of the surface of the sun was published by the U.S. government in 1853.

The College of Santa Clara in California was established in 1851 for the education of young Americans; it was started by Jesuits Father Giovanni Nobili and Father Michele Accolti with nothing but their own energy, themselves and $150 in capital. Father Giuseppe, also of Santa Clara, was renowned for his studies of electricity. He was one of the first to use carbon electric lights for streets, and he installed the first electric searchlight in the port of San Francisco. In 1866 Father Giuseppe Bayma published a treatise entitled *Elements of Molecular Mechanics* that was considered to be a hundred years before its time.

In 1841 Father Felice De Villanis was president of Rose Hill Seminary, now Fordham, in New York. Father Congiato and Father Antonio Maraschi founded St. Ignatius College, now the University of San Francisco, in 1854. Father Giuseppe Cataldo founded Gonzaga University at Spokane, Washington, in 1887 and Seattle College in 1892. Father Pamfilo da Magliano, along with other Italian Franciscans, established St. Bonaventure College and Seminary in 1855.

The sisterhoods also established numerous schools and academies. Perhaps the most well-known accomplishment of an Italian woman, though later, was that of Mother Cabrini, who founded her Sisters of the Sacred Heart in 1880. This blessed person, along with all her remarkable women, founded schools and hospitals throughout America. Mother Cabrini, also known as the Patron Saint of the Immigrants, was canonized the first American saint in 1946.

These missionary-educators founded churches, schools, hospitals and orphanages. They worked so very hard and asked nothing in return . . . except the salvation of souls for the greater glory of God.

While education in the name of God predominated the early history of America, there were also valuable contributions made by secular Italian educators and learned scholars from many fields of knowledge.

The first Italian lay teacher in an American academic institution was Carlo Bellini, who taught in Williamsburg, Virginia, where his good friend Filippo Mazzei introduced him to Jefferson, Washington and others involved in the new American government. He became an American citizen, joined the Virginia militia and taught modern languages at the College of William and Mary in 1779.

Lorenzo Da Ponte, Mozart's librettist and a man of many talents, was appointed a professor of Italian language and literature at Columbia University in 1825. Pietro Bachi, a Sicilian from Palermo and author of several books on languages, first taught Italian at Harvard in 1825. After Bachi, Luigi Monti, another Sicilian, taught at Harvard and also served on the faculties of Wellesley and Vassar colleges. He wrote an Italian grammar and many articles and became the American consul at Palermo, Sicily.

Eleutero Foresti succeeded Da Ponte at Columbia in 1836 and was later appointed professor of Italian language and literature at the University of the City of New York, now New York University, in 1842. Vincenzo Botta succeeded Foresti at New York University in 1856, and his home became a literary center and salon for many artists, authors and musicians of Europe and America. Tullio Suzzaro Verdi, from Mantua, first taught at Brown University, went to medical school, became a physician and was appointed president of the board of health in Washington, D.C. In 1861, Gaetano Lanza taught at the Massachusetts Institute of Technology.

Catholic education, especially that of the Jesuits, would emerge as a dominant force in America, and these early missionary-educators, who preached the word of God in a new land, were especially responsible for this vital contribution. In spreading the gospel to a new country, these devout men of

God and humanist scholars also educated its people and civilized its native population.

THE CIVIL WAR

By 1860, Italians could be found all across America. Most were settled in New York, California and Louisiana: but many had gone to places such as Boston, Charleston, Key West, Memphis, Mobile and Philadelphia. These early Italians lived in harmony with other pioneering immigrants, and in fact often intermarried. The later Italians, as well as other foreign-born who came to this new nation in the early nineteenth century, had to prove themselves before they were accepted, especially during the mass migrations.

The crises of Civil War gave the foreign-born a special opportunity to achieve acceptance. Among these foreign-born, the number of officers of Italian origin was the highest. More than two hundred Italians served in both armies, though most sympathized with the Union Army. Many of the Italians who fought were political exiles, some of whom rushed from Italy to America to join the Union Army, whose cause most of them supported, likely because it resembled the Italian need for national unity.

Even Giuseppe Garibaldi, the valiant and courageous freedom fighter of Italy's own movement to unify, the Risorgimento, considered signing up on the side of the Blue. In fact, later in the war, when President Lincoln faced his darkest moments and yearned for a quick victory, he offered Garibaldi a commission as brigadier general.

The new Italian government followed a policy of neutrality but in 1865 the people of Rome sent a stone from the wall of Servius Tullius, famous as the Roman Solon who introduced a military classification of citizen, to President Lincoln as a symbol of their deep love and admiration for him as a champion of liberty.

Francis Spinola, a man of vivacity, versatility and a strong devotion to American principles, served in the U.S. Congress for three terms and was admired for his loyalty, patriotism and eloquence as a speaker. Known as "Shirt Collar Spinola" because of the large shirt collars he wore, he made a famous dramatic speech in the New York Senate the day after the capture of Fort Sumter calling for that state's support for the Union and soldiers for its defense.

A strong man and an inspiring leader, Spinola was the voice for the masses of New York in the war, and the support of other states was swayed in favor of the Union by the actions of the Empire State. President Lincoln appointed him brigadier general, and he distinguished himself as a hero on the battlefield, though he had no military training. After the war, Spinola retired to private life in Brooklyn. When he died in 1892, both the House of Representatives and the Senate adjourned to commemorate him.

General Luigi Palma Di Cesnola was awarded the congressional Medal of Honor for his distinguished service in the war. He would go on to become the illustrious director of the Metropolitan Museum of Art in New York. Enrico Fardella, a Sicilian, was promoted to brigadier general for distinguished service at Plymouth, North Carolina. Charles De Rudio rose to colonel and fought with General Custer in the war against the Indians. Father Leo Rizzo da Saracena served as chaplain in the Union Army and later became president of St. Bonaventure College.

Of special note, Italian Americans formed a special regiment called the Garibaldi Guard that fought on the side of the North. They fought bravely and distinguished themselves, especially at Gettysburg. Five hundred Italian Americans served the South in Louisiana's European brigade. Eduardo Ferrero was the only general to command an all-black combat division.

Italian Americans also fought with distinction in both naval forces. Louis C. Sartori served as a commander in the Union navy and became commodore in 1873. Charles Sartori, his brother, also served in the Navy as acting assistant surgeon.

Through their valorous action and loyal service to the Union, Italians won a position of respect in the American community. America asked these immigrants to prove themselves, and they did—with blood and glory.

America's war with itself to maintain its own unity as a nation took place just at the time when Italy was becoming unified and experiencing its own internal strife. But the Italy that had just been unified around 1861 after a hundred years of turmoil and after centuries of decline from the mid-sixteenth century was a very different Italy from the Italy that brought the world the Renaissance. And this would have great significance to America.

GALILEO, CONDEMNED TO DEATH . . . ALMOST

The birth of a new and more highly evolved civilization results from the expansion of knowledge, the broadening of intellectual horizons, an increased understanding of the laws of nature, a greater mastery of the environment and a raising of consciousness about how mankind perceives itself in the world. Central to this process is the use of reason as the basis for observing the world, drawing conclusions, conceiving theories and experimenting to arrive at the truth about reality.

If one looks at the history of the Roman Empire, the first development of a new civilization different from all others, it is not altogether clear why reason plays a larger role in all dimensions of Roman life than emotion, intuition and belief systems, religious or otherwise. The Romans were a practical people, less concerned with philosophical speculation about the ultimate mysteries of life and the fundamental principles of life than with what could be achieved in the here and now. However, the Romans seem to have been somewhat indifferent to science, even though they brought the world such great engineering achievements as aqueducts, buildings and military inventions.

After the fall of Rome, Christian civilization seemed not at all interested in any scientific study of the world and man's place in it. Christians seemed predominantly concerned with the life of the soul, its eternal salvation and its lot in the afterlife. The curious irony of that period when Christianity saved Italy from darkness is that it was the great theologians and their commitment to rational thinking as a means to enhance the spiritual truths of their religion that saved the use of reason. And reason would be the basis of the Renaissance, the scientific method, the birth of a new civilization and the dawn of the modern age.

By the beginning of the fifteenth century, the total scientific achievement of the world was relatively small. Henceforth, however, monumental scientific achievements would change the world. In the time between the discovery of America and the mass migrations of the late nineteenth century, Europe and America experienced vast cultural, political, economic, religious and social change. The humanistic Renaissance and the creativity it unleashed on the world marked the beginning of the modern world. A significant result of this age of discovery and invention was the birth of the modern scientific method.

While the sailing ships of Columbus, Vespucci, the Caboti and da Verrazano were driven by the Italians' dynamic quest for discovery and by religious fervor, the winds that filled the sails and blew them to America were knowledge, reason, experimentation and the power of science. This too was precious cargo brought to the world.

Perhaps the greatest scientific contribution to America of Italians was its very discovery. In terms of the victory of hard reason over superstitions, Columbus's "Enterprise of the Indies" stands at the top, along with putting a man on the moon by means of spaceship called, appropriately, *Columbia*.

What is happening scientifically in Italy has always had a bearing on what is happening in America. Galileo was the father of modern science, and around his concepts, thinking and devotion to this new idea called science grew a community of kindred souls throughout Europe. While Leonardo da Vinci and his contemporaries were supporting one another in the fight against the demons of superstition, irrationality and religious intolerance, Galileo was isolated except for a few close friends and disciples.

In 1632, Galileo published his *Dialogue on the Two Chief Systems of the World*, which outlined the contradictory systems of Ptolemy and Copernicus. He presented his own conclusions that the earth did indeed go around the sun. In doing so,

Galileo denied the validity of intuitive conclusions without evidence, questioned authority, criticized dogmatism and attacked revelation as the source of truth. Worst of all from the point of view of the classicists who made up the scientific establishment, he published his findings in Italian rather than in Latin, thereby putting important information about scientific matters directly into the hands of those who, according to these critics, had no business having it, and who without proper guidance might draw improper conclusions from it. For this, he was arrested by the Inquisition, put on trial and condemned to die. When he later recanted, only publicly, he returned home and lived out his life in isolation in 1642.

What Galileo had done for the world, however, was to create a revolution, inaugurate the scientific age, open the door to empiricism and give birth to the Age of Reason. He would have his revenge in history, however, since the growth of science would later wreak havoc in the church.

Galileo apparently corresponded with some of the Puritan settlers of Massachusetts, especially with John Winthrop, who had traveled to Italy before 1629. Galileo's tradition of scientific inquiry carried into the seventeenth century when other scientists tried to apply the method outlined in his "heretical" *Dialogue*. His disciple Evangelista Torricelli experimented with magnetism, sound waves and light transmission and invented the barometer in 1643. Giovanni Domenico Cassini became a leading astronomer and in 1667 became director of the Paris observatory.

One of the most dramatic examples of the failure of history to reward important work properly may be the lack of recognition afforded Francesco Redi. Until well into the late seventeenth century, virtually all medical science believed in the theory of spontaneous generation, which held certain life forms could spring spontaneously from others, of an entirely different kind. The example cited was the mysterious appearance of maggots in decaying meat, as if produced by the meat that had previously contained no maggots. Redi, a poet, naturalist and physician to the court at Tuscany, posited that maggots were the first stage in life of certain flies who laid their eggs on decaying meat. By covering meat with cloths—and thus keeping the flies away—Redi proved that life forms can only come from parents of the same species and do not generate spontaneously. Without Redi's experiments, chronicled in his work *Generation of Insects,* medical science could have not freed itself from the fallacious theory of spontaneous generation and preceed instead on the proper assumption that disease was communicated from person to person because, and only when, germs managed to get themselves transported from one person to another. Though Redi was recognized in his life time (he helped found the Academia del Cimento in Florence, which served as a model for the Royal Society of London), he is seldom mentioned today when the giants of medical science are called.

Other Italians of the time important in medical research were Marcello Malpighi, a physician-scientist who was the first distinguished microscopist, and Giorgio Baglivi, an outstanding medical doctor of this period. They, like Redi, were ardent proponents of Galileo's scientific experimental method.

Italian books on many scientific subjects, the best in the world at the time, were found in the libraries of the early Pilgrims such as Cotton Mather and William Brewster. The Patriotic Society of Milan contributed many books to the American Philosophical Society, which was the first scientific institution in the United States. Several Italians joined as members—for example, the famous Count Castiglioni, Lucien Bonaparte and Carlo Botta, who would write one of the first histories of the American Revolution.

By the end of the eighteenth century, Europe was ablaze with scientific research, discovery, investigation, experimentation, innovation and invention. The Age of Reason and the Age of Enlightenment, along with social, political and religious upheavals, had changed the world. The revolutions in Europe and America created a new intellectual environment, and inquisitive thinkers felt free to express their ideas without a fear of losing their liberty. Many scientists took up the cause of Galileo and carried it gloriously into the future.

A community of brilliant thinkers, inventors, humanists, scientists and philosophers dedicated to free thinking, reason, liberty and science thus evolved in Europe and America. In the

French Enlightenment some were called *philosophes*, and in Italy some were called *abati*. Scientific inquiry and excitement over experimental discovery captivated creative thinkers on both sides of the Atlantic.

Thomas Jefferson and the other Founding Fathers were in close touch with Italian scientists: this was especially true of Benjamin Franklin, who corresponded avidly with his Italian colleagues across the Atlantic. He could read Italian and maintained a lively scientific correspondence with Alessandro Volta after they met in Paris in 1782. Volta was experimenting with transforming chemical energy into electrical energy, and in 1800 invented the Volta pile. This was the first energy device in the form of a battery to produce electricity in specific quantities and was vital to the further study of electricity. The volt is named for Alessandro Volta.

Luigi Galvani had also been working with this strange new form of energy, and the descriptions of his exciting experiments fascinated scientists, amateur or professional, in Italy, America and the rest of Europe during the 1790s. The words galvanometer, galvanism and galvanize are all derived from Galvani's name.

Lazarro Spallanzani studied various animal functions such as blood circulation, digestive processes, respiration, fertilization and reproduction. He performed the first artificial insemination and is hailed as the first great experimental physiologist.

Giuseppe Lagrange, a mathematical genius, was a professor of geometry at age sixteen and helped found the Academy of Sciences in Turin in 1758. His book represented an intellectual climax of the Enlightenment. During his time he was considered the leading European mathematician.

During the nineteenth century, more scientific interchange began to occur between America and Italy. Giuseppe Tagliabue came to New York City in 1831 to set up a manufacturing plant for thermometers and other glass instruments. He learned this from his uncle Cesare of Como, Italy, who is reputedly the first to manufacture thermometers in quantity. Tagliabue devised many instruments for the U.S. Coast and Geodetic Survey.

Experiments with electricity dominated the work of many

nineteenth-century Italian and American scientists. These studies were focused on the harnessing of electrical energy for practical usage. In Italy, Luigi Brugnatelli invented electroplating in 1805. Antonio Pacinotti invented the Pacinotti ring in 1858 and the first dynamo in 1860. Galileo Ferraris built transformers, developed polyphase current in motors and discovered the rotary magnetic field. Augusto Righi analyzed magnetism, electrical conductivity and electrical waves, thereby paving the way for Marconi's wireless transmissions. His experiments into the structure of matter and radioactivity helped make the scientific leap forward to the study of nuclear energy.

Amadeo Avogadro, a gifted physicist and mathematician, made startling discoveries about the property of gases. His hypothesis, now known as Avogadro's law, speculated that under the same conditions of heat and pressure equal volumes of all gases contain the same number of molecules (this number is now known as Avogadro's number). Avogadro's work was not accepted in his time, but fifty years later Stanislao Cannizzaro demonstrated that atomic weights could be determined using Avogadro's law, and the law has since become one of the principal underlying concepts in the atomic theory of matter.

In 1846, Ascanio Sobrero discovered nitroglycerin, from which Alfred Nobel later developed dynamite. In 1852, Eugenio Barsanti and Felice Matteucci invented the internal combustion engine. Giuseppe Pizaai, an astronomer, discovered and named the first known asteroid, Ceres. Giovanni Schiaparelli, another astronomer, discovered and measured the rotations of Mercury and Venus, studied meteor clusters and described canals on the surface of Mars in 1877.

In 1876, many Italian scientists attended the International Centennial Exposition held in Philadelphia, and they were impressed. One of them, Giuseppe Bellanca, became a pioneer in aviation; his monoplane, the *Columbia*, was the first cabin aircraft to cross the Atlantic. The Bellanca two-seater airplane is still popular among flying enthusiasts.

Quirico Filopanti, a scientist also interested in airplanes, came to America in 1849 and returned to Italy in 1866 to join

Garibaldi in his fight to unify the country. He later returned to America in search of funds for his experiments in aviation.

Dr. Felix Formento, a scientist born in New Orleans in 1837, served as chief surgeon of the Louisiana Confederate Hospital at Richmond, Virginia, during the Civil War. He wrote many medical books and later became the president of the American Public Health Association. In 1890, Dr. Antonio Lagorio, born in Chicago in 1857, established the first Pasteur institution in the West at Chicago. E. O. Fenzi, a famous horticulturist, introduced plants from all over the world to the fertile land of sunny California.

Perhaps most fascinating, and unfortunately most tragic, is the story of Antonio Meucci, born in Florence, who came to the United States in 1850. He had been experimenting with the electric transmission of the human voice through his *telettrofono* since 1849 and he had filed patents for many other inventions. In 1860, Meucci played "La Marseillaise" over a wire at a great distance from its source.

Unable to finance a patent on his invention, called in English the telephone, Meucci settled for a caveat in 1871, but could not afford to renew it in 1874. Alexander Graham Bell announced his invention of the telephone in 1876, and Meucci cried foul. A series of complicated lawsuits and countersuits ensued, but the pathetic Meucci died a broken man in 1891 with his case on appeal, never to be won. Meucci felt his work was stolen by Bell, but could never prove it. But whether or not Bell came to his discoveries independently, Meucci has never been properly credited with having been the earliest inventor of the telephone.

What a lovely touch for Italian Americans if people had been making their checks for telephone service payable to the Meucci Telephone Company over the last one hundred years!

The tradition of scientific achievement during the time before the mass migrations, instigated by Galileo's genius and steeped in a heritage of Renaissance creativity, would continue into the twentieth century with great vigor.

4

THE GOLDEN DOOR

IMMIGRATION

IMMIGRATION CAN be defined as "the act of moving for one's permanent settlement to a country where one is not native and, in doing so leaving one's own country of origin." This single word and this singular conscious act on the part of millions of Italians would comprise a seminal achievement for the course of Western civilization and would change the history of America. The ships that reached the shores of America with millions of Italians in the late nineteenth and early twentieth centuries were carried on a tidal wave of Italian culture and civilization.

Immigration has *always* been an integral part of Italian life. During the time of the Roman Empire, Italian colonies were scattered throughout the then-known world. Conquests, migrations, invasions and the assimilation of many tribes, peoples, regions and city-states all contributed to the formation of what became the Italian nation.

During the Roman era, from the third century B.C. on, Italian colonists by the hundreds of thousands emigrated from Italy. Many traveled to the rich countries of the eastern Mediterranean; under Caesar and Augustus the government provided free public land grants to its citizens settling in the empire. These emigrants succeeded in romanizing many peoples and lands that would become future European nations such as England and France.

The next major Italian migration, more sizable than the

previous one, was the result of military expansion during the three hundred years of the *Principate*, from Augustus to Diocletian. Whole cities—for example, Cologne, Mainz and Vienna—sprung up next to military encampments. This large-scale all-encompassing migration essentially created the homogeneous culture of the third century A.D., which made Rome-Italy one single and unified nation. The Edict of 212 A.D. granted Roman citizenship to all inhabitants of the empire, a cherished prize at the time.

However, with the collapse of the Roman Empire in 476 A.D., the trend in migration was reversed, and for almost eight hundred years, with the ensuing deterioration of the country, Italy was invaded by barbarian hordes, zealous infidels and foreign rulers, all of whom plundered and savaged the glorious Roman-Italian nation. Italy was plunged into the darkness of the Middle Ages.

During this calamitous time of invasions, wars and conquests by outsiders, Italians could try only to survive somehow the intrusions, and to assimilate the foreigners into their world. Much of the creative spirit and many of the special qualities of the Italian people were forged in this history of cross-cultural exchange.

The emigration of Italians to other countries, especially to those of western and central Europe, increased again from the eleventh to the fifteenth centuries, during the time of the Renaissance. This movement began with the rise to prominence of three very important and powerful maritime cities of northern Italy—Pisa, Genoa and Venice. Valuable interchange with other peoples through trade and the Crusades brought further expansion of the Italians from Europe to the East. In southern Italy, now a relatively strong unit of previously weak and small states, the rulers set out to expand their territory. Imperialistic and political in nature, this drive to expand created tension and turmoil but also culturally connected the Italian civilization with the Byzantine and Islamic civilizations of the Near East and North Africa.

Until the end of the fifteenth century and throughout the Renaissance, Italian expansion, mainly through trading activity, reached out of Italy, especially to Europe. Italians monopolized commerce and the manufacturing of goods. Wherever Italians went, they stimulated economic progress and brought an Italian culture that always benefited the country of migration.

In the second half of the fifteenth century, the expansionist efforts of Italians began to slow due to political and economic problems. Italy lost the dynamism that had charged her people from the eleventh through the fifteenth centuries. Ironically, Italy's greatest export, the Renaissance and its remarkable achievements in the arts, humanities and sciences, would become a major element in Western civilization, but in the process, the Italians would be depleted. The developing nations of northwestern Europe would carry on the splendid achievements of the Renaissance, while Italy would be left a country on the verge of collapse. Unfortunately, Italy remained a prized possession and the battleground for foreign powers trying to rule the country over a period of four hundred years. These conquerors would find, however, that while they could rule Italy, they could not rule the Italians.

Sadly, it would be four centuries before Italians would venture forth to new lands in great numbers to share with the world the benefits of their culture, heritage and experience. But when they did, for altogether different reasons, the world would once again be changed.

THE RISORGIMENTO

The creative spirit of the Italian people would be reignited in the crucible of the American experiment and Italian migration. Italians would once again discover America, this time, however, coming not from a land of relative plenty as did Columbus and Vespucci, but from poverty, disease and catastrophe, for the Italy that spawned the mass migrations of the late 1800s and early 1900s was very different from the Italy that nurtured the golden age of the Renaissance and the birth of Western civilization. The greatness, wealth and prosperity of Renaissance Italy had declined gradually and steadily from the mid-sixteenth century until the Risorgimento of the mid-eighteenth to mid-nineteenth century, Italy's great national revival and unification. Thus Italy became simultaneously one of the youngest of the modern republican nation-states and one of the oldest of Western cultures.

Many complex historical events created the circumstances that led to the great mass migration from Italy in the late nineteenth century. Italy, at the time of its final unification between 1859 and 1861, had just experienced four hundred years of chaos, turmoil and disaster in every dimension of life, one hundred years of which were spent in a strife-torn struggle to unify as a nation. The wars waged by European powers over Italy, the domination of the Roman Catholic Church over the lives of Italians, the great religious upheaval of the sixteenth century, an economy in total ruin and a series of disastrous events, natural and man-made, all combined to create a revolution that left Italy a place to *escape*, not to live in. To understand the context of this great migration and why this happened, we must go back to the early days of Mediterranean civilization.

In the time of the Etruscans and the Roman Empire, Italy sat at the very center of the Mediterranean and thrived as the center of world commerce. Thus powerful rulers and warring monarchs sought to invade and conquer this rich country. The Roman emperors fought off these invasions with great success, united many disparate peoples and from 270 B.C. until 476 A.D. ruled a huge empire. Then Italy-Rome was attacked from the north by the Germanic tribes—Franks, Lombards, Ostrogoths and Visigoths—and from the south by Austrians, French, Germans, Muslims, Normans and Saracens. Ultimately these invaders would achieve victory, conquer the Italians and destroy the Roman Empire. The sacking and looting of Rome by Alaric and the Visigoths in 410 A.D., foretold the end of the world as Rome had created it.

Most significant for the collapse of Rome and for the world in the long run was the birth of Jesus Christ in Judea, a distant Roman territory under the power of Pontius Pilate, the Roman procurator for that area. This simple carpenter, who claimed to be the Son of God and who preached a simple message of charity and love, would play as much a role in the fall of Rome as the invading hordes. At a time of military valor, when the rich held great power and an empire had been built on the idea that to prevail and prosper one must kill one's enemy, the teachings of Jesus shook the mighty foundation of the powerful Roman empire.

Christ was crucified and the disciples of this holy man gave birth to Christianity, now a religion with over one billion members, over one fifth of the world's population. However, in the beginning of the history of Christianity, it was to *Rome*, the crossroads of the world, that the followers of Christ, now called Christians, went to spread the teachings of Christ and the Word of God.

Over many centuries Rome became the center of the Christian church. The bishop of Rome became the Pope, the head of the whole church with the absolute authority of a monarch over the Italians, including the right to collect taxes, and the church became the Roman Catholic Church. The church, centered in Rome and Roman life, was strongly imbued with Roman customs, traditions, symbols, icons and rituals. This original church has endured as a faith, a belief system and an institution to the present day.

Christianity/Catholicism thus became a significant power and a dynamic force shaping the destiny of mankind. At the core of its influence was a centralized hierarchical structure in which each congregation was organized on a democratic basis with a certain autonomy. However, the authority over men that the church exerted was channeled into *political* alliances, especially in 800 A.D., when Carolus Magnus, Charlemagne, was crowned emperor of Rome by Pope Leo III.

During Charlemagne's rule and after, chaos reigned in Italy, triggered by a new wave of Viking invaders and internal divisions among Charlemagne's descendants, who would later split the empire into what is now France, Germany and Italy. While confusion and corruption reigned in Rome, the popes wielded great independent temporal power. Feudalism was born at this time as a system providing some security from foreign invasions, tyranny, cruelty, poverty, ignorance and internal civil strife.

The key element to feudalism was the relationship one had with the land, the primary, if not the only basis of economic survival. The job of maintaining law and order in this troubled time fell to the local dukes, marquises, counts and bishops and abbots, whose monasteries served as protection. Thus the clergy, almost by default, became independent rulers. While the feudal system eliminated equality and restricted liberty, it enabled the populace to survive.

In 952 A.D. the German king Otto the Great defeated Berengar II and was crowned king of Italy. His reign established the Holy Roman Empire on the religico-political unifying principle of "one pope, one emperor." This would last, in a manner of speaking, until 1806, though in name only for some of these centuries. By the nineteenth century, the power of papal succession had created such a strong political alliance that it ruled Europe, and its rule would have to be broken at great cost to the Italians and Italian life.

To add to the historical confusion of this time, and to explain a great divisiveness between Italians, Italy was not ruled by one monarch and Italians were split into two separate and distinct peoples. The North developed into independent city-states such as Genoa, Milan and Venice and were ruled by powerful, wealthy families. Many of these northern city-states prospered and remained independent until the seventeenth century. The South, however, predominantly a rural area without strong urban centers, remained prey to invaders; its people absorbed an exotic mixture of foreign cultures. Southern Italy was dominated by the Spanish from 1522 into the nineteenth century.

During this long era of foreign rule, the wealthy, privileged landowners totally controlled the destiny of their tenants. They held the power of life and death over the southern peasant farmers, or *contadini*. While the less restricted and more dynamic northern Italians became more worldly and cosmopolitan, the poorer and immobilized southern Italians remained under the power of the controlling landlords, thus denied any hope of economic advancement. When Italians, northern and southern, came to America, these cultural differences would remain; worse, they continued to cause problems for the already grief-ridden immigrants, especially the southern Italians.

At the time of America's War of Independence in the 1770s, Italy was divided into three separate parts. The central part was called the Papal States and was controlled by the pope. The northern part was composed of city-states under the hegemony of the Austrian Empire. The southern part was called the Mezzogiorno and was under Spanish rule. In spite of this, Italians continued to fight for their national identity and rebellions broke out throughout the 1700s. Many of the leaders of these rebellions, often driven into exile, served as inspiration to Americans struggling to throw off English rule.

Ironically, the American and French revolutions helped the Italians in their fight for independence. Napoleon Bonaparte, who was born not in France but in Corsica, upset the balance of power in Italy in 1796. Napoleon, as part of his plan to conquer Europe, invaded Italy, seized control, and drove the Austrians, the Spaniards and the pope out of power. French politics thus played a role in the lives of Italians, albeit a short-lived one. When Napoleon was defeated by Wellington in 1815, control of Italy returned very much to its previous status. Italy now consisted of the Kingdom of Sardinia, including Genoa, Piedmont, Sardinia and Savoy; the Papal States; Tuscany, consisting of a series of smaller duchies in north central Italy; Lombardy; Venice; and the Kingdom of the Two Sicilies, including the area around the city of Naples and all of Sicily.

By now, the successful revolutions in America and France had inspired the Italians to cast off the yoke of oppression and seek freedom from all foreign domination. After the Napoleonic wars, the shift in power had set the stage for revolution. When the French populace overthrew Bourbon rule in 1831, costing the pope French military support, the Italians revolted against the Papal States.

In Bologna, a republic was proclaimed, but Austria stepped in and squelched it, placing the city under military control. Rebellions in Naples and Piedmont erupted but were brutally suppressed, again by the Austrians. The ruthless application of force and the repressive policies of the Austrians especially angered the Italians. This anger would give rise to the Italian unification movement, or the Risorgimento.

Giuseppe Garibaldi, Giuseppe Mazzini and Count Camillo Benso di Cavour were the three great heroes responsible for the success of the Risorgimento. In America, philosophers, statesmen and the people followed this movement with intense interest. Mazzini particularly was admired and respected by leading American intellectuals and liberals. Garibaldi even lived for a time in Staten Island, New York, as a celebrated exile and a friend of Antonio Meucci.

Mazzini provided strong leadership to the movement, and his underground political fighters, Giovine Italia (Young Italy), for a brief time drove the Austrians out of Italy in 1831, the same year Charles Albert was proclaimed king of Sardinia. Mazzini tried to convince Albert to lend his support to the movement but he refused, and although he later declared war on Austria and granted his people a constitution in 1848, a year later the Austrians crushed this move.

After this defeat Charles Albert abdicated his throne in favor of his son Victor Emmanuel II. Meanwhile, in the Papal States, Pope Pius IX, threatened by the revolutionary movement, first allowed some reforms, but then revoked them. However, Garibaldi, an early follower of Mazzini, led an army into Rome in 1849 and before Pius could act against him proclaimed Italy a republic. The pope left Rome, but the French came to his rescue and reestablished the papal authority.

While Mazzini provided inspired leadership and Garibaldi provided military skill, Count Cavour used diplomacy and statesmanship instead of revolutionary force to win Italy's fight for independence. In 1852, Cavour was named prime minister by Victor Emmanuel II, new king of Sardinia-Piedmont. Cavour formed alliances with Great Britain and France, and even sent Sardinian troops to fight alongside the French in the Crimean War, thinking to earn France's help in ejecting the Austrians from Italy. He then struck an agreement with Napoleon III of France in 1858 for a joint declaration of war against Austria.

Napoleon III betrayed Cavour and negotiated a treaty with the Austrians that awarded Nice, Lombardy, Sardinia and

Savoy to France. Cavour resigned as prime minister in protest, but returned soon and negotiated a new agreement with Napoleon III that gained Romagna, Parma, Modena and Tuscany for the kingdom of Sardinia-Piedmont.

In 1860, while Cavour carefully negotiated, Garibaldi excitedly raised an army, dressed his troops in bright red shirts, took control of Sicily, charged victoriously into Naples and won control of that territory, and then marched on to take Rome. However, Victor Emmanuel, fearing the French would intervene to save the pope, denounced Garibaldi and sent his troops to stop him. Garibaldi surrendered, but Cavour—under the pretext of protecting the pope from revolutionary forces—sent the Piedmont army across papal territory and proclaimed Sardinian dominance over all of northern Italy except Venice. In the south, the pope still controlled an area around Rome.

In 1866, just when the movement to unify Italy seemed doomed, Italy allied with Prussia to defeat Austria in the Seven Weeks' War, and this victory returned control of Venice to Italians. In 1867, Garibaldi mounted another assault on the Papal States, but French forces repelled the attack. In 1870, Napoleon III suffered serious losses in the Franco-Prussian War, and the French military protection of the Papal States lost its credibility. On September 20, 1870, Garibaldi and his Red Shirts marched victoriously into Rome. On July 2, 1871, Rome was proclaimed the capital of a united Italy. At long last, after centuries of foreign domination, the Italians ruled their own country once again!

The changes that came in this era—the emancipation of the suffering masses, establishment of the principle of equality under law, establishment of religious tolerance, a lessening of censorship, the end of papal control and ecclesiastical jurisdiction, the secularization of education, and economic reforms based on free enterprise—all amounted to a revolution, from which would be born the Italian Republic and a democratic constitution.

However, the newly unified Italy faced many serious problems whose roots went back centuries. Years of foreign domination and disparate loyalties had made the Italians a collection of different peoples with opposing points of view. The continued refusal of the papacy to give final, formal recognition to the Italian state reinforced these divisions. The profound differences between the poverty-stricken South and the wealthier North widened. Though unified, Italy seemed curiously at war with itself. This led Garibaldi to observe: "It has taken a hundred years to unify Italy. It will take another hundred years to unify the Italian people."

Unfortunately for Italy, unification and independence did not end inequities and injustices. The glorious victory of the Risorgimento, the great Italian revolution, was in many ways a disaster for the Italian people, especially those from southern Italy.

Fortunately for America, for the first time in four hundred years, Italians would again venture forth to new lands in great numbers, this time in search of a better life, to the Land of Opportunity *oltremare*—beyond the sea.

OLTREMARE—BEYOND THE SEA

Ironically, the torch carried by the Italian people in the name of liberty would scorch those that shed blood for it. While Italy had been united by the courageous efforts of the Risorgimento, this unification was in name only. Each area of Italy had developed its own unique and special history, customs, traditions, dialects, attitudes, values, beliefs, philosophies and problems.

The political, social and economic divisions and differences within Italy that had existed from the days the Roman Empire were *heightened* by Italy's reunification. Unable or unwilling to continue to endure the persistent hardship, between 1880 and 1900 5 million Italians immigrated, and between 1900 and 1920 another 10 million fled Italy. By 1970, approximately 5.2 million Italians came to America.

Prior to the mid-1870s, most immigrants to the United States came from western and northern Europe. Between 1820 and 1860, hundreds of thousands of English, Germans and

Irish migrated to America in the first mass migration to America. These early immigrant groups established themselves in a social pecking order that would cause clashes and conflicts with later immigrants from Europe. In time, these first immigrants, along with the Americans who had been here from early days, would look upon the later immigrants as "invading hordes" threatening the special character of American life. Those Italians who left the poverty, suffering and ignorance of the old world for a life in the new world would encounter prejudice, discrimination and ignorance of a new type.

After national unity came to Italy around 1870, most of Italy had to recover from four hundred years of chaos, foreign rule and wars, a hundred years of which were committed to the reunification movement and struggle for independence. The nineteenth century in Italy was a time of great change, of political revolution, of wars and bloodshed, and of repression.

As a consequence of the final unification of Italy, many educated Italians experienced a personal sense of broadened horizons beyond the bounds of their traditional horizons, whether political or economic, public or personal, emotional or intellectual. The reawakening of Italy was as much a personal experience for Italy's people as it was a national experience for Italy's citizenry. Just as in a certain way the Renaissance marked a rediscovery of Roman values, tradition and heritage, the Risorgimento brought with it revival of a powerful culture that had been fragmented by political forces for three centuries.

After unification, Italy began its rebirth into the modern industrial world, the very world the Renaissance had helped to create, but for historical reasons Italy had missed out on. Italy now had to catch up with modern industrial nations, though it might take a century, but when it did, it did so with her own unique creative spirit. Ironically, the unification movement itself contributed to the mass exodus from Italy to America in the late nineteenth century.

The decision to leave Italy was more than simply a weighing of internal oppressions against external opportunities. Migration had always been part of the Italian character, especially for northern Italians, who were the first to arrive in America in the time before 1880. Northern Italy had always been more advanced than the poor agrarian South, and northern Italians were more worldly, cosmopolitan and experienced with travel to other countries. Most were already quite involved with world affairs as traders, merchants and businessmen dealing with other cities and countries.

The unification of Italy was beneficial to the North, though for many reasons unfairly so. The events after the Risorgimento triggered economic prosperity and rapid industrialization in the North, especially since the new national government in Rome was oriented toward the North and dominated by northerners. These new leaders of a revived nation primarily concerned themselves with holding on to their newly created power and ignored many of the old problems created by centuries of abuse.

With their eyes firmly fixed on the future of the new Italian nation, governmental leaders were blinded to the critical and centuries-old crises of its past, and this primarily meant the problems of the South, the *Mezzogiorno*.* Not only did the government of Rome spend huge sums to run itself, it demanded that its financial excesses be paid by the already overburdened southern Italians, whose problems required, but did not get, the attention of its government.

All throughout the 1800s, even before the great migrations of the last two decades of the century, many Italians left Italy. Some went to neighboring countries, but most crossed the Atlantic to North and South America. Many of the northern farmers immigrated to South America, especially Brazil and Argentina. However, in the late 1800s, a yellow fever epidemic in Brazil and political crises in Argentina and Paraguay dissuaded Italians from emigrating to these countries and encouraged them to turn toward North America.

Northern Italians also left Italy as industrialization established itself in the northern urban areas, several of which, like Milan, would eventually become modern twentieth-century

---

* The word *Mezzogiorno* means, literally, "noon," but is also used to describe the South of Italy. A similar idiomatic use exists in French, where the word *Midi*, ("midday") also describes the South of France.

metropolises. In 1848, the discovery of gold in California lured Italians to America, as did the rich, fertile soil of the west coast, where Italians would create the prosperous agricultural and wine-making enterprises. Fishing and trading also attracted many Italians, especially in port cities such as San Francisco, Boston and New Orleans.

While Italians of the North were not having as tough a time surviving in Italy as those of the South, Italy had a depressed economy and whatever economic growth there was just could not keep up with the expanding population. Pure and simple, opportunity was elsewhere, and before 1880 over a million emigrants, mostly from northern Italy, packed up and left their homes for other countries, especially the United States. They would be followed later from 1880 to 1920 by millions of fellow Italians from southern Italy.

Italian American community life in America began to emerge during the 1850s, as Italian artisans, journalists, tradesmen, skilled craftsmen and political exiles came from the embattled regions of an Italy still in the throes of the unification struggle. Many of the political refugees especially became responsible, effective leaders of the Italian American communities of large urban areas, especially New York City.

During this time, most of these children of Italian immigrants had no formal education and had to work to help support their poverty-stricken families. Through the efforts of native American reformers, who later played a major role in the lives of Italian immigrants, and of an outraged Italian American community, these abuses of child labor were eventually outlawed by legislation. The American Catholic church also failed to provide education for these children, one of its many failures in dealing with its Italian members.

That the Catholic church exerted very little effort to help the Italian immigrants socially, even though most Italians were devout Catholics, is an historical curiosity. Before 1880, there were very few Italian priests in America, even though there had been many Catholic missionaries to the frontiers in America. The church was predominantly Irish and had no use for these vulgar, non-English-speaking foreigners with pagan rituals who were supposed to be Catholic. When the southern

Italians, who were even stranger in their religious practices than the northerners, arrived later, all hell broke loose between the Irish clergy and their new Italian parishioners.

The reform movement in America and the native American humanitarians helped the Italian immigrants, as did Protestant ministers and laymen, thus accounting for the number of Protestant Italians in America. While these early Italians welcomed the support of sympathetic government officials, the generosity of American philanthropists and the social benefits offered by the Protestants, they preferred self-help to charity. So they established mutual benefit associations to provide financial, educational and medical assistance to other needy Italian Americans.

By the 1870s, enclaves of Italians were emerging in the big cities; such an enclave was referred to as Little Italy, the most famous being that around Mulberry Street in New York City. At this time, life for Italian Americans was very difficult. Americans of this period were fervently devoted to the accumulation of wealth and property rather than to social causes. America was committed to industrial growth, and the captains of industry were given free reign to exploit natural and human resources for their private gain, thus causing great human suffering, especially among the immigrants.

In addition to having to endure horrid housing conditions, inhuman working conditions and exploitative wages, unskilled Italian laborers in the urban industrial areas and coal-mining regions found themselves in natural conflict with an earlier migrant group, the Irish. The bitter competition for jobs, for neighborhoods, for the meager gleamings left to the immigrant groups as America produced its great wealth brought violence, and fighting broke out between these two groups.

The 1870s was a terribly troubled time for America. The forces of industrialization and urbanization were sweeping the country just as a maelstrom of Italian migration was gathering strength. This was a time of confusion, dislocation and hostility, and native Americans looked for scapegoats to pin the blame on for the widespread social unrest and consequent violence gripping the country. It is in this period, to the misfortune, pain and anguish of the Italian American, that the myth of Italians as lawless gangsters had its roots. This myth, formed during the 1870s, would become a pernicious negative stereotype by 1881.

Thus to the problems of mere survival in the new land were added the abuses due to prejudice against Italian Americans. And this prejudice would transfer to the millions of southern Italians soon to come to America, but with the extra added attraction of the Mafia myth, according to which Italians were heartless killers, vicious criminals and members of a secret society of evil.

Fighting against nativism and xenophobia, burdened with fear, discrimination and prejudice, and cursed with terrible economic difficulties, northern Italians made up the majority of slum dwellers in the Little Italies across the land during the 1870s. Yet by the 1880s many had became respectable and even successful, and many had unobtrusively joined the mainstream of American life.

Human nature being what it is, many of these northern Italians, now securely successful and socially accepted, would forget their own experience of poverty and prejudice, and deprecate the character and habits of the southern Italian immigrants of the next huge wave. These southern Italian immigrants, unlike any other people who had come to America, unlike even their own fellow countrymen and women from the North, would soon replace the northern Italians as the focus of racist violence and humanitarian concern in America.

ISOLA DELLE LAGRIME—ISLAND OF TEARS

During the 1880s a human tide of immigrants from Italy continued to flood American shores, but this time the immigrants were from southern Italy, the Mezzogiorno, described at the time as a land that time forgot.

Right through unification and beyond the South remained firmly entrenched in a feudal agrarian economy on which over 80 percent of the people depended for a living. Thus, the southern *contadini,* the peasants, were locked into a land system that offered no hope for personal betterment, victims of a government policy committed to the expansion of the North at the expense of progress for the South.

The rule of the South by the North created political chaos as well as economic disaster for the South. The dream of unification became a nightmare for southern Italians, and instead of the welcome relief expected by the peasant population, things grew worse. Rather than bringing order to the whole of the nation of Italy, unification brought more inequality and greater political disorder. In addition to the unfair tariff laws and other acts deliberately favoring the industrialized North over the agrarian South, graft, bribery and corruption on the part of local public officials in the southern provinces further worsened the situation.

To add insult to injury, many of the absentee landlords, who with the connivance of corrupt officials grew rich on high rents and unfair terms imposed on the southern peasants, were from the North. These arrogant landlords shared pitifully little of the wealth extracted from the land, provided unsteady employment and never reinvested their profits back into the area.

Then to the economic crises created or perpetuated by the callous indifference of the new government in Rome were added every conceivable form of natural disaster. Rain, when it did fall, fell in the wrong seasons and in torrents, cascaded down the hills and carrying off precious topsoil. This in turn spawned malarial swamps in the lowlands. Blighted land, deforestation, the lack of any natural supply of water or any kind of irrigation system—all these combined to put farming in a disastrous state. The southern Italian peasants now faced a life of squalor, poverty and bondage to a ruined land. And to add insult to injury, they could not even *own* this miserable land.

Malaria, pellagra, cholera, sickness and disease reached epidemic proportions. Phylloxera, a kind of plant lice, destroyed the vineyards and thousands of acres of crops. To unemployment, poor wages, substandard housing and lack of education, were added famine, earthquakes, droughts, heat waves, floods, soil erosion, crop destruction and volcanic eruptions. To make matters worse, there was a population explosion in southern Italy at the time.

Even circumstances outside Italy and beyond their control hurt the southern Italian economy. France levied a high tariff on Italian wine, making it too expensive for Frenchmen to buy, so the southern Italian wineries of Apulia, Calabria and Sicily faced financial disaster while northern Italians continued to buy French wine. Ironically, because Italian immigrant farmers had become so successful growing in California and Florida those same crops they had grown in Italy, the United States started to reduce its importation of fruit from southern Italy. Even the sulfur trade of Sicily, which exploited small children to carry ores from the mines, fell on hard times.

The southern peasants rioted in protest against their miserable conditions, but to no avail. They were left barely able to survive. Life for the southern Italians was absolutely unbearable. The uncaring, northern-dominated government in Rome, the catastrophic economic ruin, the political disorder, the oppression of the poor, and a phenomenal barrage of natural disasters all added up to one thing—*hopelessness*. And the message in all this misery, this *miseria*, though painful, was also clear—"Seek opportunity elsewhere!" And the land of opportunity was *oltremare*, beyond the sea.

Thus, for these poverty-stricken wretches, immigration meant liberation and a better life. The southern Italian peasants had had enough of poverty. They were now ready to leave the homes and villages they had lived in all their lives to venture forth to an unknown land.

Immigration for the southern Italians was a soul-wrenching experience. Unlike many northern Italians, who were more experienced with the ways of the world, these socially handicapped southerners came from a stagnant and stratified provincial culture and had had no experience whatsoever interacting with the outside world; few, if any, had had relations with peoples beyond their immediate region. In fact, for most *contadini* the trip to America was the first trip outside the village where they had been born and spent all of their lives.

While southern Italy remained locked in the grip of a depressed economy, dominated by an oppressive government, constantly on the verge of ruin and suffering ceaselessly from poverty, the clarion call "America! America!" rang throughout the *Mezzogiorno.* Steamship agents and American labor recruiters, along with *padroni,* or labor contractors, scoured the southern Italian countryside for human beings to send to America as laborers.

These proclaimers of a new life and of salvation from starvation charmed the poverty-stricken peasants with stories of wealth, prosperity, freedom, liberty, equality and, jobs across the sea. They painted a picture of the United States as a land of plenty where the soil was rich, work was abundant, wages were high, taxes were low, military conscription did not exist, the opportunities were infinite and the possibilities were endless. America promised a better life, for *nothing* could be worse than what they were currently enduring. And so America called to these poor peasants, and they answered enthusiastically, and by the millions.

The southern Italians sold all their earthly possessions to set sail for America. Many fully intended to discover their riches in the promised land, then return to their homes and lead more comfortable lives. Some did become rich and returned. Others became destitute and returned. Most stayed in the United States, and most prospered.

By the 1870s it took a steamship only ten to fifteen days to cross the Atlantic. Also, trade between North America and Italy and Europe was growing rapidly. Several European shipping lines provided passage on steamships from several Mediterranean ports to New York and Boston.

Almost 90 percent of the Italian immigrants crossing the Atlantic did so crammed like cattle in steerage, which was the cheapest passenger section of the steamers. The trip to America was a hellish odyssey. They found themselves jammed into narrow double-decker beds on awful mattresses in overcrowded, poorly ventilated and stench-filled compartments. The ten-to-fifteen-day voyage across the sea to the promised land was in fact an anguish-filled eternity of rotten food, bad smells, seasickness, foul bathroom facilities and maltreatment by uncaring or hostile crew members. Whenever they could, these poor wretches spent their time outside on the decks of the ships to escape the horrors of the lower depths.

For the vast majority of the millions of immigrants, the port of destination was New York City. What a wonder it must have been for these peasant farmers from the land that time forgot, a stricken land of scorched earth, to steam into the Verrazano Narrows, sail by the Statue of Liberty and set foot on the land where "the streets were paved with gold."

Starting in 1892, the first step in the land of opportunity that these Italians took was onto Ellis Island, the hub of disembarkation for the millions entering the United States. During the most crowded times of immigration, many were herded onto barges like cattle to await their chance to set ashore on the pier leading them to the main entry point of Ellis Island. From the main entrance, all the poor, ill-clad, illiterate, non-English-speaking peasants were herded upstairs through a nightmarish maze of corridors in the Great Hall, where they were unceremoniously stripped naked and brusquely examined for contagious diseases, physical deformities and mental disorders. Those who passed were then shuffled to the registry section, where with the help of an interpreter they had to answer an array of questions. Those who failed either the medical examination or the questioning faced the worst and most feared calamity—a forced trip back to Italy. Those who passed all the tests, about 95 percent of the Italian immigrants, were approved for entry and given their ticket of admission to America.

Italian immigrants called Ellis Island *Isola delle Lagrime,* the "Island of Tears," for it was here that their greatest dreams or worst fears would be realized. This was the final point for the immigrants in their journey beyond the sea, but it was also the point on which balanced entrance to America and the promised land or deportation back to Italy.

The Statue of Liberty lit the way through the passageway to America, but it was the Great Hall that opened the golden door to opportunity in the promised land. If one could only get through that door, salvation would be won, liberation would be

achieved, victory would be gained, and life would be better. Or
so the peasant immigrants from southern Italy thought when
by the millions they walked through the golden door of Ellis
Island.

MEZZOGIORNO

The southern Italians arrived in America bewildered and
afraid, unable to speak English. After they had somehow
managed to survive the indignities of medical inspection and
interrogation, and after they were released from Ellis Island
into America, they were ferried to the Battery section of
Manhattan or to New Jersey train terminals to carry on their
journey to places all across the country, places they could only
dream of or imagine back home.

When they arrived in America, free at last from the misery
and oppression of Italy, they were hardly prepared to live,
much less survive, in this exotic, fast-paced urban environment.
The agrarian, rural and feudal society of southern Italy was
highly stratified and completely cut off from the modern
world. Modern industrial life was as foreign to these isolated
and seemingly backward people as life on Mars.

The culture, traditions and life-styles of the *Mezzogiorno*
simply did not provide the survival skills for the strange new
American society. These peasants, who seemed to step right
out of the pages of a medieval passion play, were thrown into
the boiling caldron of a melting-pot America and challenged to
a life-and-death struggle to survive in the highly competitive,
basically democratic, primarily industrial and modern new
world. No two cultures could have been more different!

Upon arrival, the immigrants, most of them penniless, were
immediately assaulted by enterprising Italian Americans who
offered various services to their fellow *paesani*. Many of those
extending the hand of friendship turned out to be cheats and
con men. Those who were reputable provided transportation,
changed Italian money to American, offered employment,
recommended living quarters and gave valuable advice. Later,

agencies of both the Italian and American governments and of the local Italian American community were organized to provide these services at Ellis Island.

While the literature and guidebooks given to the immigrants at Ellis Island urged them to head for farms in the southern and western states, most of them settled in the cities of the northeastern states, including New York, New Jersey, Pennsylvania, Connecticut and Massachusetts. New York City, Philadelphia and Boston in the Northeast, Chicago in the Midwest, New Orleans in the South and San Francisco in the West all became major centers for Italian immigrants.

In these times of stress and turmoil, in a foreign and frightening country, and in an unfamiliar urban environment, the southern Italian immigrants sought security in the familiarity of their own self-created, though not always by choice, communities. Back in Italy, their lives had always revolved around a tightly knit extended family and around their *paese*, or home area.

These Little Italys provided the same closeness, security and community life that they were familiar with in the old country. Here they gathered with *paesani*, people from the same region who spoke the same dialect and practiced the same customs. In these ethnic neighborhoods, the immigrants, along with their families and friends, sought protection and safety from an alien world, thereby insulating themselves from the *Americani*, who were so different from them. Thus most of the southern Italians remained in these Italian enclaves, where the slum housing, though old and crowded, felt safe and secure. Most of all, it was home for these struggling new Americans, and home is where the Italian family lives and thrives.

Southern Italian immigrants brought with them the culture, traditions and folkways of their native lands, and conscious of it or not, they also carried within their souls a brilliant heritage that had somehow survived for centuries, that was now surviving the journey across the sea in the holds of rat-infested steerage, and that would still survive the calamities, clashes and connections with American culture.

Centuries of conquests, invasions, crises, abuse and exploitation had created within the Italians a dependence on the family as the only truly secure institution. To the southern Italian, the world was divided into three basic kinds of relationships: that of family members, or *la famiglia;* that of godparenthood, or *comparatico,* meaning close friends of the family who became members of the family; and the rest of the world, all strangers, or *stranièri.* During this period of mass migration, especially in the early decades, the family provided the foundation for the survival and eventual success of Italian immigrants in America.

Unfortunately and ironically, although northern Italians had immigrated a generation before the southern Italian *contadini,* they did not offer any help to these new immigrants. Ancient prejudices and different customs and dialects continued to separate the two groups. To northern Italians, the "problem" of the South seemed transplanted thousands of miles from home. Northerners viewed themselves as more sophisticated and urbane than the country-bumpkin southern Italian farmers and peasants, so they tried to avoid any connection or association with them. They forgot their own experiences in the struggle to survive and how much they could have used a leg up. Now that others were fighting those same battles they had little interest in the obstacles to be overcome.

The differing physical features of each Italian group also set them apart. While most northern Italians were fair-skinned, reflecting the Germanic component in their background, most southern Italians were darker, reflecting their combined Spanish, Arab, Moorish, Greek and French ancestry. The swarthy features of the southern Italians also set them apart from the fair-complected Anglo-Saxons who dominated America at the time, and with whom these immigrants would bitterly clash.

The white Anglo-Saxons thought they were superior to these "unwashed hordes" invading a lily-white America, an America they had built. So totally disregarding all non-British elements in American society, they sought to maintain an imagined purity in the national character, much to the detriment of all concerned.

During the forty years of the mass migrations from 1880 to 1920, there was widespread violence, economic dislocation and fear, prejudice, discrimination and racism. America was on the industrial warpath, and the United States was changing from a rural nation into an industrial giant. From the 1870s, native Americans used Italians as scapegoats to explain the chaos and to blame for the violence. So the perception of the Italian as a lawless gangster that had haunted the previous generation of northern Italians now evolved into a full-blown stereotype and descended with a vengeance on the poor southern Italians. By 1881, this notion of a lawless Italian had fully crystallized in the minds of non-Italians, especially those of white Anglo-Saxon Protestants.

The myth of Italian criminality can be traced to the history of the Italians' relation to authority and the Mafia, though several legends tell variations of a similar theme. Generally, the origin of the Mafia is traced to nineteenth-century western Sicily, when Spanish misrule and oppression, along with a choatic feudal system, created a desperate need for a workable system of law and order. Landowners, believing as they did in the medieval concept that the dignity of the individual compels him to administer his own law, hired clandestine groups as guards and law enforcement officers, known as mafiosi, to protect their homes and families from marauders and foreign rulers. The mafiosi expanded upon their work and actually enforced a more equitable form of justice than that provided by so-called legitimate government.

Because the Mafia operated extralegally, special security was required. Bound by a blood oath of *omerta,* not to seek justice by any legal institution, the Mafia became a way of life containing the seeds of criminal clandestine activities. Because power corrupts, the mafiosi became a law unto themselves, exacting tribute from landlords as well as peasants. Then they began extortion by threat, smuggling, selling "protection," fencing stolen goods and other criminal activity.

According to other interpretations, the Mafia dates back to the eleventh century during the Norman domination of Sicily. After the rape of a young Sicilian virgin by the French, a clandestine group sought vengeance and justice, taking up the cry "Morte Alla Francia Italia Anèlla" ("Death to France, the cry of Italy.") The legend of the Sicilian Vespers comes from this story also.

Whatever the origin of the power of the Mafia over the lives of southern Italians, the fact remains that mafiosi also came to America as immigrants in the 1880s and they exploited their own by selling protection, smuggling and organizing prostitution rings. They gained commissions by controlling the emigrant trade, thus tainting innocent immigrants with unfair labels of being mafiosi as well. Thus began the idea of the southern Italian as a criminal type, and while there were unquestionably some Italians who did become criminals Italian Americans were much more the victims of the Mafia than its criminal agents.

This misperception created hysteria and violence. Lynchings actually took place in Colorado, Pennsylvania and Louisiana. The most famous lynching took place in New Orleans in 1891 when eleven Italians were killed after nine of them were acquitted for the murder of the chief of police. This incident, covered widely in the press, sealed the Italian immigrants' fate, for it fostered the untruth that the Italian Mafia had established its criminal conspiracy within the Italian American community. Essentially it publicly sanctioned hating Italians, and events like this actually led to the later enactment of restrictive legislation against Italians.

Italian communities responded with cries of outrage, expression of pride in their heritage and proclamations of contempt for such primitive thinking. What a far cry this blind prejudice was from the democratic heritage and gospel of liberty and equality for all that had beckoned those longing to be free. These poverty-stricken, vilified representatives of a proud and illustrious civilization would have to struggle hard indeed for justice, social recognition and economic success. Their victories would be won in spite of this negative stereotype which would persist, though in modified form, throughout Italian American history.

This dilemma of trying to live as honest, upright and moral citizens while being presumed by the general public to be inclined toward lawlessness has haunted the Italian immigrants and continues today as a serious issue for Italian Americans. Most Italian immigrants were not lawless criminal gangsters, but lived fully legal lives. Their pride in their own moral rectitude made them outraged at any hint they were mafiosi, the very criminals who victimized the Italian American communities.

The Italian value system always revolved around the family and has survived throughout all assimilation and acculturation. The Italian nature reflects a highly moral character with the family as the central focus. Live your life with honor, so that it will command respect for you, be proud of everything you do—for your family, your work, and your life. Italians take intense pride in their work, art or craftsmanship. They are diligent, committed and hard-working people, and they are fully as honest as any other ethnic group. Italian values were and still are those of love, honor, pride, respect, dignity, thrift, honesty, integrity, and justice for all. Close-knit family ties, a strong community feeling and a passion for life, work and family were vital to the Italian immigrants' value system. Not exactly a set of values that defined the criminal element they were described to be!

In spite of the negative image foisted on them, in spite of the cultural clash with a predominantly white Anglo-Saxon society, in spite of language differences, ridicule, prejudice, discrimination, violence, ignorance, cruel exploitation, and in spite of their total and absolute lack of preparation for living in a modern industrialized world, these Italian immigrants survived and succeeded.

The peak years of the Italian immigration were 1900 to 1914, when more than two million Italians came to America. The government of Italy now encouraged emigration as a means of lessening the strain on its own economy. To improve its image overseas and to strengthen the possibility for admittance of the emigrants, the Italian government established requirements in 1901 for those wanting to leave Italy. Before this date, Italians had been permitted to emigrate without any special papers or permission, hence the term WOP—"without papers." It also imposed a tax on prospective emigrants and denied a passport to anyone convicted of a crime. It created a general emigration office to oversee all facets of emigration. These efforts paid off: Italian immigrants had the lowest rejection rate of any ethnic group seeking entrance to the United States.

Unfortunately, the nativist thinking of the 1880s and 1890s finally took precedence in the minds of Americans, many of whom had become angry and disgruntled by the "invading hordes." They believed immigration should be limited and backed the restrictive immigration legislation enacted in the twentieth century. In 1917, Congress passed a law requiring a literacy test for admittance to America. When this failed to stem the tide of immigration after World War I, Congress passed laws in 1921, and again in 1924, that set quotas or limits on immigration. To try to protect the mythical national character from corruption, yet simultaneously protect themselves against the charge that the law discriminated against any particular ethnic group, the drafters of most of this immigration legislation set quotas on immigration from each country in proportion to the number of people from that country already residing in the United States.

As a consequence, this legal effort to restrict immigration benefited the Italians; so many of them had already immigrated to America that the Italian quota was in fact high. Also, the quota did not restrict the immigration of spouses and children of U. S. citizens, so many Italian men became citizens in order to allow their families to immigrate more easily. As a result, Italians were able to come here at a rate three times the yearly quota.

However, the new life in America did not fulfill the dreams of all the Italian peasants who came to the United States. Almost half of the more than 4.5 million Italians who came here between 1876 and 1924 returned home to Italy, but the relative wealth and success of those returning emigrants continued to inspire other Italians to come to America.

To these poverty-stricken southern Italian immigrants, America was a chaos. Fortunately, they had hidden deep within their souls a heritage of a rich culture, but which lay dormant, awaiting reawakening. Perhaps more significantly, the Italian character, convoluted by centuries of changes and disasters, had essentially stayed intact and was actually strengthened by centuries of crisis, catastrophe and calamity.

The mass Italian migration to America happened to occur when the forces of industrialization and urbanization were sweeping this country, and the Italian immigrants would willingly or unwillingly be swept into this cyclone. This powerful synergy of different forces and complex cultural interaction would forge a dynamic crucible of creative change that would affect life in America forever.

The Italian immigrants' pride in their traditions, faith in themselves and confidence in a better tomorrow gave them some comfort in a hostile world and a powerful energy to conquer that world.

5

AMERICA

PASSAGE

IN THE changeover from one culture and life-style to another, there always seems to be a transition period in which the people who are experiencing the uprooting and violent change find themselves straddled between two worlds, with one foot firmly planted in each. In such a confusing time, people confront problems and face life no longer fully governed by their old values, but not yet governed by the new. The result of this clash of values is internal conflict, a painful addition to all the other problems that attend relocation.

For Italians, this perplexing time of integration into American life was long and difficult, to a great extent because their own value system had been ingrained in them so deeply and for so many centuries. Italian immigrants clung desperately to their old ways out of fear as the expansive new ways of this strange new world, so unlike the almost feudal customs of the old country, took hold within them.

The immigrants had not only to endure the passage across the sea to a new world but also to change their life-style from that appropriate for a rural, agrarian environment in a static, closed society to that suitable to an urban, industrial environment in a dynamic, open society. This conflict between old ways and new forced Italian immigrants to hold on to their old-world values for dear life, even while trying to create new lives for themselves based on new-world values.

Thus the integration of Italians into mainstream American life has been a truly ambiguous, complex and elusive process from the very start. Assimilation began slowly before World War I, proceeded slowly through World War II with most second-generation Italian Americans, and then progressed vigorously after World War II with third-generation offspring.

Integration, to the first generation Italian Americans, represented an assault on their old-world values. However, to the *children* of these first Italian Americans, integration meant full participation in American life. It also meant forgetting old-country mores and forsaking old-country customs and traditions in favor of those common to their new country. Becoming American would lead to financial security and social progress, these two combining to allow a major step up the ladder of success.

While the first-generation Italian Americans were struggling to survive in America, still clutching to their breast, with great fervor, the familiar ways of the past, the sons and daughters of immigrants were busily casting off the shackles of the old country and passionately embracing the customs of the new. They may have had nothing and they may have felt like aliens, but they were also captivated by the excitement of this new world, the thrill of American life and the window of opportunity opened to them.

Life in America was indeed different for the children of immigrants. At the time of this vast influx of foreigners to America, the social, educational, religious and civic institutions sought to "Americanize" all ethnic groups. America and its special, relatively new and quickly evolving culture was seen as a great homogenizing machine that blended different nationalities into a unity so that none of the individual groups could be recognized as foreign.

So it was that Italian children, like other ethnics, were urged to forsake the ways of their parents. To the Italian kids, this meant giving up *la via vecchia,* the old way, for the new, *la via nuova,* and this also meant pain, suffering and humiliation.

Sadly, in their first attempts at assimilation, many children of immigrants were ridiculed for their behavior by their American friends, were teased mercilessly about their foreign ways or funny names, and were made to feel embarrassed at their backward, ignorant and old-fashioned parents who dressed strangely and refused to act like Americans.

No matter how conflicted, Italian children did renounce the ways of the old country and threw themselves headlong into becoming Americans. However, in casting off their old values and taking on the new, they also found themselves overwhelmed by the forces of American life, some of which were viewed by parents as "foolish distractions" or "crazy notions" filling the heads of Italian kids. Some of these kids became "more American" than the Americans, and some even changed their names.

However, to Italian Americans, this new American way of life also meant the fulfillment of materialistic desires, the drive of free enterprise, the spirit of capitalism, the motive of profit, the compulsion for success, the allure of consumerism, the influence of advertising and the demand to produce. Horatio Alger was their hero.

Thus, to the children of immigrants, the second-generation Italian Americans, integration meant *becoming American* and participating fully in American life. And their parents had come to America to give them this opportunity for success and to fulfill the great American dream. To achieve that dream, the children and their children's children had no choice but to change, to become American. They would emerge victorious from this painful process, but in order for them to gain a new life, much of the old had to be set aside, perhaps to be taken up again later. For now, the sons and daughters of Italian immigrants would forsake the old and embrace the new, while their parents clung dearly to the old.

Most Italian immigrants had come from a rigid, closed, static and hierarchical society, predominantly rural and agrarian in nature, and absolutely limited in terms of opportunity for advancement or personal fulfillment. At the time of the mass emigrations, there was simply no chance for success and no hope of any kind for a rewarding life in Italy. In America, they were thrown into a free, open, dynamic, egalitarian and democratic society, predominantly urban and industrial in nature, and totally unrestricted in terms of opportunity for advancement and personal development. If ever America was committed to any one thing, it was to the spirit of individual progress, accomplishment, achievement and success.

This clash of two worlds, this collision of two cultures and this conflict of value systems created chaos and turmoil for the Italians in America. In Italy they had been resigned, stoic and quietly persevering in the face of futility, serving family at the expense of self. Life in America made them individualistic, aggressive, dynamic and committed to succeed in whatever opportunities came their way in this new world. America unlocked a powerful force within the Italian soul that for centuries had been deeply suppressed. In America, this powerful force came alive and exploded.

What good fortune America was for Italians! And what good fortune Italians were for America!

MELTING POT

America! America! A *new* world, a new kind of world, a world based upon freedom, equality, justice, life, liberty and the pursuit of happiness; the great democratic experiment in self-governance; a new idea of nationhood, a nation conceived in liberty and dedicated to the proposition that all men are created equal; the egalitarian country committed to equal opportunity for all its citizens; a nation of one from many, including everyone and excluding no one.

Italy. An *old* world but a new nation, a country that had spawned the Roman Empire; attended the conversion of Europe to Christianity; experienced for humankind the Age of Faith, the golden age of the Renaissance, the Great Age of Discovery, humanism and the Age of Reason; had been the first home of classicism and of dynamic democratic concepts such as equality under the law; and finally a newly unified nation spiritually exhausted by the Risorgimento. Then, overwhelmed by the problems at hand, it lost tens of millions of its poverty-stricken populace to other countries abroad, mostly to America, the land beyond the sea and the new melting pot.

If any country knew and understood historically what it meant to be a melting pot, it was Italy, since to a greater degree than any other country Italy had assimilated many different tribes of people and many diverse ethnic groups. Many peoples of the ancient world shared in the creation of the Italian race.

The Roman Empire completely absorbed or amalgamated every one of the distinct peoples who came to settle in the Italic peninsula after the Etruscan, Celtic and Illyrian invasions. Italian history began with the Etruscans, who probably immigrated from Asia Minor and dominated most of northern and central Italy until 396 B.C., when their walled city of Veii fell to the Roman dictator Marius Furius Camillus. Meanwhile Greek colonies and states had dominated the lower peninsula and Sicily. Thus the Etruscans to the North and the Greeks to the South significantly influenced what became known first as Roman civilization and then as Italian civilization.

Romans conquered and then absorbed numerous peoples and tribes into a unified Roman state. Foreign colonies brought immigrants from every corner of the immense expanse of imperial holdings, including the Near East, Syria, Palestine and Egypt, and the Roman provinces of Asia Minor, which spread oriental culture throughout the empire.

In 211 A.D., Emperor Caracalla's *Constitutio Antoniana* conferred Roman citizenship on all inhabitants of the provinces, making formal and legal the universalism of Roman expansion. The population of the Roman Empire, linked together by a truly amazing bureaucracy and infrastructure, included all races of the world, and Rome the city was not only the central organizing focus of the empire but the living symbol of a universal, world-embracing cosmopolitanism. What had become a national or imperial evolution of an empire out of a state had now become a universal institution. To be a Roman citizen then was truly to be a citizen of the world.

When Emperor Constantine recognized Christianity as the

Roman state religion in 323 A.D., another form of universalism was singularly created and established for all of history. Christianity became inevitably linked with Roman history, thus establishing another universalism, this time religious. When Christianity later split into various denominations, the dominant form became Catholic, which means universal. What had been a regional or papal church had now become a truly universal institution.

Thus two systems of expansive and cosmopolitan universalism became integral parts of Italian civilization—that of the secular and global universality of Roman citizenship and that of the religious and spiritual universality of the Roman Catholic faith.

Rome was thus the fountainhead of two universal institutions that survive in one form or another as major influences in modern times. While these were the source of great pride for Italians, they were also the source of great tragedy for Italy. Rome would become the capital of Italy *and* the seat of worldwide power of Christianity, the largest religion in civilization.

Both of these powerful universal forces would continue to shape Italian history and values. With the fall of the Roman Empire in 476 A.D., Italy was invaded, divided, conquered and fought over for almost fourteen centuries. First came the ravaging hordes and barbarian invaders, including Visigoths, Huns, Vandals, Herulians, Ostrogoths, Franks and Lombards. In 568 A.D., Italy was partitioned between Lombards and Byzantines.

Invasions of Italy continued—the Saracens, Moslems, Normans, Magyars, Germans and even Vikings. The centuries of the Renaissance were characterized by the rise of independent city-states to which many Europeans were drawn. From the fifteenth century on, Italy became a country fought over for four centuries by foreign invaders including Ottoman Turks, French, Spanish and Austrians.

So Italy itself was also a melting pot that absorbed and assimilated every conceivable diverse ethnic, cultural and religious background, history and heritage. The coalescing of these divergent forces, values, customs, traditions, faiths, attitudes and philosophies, along with lots of exotic foreign interconnections and cross-cultural fertilizations, made what we call Italians.

Thus Italian consciousness for the whole history of the country, from the universalism of the Roman Empire and the universalism of the Christian, then Roman Catholic, Church, has been worldly and cosmopolitan. The assimilative power and all-embracing nature of the Roman Empire has evolved into an Italian people with a consciousness transcending tribal and racial distinctions in favor of a universal humanism.

Thus Italy became a true melting pot country, what would now be called a pluralistic society, throughout its long history of migrations, external and internal, invasion by alien groups, and domination by foreign powers. Not only had Italians become cosmopolitan in the process of assimilating many different cultures, but the whole experience of Italians had been shaped, colored and influenced by their own emigration to other lands, where they consistently contributed to their new places of residence. They felt at home in any corner of the world.

At first glance, it may be difficult to imagine that the millions of poverty-stricken immigrants fleeing an Italy racked by four hundred years of chaos were anything like the cosmopolitan travelers of the Roman Empire, the great humanists of the Renaissance or the adventurers to the New World. However, it is not hard to understand that these Italian immigrants carried within their souls a sort of cultural memory that included a *value system* for survival in foreign lands firmly founded on the strength of a transcendent spirit, a universal cosmopolitanism and a basic humanism.

Would these Italian immigrants feel at home in *this* corner of the earth, the corner called America?

THE CRUCIBLE

America was a chaos for these bewildered Italian immigrants lost in a strange land and unable to speak the country's language. Life had been a horror in the old country, but at least the pains, problems and disasters were familiar ones. Here they were trapped between two powerful cultures, each antagonistic to the other. However, if the hard dues were paid America promised an opportunity to escape one's destiny and overcome poverty. What had been an impossible dream in the old country was now a feasible possibility in the new one. In fact, everything was possible here in America, much more in fact than the immigrants had dared to dream.

These seemingly rural country bumpkins from a medieval southern Italy were confused and frustrated at being characterized as lazy and frivolous, and "a hybrid race of good-for-nothing mongrels," a menace to society, and at the very least, foreigners with strange folkways and traditions. Faced with being thought of as alien and inimical visitors from another planet, these children of Columbus could take solace only in an inner strength coming from a proud history. They had faith in their own survival skills, refined with great pain over the centuries; in their own creative abilities, honed by countless crises and calamities; and in their stoic confidence in a better tomorrow—for better or worse, *life is to be lived,* no matter how tragic or comic, dramatic or catastrophic.

What courageous and enterprising spirits these new pilgrims must have been to endure a long, difficult and painful ocean voyage, packed like cattle into the horrors of steerage, to come to a new country where they had no friends or family and where the native population openly vilified them. Pilgrims fleeing opression met only Indians. What truly exceptional individuals these later-day pilgrims must have been!

No other ethnic group has had as broad, varied and extensive an influence on American life as have the Italians. Since Columbus discovered America, Italians have been coming here and making valuable contributions to its birth, growth and development. The Italians who came before the mass migrations of the late 1800s and early 1900s, as we have seen, had contributed to America far out of proportion to their numbers.

The extensive influx of Italians has had an amazing and remarkable influence on America. Certainly some of this impact is purely the result of the unusually vast number of Italian immigrants who came to America—over 5 million in the last hundred years. Though the demographics are disputed, the 1980 census counted 12 million Americans of Italian ancestry, and estimated that one in every twenty Americans is a descendant of Italian immigrants—23 million or so Italian Americans. If only through sheer numbers, the Italian legacy is profound and significant, but in fact the Italian influence is actually greater than would be expected from even these large numbers, and it lives on. Today Italian Americans can look back on a history of success and achievement in the adopted land of their ancestors.

Through their creativity, passion and energy, Italian American men and women have always contributed to American civilization. Italian ideas, values and philosophical speculations, revolutionary in concept and expression, had a significant effect on our nation's progress. From the time of Columbus, Italian Americans have been channeling their energy into the forging of this great democratic nation.

Yet Italian Americans are baffling when it comes assimilation, and are sometimes referred to as "unassimilible." They may have accomplished the impossible in that they have succeeded in integrating themselves into American life while somehow simultaneously preserving the values, traditions and characteristics they inherited from a rich and splendid culture. While remaining fiercely independent and wildly individualistic, they have joined the cultural mainstream and made impressive contributions to American life.

Italian Americans are unique as a group, yet an absolutely integral part of the American nation and the family of man. At the core of this seeming paradox of uniqueness and integral participation in the process we call living is a basic humanness and a creative life force unmatched by any other ethnic group.

The heritage of contributions to come from the "mongrel horde" invading America would far surpass any previous histories of contribution. Lady Liberty extended her arms to a bereft people seeking salvation from beyond the sea, and they came by the millions. The Red Sea parted and the Italians crossed over to the Promised Land.

6

LABOR

ITALIANS WERE lured to America by exciting tales of this new world. The central driving force of emigration was the need to escape poverty. After arrival in America the immigrant's goal was to find a job, work hard and save money, but many Italians had trouble finding work in rapidly industrializing America because they lacked the necessary skills and education. More than half of the southern Italians who arrived were totally illiterate; within the medieval feudal system of southern Italy education was a privilege available only to would-be priests and the sons of wealthy landowners. Most of those who came to America were peasant farmers, or *contadini,* and while some did go to work on American farms, the vast majority traded in their Italian hoes for American picks and shovels.

For these immigrants, the American dream was in their *hands,* hands to be used for manual labor. At the end of the nineteenth century, jobs were plentiful in America, and immigrants provided the huge force of laborers needed to build and retrofit the cities of this rapidly growing industrial nation.

While Italian Americans were good at farming and farm life was preferable to city slum life, the farms were no match for the expanding and thriving cities when it came to jobs and earning potential. Success was to be won in the urban centers, in the cities, big and small. Italian immigrants knew that the economic and financial rewards of industrial employment were

98

the key to survival, the not-so-magic carpet to prosperity . . . and perhaps the key to owning land, the last impossible in the old country.

Italian communities sprang up not only in the major cities but all across America from the Appalachians to the Rockies, especially near rail yards where grocers, shopkeepers, saloon-keepers and boardinghouse owners set up business. These became active, thriving centers for the immigrant labor force moving across the country. New York, Illinois, Pennsylvania, California and Louisiana offered the best pay and attracted many Italians. Employment opportunities were abundant, since every state in the Union depended on immigrant labor to perform the myriad tough, low-paying jobs of an expanding country on the move.

The Italian American labored for his family, which, as in the home country, remained the central focus of his energies. The home was the hub of Italian life. Domestic values took precedence and governed all of life's decisions. Extended families provided help to needy relatives and to those closely related to the family through *comparatico,* or godparenthood. A man worked hard for his family, both for love and because this is how he earned the respect of his community.

The great mass migration to America continued through the turn of the twentieth century, a time when progressive movement for social reform swept across the nation. This concurrence of Italian immigration and the rise of American progressivism is critical to understanding the Italian American experience. In fact, the progressive reform movement was just as much a result of the huge influx of Italians and other ethnic groups as it was a flowering of American thinking in a newly born and modern, growing industrial society. Italian labor provided a vital energy in transforming America from a rural, agrarian country into a giant twentieth-century industrial power.

Italian Americans clustered in Little Italys where they could maintain a life-style familiar to them and similar to that of their hometowns and villages. Their strong feeling for community, or *campanilismo,* drew them together in these enclaves, where they created local trades and businesses, thus fulfilling the

Italians' need for living close to their work. These safe havens, while basically slum dwellings, also provided shelter from racial discrimination from non-Italians. Italians from different parts of Italy spoke different dialects and had different folkways.

Italian Americans, because of their strong sense of neighborhood and community, were some of the first to recognize the power and value of collective and organized community action to address the problems of an urban industrial society effectively. In addition to progressive social reformers from the United States, socialists and political activists came from Italy to initiate reforms of their own.

Italians founded mutual aid societies and fraternal organizations such as the Society for Italian Immigrants and the Order of the Sons of Italy in America to help the newly arrived immigrants. The Italian government established the Italian Benevolent Institute in New York City for temporary immigrant housing. By 1920 there were more than 2,500 Italian mutual aid societies and fraternal organizations across the country that provided help and a sense of security to Italian immigrants.

The Italian language press also helped the immigrants acclimate themselves to American society, especially through daily and weekly newspapers written almost completely in Italian. These journals brought news of life in the old country, offered advice on solving the many problems of survival in the new country and kept the immigrants up-to-date on social, cultural, political and recreational happenings. They also published articles on the glorious Italian heritage to instill a sense of ethnic pride in expatriated immigrants.

In 1849, Secchi de Casali had founded *L'Eco d'Italia,* the first Italian-language weekly newspaper in the country, and this paper spoke for and to the Italian community of New York for almost three decades. In 1879, Carlo Barsotti founded *Il Progresso Italo-Americano,* the first Italian-language daily newspaper, in New York. Later on *Il Progresso* would grow into the largest and most influential Italian newspaper in America under the ownership of Generoso Pope, reputedly the first Italian American millionaire. By 1922, almost two hundred Italian papers were published, including Cleveland's *La Voce del*

Popolo, Chicago's *L'Italia,* Philadelphia's *L'Opinione* and San Francisco's *L'Eco della Patria.*

During these difficult early years, Italian values dominated the lives of the immigrants. First came hard work to earn money, then the thrifty use of it and finally the saving of it. Italian families handled the management of their meager earnings very well and lived carefully within tight budgets. Italian mothers and housewives took immense pride in making do with little and in providing healthful meals on small food allowances.

Progressive social reformers praised these amazing women as ideal and excellent parents. Their seemingly endless energy, compassion, love, thrift, dedication, fierce loyalty and genuine care and affection for their children were held up for respect and admiration. These women, now our grandmothers, seemed indeed to have been a breed apart.

By the start of the twentieth century, the effect of the progressive social reform movement was being felt in America, and Americans were becoming more tolerant of and friendly to these "unwashed masses" whom they had been erroneously characterizing as criminals, agitators or anarchists. Of course, Americans also realized that the phenomenal national growth and expansion, enhanced by an unprecedented and pervasive optimism in the country, required, demanded and was getting its essential labor from these immigrants. Now, more than ever, Italians were filling an insatiable, practical and valuable need. The industrial requirements for growth and expansion swallowed the mass migration from Italy just as America entered an era of optimism, progressive reform and social justice, which were, in fact, the by-products of this very industrial evolution.

Social reformers expressed respect and admiration for the moral and social character of these southern Italian immigrants, who seemed so proud of their work, so devoted to their families and so determined to improve their economic status. Here, indeed, was the very personification of the American spirit and a poignant manifestation of the American dream. The reformers praised these Italians for their diligence, thrift and family ties; they lauded the Italian parents as ideal; and they hailed Italian children for their enthusiastic desires to become Americans and achieve success.

The first step toward success, indeed toward survival, was the finding of a job. While a large majority—more than 75 percent—of the southern Italians who had immigrated were peasant farm workers, most wanted to escape farm life, which represented the oppression and poverty they had fled. Thus, most sought other occupations in America if only to put their painful pasts behind them.

The majority of these immigrants settled in industrial states such as New York, Pennsylvania and New Jersey, and took those jobs with the railroads and construction businesses that were just being vacated by the Irish immigrants who were moving on to skilled jobs. Many followed the Jewish immigrants into the garment industry, some sold fruit and vegetables from pushcarts, some took menial jobs as organ grinders, peddlers and bootblacks, and others opened small neighborhood stores.

These new Italian Americans cut timber, harvested crops and canned foods. They toiled in the coal mines of Pennsylvania, West Virginia, Kentucky and Illinois. They worked the copper and silver mines of Arizona and Colorado, and the iron mines of Minnesota and Michigan. They made steel in refineries. They worked in the slaughterhouses and stockyards of Chicago and Kansas City. They made cigars in Florida. They created a huge fishing trade in northern California, especially in San Francisco and Monterey. They worked in glass and shoe factories.

Italian women swarmed the New York garment industry in large numbers and would later play a vital and significant role in the unionization of that industry. They still comprise a large percentage of those in the clothing trade. In New York and New Jersey, Italians cut cloth and sewed and pressed garments in the sweatshops. They manufactured silk and textiles, especially in the factories of New England.

Mainly they built. Italian immigrants swung picks and shovels, dug dirt, mixed cement, climbed scaffolds and carried bricks. They built roads, subways, canals, sewers, bridges, tunnels, railroads, ships, reservoirs and streets. They paved those streets that were supposed to be made of gold! And they built America.

For their families and for their country, the Italian immigrants labored. Their limited education restricted almost all *contadini* to unskilled work. Most Italian immigrants on the east coast found work through Italian contract agents called *padroni*. Back in Italy, the *padroni* had scoured the countryside for laborers to send to America, luring them over with promises of a better life in the land of plenty. In America, the *padroni* assumed a great deal of power as middlemen between employers and workers. They also became leaders of the immigrant communities and functioned as bankers, interpreters and advisors to the newly arrived immigrants.

Unfortunately, the *padroni* exploited the Italian workers mercilessly, but as labor agents they directed the broad distribution of Italians all across America, in cities where they worked industrial jobs and in rural areas where they worked the farms. The *padroni* became very powerful politically, even though their motivations—to make profits from the contracting and exploiting of cheap Italian labor—were less than pure. However, without the *padroni*, there might not have been any labor for the immigrants. The padrone system was full of evils, but it was also vital to the survival of these peasants from Italy.

In 1897, the *padroni* controlled almost two-thirds of New York's Italian labor force, especially in the construction trades. At the turn of the century, Italians made up nearly the entire labor force responsible for building the New York City subway system and manned most of the sand and gravel mines that provided the mortar for this amazing and extensive construction project.

The padrone system did not last long. As soon as the Italians could find work themselves, they turned away from the *padroni*.

By the early twentieth century, in spite of the prejudice and discrimination they had had to endure, Italian immigrants had not only provided America with a huge labor force to build a new highly industrialized nation, but had begun their own journey up the ladder of success. Within one short generation in America, they had proved that hard work, diligence, determination, respect, pride, perseverance and family devotion paid off. This initial success would blossom and expand all across America and into every field of endeavor, from manual labor to high technology. The same hands that sweltered on the handles of picks and shovels would also guide the first man onto the Moon. The progeny of these poverty-stricken immigrants from the land that time forgot would indeed reach for the Moon, and get it, but they had to work hard for it.

By 1918, there were an estimated three million Italian Americans and most of these were swelling the rank and file of a huge labor force. The progressive reform movement continued to direct the national consciousness toward social justice. Prominent Italian Americans, such as Antonio Stella, Rocco Brindisi and Gino Speranza, also worked for reform. American liberalism was moving the country forward on a foundation built by Italian and native-American progressive reformers and driven by a force of a heavily Italian-populated labor movement.

At first, however, Italian workers had serious problems with the labor unions and the strike method of attaining concessions from employers. Seeing Italians as less than human and exploiting the desperate need of new immigrants to make a buck, employers recruited recent arrivals as scabs and strikebreakers to fight the newly formed labor unions. Some immigrants were unaware that they were being used as strikebreakers and were bewildered by the violence, hatred and abuse heaped upon them by union workers.

Italian immigrants often found themselves trapped in a terrible dilemma—if they refused to strike against abusive and oppressive employers who were exploiting the workers, they were attacked for sabotaging the labor movement, and if they joined the strikers they were attacked for being agitators, bloody anarchists or desperate criminals.

The Italian workers, though conflicted about their involvement in unions, were not anti-union. Motivated by the drive to make money and pushed by the basic economic pressure of survival, they first joined those unions that had developed strong bargaining power. They also seriously sought to change and uplift the terribly degraded status of American laborers in the nineteenth century.

They were damned if they did and damned if they did not join the unions, but most Italian laborers did eventually join and many became directly involved with the growth and success of the labor movement, both within the rank and file and as leaders. Those early, confusing and bitter incidents where they had been strikebreakers had occurred in strikes with coal miners in Pennsylvania, meatpackers in Chicago and garment workers in New York. As a result, some of the unions even barred them from joining, but soon the Italians broke these barriers of prejudice and became enthusiastic union workers and supporters of union causes. And Italian women played a vital role in the unionization of America, especially in the apparel industry, even though family escorts made it difficult for union organizers to approach them.

In 1910, a fiery young Sicilian woman set off a strike against the clothing manufacturers in Chicago and this signaled a major step forward for the garment industry. Three Italian Americans led the strike: A. D. Marimpietri, Emilio Grandinetti and Giuseppe Bertelli, all of whom were hailed as "the apostles" of socialism and labor organization among the Italians. This strike was squelched and, while it failed, it did set the stage for the creation of the Amalgamated Clothing Workers of America, in which Marimpietri participated so valuably.

The A.C.W. founded by Marimpietri and others would, within a decade, totally organize and unionize the garment workers of Chicago and establish standards for wages, hours and conditions in the shops. So the very workers who had been accused of sabatoging the union movement in the clothing industry achieved some of the earliest significant economic gains and brought about sorely needed improvements. Even Samuel Gompers, himself an immigrant, who became the father of the American Federation of Labor, had characterized Italians as "the wrong kind of immigrants" and blamed them for the perpetuation of horrible labor conditions. The Italian workers, along with Jewish and Polish immigrants, had to prove themselves in the labor movement, and they did.

On March 25, 1911, tragedy struck the Triangle Shirtwaist Company factory in New York when a fire broke out. Hundreds of garment workers were trapped in flames and smoke as they fought each other in a futile attempt to escape down through the one fire exit that had not been locked. Most were driven to jump to their own deaths in frantic, horrifying leaps from the top-floor windows of the ten-story building. One hundred fifty-four men and women, boys and girls, died in this fire, more than one-third by jumping from windows and tearing through hastily spread-out nets below. Most were incinerated in the inferno created by the concentration of fire and smoke within rooms and corridors.

This tragedy marked the turning point of the labor movement, making the need for strict labor regulations all-too-painfully obvious. The dispute over whether unions were necessary to protect workers came to an end, though in a most unfortunate way. The Triangle Shirtwaist Company fire also occurred just when the International Ladies Garment Workers Union (ILGWU) was about to consolidate its newly established power.

Luigi Antonini, a prominent union leader and persuasive spokesman for labor in the strike of shirtwaistmakers in 1913, started to organize Italian American garment workers. He edited *L'Operaio,* a union magazine, and helped make Local 89 the largest in the ILGWU. Later he fought against fascism and served as a state chairman of the American Labor Party. He also joined with John L. Lewis of the United Mine Workers and Philip Murray of the Steel Workers to form the Congress of Industrial Organizations or the CIO. When he broke from the American Labor Party, he helped to found the Liberal Party.

The struggle of the ILGWU to gain better pay and decent working conditions was integrally related to the rise of Italian American women from sweatshop status to respectable industrial citizenship. The union succeeded in providing economic gain, improved working conditions and workers' benefits where charitable organizations, churches, social-service programs and even the law had failed.

Whole families endured the long hours, despicable treatment and low wages of the sweatshops to survive and advance economically. Again the family unit took precedence in the evolution of the Italian American, when parents, grandparents, children, uncles and aunts all worked together on piece-meal clothing bundles at home. During strikes, husbands and wives, mothers and fathers, sons and daughters all waved banners, marched and picketed for union causes.

Curiously, Italians would sometimes declare strikes to celebrate special religious holidays, such as the feast of St. Joseph on March 19. Felix D'Alessandro attempted to organize an Italian national union under various names such as The International Laborers' Union, The General Laborers' International Union and The Laborers' Union, but these efforts failed.

Italians mainly participated in union activities and strikes within their own trades. Arturo Giovannitti rallied a strike of fifteen thousand immigrants against the American Woolen Company at Lawrence, Massachusetts, in 1912. Waving the banner of the Industrial Workers of the World (the Wobblies), Giovannitti and other Italian labor leaders and workers led this famous textile-workers strike in a dramatic demonstration that attracted national attention to the horrendous working conditions and the illegal use of child labor rampant in the New England garment industry. In 1913, Carlo Tresca, another energetic labor leader, organized a strike against the silk mills of Paterson, New Jersey. August Bellanca organized the Italian workers of the Amalgamated Clothing Workers of America, George Baldanzi became president of the Textile Workers of America and James Petrillo became president of the Musicians' Union.

Socialists and revolutionaries naturally gravitated to the labor movement for socio-political reasons. Many devoted their energies to organizing unions, setting up organizations and fighting for rights and for better wages for all people, not just Italian Americans. August Bellanca and Luigi Antonini, perhaps the most prominent Italian labor leaders from the 1920s to the 1960s and founders of the Italian American Labor Council, considered themselves socialists. However, they followed the fundamental philosophy of American organized labor, whose goal was the improvement of the conditions of the laborer in a free-enterprise economy and a democratic society. Serafino Romualdi was responsible for establishing an international labor movement free of Soviet influence after World War II.

Italian revolutionaries included left-wing socialists, anarchists and syndicalists and many joined The Industrial Workers of the World, which promoted strikes on behalf of the workers. Gaetano Bresci, an anarchist, had lived in America before taking the life of King Humbert I of Italy. Edmondo Rossoni, who later became a powerful fascist and Mussolini collaborator, had agitated in the United States. Most Italian left-wing socialists and those who were communists after 1918 either left America or changed their minds about their beliefs as time went by. Many heavily influenced the achieving of fair and equitable treatment for the workers.

Socialist-minded Italian Americans contributed significantly to the expansion and success of the labor movement and assumed top leadership positions through World War II and after. However, as Italians became successful, got educated and moved into mainstream American life, a new breed of union leader evolved that would significantly influence the labor movement in America.

Anthony Scotto was president of Local 1814 of the International Longshoreman's Association and the son-in-law of "Tough Tony" Anastasia, brother of mobster Albert Anastasia. Scotto represents this new-breed combination of tough-guy union boss and sophisticated labor leader. Constantly fighting accusations of being Mafia controlled, he strove in the 1950s for union reform and became a real powerhouse of labor and a political activist for liberal causes. He became one of America's most progressive labor leaders. This tradition of powerful union organizing and progressive labor leadership would continue to present times.

Robert A. Georgine now serves as the president of the Building and Construction Trades Department of the AFL-CIO in Washington, D. C., one of the most powerful positions in labor. Georgine has become a major guiding force in the labor movement.

In spite of discrimination and after the initial conflicts of early immigrants with fledgling unions, the Italian Americans committed themselves enthusiastically to the labor movement.

They almost equated union membership with American citizenship and in their desperate desire to become American championed the cause of the workers of America and helped make the labor movement a great American success.

The poverty-stricken peasants from Italy were blessed with passage through the golden door to America, but America was blessed with the pride these Italian immigrants took in their work and in their work associations, the same pride that had inspired Italians for centuries no matter what the job.

7

FARMING

NEW WORLD CONTADINI

THE ITALIAN immigrants who sought escape from the rural
and agrarian poverty of southern Italy settled mainly in the
large urban areas of America, many never again wanting to
see a hoe or a rake. Indeed, between 1860 and 1900, almost
36 million immigrants from all countries flooded America's
cities, and of these only 9 million went to farms. The Italian
peasant farmers who fled to America's cities became part of
a wider trend of American farmers moving to urban centers
in the late nineteenth century, leading to a serious and acute
shortage of farmers and farmhands that hurt agricultural
America at this time.

Social reformers thought that dispersing the immigrant
population would help solve the farm problem while also
alleviating the overcrowding of urban slums and freeing the
immigrants from the exploitive yoke of the padrone system.
At this time, many Americans valued the agrarian tradition
and agricultural way of life as the highest form of American
life and cherished the farms as the last strongholds of
honesty, morality and virtue. The attempt by agrarian
promoters and social reformers to divert Italians to
America's farmlands was largely a failure, though many
immigrants did turn to agriculture and some did so with
great success. By the turn of the century even the Italian
government, through its Italian Commission of Emigration,

joined the social reformers in urging Italians to settle in rural areas rather than in cities.

As it turned out the experience of the Italians who went west and to California was rather different from those who settled on the east coast and in the urban centers of America. The closed nature of Italian American society and the clannishness of the Little Italys was less evident among Italians who settled on the west coast. These immigrants had arrived with enough money to travel across the country, some with enough to buy land, though, of course, most did not have enough to meet the needs of their growing agricultural enterprises.

The growth of Italian farm colonies took several courses. In the best cases, the successful Italian farmer solicited others to join him; in the worst cases, some carefully planned and officially supported rural colonies failed completely. However, many Italian groups and their farming ventures did succeed and prosper.

In the mid 1800s, the California gold rush attracted many foreigners, including Italians, in search of adventure and riches. By 1870, almost two-thirds of those who had migrated to California were foreigners, most of whom eventually settled in the San Francisco area. By 1920, Italians represented 11.7 percent of California's foreign population and were, by far, the largest ethnic group in the state.

The rich, fertile soil of California, the mild, beautiful weather and the strong similarity of the California landscape in its coastal regions to much of Italy all drew Italians to the west coast. Italians really felt at home in California, and those who came here experienced a more positive and welcome sense of life in America than did those who settled in the dirty, urban, industrial ghettos of the east.

By 1850 so many Italians were already living in California that the King of Sardinia established an Italian consulate in San Francisco. Earlier in the 1800s, many northern Italians had come to America from the rich farmlands of Piedmont and Liguria to settle in the fertile lands of California, where they established successful fruit and vegetable farms and, especially, wineries. Even the wines being produced in California resembled those of Italy. Around 1880, more northern Italians from Genoa, Turin and Lombardy came to the "Mediterranean west coast" and started to create vineyards and produce wine. They also engaged in a variety of food-related enterprises, including the farming of fruit, vegetables and other produce.

Most important of all for the California wine industry, Italian farmers brought a heritage of old-world care and centuries of agricultural wisdom to the new-world production methods of growing grapes and making wine. The knowledge, skill and winemaking techniques of Italy became the cherished possessions of California.

Many Italians prospered in the wineries all across the Golden State. In 1881, Andrea Sbarbaro founded the Italian-Swiss agricultural colony in Sonoma county, thus giving birth to the modern wine and grape industry. Sbarbaro hired Pietro Rossi, whose chemical knowledge insured the success of this dynamic company.

In 1897, the grape crop was so large that nothing existed to hold it, so Sbarbaro had to construct a huge cement reservoir with a five-hundred-thousand-gallon capacity, the largest wine tank in the world. When it was emptied the following year, Sbarbaro held a dance in it, with an orchestra and two hundred people. This colony became totally self-sufficient as a small town, shipped its wine eastward in railroad tank-cars and dominated the United States wine market. These new methods of winemaking, production and distribution, and the success of this creative farming colony stimulated the widespread participation of Italians in the phenomenal growth and subsequent rise to prominence of the California agricultural industry.

In the 1880s, Secondo Guasti established the Italian Vineyard Company, which created the world's largest vineyard near Los Angeles, California. Guasti, who immigrated from Piedmont in 1881, planted grapes on thousands of acres in the dry, semi-arid soil of Cucamonga where others had turned away in failure. He succeeded in producing millions of gallons per year of dessert wines, such as port, sherry and angelica.

Many Italians prospered in wineries across California. Ernest and Julio Gallo represent the pinnacle of the Italian success in producing wine for worldwide consumption. Gallo's sales are a billion dollars annually now. Along with the Gallo family, there were the Petri and Cribari families of California's Central Valley, the Mondavi family of Napa Valley, the Sebastiani family of Sonoma and the Martini family at Saint Helena. Each in its own way has made vital contributions to the wine industry and together they have become major successes for Italians.

While the success of Italians in winemaking was quite phenomenal, it was not the only profitable field of enterprise for Italians. Other immigrants bought rich grazing lands from Santa Barbara north up the California coast and started dairy farming. They built a butter and cheese industry scattered throughout the San Luis Obispo, San Simeon, Cambria, Cayucos and Morro Bay coastal ranges.

In 1889, Marco Fontana, a Genoese, founded the California Fruit Packing Corporation, the largest fruit and vegetable canning operation in the world. Fontana originated the brand name Marca del Monte, now Del Monte. In 1893 Joseph Di Giorgio, from Sicily, became an importer and a grower of fruit throughout the San Joaquin Valley and then founded the Di Giorgio Fruit Corporation with his brother Rosario. Canning fruits and vegetables as well as producing them under the S & W label, Di Giorgio became the largest shipper of fresh fruit in the world and was respected as probably the most important man in that industry.

These Italians, relying on their agricultural knowledge and experience, turned to farming and to proven products such as grapes, fresh fruit, tomatoes and vegetables. They had also found truck farming to be profitable and by the end of the nineteenth century, Italian farmers were already experiencing major successes in California. In 1900, there were over sixty thousand Italians in California and over half worked in agriculture.

A thriving produce district arose in San Francisco as agricultural products were carted into open-air markets for sale to the public. Similar markets were established in the Sacramento and San Joaquin Valleys and in many other parts of California. The dramatic success of Italians in farming and marketing their products throughout California owes a debt to the financial acumen and progressive lending policies of Amadeo Pietro

Giannini, founder of Bank of America and himself a produce merchant; Giannini understood the unique banking needs of these Italian farmers and helped them become agricultural capitalists. Later, Joseph Maggio became the "Carrot King" of the United States, and Sam Perricone became the "Citrus King."

For Italians, California truly was a Mediterranean America. Alongside all these agricultural achievements, huge fishing industries sprung up, especially in port cities such as San Pedro, Monterey and San Francisco. Genoese and Sicilian fishermen brought centuries of seamanship and fishing skill to make the California fishing trade highly successful; today their names are seen along the wharves of every California port.

Italians also created a trade and distribution system for agricultural produce and fish. Many commercial-service companies in California's main growth industries were established by Italians. Italians also put their skilled and unskilled labor and artisanship to work in the construction of houses, estates, college campuses and municipal buildings throughout the state. Italian stonemasons, ironworkers, landscapers and tile-makers enhanced the beauty of all California. Both figuratively and literally, they built a great deal of California.

The present-day Italian names of places in California pay tribute to this strong Italian influence—as Asti, Lodi, Arcadia, Tarragona, Terracina, Verona and Venice. And the pervasiveness of Italian names all across the state pays homage to a deep and profound influence on the Golden State. Italian accomplishment, achievement and contribution to America reached a zenith of success in California.

Though California marked the area of greatest success, Italians also set up thriving and productive agricultural communities all across America, particularly in Louisiana, Florida, Connecticut, North Carolina, Tennessee, Rhode Island, Utah, Nebraska and Wyoming. They transformed the swampland of western New York's Hudson River Valley into successful vineyards and raised cotton, sugar cane and rice in the South. They planted vast and prolific apple and peach orchards in Arkansas and started truck farms near metropolitan areas in Texas and Wisconsin.

In New York, Generoso Pope, prominent Italian-American newspaper publisher, became concerned for the fate of thousands of southern Italians crowded into the urban ghettos and devised an unusual and creative solution to the problem. Along with Charles Landis, a wealthy philanthropist, Pope arranged low-interest loans to all southern Italian immigrants to help them realize their fondest dreams—buying their own farmland. Italians leapt at the opportunity; by the 1880s, Vineland, New Jersey, became the largest Italian community outside of Italy. To present day the descendants of these immigrant farmers make up a large percentage of the Vineland farm community.

While the slave-owning South did not appeal to the Italians who arrived before 1865, after the Civil War blacks began to migrate to the North and white farmers were leaving farming for the cities. So, southern states wooed the immigrants with special offers to work the farms. An agricultural colony was established at Yazoo Delta in 1885, at Friar's Point, Mississippi. Some Italians traveled westward beyond the Mississippi and many went to Louisiana, which attracted almost as many Italians as did California. Steamers also traveled directly from Genoa, Naples and Palermo to New Orleans, and especially Sicilians settled here. By 1910, Louisiana had over twenty thousand Italian residents.

Austin Corbin, a wealthy industrialist and owner of the Long Island Railroad, with the cooperation of the mayor of Rome, brought immigrants to an agricultural colony established at Sunnyside, Arkansas, in 1895. Five hundred immigrant families lived there, and workers of all types were brought in to this progressive colony. Unfortunately Corbin died, many Italians left the settlement, many died from malaria and other disease and Corbin's plans for what might have been one of the most successful agricultural experiments in America went unfulfilled.

However, in 1898, Father Pietro Bandini stepped in and saved the colony. Bandini negotiated to have the Italian colonists buy land in Missouri and Arkansas for only one dollar an acre. After a few tough years, on a plot of nine hundred acres of Ozark land in Arkansas, Italians succeeded at dairying, grape growing and fruit crops. They also pioneered the canning industry in Arkansas; the Welch's Grape Company, attracted by the abundance of Concord grapes, built a plant here. The town was renamed Tontitown in honor of Enrico Tonti, the symbolic "Father of Arkansas."

Italians developed successful farming ventures in Knobview, Missouri, which was renamed Rosati after Bishop Giuseppe Rosati. Italian railroad workers established a cotton colony in Bryan, Texas. In New York, the Italian colony grew grapes at Fredonia, onions at Canastota and turned wasteland into profits with fruit and truck farming in Hammonton, New Jersey. In Genoa, Wisconsin, Italians raised wheat, corn, oats, rye, barley, tobacco and dairy and beef cattle. Italian cheesemakers in Wisconsin, Michigan, New York and California, soon to be joined by the Germans, Swiss and Scandinavians, created the American dairy industry.

These early successes of Italian immigrants, who turned the lands of the American countryside into rich harvests of crops, helped social reformers and progressive thinkers to promote life on the farms as the antidote to the maladies of urban dwelling. Yet though many of the Italians did leave the overcrowded cities and prosper in agricultural America, most of the southern Italians who migrated, of which more than 75 percent had been farmers, saw farm life, for all its mythical value, as the oppressive life they had just fled. Thus, most stayed in the cities.

The Italian immigrants also knew that the economic rewards of industrial employment represented a more reliable road to success, prosperity and, eventually, even to owning land. By 1900, within one generation of immigration, urban Italians clearly showed signs of upward mobility and the progeny of millions of immigrants would become educated and flood the professions. And America would become more accepting of these "unwashed masses."

8

SPORTS

"Crazy Notions"—Sports

Part of the "American craziness" or *pazzia Americana* was a strange contest of strength where people beat each other up, called boxing, and a funny game where grown men hit and chase a little white ball around a field, called baseball.

American sports, one of the craziest of the new-world notions to invade the hearts and minds of Italian kids, fascinated these children and represented a way up the ladder of success and out of the ghettos and slums where they seemed penned up. Italian kids seized on these strange new games not only for fun and possible careers, but because, plain and simple, they were American; more than anything else, the immigrants' children wanted to be American. In fact, in some ways, they became more American than Americans.

Sports fascinated Italian American children and participation in sports was an Americanizing process, thus reducing prejudice and conferring acceptability on Italians as Americans. Sports also bestowed glamour, wealth, pride and self-worth on those who succeeded at them. So, with one foot planted in the past and the old country, the second-generation Italian American progeny of immigrant parents stepped enthusiastically forward into the future by planting the other foot in the sports arenas and baseball fields of America.

117

BOXING

Boxing was one of the first sports to attract Italian Americans. Rocco Barbella, born in 1922 in New York City, left school in the seventh grade to hang around a gym and become a boxer. After service in the United States army, he returned to the ring to become the middleweight champion of the world—as Rocky Graziano. He became famous for his "unscientific" style of scrapping. His dramatic and exciting battles with Tony Zale have become boxing legend, and his life was portrayed by Paul Newman in the film *Somebody Up There Likes Me.*

Rocco Francis Marchegiano, born in 1924 in Brockton, Massachusetts, first wanted to play baseball but began to fight recreational bouts while in the service in 1943. In 1947 he tried out for the Chicago Cubs but was turned down because of an arm injury he had received in the war. Rocky then boxed in amateur contests with his friend Al Colombo as second and Gene Caggiano as his manager. In 1951, as Rocky Marciano, he knocked the famous former world champion Joe Louis unconscious with a classic right cross and later became champion himself. His sensational thirteenth-round knockout of Jersey Joe Walcott in 1952, which won him the title, was one of boxing's greatest bouts of all time. Marciano retired with forty-nine victories, of which forty-three were knockouts, as boxing history's only undefeated heavyweight champion of the world; his record of forty-nine consecutive victories has never been equalled. Rocky died in a tragic plane crash in 1969, at the age of forty-five.

"Two-ton" Tony Galento was a huge brawling heavyweight boxer in the 1930s who fought 114 fights between 1929 and 1944 and who coined the phrase, "I'll moider da bum." Galento weighed in at two hundred to two hundred and forty pounds on a 5'11" frame and fulfilled his prediction eighty-two times with fifty-two knockouts. In 1939, he knocked Joe Louis, the defending champion, to the mat but could not wrest the crown from Louis. Galento was born in Orange, New Jersey, the son of Italian immigrants. He quit school after the sixth grade to work as an iceman and made his boxing debut at fifteen in an amateur contest with a KO in the first round. He turned pro two years later in 1929. After a rough and tumble boxing career, he became a professional wrestler in 1944 and then an actor with small parts in films.

Perhaps the most powerful and persuasive influence of any Italian American on the pugilistic profession was not in the center of the ring but in the corner, and that honor goes to the famous manager Angelo Dundee, born Angelo Mirena, Jr. in 1921 in Philadelphia. In the 1930s, his older brother Joe began to box professionally and took the name "Dundee" as did his brother Chris, his manager. Angelo joined his brothers in the fight business in 1948. Dundee became the top cornerman in the business with nine world champions to his credit, including Muhammad Ali, Sugar Ray Leonard, Jimmy Ellis, Willie Pastrano, Carmen Basilio, Luis Rodriguez, Ultiminio (Sugar) Ramos, Jose Napoles and Ralph Dupas. Outgoing and upbeat, Dundee does not fit the image of the rough and tough, cigar-smoking manager. His sunny disposition helps him blend with a fighter to create a strong, positive rapport out of which comes the key to bringing out the best in a man. Angelo Dundee still produces the best champions in the fight game with his winning philosophy.

BASEBALL

Baseball, the "great American Pastime," also fascinated the children of immigrants as a "crazy idea" running through their heads. Games played on empty sandlots across America by all immigrant groups brought kids together under the banner of good old American fun and games. It didn't matter in these neighborhood lots what your ethnic origin was as long as you could hit the ball, the baseball.

Joseph Paul DiMaggio, known as the "Yankee Clipper" and voted the "greatest Living Player" of baseball in 1950 was born in 1914 in Martinez, California, near San Francisco, the eighth of nine children of an Italian fisherman. He began, along with his brothers and many other neighborhood kids, to play baseball as a child in the lots of San Francisco. He won a position with the New York Yankees in 1936 and catapulted the

Yankees to ten World Championships from 1936 to 1951, ending his career with a .325 lifetime batting average and 361 home runs. DiMaggio was voted most valuable player in 1939, 1941 and 1947 and, besides his powerful batting, is considered by many the game's best defensive center fielder, certainly its most graceful. He was elected to the National Baseball Hall of Fame in 1955 and was by far the most internationally famous sports figure of the time. DiMaggio's publicized marriage to actress Marilyn Monroe added to his celebrity status, but the marriage ended in divorce. His accomplishments earned him a permanent place in history and in the heart of sports fans forever.

Lawrence Peter Berra, nicknamed "Yogi" by his childhood friends because he looked like a fakir they had seen in a movie, was born in 1925 in St. Louis, the son of a brickmaker. He too learned to play baseball in neighborhood sandlots and in 1946 made the majors when the New York Yankees brought him aboard. He played seventeen years for this team and set many World Series records as a formidable bad-ball hitter who was especially reliable in the clutch. He was three-time American League most valuable player. He then managed the Yankees and the New York Mets, winning championships with both teams. Yogi also became vice president of the Yoo-Hoo Beverage Company. One of baseball's all-time great characters, Yogi kept the game fun and interesting with his colorful malapropisms and down-to-earth sports wisdom. In response to a player's lament, after a bad turn in a game, that it was now all over, Yogi came up with perhaps his most famous line of wit and wisdom: "It ain't over till it's over." As applicable to most of life's discouraging moments as it was to this baseball game, the line is now as much a part of American lore as many lines of Twain and Lincoln.

Joe Garagiola was one of Yogi Berra's sandlot baseball friends and was born in 1926 in St. Louis where he too yearned to play professional ball. He began his career with the St. Louis Cardinals in 1946 and left in 1951. Also a terrific catcher, Joe then played for the Pittsburgh Pirates, the Chicago Cubs and the New York Giants. When he retired from active play, he became famous as a sports announcer for NBC television. He was also one of the hosts of the "Today" show in its early days. Sometimes referred to as the Will Rogers of baseball because of his quips and witticisms, Joe captured the humor in his former profession in his book *Baseball is a Funny Game.*

Phil Rizzuto, known as "Scooter" for his quick, agile moves as a shortstop, was born in 1918 in Brooklyn, New York. He played for many years for the New York Yankees, turning many base hits into double plays as an infielder. One of the game's finest infielders, he played in nine World Series and was the American League's most valuable player in 1950. Phil also left professional baseball to become a sports announcer for the Yankees. He then went on to become a successful spokesman for the Money-Store.

Anthony Richard Conigliaro, born in 1945 in Revere, Massachusetts, so well known to baseball fans that he is referred to simply as Tony C, began his career in baseball at age four when his father Salvatore introduced him to a ball and bat. He joined the Little League and by high school he was batting .600. In 1964 he became a major league player with the Boston Red Sox. By 1965, Tony C was the American League home run king, and in 1967, at age twenty-two, he became the youngest player ever to have hit 100 career homers. However, he was hit in the eye by a pitch in the 1967 pennant race and was seriously injured. He was told he'd never play again, but made a miraculous comeback, hitting 22 home runs and batting in 82 runs in 1969, and hitting 36 home runs and batting in 116 runs in 1970.

Ed Abbaticchio, born in 1877 in Latrobe, Pennsylvania, was considered to be the first Italian American to play in the major leagues. Abbaticchio started his career with the Philadelphia Phillies in 1897. A second baseman and shortstop, he went on to play with the Boston Braves and Pittsburgh Pirates, compiling a lifetime average of .254 in eight seasons. Abbaticchio also played football and was credited by the famed coach Fielding Yost with having developed the spiral kick.

Babe Pinelli was born Rinaldo Angelo Paolinelli in San

Francisco, California, and gained fame as a baseball umpire. In his last-ever game behind home plate, he handled Don Larsen's perfect game in the 1956 World Series, calling the famous third strike on Dale Mitchell to end the classic contest. Pinelli had been a longtime major-league player, a good-hitting third baseman for the White Sox, Detroit Tigers and Cincinnati Reds from 1918 to 1927.

Vic Raschi was born in 1919 in West Springfield, Massachusetts. A mainstay of the New York Yankees' pitching staff on five straight World Series champion teams from 1949 to 1953, Raschi won twenty-one games three years in a row. Nicknamed "The Springfield Rifle" because of his powerful arm, Raschi had a 132–66 lifetime record with 26 shutouts. Along with Allie Reynolds, a Native American Indian, Raschi gave the Yankees one of the best one-two pitching punches of that era. Raschi's five career World Series wins are eighth on the all-time list.

Famous managers include Billy Martin, whose volatility and passion for his team and the game of baseball keep both exciting and dramatic, while Tommy Lasorda of the Los Angeles Dodgers is considered by Angelenos the best manager the game ever had. Today, Tommy Lasorda is unquestionably the unofficial ambassador of baseball, having been with the Dodgers both in Brooklyn and Los Angeles for over thirty-six years. Ever since he was a kid growing up in Norristown, Pennsylvania, Tommy yearned to become a major league baseball player and his dream came true when he was called from the bull pen with the bases loaded and two outs to pitch to Yogi Berra, one of his heroes, at Yankee Stadium. Tommy is considered the dean of major league managers and over his long career with the Dodgers went from player to scout, coach and then manager to one World Championship in 1981, three National League titles and five division titles. Tommy's warm, personal style, paternal, caring interest and positive, winning attitude have endeared him to fans and players alike. He was named Manager of the Year four times and managed in three World Series and three All-Star games. His passionate love for the game has truly made Tommy "Mr. Baseball" to fans everywhere.

FOOTBALL

While boxing and baseball captured the hearts and minds of the immigrants' children and then their grandchildren, football as a career did not become possible until education and college became important to Italian Americans. This participation of second-generation children in academic life beyond primary schools began to take root after World War I, carried into the 1920s and 1930s, and reached grand proportions after World War II. Education was a golden key to opportunity not just in academic, professional and social success, but also in sports.

"Winning isn't everything, it's the only thing." With these words and the competitive philosophy they express, Vincent Thomas Lombardi became the number one coach in professional football history and inspired a generation of football players and corporate managers. Vince Lombardi was born in Sheepshead Bay, Brooklyn, in 1913. He enrolled at Fordham University, where he became a notoriously aggressive lineman and one of the "Seven Blocks of Granite." He returned to Fordham as a coach in 1947, where he introduced the T-formation offense. In 1954, he became offensive coach for the New York Giants and, with his famous T attack, led the Giants in 1956 to their first NFL championship since 1938. In 1959 he signed aboard as head coach and general manager of the Green Bay Packers, a team then considered the Siberia of football. Under Lombardi, the Packers won the Western Conference titles in 1960, 1961 and 1962, the NFL championship in 1961 and 1962, the first Super Bowl in 1967, and three world titles in 1965, 1966 and 1967. Just after taking over the Washington Redskins, this miracle worker of football died in 1970 and all the sports world mourned his passing.

Alvin Ray Rozelle, nicknamed "Pete," was born in South Gate, California in 1926 and became commissioner of the National Football League in 1960. Pete went to the University of San Francisco, got a B.A. in 1950 and stayed on as assistant athletic director for two years. He worked briefly as publicity director of the Los Angeles Rams, left in 1955 for a private firm and returned as general manager in 1957. The NFL selected Rozelle as commissioner in 1960. Though faced with many complex and critical crises during the period of the game's greatest growth, Rozelle ruled the giant industry of football with so fair, firm and judicious a hand that he gained the respect and admiration of owners, players and fans alike. He also piloted the game toward unbelievable popularity and amazing financial success.

Joe Paterno, considered one of the best college football coaches in history, was born in Brooklyn in 1926. At Brooklyn Prep Joe started to show his ability in football and though he went on to Brown University, he was called to serve in the army during World War II. He returned to Brown and in 1949, as a senior, he proved his worth with an eight to one winning record. Paterno became head coach of Penn State in 1965 at age thirty-nine where he became a legend. He led Penn State to eleven major bowl games, inspired four perfect seasons, produced many All Americans and developed forty-eight players who entered the National Football League. He became the nation's most successful college football coach, won 82.9 percent of all his team's games and was twice honored as coach of the year. Though Paterno was offered important and lucrative positions with professional teams, he has turned them down in favor of his commitment to college football and his desire to unite academic excellence with athletic performance.

Franco Harris, a black Italian American, was born in Fort Dix, New Jersey, in 1950, the son of Cadillac, a former American serviceman, and Gina, an Italian woman from Lucca, Italy. Harris excelled in football at Pennsylvania State University and in 1972 was signed to the Pittsburgh Steelers of the NFL, a consistently losing team. Harris was named rookie of the year in 1972 and quickly became a record-breaking rusher. With Harris, the Steelers won their first divisional title in forty years and then won two league championships in 1974 and 1975. Harris held the record for the most yards gained in a Super Bowl, 158 against the Minnesota Vikings in 1975. Harris's devoted and fervent fans proudly call themselves "Franco's Italian Army."

Perhaps one of the proudest moments for Italian Americans was the Super Bowl of 1984 when the quarterbacks squaring off against each other were *both* of Italian ancestry—Dan

Marino of the Miami Dolphins and Joe Montana of the San Francisco 49ers. Their battle on the football field was followed up by a national advertising campaign for Coca Cola that played on the friendly rivalry of these two star players and endeared them to the hearts of all Americans, especially Italian Americans.

In 1984, Dan Marino was the highest rated quarterback in the NFL. He had played for the University of Pittsburgh where he became the most acclaimed college quarterback in the country. Picked by Don Shula for the Miami Dolphins, he passed for an amazing forty-seven touchdowns in his first twenty games; just for reference, it took Joe Namath three seasons to reach his fiftieth touchdown pass completion. Marino's relaxed style, his personal manner and demeanor, set him apart as a personality as well as a top player. His talent, charisma, natural leadership and courage on the field all make him a highly successful football pro.

Joe Montana had also become a leading passer in the NFL by the early 1980s when he took over as star quarterback for the San Francisco 49ers in 1980. Montana grew up in Monongahela, an area in southwestern Pennsylvania that had produced many other sports greats—for instance, Joe Namath, Johnny Unitas, George Blanda and Stan Musial. He played a spectacular college career at Notre Dame and became an All American. He set a San Francisco record for pass-completion percentage and led his team to victory of the 1984 Super Bowl against his fellow Italian American Dan Marino. While the San Francisco 49ers may have won the game, the victory was a win for all Italian Americans.

Nick Buoniconti was born in 1940 in Springfield, Massachusetts. The epitome of a winning linebacker during his career with the Patriots and Dolphins, Buoniconti was the centerpiece of the Dolphins' "No-Name Defense" on three successive Super Bowl teams, including back-to-back NFL champions. Selected All-Pro six times, the former Notre Dame star is now a successful business executive and co-host of HBO's weekly NFL magazine show.

Daryle Lamonica was born in 1941 in Fresno, California. A former Notre Dame quarterback, Lamonica began his pro career with the Buffalo Bills in 1963, then was traded to the

Raiders in 1967. Many called him "The Mad Bomber" for his penchant for trying to win the game with one long pass, but Raiders quarterback Lamonica knew exactly what he was doing as he kept his team in contention in the late 1960s and early 1970s. A four-time All-Pro who was AFL player of the year in 1967 and 1969, Lamonica led his team to Super Bowl II in 1968 against the Green Bay Packers.

Lou Little was born in 1893 in New York City. Little, whose original name was Luigi Piccolo, was a member of the National Football Foundation Hall of Fame. He coached Columbia University's football team from 1930 until his retirement in 1956. He was best known for developing a long string of outstanding quarterbacks. Little's teams pulled a number of major upsets, including triumphs over Stanford in the 1934 Rose Bowl game and a one-point win over Army in 1947, snapping the Cadets' thirty-two game unbeaten string. In January 1955, Little was given the Coach of the Era award by Scripps-Howard newspapers.

Brian Piccolo was born in 1943 in Pittsfield, Massachusetts. An inspiration to those who followed him into football, Piccolo lived a life tragically cut short by cancer on June 16, 1970. He had strived to become the best during his football career and showed courage and dignity in the face of death. Piccolo led the nation in rushing at Wake Forest College, totaling 1,044 yards during his senior year in 1964. Drafted by the Chicago Bears, he backed up Hall of Famer Gale Sayers for five seasons, gaining 927 yards rushing and catching 58 passes.

Andy Robustelli was born in 1926 in Stamford, Connecticut. Robustelli was one of the best examples of the pro football "ironman" type, missing only one game in fourteen years with the Los Angeles Rams and New York Giants. He was a centerpiece of the Giants' original "Fearsome Foursome," earning All-Pro honors seven times. The Maxwell Club named him NFL player of the year in 1962.

As of 1985, there have been four Italian American football players who have won the Heisman trophy: Alan Ameche, Joe Bellino of Navy and John Cappelletti of Pennsylvania State, all of whom went on to successful professional careers in football; and Vinnie Testaverde, the spectacular quarterback of the University of Miami.

WRESTLING

Wrestling also attracted immigrant children as a means of achieving sports success and some boxers, such as Primo Carnera, switched to wrestling after careers in boxing. In this sport, one name stands out above all the rest as a symbol of success. The rhythmic chanting of that name rocked wrestling rings for years—"Bruno! Bruno! Bruno!"

Bruno Sammartino grew up in Pizzoferrato in central Italy, where he learned to wrestle from Giovanni Batisti, once the great Greco-Roman heavyweight wrestling champion. After a life of starvation and poverty in wartime Italy, Bruno came to America at age fifteen with his family. He arrived weighing ninety-three pounds, suffering from malnutrition. He mowed lawns, worked in construction and lifted weights in Pittsburgh; by 1959 he had turned professional wrestler. He became the world champion in 1963, just three-and-a-half years later, and stood 5'11" tall with a fifty-eight-inch chest, twenty-one-inch biceps and a thirty-eight-inch waist. An amazing athlete, Sammartino held the World-Wrestling-Federation championship title for eight years. Matches featuring Bruno created complete pandemonium in wrestling houses everywhere. His fans loved him and respected him for his good sportmanship as well as his wrestling skill and style. Sammartino's brilliance as a wrestler symbolized the athletic prowess of the sport rather than the buffoonery, clowning and showmanship of wrestling today.

Antonino Rocca also became a world-famous heavyweight barefoot wrestling champion. Rocca was born in 1928 in Traviso, Italy, and grew up in Rosario, Argentina. He became a star rugby player at the University of Rosario before deciding to enter professional wrestling. He weighed 224 pounds and was known to sleep ten-to-twelve hours a day regularly and, before a bout, as long as forty-two hours. Rocca claimed that the secret of long life was good circulation of the blood and that he would live to be 150 years of age. He died at 49 in 1977.

GOLF

In golf, Gene Sarazen, or Eugene Saracini, born in 1902 in Harrison, New York, played with Harry Vardon, one of the patron saints of the game, Bobby Jones and Walter Hagen. Sarazen made history and established long-standing records in golf. He won the United States Open in 1922 at Skokie near Chicago and in 1932 at the old Fresh Meadow in Queens, New York. Sarazen is famous for the most spectacular shot in golf history—a double eagle at Augusta National's fifteenth hole during the final round of the 1935 Masters. In 1973, at age seventy-one, he recorded another sensational shot—a hole in one on Troon's 126-yard eighth hole during the British Open.

Very few can match the dramatic and uplifting *double* comeback story of Ken Venturi, born in 1931 in San Francisco, California. Venturi's father Fred ran a pro shop at Harding Park golf course where Ken played regularly. Venturi turned pro in November 1956 and quickly became a big money winner. In one year, he won both the British and United States Golf Open and continued to win major tournaments through 1960. His victory in 1960 in the Milwaukee Open was his last for almost four years, a period during which he was assaulted with a series of physical ailments.

His first comeback peaked in 1964 with the Thunderbird Classic at the Washington Country Club. Venturi was suffering with heat prostration and could barely hold his putter, but amazingly he shot a seventy to win first place. His comeback earned him *Sports Illustrated* magazine's Sportsman of the Year award, the Comeback of the Year award by Associated Press and Player of the Year award by the Professional Golfer's Association. However, later that year, after more victories, Venturi developed painful problems with his hands and fingers and had to drop out of competition again. In 1965 he had his hands operated on and soon took up his clubs in yet another comeback. He won the Lucky International Open Tournament in 1966 back at his hometown of San Francisco. Venturi, a handsome man, six feet tall and 170 pounds, and a gifted athlete with an iron will and absolute courage, in 1966 was awarded the Ben Hogan trophy by the Metropolitan Golf Writers' Association in New York, an award presented to a golfer who has overcome a physical handicap.

Donna Caponi was born in 1945 in Detroit, Michigan. A star women's golfer, Caponi was a precocious title winner. She captured the U.S. Open in 1969 and 1970, the LPGA Championship in 1979 and 1981, and the Dinah Shore Colgate Open in 1980. Caponi had five tourney wins in 1980 and most consecutive holes without a bogey—fifty. She is one of several Italian American women who are quickly becoming top sports stars.

BASKETBALL

In basketball, Jim Valvano grew up in the streets of Corona, Queens and started playing for Rutgers University. By his senior year, he was captain of a basketball squad playing in the semifinals of the National Invitational Tournament. Later, Valvano coached the Iona team into a championship squad, but then left to coach the North Carolina State basketball team in the Atlantic Coast Conference. A top collegiate basketball coach with a fiery, competitive spirit, Valvano has never forgotten his roots. In an interview with *The New York Times*, he said: "When I went to Iona, I saw myself in that school. I saw ethnic and Italian kids, first-generation college kids trying to make it. That's who I am. That's me, kid."

Forrest S. (Red) De Bernardi was born in 1899 in Omaha, Nebraska. De Bernardi was an AAU All-American basketball player from 1921 to 1923. He led the Hillyards to AAU titles in 1926 and 1927. In eleven AAU tournaments, he was named All-Tournament seven times and All-American at three positions. He was selected an All-Time All-American in 1938.

Hank Luisetti was born in 1916 in San Francisco, California.

The first player to score 50 points in a basketball game, this All-American at Stanford University revolutionized basketball with his one-handed set shot. He broke the national scoring record with 1,596 points at Stanford, at a time when basketball teams were hard pressed to combine for 50 or 60 points in one game.

HOCKEY

In 1980 the United States Olympic hockey game win over the Soviet Union at Lake Placid, New York, filled American hearts with pride. The players were all relatively young and inexperienced but they rushed to the gold-medal win with a series of astounding upsets, culminating with their surprise victory over the Russians. They were led by their team captain and an Italian American, Mike Eruzione, who during the award presentation joyously called out to his teammates to join him on the award stand. While this win brought Eruzione instant fame, four lucrative promotional contracts, and speaking engagements across the country, he played only a bit of minor league hockey and soon quit the game, but with an emotional and athletic high that could never be duplicated and an experience that helped all America feel good about itself.

Phil Esposito, from Sault Sainte Marie, Ontario, played professional hockey for 18½ years in the National Hockey League before retiring in 1981. He played for Chicago and then the Boston Bruins, winning his first Stanley cup in 1970 with the Bruins, the team's first since 1941. He helped the Bruins win the Stanley cup again two years later. Esposito was traded, to his disillusionment, by the Boston team, but disappointment was soon replaced by the exhilaration of reshaping his career with the New York Rangers. By the end of his career, Esposito had racked up an amazing 1,590 points, second only to Gordie Howe, had scored 717 goals, also second to Howe, and had placed third in career assists with 873. In September 1984, he was inducted into the Hockey Hall of Fame. A five-time winner of the Art Ross trophy as the NHL's top scorer, Esposito is making his mark as general manager of the

New York Rangers. Perhaps most memorable to American fans were the series of three straight victories over the Soviets in 1972 in Moscow.

Tony Esposito was also born in 1944 in Sault Sainte Marie, Ontario. For 15 years, starting with a stellar rookie season with the Blackhawks in 1969, Tony Esposito was a formidable adversary for his brother Phil as a goalie. Tony Esposito made shutouts commonplace, earning the nickname "Tony-O." He made NHL All-Star ten times and represented Team Canada in international competition in 1980 and 1984. Esposito currently is a representative for the NHL Players Association.

ICE SKATING

Also on the ice, Linda Fratianne from Northridge, California, competed at age fifteen in the U.S. Ladies Figure Skating Championships in 1976 and won the U.S. title in 1977 and 1980. Linda has been hailed by some as perhaps the most technically proficient woman skater in the world and is one of the few women in ice-skating who routinely performs triple jumps.

Fratianne, daughter of an L.A. municipal court judge and one of five children, started to skate at age nine, a very old age for an aspiring champion, but leapt from the juvenile class to senior ladies division within three years. At 5'1" and weighing ninety-five pounds, Linda is a brilliant technician. She won the World Figure Skating Championship in 1977 and 1979, in the 1980 Olympics she capped her career with a Silver Medal, after having won more than one hundred and forty tourney championships.

At age twenty-two Brian Boitano, from Sunnyvale, California, captured the men's singles title at the annual World Figure Skating Championships for three consecutive years from 1986 to 1988. In the freestyle final at the World Championships in Geneva, at the age of twenty-two, Brian shot to first place on the strength of a dynamic and bravura jitterbuging performance to the music of Gershwin and the blues. Boitano performed so magnificently that his teammate, Debi

Thomas, the first black world champion ever in skating, gave a performance that included four triple jumps and a tricky triple-double toe-loop combination. A lovely example of one teammate inspiring another to great heights.

In 1988 Brian Boitano captured for men's figure skating the gold medal while Debi went on to become the bronze medalist in the 1988 Winter Olympics.

BODYBUILDING

Perhaps one of the most influential men in the field of sports and bodybuilding was the world famous Charles Atlas, born Angelo Siciliano in 1894 on a farm near Acri, Italy. Angelo and his family immigrated to Brooklyn in 1904, but he was a very weak and sickly child who got beaten up severely one night by a bigger kid. This incident caused Angelo to start exercising at a local gym. On a trip to a zoo one day, Angelo happened to notice a lion, confined to a small cage pitting one muscle against another. In this moment of inspiration, Angelo got the idea that changed his life and the lives of many others. Through the use of a system he called "dynamic tension," Siciliano built his own muscular body and in 1922 was named by *Physical Culture* magazine the "World's Most Perfectly Developed Man." One day someone remarked to Angelo that he looked like a statue of Atlas at a local bank and Angelo Siciliano, the Coney Island janitor, then became Charles Atlas, the bodybuilder.

In the early 1920s Atlas modeled and then in 1929, started selling a correspondence course in bodybuilding. Atlas then ran ads in comic books, newspapers and magazines that showed the ninety-seven-pound weakling getting sand kicked in his face and losing his girlfriend to a bully. After the Charles Atlas course, the weakling, now a muscular he-man, returns to the beach, slugs the bully and recaptures his girl who sighs, "My hero!" With his system of "dynamic tension" and his even better sense for good advertising, along with a passionate desire to help others build strong, muscular bodies, Angelo Siciliano or Charles Atlas founded the bodybuilding business.

GYMNASTICS

In gymnastics, the beautiful fireball of energy, Mary Lou Retton, became the dynamic Olympic gold medal gymnast and endeared herself to all Americans. Born in 1968 in Fairmont, West Virginia, the youngest of five children, she was the great-granddaughter of an Italian immigrant coal miner. Retton began taking gymnastic classes as a student at West Virginia University and soon learned that her true talent, because of her diminutive size, was as a powerful and explosive sprinter. Retton developed her own unique and special gymnastic style, which revolutionized the image of a gymnast, turned it away from more balletic and traditional movements toward those more dynamic and dependent on power, speed and agility. Her coach describes her as "a little flyer."

Over the years, Retton won contest after contest, grooming herself for the 1984 Olympics games. She performed brilliantly in her category and won the gold medal, evoking an explosion of joy and love from Americans everywhere. Retton became an overnight celebrity and was named "Sportswoman of 1984" by *Sports Illustrated* magazine. In 1985 she became the first gymnast to be elected to the United States Olympic Hall of Fame.

HORSE RACING

In horse racing, Eddie Arcaro, born in 1916 in Cincinnati, became one of racing's best jockeys. Arcaro quit school at age fourteen and worked at the track for three years learning about riding horses. He ran his first winning race on a horse called No More in Chicago in 1933. His career as a jockey from 1931 to 1962 was punctuated by records that established Arcaro as the king of horse racing. He was one of only two jockeys to ride five Kentucky Derby winners, he rode six Preakness Stakes winners and six Belmont Stake winners and he rode two Triple Crown winners to victory, including Whirlaway in 1941 and Citation in 1948. Arcaro's earnings surpassed 30 million dollars, more than that earned by any other jockey ever. His career, spanning thirty-one seasons, featured 24,092 mounts, of which 4,799 were winners. Arcaro then became a successful television news commentator for ABC Sports.

Carmine Abbatiello, born in 1936, grew up in Staten Island, New York. Under protest by his father, who wanted him to have an education, Carmine dropped out of high school and then discovered the world of horse racing, inspired by his brother Tony's interest in it. After falling on his nose trying to ride a rodeo pony, Carmine climbed astride the more stable sulky and rode his way to a record-breaking career as a top harness racer.

Abbatiello has been one of the sport's leading money winners. In eleven of the years from 1968 to 1981, he won purses of 1 million dollars or more, with his best year being 1980 with 3.3 million dollars in winnings, of which he gets 5 percent. By 1981, he ranked second in career wins with a 4,723-career-win record and third in money won with almost 30 million dollars. He is considered an aggressive, driving, almost-perfect and top-performing athlete of the sport. His confident, passion-for-winning attitude has made him the most sought after driver in New York.

AUTO RACING

Auto racing has always been an enterprise that gets the juices flowing and the blood rushing for Italians. The name Ferrari virtually personifies the thrill and excitement of race cars, with Enzo Ferrari being the pre-eminent designer of fast, winning cars in the world along with Lamborghini and Maserati.

Yet, Mario Andretti's name personifies the ultimate name among race-car drivers. Andretti, born in Montera near Trieste, Italy, in 1940, moved in 1955 to Nazareth, Pennsylvania, where his father worked in the textile industry. He and his twin brother Aldo had learned auto-mechanic skills in Italy and, against the protest of their father and unbeknownst to the family, raced secretly.

Mario and Aldo worked in a garage and rebuilt an old Hudson to race in stock-car contests, winning many times. In

1959, Aldo was hurt in a crash and the boys' father finally learned of their clandestine driving. The father's anger was so great that Mario left home to continue racing. Later father and son reconciled, but racing cars was now a way of life for Mario.

Andretti joined the United Racing Club and then won eleven races in 1963 driving midgets. In 1964 he hooked up with the United States Auto Club and in 1965 won the U.S.A.C. national championship. He placed third in the Indianapolis 500, which brought him the Wetzel Rookie-of-the-Year award. In 1966, Andretti won eight championship races and the U.S.A.C. title for the second year in a row. In 1969, he raced fellow Italian American Andy Granatelli's turbo-powered Ford to a successful number one victory and to a new speed record of 156.867 m.p.h. for the event. Andretti went on to win the ultimate race, the Grand Prix of Europe, and to establish himself as the best race-car driver in the world.

The other two Italian American race-car drivers who have won the Indianapolis 500 are Ralph De Palma and Peter De Paolo. Ralph De Palma was born in 1882 in Troia, Italy. After immigrating to the United States in 1893, De Palma became one of the early stars of auto racing. He was crowned racing's national champion in 1912 and 1914, driving in ten Indy 500 races and winning in 1915. He held the record of having led the Indy 500 for more laps (613) than any other driver. Also an accomplished engineer, De Palma helped design and build the Packard V-12, which he drove to a new land speed record of 149.87 m.p.h. at Daytona Beach in 1919.

Peter De Paolo was born in 1899 in Philadelphia, Pennsylvania. De Paolo was the first man to exceed the 100 m.p.h. mark for average speed at the Indianapolis 500, winning the 1925 Indy 500 with an average speed of 101.13 m.p.h. De Paolo and his uncle, Ralph De Palma, were the first to be inducted into Auto Racing's Hall of Fame.

TENNIS

On the tennis courts, there is one South American of Italian descent who is being heralded as one of the game's future stars—Gabriela Sabatini, born in 1970 in Buenos Aires, who in 1985, at age 15, beat four of the top ten players in the world. Sabatini already expresses qualities of tennis greatness with her sixth sense on the court, her feel for the play of the ball, her coolness under pressure, her knowing when to end a point quickly and her instinct for attacking when she herself is most vulnerable.

Fans and other tennis pros alike all agree that Sabatini has that special something, that quiet confidence in herself, that knowing she's good and that tennis genius, all of which make for a great player. She also has a unique beauty and special magnetism on the court that have endeared her to the crowds and attracted lucrative endorsement contracts, especially with the Italian clothing designer Sergio Tacchini.

BOWLING

Basil "Buzz" Fazio was born in 1908 in Aultman, Ohio. Winner of more than thirty bowling championships, Fazio was a top competitor in the 1950s. He was honored many times by the *All-American Bowlers Journal*. Fazio was elected to the Bowling Hall of Fame in 1976.

Enrico "Hank" Marino was born November 27, 1889. Winner of every major tournament in pro bowling's early years, Marino was selected "Bowler of the Half Century" in 1951. Marino was the first bowler inducted in Bowling's Hall of Fame.

Carmine Salvino was born in 1933 in Chicago, Illinois. One of the greatest pro bowlers of all time, Salvino won eighteen Professional-Bowlers-Association championships in his long career. He was a five-time *Bowling Magazine* All-American and sported five sanctioned three-hundred games in his career. He compiled a two-hundred average in more than thirty years of bowling. Salvino was elected PBA president in 1985. The colorful kegler is a member of numerous Hall of Fames: the Illinois Bowling Hall of Fame, PBA Hall of Fame, American Bowling Congress Hall of Fame and Chicago Sports Hall of Fame.

Andy Varipapa was born in 1891 in Carfizzi, Italy. Varipapa was one of the greatest bowlers of the 1940s and 1950s. He was named "Bowler of the Year" in 1948 by earning induction into the American Bowling Congress Hall of Fame that same year. He specialized in trick-shot bowling.

BILLIARDS

Willie Mosconi was born in 1918 in Philadelphia, Pennsylvania. Mosconi was the world billiards champion fifteen times through the 1940s and 1950s. The most recognized billiards player in the world even today, Mosconi holds the record for the highest billiard run, 526 in a 1954 exhibition. He is the holder of the Tournament High Grand Average, 18.34 in Chicago in 1950, and holds many world records.

SPECIAL MENTION

Bud Furillo of Los Angeles brings his love, enthusiasm and knowledge of sports to a huge and loyal audience on his radio show throughout southern California. He is the pre-eminent sportscaster in this area.

Chet Forte is one of the top sports directors in television today. He has been the man in the control truck for Monday night football since its inception in 1970. He is also the chief director for the World Series, the All-Star games, the Indy 500, the Kentucky Derby and the Olympic telecasts. He has won nine Emmy awards for his directorial excellence.

As a curious footnote in the history of sports endeavors, it was Maria Spelterina who walked across Niagara Falls on a tightrope in 1876, at the age of twenty-three. Suspended over the raging and pounding waters on a 1,100-foot rope, she made the death-defying crossing and even danced a bit to waltz music being played by a band along the shore. She made a second trip across, this time with baskets on her feet, in eleven minutes and back in ten. On her third trip she was blindfolded and her fourth was made with her wrists and ankles hand-cuffed.

In the circus, we have the famous Zacchini family, the human cannonballs fired from twenty-three-foot cannons triggered by Papa Edmondo Zacchini. As the *New Yorker* magazine of July 17, 1965 put it, "In the past, his six brothers, his two daughters, three of his four sons, and his daughter-in-law have all blasted off professionally; in fact, it seems unlikely that there has been a moment in the last thirty-five years when one Zacchini or another was not passing rapidly through the air over some part of the United States."

9

GOVERNMENT AND POLITICS

THE POLITICIZATION of the Italian immigrants and their children, slow at first, was the first significant sign that Italians were dropping their old Italian ways, taking on new-world ways and integrating themselves into the mainstream of American life. The sense of alienation and separateness from American ways they previously felt was coming to an end; Italian Americans now ventured forth on new horizons and involved themselves with the broader American community.

Generally speaking, the southern Italian immigrants were influenced by the memory of their negative political experiences after the unification of Italy in 1870. The new Italian government in Rome and its political mechanisms did nothing for the peasants of the South except to make conditions worse for them. The immigrants who came here during the mass migration carried this sense of futility about politics with them to the shores of their dreamland.

In the late nineteenth and early twentieth centuries, the only expression of political organization within the Italian American community was that of the *padroni* system. Ostensibly labor bosses or employment agents, the *padroni* were involved only with providing a means of making a living for the immigrant and delivering a fully able worker to the employer, but the *padroni* became more than just suppliers of bodies

139

They became vitally involved with the lives of their workers by providing services, offering advice, making suggestions and in many different ways helping the immigrant survive in a new land.

The *padroni* also exploited the immigrant workers mercilessly. This, once again, confirmed in the minds of the peasants the tendency of those in authority to wield power unfairly and to the detriment of those subject to that authority. However, without the exploitive *padroni*, there may have been no jobs for the immigrants. Thus, the padrone system was seen as a necessary evil, though not all *padroni* were unfair or unethical.

Some *padroni* became effective political leaders of the community. They broadened their influence and took on roles beyond their original scope by aiding the immigrant in obtaining citizenship and by securing votes for political machines. This ability to effect the outcome of elections was quickly noticed by the American politicians and brought more labor commissions from various employers, thus creating a cycle of ever-increasing power wielded by the *padroni*.

Because the *padroni* had to be attuned to the needs of the American labor markets specifically, and the needs of the American society generally, many of them became talented, aware and knowledgeable in the dynamics of the American social, political and economic systems. They developed a sense of what made the country and its society run, through an understanding of its political power, social status and economic structures, and perceived, correctly, how to put this new knowledge to work. Though all this was done mainly for personal gain of the *padroni,* the immigrants would benefit from the increased skill of the *padroni* to work the American system.

As the rise of the Italian immigrants out of the lower economic ranks pushed the *padroni* up before them, the latter began to shed their original roles as simple employment agents and took on additional roles as political and communal leaders. As they achieved political influence, they could offer government jobs in exchange for support. These newly formed Italian leaders well understood that once the immigrant population became Americanized and moved into the mainstream, they would still need political direction and access to channels for economic growth. The immigrants themselves knew this and supported the political ambitions of their leaders for the *padroni,* as opposed to the American bosses, owners and leaders, were at least of their own kind.

Thus, the padrone system evolved into a political process that significantly shaped the life of Italian Americans. As the padrone system ceased to dominate the immigrant work experience, it simultaneously stopped producing all the leaders of the Italian American community. The new leaders were more organically evolved from the Italian American community and their success within the larger society brought increased self-esteem and a sense of glory to Italian Americans as a group. Perhaps for the first time in the new country, Italian Americans began to experience a positive sense of self-identity as a group. They now started to feel that they belonged in America.

Other early influences in the political life of the Italian Americans were the various revolutionaries, left-wing socialists, syndicalists and anarchists who came to America, some as political refugees. However, "anarchism" as a term used for a political ideology had many different meanings at this time. The anarchists of this era were very different from the Leninist Communists or Russian Bolsheviks who had repulsed most Americans.

It was a failure of most Americans to make this distinction that sealed the doom of two anarchists, Nicola Sacco and Bartolomeo Vanzetti, the celebrated Italian Americans accused of murder in a payroll holdup in 1920. They were executed in 1927, but their guilt remains in doubt. This case seems in historical perspective to have been rooted in prejudice toward Italian Americans, as well as in a profound misunderstanding of the kind of anarchism advocated by the unfortunate Sacco and Vanzetti.

When it became vitally important to file proper papers, seek citizenship and put the power of their vote to work for themselves the immigrants were pressed into political action. The labor movement mobilized many others into concerted action. As the immigrants became more Americanized, and they were motivated to pull themselves out of poverty, unionization became a viable, pragmatic means of doing so.

Socialists, in particular, gravitated to the drive for unionization, but again many Americans failed to make a necessary distinction—this time between democratic socialists and Moscow-dominated communists. At the core of their American socialist philosophy was a genuine *humanistic* concern for all people, a concern that focused especially on bettering the lot of the workers. These early socialists worked feverishly to improve labor conditions in America, but they did so by remaining within the principles and dictates of America's free-enterprise system and its democratic form of government.

World War I also expanded the political consciousness of many early Italian Americans, as thousands either returned to Italy to fight in the armed forces or joined the American Expeditionary Force. This participation in the war and its aftermath of peace conferences created greater interest in politics as well.

The powerful political machinery of the strongly rooted urban Democratic Party did not miss out on the voting potential of the immigrants and deliberately sought to help them through neighborhood wards and local community involvement. This is why so many Italian Americans became Democrats in their early years of American life. Many Italians who left Italy did so because they resented their lack of influence in Italian life and sought the freedom from arbitrary domination in a democratic America. This compelling desire for democracy would carry forth through World War I and into World War II, when Fascism under Mussolini would drive many more freedom lovers from Italy to American shores.

The later waves of migration—before, during and after the period of Fascist repression—consisted of more politically sophisticated, better educated and more intellectual Italian immigrants. Most were professionals—doctors, lawyers, artists, journalists, scientists, teachers. The evolution of Italian American political attitudes took a shift both toward conservatism and toward the Republican Party among second-and-third-generation children of early immigrants, and among new arrivals as a result of more active participation in the political process of the higher social status and greater economic advancement and of the more affluent status of these immigrants. Over the years, many Italian Americans who had long family loyalty the Democratic party remained in the party, but gravitated toward the conservative wing of it.

Another factor in the switch toward conservatism and the Republican Party was the role of the Irish in both the political power base of the Democratic party and the monopoly the Irish held in the hierarchy of the Catholic Church. Many Italians converted to Protestantism when the Protestant ministers and laity championed social-reform programs to help the immigrants. Others switched their political allegiance to the Republican Party when faced with the iron-fisted political machinery that effectively shut them out of control of the Democratic Party.

Though at first the political consciousness of the Italian immigrants was very low—more a consequence of a long history of negative political experience than of the new realities of American life—the first- and second-generation Italian Americans learned very quickly about political power. They adapted pragmatically to the exigencies of political realities and changed creatively to take advantage of the American democratic system and the process of government. Education also played a major role in the growth and development of the Italian American political consciousness.

Once Italian Americans reached a more sophisticated awareness of political realities and threw themselves into the political arena, seeking government positions and using the electoral process to advantage, there was no holding them back. The influence of the Italian Americans in politics and government is now felt profoundly throughout America, at every level from local to state to national to international.

Onorio Razzolini was perhaps the first Italian to hold a public office in the United States. He was appointed Armourer and Keeper of the Stores of Maryland. William Paca, one of the signers of the Declaration of Independence, was one of fifteen senators in the first Maryland state legislature. In 1778 Paca was made judge of the General Court of Maryland, and in 1780 he was appointed Chief Justice of the Court of Appeals in

Admiralty and Prize Cases by Congress. President George Washington appointed Paca judge of the Federal District Court in 1789. Paca also served as governor of Maryland for three terms from 1782 through 1785.

In 1837, John Phinizy, the son of an Italian immigrant named Ferdinando Finizzi, became the first Italian American to be elected mayor of an American city, Augusta, Georgia. In 1839, Charles Del Vecchio became the first Italian American Fire Commissioner of New York City. In 1900, Andrew Houston Longino was elected governor of the state of Mississippi.

Francis B. Spinola, known as "Shirt Collar Spinola," a man of vivacity, versatility and strong devotion to American ideals, served in the United States Congress for three terms and was respected and admired for his eloquence as an orator. Spinola, a Democrat from New York, was the first Italian American congressman in the United States. His impassioned speech in the New York Senate the day after the capture of Fort Sumter had assured mass support for the Union in the Civil War. When he died in 1892, both the U.S. House of Representatives and the Senate adjourned to commemorate him.

From 1891 to 1895, Anthony J. Caminetti, a Democrat, served in the United States Congress from the state of California; and in 1913 President Woodrow Wilson appointed him Commissioner General of Immigration.

The political awareness of Italians here in America between the early twentieth century to the beginning of World War II was also shaped by intensified feelings of pride in Italy, or *Italianita,* which was being rekindled by the Fascist dictator Benito Mussolini. This newly discovered sense of pride in a country that heretofore was a broken, strife-torn and economically depressed landscape of catastrophe explains why so many Italian immigrants expressed allegiance to Italy and to *Il Duce* during the decades before World War II.

Mussolini's imperialistic dictatorship attracted the sympathy and support of the Italians in America, not because of its political and military aspirations but because of the reawakened pride and patriotism it encouraged. Mussolini had instituted many needed social reforms in Italy, had "made the trains run on time" and had mobilized Italy into a prominent player on the stage of European power politics. His decision to cast the lot of Italy with Adolf Hitler, thought by many of the time to symbolize the wave of the future, doomed his party to its death and his country to two decades on abject suffering.

The climb to power of Mussolini and his Italian ventures did help to politicize Italian Americans, at first on the basis of pride in Italy. However, with Italy's declaration of war against the United States in 1941, all feelings of allegiance to Italy by Italian Americans were put aside. Italian Americans were Americans first, and their allegiance was to the flag of the United States. They would without any great agonizing shed their blood and give their lives in a battle to the death between America and it allies and Italy and its allies. In the end they served Italy as well as America's allies, liberating it from the yoke of Nazi and Fascist domination. Mussolini's rekindling of political pride did have a powerful effect on Italian Americans, but not the effect *Il Duce* originally envisioned.

While the year 1940, when Mussolini joined Hitler in the war, stands as a pivotal turning point and a crisis-filled year for Italian Americans Mussolini's declaration of war on the United States in the wake of Pearl Harbor in December 1941, truly stunned Italian Americans. After the initial shock of such lunacy—the Axis pact required only that each member go to war if either of the other two were attacked, not if one of the others did the attacking—Italian Americans immediately embraced the ideals of democracy and absolutely committed their allegiance to America. For the Italian Americans, any previous conflicts or questions about political loyalty were immediately resolved. In 1943 when the American forces landed on Sicilian shores and then on the Italian mainland, the Italian American soldiers clearly envisioned themselves as liberators of the country from which their parents and grandparents had come. In place of any old political conflicts came a quantum leap upward in the shaping of their political consciousness. The fruits of this newly evolved awareness would blossom to have great national impact after World War II.

During the war, many political refugees sought protection and a better life in America by escaping to America from

Fascist Italy. Italian Americans on the home-front, from Democrats to socialists to revolutionaries to organized labor, helped those refugees who came here. In fact, even in Italy there was a substantial anti-Fascist effort not only on the part of the Italian partisans but within the military, the Vatican and the within the general populace to help political and religious refugees, especially the Jews, escape to America. When France was occupied and Paris fell, New York City became the center for exiles who had left Europe to escape Nazism and Fascism. The Mazzini Society was founded in America, as a counterweight to fascist influence, working to establish a republican democracy in Italy. After World War II, the political energy and power of the Italian Americans would erupt into a dynamic force to be seriously reckoned with, both nationally and internationally. Italian Americans would explode on the political scene in just a few decades.

Before this, the truly significant political contributions on a national scale from Italian Americans began with the career of one of the most universally respected politicians the country has ever seen. Fiorello Henry LaGuardia, born in 1882 on New York's Lower East Side, rose to power and gained national prominence as a gifted government leader and shrewd politician. In 1901, he worked as a clerk in the American Consulate in Austria-Hungary and in 1904 he served as an interpreter at Ellis Island. By 1915, with his law degree won, he was appointed Deputy Attorney General of New York and by 1916 he was elected to the United States House of Representatives.

Fiorello, known as "the little flower," had become the most prominent Italian American in the country. By the time he died in 1947, he was a Foreign Service official, a World War I bomber pilot, and was re-elected in 1933 to the office of mayor of the City of New York, the highest elected office ever achieved by an Italian American, and was re-elected to Congress after the war on the Republican ticket. Fiorello was known as a self-made man, loved for his warm, compassionate nature and respected for his brilliant mind. He represented the Italian American aspiration at its very best. A supporter of much of the New Deal program, even though a registered Republican, and a close personal friend of Franklin D. Roosevelt, LaGuardia was loved by all New Yorkers and admired nationally by all Americans. LaGuardia was a national statesman, rather than a politician, a humanist rather than a governor and an inspirer rather than a commander.

Elsewhere throughout America, other Italian Americans were beginning to fill powerful seats of government. In 1931, Angelo J. Rossi became the first Italian American mayor of San Francisco and the first of a major American city. He was a businessman born in the United States of Italian parents; he ran for office as a progressive Republican. He was an active man who vigorously participated in Italian American events and organizations. Rossi served till 1944; he was admired, liked and respected throughout the West.

Elected in 1968 and 1972, Joseph L. Alioto served as mayor of San Francisco and his electrifying nominating speech in 1968 for presidential candidate Hubert Humphrey at the famous Democratic National Convention in Chicago catapulted Alioto to national prominence. George Moscone also served as mayor of San Francisco in the 1970s, until he and the city supervisor Harvey Milk were tragically shot to death by a disgruntled colleague.

Vincent Impelliteri was elected president of the New York City Council in 1945. In 1950, he was along with Ferdinand Pecora, Edward Corsi and Vito Marcantonio, one of four Italian Americans who ran for the office of mayor of New York City. Impelliteri won on the Independent ticket of the Experience Party and became the second Italian American to hold the mayor's office. In 1949, Carmine G. DeSapio became the leader of New York's Tammany Hall and grew in power as a political boss wielding national influence.

Italian Americans have captured many state houses by winning governorships throughout the country. Andrew Houston Longino in 1900 was the first Italian American elected governor, of the state of Mississippi. Though not perceived as an Italian American, Alfred E. Smith or Alfred Emanuele Ferrara was elected governor of New York State in 1918 and served four terms. In 1928 he ran on the Democratic ticket as the first Roman Catholic candidate for president but was defeated by Herbert Hoover. His tenure as governor brought many reforms, and he was a deeply liked though forceful leader. The first Italian American governor perceived as an Italian American was John O. Pastore, who was elected governor of Rhode Island in 1945. He served two terms and then in 1950 became the first Italian American to be elected to the United States Senate, at the time the highest elective office ever won by an Italian American. Pastore was also the keynote speaker at the Democratic National Convention in 1964.

Charles Poleti was elected lieutenant governor of New York State and served from 1939 to 1942. When Herbert Lehman was elected to the United States Senate, Poleti served briefly as governor of New York state, though he was never elected to that position. Other Italian American governors from the post-World War II era to present day include Christopher Del Sesto, Edward Di Prete and John Notte all of Rhode Island, Richard Celeste and Michael Di Salle of Ohio (Di Salle also served as mayor of Toledo), Foster Furcolo of Massachusetts, who also served as United States Congressman, Alberto Rosselini of Washington and the first Italian American woman to be a governor, Ella Grasso of Connecticut. John Volpe, four-time governor of Massachusetts, and Mario Cuomo, governor of New York, have both achieved national prominence.

Besides John Pastore those who served as U.S. senators are Alphonse D'Amato of New York, Dennis De Concini of Arizona, Pete Domenici of New Mexico and Patrick Leahy of Vermont.

The significant rise of Italian Americans to high positions in the United States government is shown by those who have served or presently serve in cabinet positions. The first cabinet appointment was that of Charles J. Bonaparte, who served as secretary of the Navy under President Theodore Roosevelt. Bonaparte was then appointed Attorney General by Roosevelt in 1906 and in 1907 founded the Federal Bureau of Investigation. While it may have been J. Edgar Hoover who became famous as the director of the F.B.I., there is a certain irony in the fact that an Italian American founded the bureau years later . . . the F.B.I. played a major role in the criminal investigations of the Mafia, and in its zeal to indict those suspected of organized crime, unfairly harassed law-abiding Italian Americans.

The next cabinet appointment came when Judge Paul Rao was sworn in as Assistant Attorney General of the United States in charge of the Customs Division in 1941. Rao's meteoric rise to become the top expert and Chief Justice of the United States Customs Court in 1948 is discussed in our section on law and jurisprudence.

In 1953 President Dwight Eisenhower appointed Rocco Siciliano, at age thirty-one, the first Italian American Assistant Secretary of Labor. Siciliano came from an Italian family in Salt Lake City, Utah, graduated with honors from the University of Utah and received his law degree from Georgetown University in Washington, D.C. He served in World War II as an infantry platoon leader and won the Bronze Star along with many other decorations. Siciliano worked for the National Labor Relations Board and the U.S. Employment Service, where he gained much valuable experience in labor problems. In 1957 Siciliano later became the first Italian American ever named Special Assistant to the President. With responsibility for personnel management, Siciliano served as exclusive advisor on personnel matters for the nation's largest employer, the federal government, with over 2,100,000 employees.

In 1959, Siciliano left his government position to work in private industry and the law profession. However, in 1969, President Richard Nixon called upon him to serve as the Under Secretary of the U.S. Department of Commerce, where he worked till 1971. In 1971, he left government to serve as president of Ticor, a diversified financial services company that included the nation's largest title insurance company.

Edward Corsi, born in Capestrano, Aquila, Italy in 1896, came to America in 1906, received his law degree from Fordham University in 1922 and distinguished himself in public life as an executive in the government, an author and a leader. He became supervisor of the U.S. Federal Census in Manhattan in 1930, U.S. Immigration Commissioner at Ellis Island from 1931 to 1933 and commissioner of Immigration and Naturalization from 1933 to 1934. His public service included positions as chairman of many boards, committees and commissions. From 1943 to 1955 he served as Industrial Commissioner of the State of New York and in 1955 as assistant to the U.S. Secretary of State. Corsi authored many books and articles and was an editorial writer for various newspapers and magazines. Although Corsi was not actually a cabinet member but an assistant to the secretary, his achievements in government service were significant.

Anthony Celebrezze, born in Anzi, Italy, the ninth of twelve children, came to America in 1914 at age four, grew up in Cleveland, Ohio, and received his law degree in 1936 from Ohio Northern University. During World War II, he served with the United States Navy in the South Pacific as a seaman first class. He practiced law until 1950, when he was elected to the Ohio State Senate. Celebrezze served as mayor of Cleveland from 1953 to 1962. In 1962, President John F. Kennedy appointed Celebrezze Secretary of Health, Education and Welfare. Celebrezze served with distinction in the position and was retained as Secretary by President Johnson. He left the cabinet in 1965 to accept an appointment as a federal appellate judge of the Sixth Circuit Court of Appeals.

Edward Re served as Assistant Secretary of State for Educational and Cultural Affairs in President Lyndon Johnson's administration from 1968 to 1969 and distinguished himself as a judge of the United States Customs Court. He too is discussed in our law and jurisprudence chapter.

Monsignor Geno Baroni was appointed an Assistant Secretary in the Department of Housing and Urban Development by President Jimmy Carter in 1977. Monsignor Baroni had headed the National Center for Urban Ethnic Affairs, fought to advance the rights of minorities and to upgrade the status of all ethnic groups in America. He was also the founding president of the National Italian American Foundation in 1976 in Washington, D.C. Baroni's passionate concern for Italian Americans and his loving humanism endeared him deeply to those of us who were gifted with his friendship.

Joesph Califano, Jr. was appointed Special Presidential Assistant in 1965 by President Lyndon Johnson. He was later selected by Jimmy Carter to serve in the cabinet position of

Secretary of Health, Education and Welfare. In 1965, Joseph Sisco was confirmed as Assistant Secretary of State for International Organization Affairs. Sisco had received his M.A. degree and Ph.D. in international relations by 1950, served as an officer with the Central Intelligence Agency and then joined the State Department staff, specializing in United Nations affairs. From 1951 through 1965 he served in various positions of leadership in the State Department. Sisco continues to play a key role in foreign relations, especially with respect to the United Nations and relations with the Middle East and Russia. Frank Mercurio served as commissioner in the U.S. Labor Department. Benjamin Civiletti served in the cabinet position of Attorney General in 1978.

Frank Carlucci also has served in several top government positions, including deputy director of the Central Intelligence Agency, deputy Secretary of Defense under Casper Weinberger and director of the National Security Council, the President's chief national security advisor. Carlucci was appointed Secretary of Defense in 1987.

John A. Volpe was Secretary of Transportation under President Nixon. Volpe was born December 8, 1908 in Wakefield, Massachusetts, the oldest of five sons. He had to work as a plasterer to help his father's failing business, in 1928 enrolled at the Wentworth Institute and majored in architectural construction. Volpe used his hard-earned savings of five hundred dollars to create the Volpe Construction Company, which prospered over the years. He closed his business during World War II and joined the Civil Engineer Corps of the Navy and left the service in 1946 as a lieutenant commander. Volpe reopened his construction business and built schools, hospitals, shopping centers, public buildings and military installations; in 1953, he was named Massachusetts Commissioner of Public Works. He was then named the first Federal Highway Administrator by President Dwight Eisenhower in 1956. In 1960, he was elected governor of Massachusetts, was defeated in 1963, and then went on to win and serve two more terms.

In 1969, President Richard Nixon appointed Volpe Secretary of Transportation. While Volpe had already realized his dreams of creating a prosperous business, of serving as governor of a state and as a cabinet member in the White House, he was appointed ambassador to Italy in 1973, thus forming the marvelous completion of a great cycle—the son of a hardworking, determined Italian immigrant laborer struggling in America now returning to represent the United States in the land of his forebears. Volpe continued both his commitment to American ideals and his respect for his cherished Italian descent by serving as president of the National Italian American Foundation. In 1982, he was asked by President Reagan to serve as chairman of the Presidential Commission on Drunk Driving. He was awarded the Presidential Citizens Medal "for the fine work and report" of his commission. He then served as chairman of the private sector National Commission Against Drunk Driving in 1984, which was responsible for saving tens of thousands of lives on our highways.

Finally, while not a cabinet appointment, Jack Valenti served as Special Assistant to President Lyndon Johnson and was later appointed president of the Motion Picture Association of America. Valenti's power as an ambassador of American culture is expressed through the force of every American movie that carries our values, ideas, life and culture throughout the globe.

Ella T. Grasso, born in 1919 and named Ella Rosa Giovanna Oliva, became the first Italian American woman to be elected governor. She grew up in Windsor Locks and achieved high academic grades at Mt. Holyoke College in Massachusetts. She married Thomas A. Grasso in 1942 and during World War II was state assistant director of research for the Federal War Manpower Commission in Connecticut. She became associated with the League of Women Voters, took an interest in Democratic party politics and decided to take positive action on issues of concern to her.

In 1952 and 1954, Grasso was elected a representative to the Connecticut General Assembly and was assistant house leader in her second term. She was elected secretary of state in 1958 for the first of three terms and evolved into one of the best-known and well-liked politicians in the state. Grasso ran for the U.S. Congress in 1970 and won; her voting record in Congress received an 80 percent rating from the liberal

Americans for Democratic Action, but her stand against abortion and her absence from a child-care vote hurt her politically with some feminists. In 1974, she was elected governor of Connecticut and came to be known as one of the most effective political warriors in the country. Ella Grasso proved to be a formidable politician and a shrewd, effective governor.

There are several government leaders and political personalities who have made very special contributions that are particularly pertinent to Italian American issues and American life. New Jersey's Peter Rodino, at his retirement, the dean of Italian American congressmen, became a congressman in 1949, played a key role in the Watergate crisis and gained national fame as chairman of the House Judiciary Committee conducting the impeachment hearings on President Nixon in 1974. His even-handed, clear-thinking and fair-minded handling of the proceedings, along with the tough legal mind of Judge John Sirica, his fellow Italian American, averted a major catastrophe for the country's republican form of government and democratic way of life. Rodino also served as chairman of the House Subcommittee on Monopolies and as ranking majority member of the House Select Committee on Narcotics Abuse and Control. His long career of distinguished achievement has inspired other Italian Americans to enter public life in government.

Mario Biaggi, congressman from the Bronx, became the most decorated policeman in the United States. During his career as a police officer from 1942 o 1965, Biaggi was wounded eleven times in the line of duty, was awarded the New York's City's Police Department's Medal of Honor and was decorated twenty-seven times. In 1967, he was elected president of the National Police Officers Association of America. He was also inducted into the association's Hall of Fame and was awarded its Medal of Honor for Valor. Biaggi's bravery and courage as a policeman stand high in the field of law enforcement, representing the very best achievements for American justice.

During this distinguished police career, Biaggi found time to complete school, was admitted to the New York Bar and retired from the police force as detective lieutenant. In 1969, he entered the House of Representatives as a congressman from New York. He serves on the House Education and Labor Committee and its subcommittees, on the Merchant Marine and Fisheries Committee, on the Select Committee on Aging and is chairman of the Subcommittee on Merchant Marine.

Beyond Biaggi's considerable accomplishments as a United States congressman is the work he has done for the Italian Americans. He is especially a fighter against ethnic bias, prejudice and discrimination, particularly as practiced in the media. He serves as chairman of the Italian American Media Institute and has sponsored legislation to prevent discrimination in the media. He serves as chairman of the Italian American Media Institute and has sponsored legislation to prevent discrimination in the media. Biaggi has always carried the banner of Italian American causes, for which Italian Americans respect and admire him.

As of this writing, Mario Biaggi has been waging a major legal battle in the New York courts. All those who have known and love Mario are hoping that he will emerge victorious and be vindicated in his struggle to exonerate himself.

Frank Annunzio, top-ranking congressman from Chicago, has been working diligently on behalf of Italian Americans for decades. He was a driving force behind the move to honor Constantino Brumidi, "the Michelangelo of the United States Capitol," with a joint resolution to dedicate a bust of Brumidi in 1968 as artist laureate of the Capitol. Annunzio also serves on the House Banking, Finance and Urban Affairs Committee, and the House Administration Committee and several subcommittees.

Annunzio was also a prime mover in the historic effort to create the National Italian American Foundation in 1976 when a huge bicentennial dinner was held in Washington, D.C. At this time several groups, including the National Italian American Coordinating Association, formed for the dinner, which helped launch this national organization to represent Italian Americans all across the country. In addition to helping create the NIAF, Annunzio organized the Italian American congressional delegation into a powerful and cohesive support group of the foundation.

Joseph Dio Guardi from Westchester County, New York, first became a congressman in 1984 and is already creating a stir with his creative ideas. Dio Guardi grew up in what is now the South Bronx, attended Fordham Prep and Fordham University, graduating in 1962. By age thirty-one, he was one of the youngest full partners at Arthur Anderson & Co., one of the world's leading accounting firms. In 1984, after a successful professional career of twenty-two years, Dio Guardi announced himself as the "Common Sense Candidate for Congress," and won.

He entered our nation's Capitol hell-bent on making our government fiscally responsible. Dio Guardi is fighting vigorously to pass necessary financial reforms in his House of Representatives bill, the Federal Financial Management Improvement act, which calls for a chief financial officer for the federal government operating as a CFO of a corporation. This progressive and far-sighted solution to one of our nation's most persistent problems may revolutionize the federal bureaucracy and how it does business.

Dio Guardi seems to embody all the best values of the new breed of Italian American. He manages to combine a deep, passionate, liberal humanism, with a strict, no-nonsense, conservative political attitude, supported by a profound and solid foundation of pragmatism, discipline, hard work and responsibility. Dio Guardi can only be described as a creative visionary, a new-age thinker with old-age values and a true man of a Renaissance.

Joseph Alioto became a national figure when he delivered a riveting speech to nominate Hubert Humphrey at the 1968 Democratic National Convention in Chicago. The inside word was that Alioto came very close to being chosen Humphrey's vice-presidential running mate then, but was not. Alioto was a beloved mayor of San Francisco and a gifted politician who could walk into a room of a thousand people, flash a smile from the dais and evoke a standing ovation to rock the house. He is also a brilliant lawyer with a huge practice and is one of the world's leading experts in international law. It was a great loss to Italian Americans and to the country when Alioto went back to private practice and left public life. He would have made a great president.

Geraldine Ferraro, congresswoman from Queens from 1978 to 1984, made history as the first woman and the first Italian American to run on the presidential ticket when she was nominated for vice president at the Democratic National Convention in 1984. Ferraro was born in 1935 in Newburgh, New York, one of four children.

After the sudden death of her father in 1943, Ferraro, her mother and her only surviving brother moved to the Bronx and later to Queens. Ferraro graduated from Marymount College in Manhattan in 1956 with a B.A. degree in English. She then earned her law degree attending night classes at Fordham University Law School and started practicing law while also raising three children. She worked as an Assistant District Attorney, ran for the United States Congress in 1978 and won.

One of the most fabulous moments for Italian Americans was the historical event when all four candidates on the national ticket—President Reagan, Vice President Bush, Walter Mondale and Geraldine Ferraro—appeared on the dais of the 1984 National Italian American Foundation Dinner in Washington, D.C. This was the first time this had ever happened and beyond the historical significance of the event was the political significance for Italian Americans. In some symbolic and important sense, this confirmed that Italian Americans had truly arrived as a force in politics to be reckoned with.

Unfortunately, the euphoria of Ferraro's being chosen as a candidate wore off early in her campaign, especially when the media began to pursue her relentlessly, with overt bias, regarding the various financial dealings of her and her husband, John Zaccaro. The cruel public attack on her and her family created sensational headlines across America, with deep, hurtful damage to Ferraro and her loved ones.

For Italian Americans, the historical significance of Ferraro's nomination is unquestioned, but her electoral experience was ambiguous and uncertain. Her nomination was clearly important for women and Italian Americans, but her candidacy unfortunately pained some Italian Americans by raising the age-old myth of Italians having some illicit or immoral past, no matter how obliquely relevant or how far back in time. One leading television news personality stated on a national show that if your name ends in a vowel you have to expect questions about possible Mafia involvement.

Whatever the final consequences of the Ferraro campaign, Ferraro made history for women and Italian Americans. Her candidacy emphasized a historical problem Italian Americans have had with negative stereotyping and ethnic bias. Hopefully this will serve to inspire other Italian Americans to strive for high public office, as well as encourage the media to try a little harder to measure all Americans against the same set of standards.

Ferraro went on to write a book about her life and in particular about her experience in running for vice president. In all our history, those who saw it will never forget the night this "daughter of an immigrant" made her speech as the first Italian American and the first woman to run for national office in July 1984. If only for this, Ferraro deserves the appreciation and gratitude of Italian Americans.

Nor will they forget the speech of another Italian American who tore the roof off the Moscone Convention Center that same week when he stepped up to the podium and told the world what it meant to be an American of Italian descent.

Mario Matthew Cuomo, famous governor of New York State, was born in 1932 in the borough of Queens in New York City, the third child and second son of Andrea and Immaculata Cuomo, who had immigrated to America from Solermo, Italy, in the 1920s. Suomo's father dug ditches and sold goods from a pushcart, then opened an Italian grocery store in Jamaica, Queens. Cuomo attended local public schools and Catholic parochial schools, and got his college degree at St. John's University. He got his law degree at St. John's in 1956, worked as a lawyer and was appointed by Governor Hugh Carey as secretary of state in 1975. After an unsuccessful run for mayor of New York City, Cuomo ran for lieutenant governor with Carey in 1978 and won. Cuomo was elected governor in 1982 and re-elected in 1986 by the largest majority in the state's history. His progressive leadership of the Empire State has brought national attention to him as a gifted statesman and made him a prime contender for the presidential nomination in 1988. Sadly, when he chose not to make the run for the nomination the media immediately started reporting rumors that he was afraid that a national campaign might flush some Mafia skeletons out of his family's closet. This after an entire career spent in the public's eye!

Cuomo's speech during the same Democratic National Convention that nominated Geraldine Ferraro in 1984 brought Italian Americans to a national consciousness on a profound and sophisticated level. His speech embodied the very principles, values and philosophy that had made him a successful governor. Somehow his very presence ratified the ideals of America and those of the Italian American.

Cuomo is a complex, deeply emotional and highly intellectual man. His intensity and enthusiasm for his beliefs and their corresponding confusions, complexities and contradictions, call to mind a philosopher or theologian grappling with the pain of the world and the push and pull of heart and mind. He is a man of action, yet reflective and speculative. For him the family is not just his own family, but the state, the country and the world. His values are quintessentially Italian American. With his accomplishments and his emergence on the national political scene, it was natural for many to realize that, as president, who could better exemplify the Italian America dream than Mario Cuomo.

There is now a strong trend toward increased political power as more and more Italian Americans are entering electoral races and committing themselves to serving the public. Also, the evidence indicates that the appeal of Italian Americans is not on ethnic grounds, even though, paradoxically, it is those very Italian American values that the electorate finds so appealing in Italian American candidates.

As a curious irony of history, we probably have already had an Italian American president, since John Fitzgerald Kennedy claimed Italian heritage on his mother's side of the family. On Columbus Day, 1962, President Kennedy was introduced by Peter Rodino and told a startled audience of Italian Americans in Newark, New Jersey:

"My grandfather, John F. Fitzgerald, who used to be mayor of Boston, and was a congressman, always used to claim that the Fitzgeralds were actually Italian, were descended from the Geraldinis, who came from Venice. I never had the courage to make that claim, but I will make it on Columbus Day here in this State of New Jersey today!"

You see, everyone wants to be Italian!

10

THE PROFESSIONS

WAR AND EDUCATION

BECAUSE ITALY's feudal system had kept so many bound to the land and enslaved in ignorance, over half of the southern Italian immigrants who came to America were illiterate. Education was a hallowed privilege available only to the priests and landed gentry. Other than among the landed gentry southern Italians could not afford to encourage children to pursue an education because they needed them to work the land and contribute to the support of the family. These attitudes transferred to America.

While other ethnic groups, especially the Jews, saw education as a means of economic salvation and an escape route out of the ghetto and toward prosperity, most Italian immigrants, especially the *contadini*, seemed unaware at first that education could be even more helpful than hard work in opening doors to financial stability and success. The first change in this shortsighted attitude was forced in 1917, when a new law required immigrants to pass a literacy test in English. Ironically, while this law was actually intended to limit Italian immigration, the Italian immigrants quickly adapted to the demands of the law and vigorously sought the education they needed to gain admittance to America. Their survival depended on it, and they adapted.

By 1903, the number of professionals entering the United States from Italy was still distinctly small. But just as Italian Americans began to gain in affluence and to accept the

160

value of education, discrimination against them started to wane. As a consequence, Italian Americans gradually entered the professions.

The key to the door of greater opportunity was education, but it was the free public school system of America that provided it. The official policy of the American pedagogical community fully expressed the value of becoming American and unbecoming Italian, and as painful as this process was for those put through it, it was an essential process in its time. Beyond the hardships of the day-to-day struggle to survive, these first Italian Americans also had to deal with nativism, xenophobia, discrimination and now "Americanization." In their climb out of poverty and up to a higher social status, these immigrants would create something new—a culture that somehow combined two contradictory worlds, reconciled two different cultures and integrated two clashing sets of values.

By the 1920s, the transition from an anonymous mass migration to an involved participation in contemporary American life had begun in full force. The Italian immigrants rose very quickly from pick-and-shovel and menial work to skilled labor, and by the 1930s they had swelled the ranks of America's enterprising small businessmen. They could be found all across America as bakers, butchers, barbers, grocers, fruit and vegetable sellers, tailors, shoemakers, masons, stone-cutters, scissor and knife sharpeners, confectioners, restaurateurs, saloon-keepers, hotel owners, carpenters, plumbers, electricians, machinists and painters.

The children of these immigrants, however, went to school, got educated, graduated and looked for something better than the immigrant experience. Some changed their names, intermarried and moved out of the Little Italys. They were clearly moving into the mainstream of American life by the time of World War II.

Yet for Italian Americans, World War II both created and resolved serious crises of identity. Italians who were broken spirited by the aftermath of the Risorgimento and of World War I came to be stirred during the 1920s and 1930s by feelings of new-found nationalist pride in Italy as a nation.

These new feelings also helped retard the process of assimilation of the Italians into American life.

Mussolini's decision to enter the war on Germany's side in 1940, and his declaration of war on the United States after Pearl Harbor, shocked Italian Americans. The feelings the Fascists had encouraged for an imperial Italian state, or *La Patria*, resolved any conflicts of loyalty and any sense of ethnic schizophrenia for these Italian Americans. Forced finally to choose, Italian Americans saw clearly that they were Americans first! Their only loyalty was to the American flag. Ironically, they were to be the liberators of the country of their parents and grandparents.

Italians are not by nature militaristic and warlike. However, Italians and Italian Americans were fighters for the cause of liberation and against the Nazi plan of world domination. In fact, more information regarding the Italian clandestine protection and saving of many Jews during the war is now coming out. Apparently the loyalty of the Italian generals to Mussolini caused them to say one thing about their support of Hitler and about their hatred for the Jews while their actual treatment and policies toward the Jews were quite different.

The Italians in Italy, especially the underground liberation forces, and the Italian Americans who came to fight on the soil of their forebears were brave, courageous and loyal to their allegiance to freedom, democracy and liberty. Even those Italians who became soldiers, many never seemed to develop the warlike attitudes of German recruits. The embarrassed, sheepish grins of captured Italian prisoners expressed the genuine joy over being released from the ridiculous wartime obligation of fighting and killing. These Italian fighters were not Nazi storm troopers or Fascist goose steppers, but farmers, shepherds, fishermen and laborers who just wanted this absurd war to end. Capture by the American forces of liberation was indeed welcome relief from the misery of fighting. In fact, perhaps as a tribute to the love the Italian population had for America and Americans, the citizens of Sicily started a movement with Salvatore Giuliano the bandit as one of their spokesmen to make Sicily the forty-ninth state!

But, for Italian Americans it was a different story. In World

War I, of the almost two hundred thousand who served, two were awarded the Congressional Medal of Honor, about one hundred received Distinguished Service Crosses and thousands sustained battle wounds and injuries. In World War II, Italian Americans racked up a splendid war record of bravery, loyalty and courage. More than half a million served in the armed forces, thirteen received the Congressional Medal of Honor and then were awarded the Navy Cross. In a curious irony of history, the Sicilian Lucky Luciano, known member of the Mafia and kingpin of organized crime, was recruited by the United States government to help the Allies with their campaign in Sicily by using his criminal connections there. His efforts helped win the war.

John Basilone of New Jersey was a Marine gunnery sergeant whom General MacArthur called a "one-man army." He was awarded the Medal of Honor for his bravery and valor fighting on Guadal-canal, but was killed in the battle of Iwo Jima and received the Navy Cross posthumously.

Donald Gentile, son of an immigrant stone quarrier, and a coal miner in Ohio, enlisted in the Royal Canadian Air Force and set his heart on becoming a fighter pilot. He then transferred to the United States Air Corps after Pearl Harbor, flew 182 valorous missions, shot down 42 German planes and emerged as a leading ace among fighter pilots.

A. Vernon Jannotta, whose father came from Copua near Naples, became a rear admiral in the Naval Reserve and had also fought in World War I. During a kamikaze attack in the Philippines, he went aboard a flaming tanker ship packed with fifty-thousand gallons of high-octane gasoline and one hundred and sixty torpedoes, rescued the crew and then stayed to put out the flames.

Gino J. Merli, a private from Pennsylvania, while serving as a machine gunner in Belgium, was attacked by a huge and savage German onslaught and found himself surrounded. He fought courageously and brilliantly throughout the night and when dawn broke the following morning, there were fifty-two enemy dead, of whom nineteen were found right in front of his gun.

Ruth Flora was one of the first Italian American naval officers serving in the United States Navy. Anthony Casamento fought against the Japanese bravely and, after a long, hard struggle to receive his due, was awarded the Congressional Medal of Honor in 1980.

At home, Italian Americans supported the war effort passionately and gave generous aid to refugees from racial persecution and to exiles from German-occupied countries. New York became a center for anti-Fascist exiles, many of whom were Italians who went on to contribute significantly to American life, especially in the sciences.

For Italian Americans, World War II changed everything. They had fought and shed their blood on those same strange foreign homelands that they had only heard about from their parents and their grandparents. This experience fighting for the "old country" of their ethnic descent and actually liberating the homeland of their forebears somehow planted the seeds for a reawakening of a new sense of identity by Italian Americans, an identity strongly related to the discovery of their Italian heritage. The war made Italian Americans discover Italy, and along the way they began to re-discover their identity.

In America, gone were discrimination, bias and prejudice toward Italians, even though these problems would take another, perhaps more subtle, shape later when the media became a dominant force in American life. For now, gone was the pain and disdain experienced by the Italian American immigrants. Gone also were the underlying constraints of nativistic and xenophobic Anglo-Saxon biases. The Italian American conquering heroes that returned from the war that made the world safe for democracy were American heroes first and foremost.

Now, these ambivalent sons and daughters of poverty-stricken immigrants were unequivocally, full-fledged Americans, and they had proved it with their blood and heroism. After the war, America's atmosphere was jubilant, victorious, heroic, proud, new, liberal, democratic and expansive. America was an unlimited horizon of opportunity and America welcomed these conquering heroes, these *American* heroes, with open arms, ticker-tape parades and, perhaps most of all, with the G.I. bill, which altered educational opportunities to the returning soldiers.

Education was now available to a huge population of Italian Americans and would become a magic carpet carrying them into the professions, into corporations and into their own businesses on a vast, huge scale. And in just two generations of being Americans, Italians who had been seeking relief from the poverty of the old world would now experience the affluence of the new world. The architectural, artistic, clerical, educational, financial, industrial, journalistic, juridical, legal, medical, political, scientific and social-service spheres of life became saturated by the children and grandchildren of the Italian immigrants, as well as by those who fled Italy during the war. The Italian American soldiers, fresh from the victory of a world war fought to liberate the country of their ancestry, were invigorated and charged with boundless energy to succeed.

EDUCATION

Prior to the mass influx of Italian Americans into the professions at large after World War II, there had already been a tradition of accomplishments within many spheres of professional activity. This was actually true of education itself.

The remarkable history and tradition spearheaded by the zealous missionaries from the days of Columbus and continued by the intellectual Jesuits, was carried forward by teachers, scholars and thinkers from Italy during the nineteenth- and twentieth-century mass migrations. The substantial participation in and contribution to the world of educational endeavors would explode into an extensive array of amazing accomplishments in all disciplines of knowledge, especially in the twentieth century. This heritage of a quest for knowledge would be carried on by a multitude of Italian American scholars, teachers, educators, philosophers, and intellectuals. And, this tradition of learning permeated the evolution of Italy as a country and produced significant advances in the world of academe dating back to the centers of learning and seats of wisdom that flourished in Roman times, the Middle Ages and the Renaissance.

On June 25, 1678, in Padua's great cathedral, Elena Lucrezia Piscopia Cornaro became the first woman Ph.D. in the world by defending two philosophical theses before a throng of scholars and townspeople. Antonio Genovesi became the first Italian and European to hold a university chair in economics in 1754.

Maria Montessori, born in Chiaravalle near Ancona, Italy, in 1870, gained a worldwide reputation as a foremost educator with her unique methods of childhood learning. Montessori became a leading psychologist and opened her first "Casa dei Bambini" in 1907 where children discovered for themselves the nature of the world. She pioneered progressive education in the world and based her methods on a primary concern for the development of the individual human personality, a concept first advocated by another Italian, Vittorino da Feltre in the fifteenth century.

The tradition of a fine liberal arts education in the many Catholic schools, colleges and universities persists to present day, especially in the Jesuit institutions. Many of the leaders we see today emerging as powerful voices in the shaping of our country's future have had the benefits of the intellectually rigorous Catholic schools and Jesuit training.

Lorenzo Da Ponte, priest, linguist and musician, was Mozart's librettist and wrote *Don Giovanni, Figaro* and *Cosi Fan Tutti*. He came to America from Venice in 1805 and became the first teacher of the Italian language in New York at Columbia College in 1806. He also promoted Italian opera by building New York's first opera house in 1833 and was of Italian-Jewish descent. Father Samuel Mazzuchelli was an architect and philologist as well as an educator. He wrote a book of prayers in the Winnebago language in 1833 and this was the first work published in any Sioux language. He also built the first Catholic churches in Iowa and Wisconsin. Father Gennaro De Concilio came to America in 1860 and became a professor of Logic at Seton Hall University in New Jersey. He wrote the famous *Baltimore Catechism*, which was used extensively in Catholic schools across America.

Italian Americans also founded secular academic institutions in keeping with a passionate desire for the learning, teaching and sharing of knowledge. In 1778, Carlo Bellini, friend to Thomas Jefferson and Filippo Mazzei, became the first Italian professor in the country as a teacher of Romance Languages at William and Mary College. Nicholas Biferi, as well-known harpsichordist who performed recitals in New York City, created a music and dance school for young ladies that was the first of its kind in America.

Mario Cosenza became the first Italian American dean at Brooklyn College, and he promoted the teaching of Italian in high schools and colleges across the nation. In 1913, Angelo Patri, who had educated millions of parents in his newspaper columns on how to raise children, became the first Italian American school principal with his appointment at Public School 145 in the Bronx.

Max Ascoli came to the United States in 1931 after an illustrious, though controversial, career teaching jurisprudence at Italian universities. He joined the graduate faculty of the New School of Social Research in New York City, edited and published *The Reporter*, a liberal magazine, and has written several books.

Mario Pei became a world famous linguist at Columbia University.

Peter Sammartino created Fairleigh Dickinson University in 1942 during the difficult years of World War II. Truly a Renaissance man, Sammartino graduated college at the age of twenty, taught highly gifted boys, wrote prolifically and edited a magazine. He became president of New Jersey's Association of Colleges and Universities and the International Association of University Presidents, served on the President's Committee on Higher Education in the United States and he was the person responsible for creating the campaign to restore Ellis Island. Sylvia Scaramelli, Peter's wife, was also a remarkable educator who worked enthusiastically with him to make Fairleigh Dickinson a strong university.

Leonard Covello was born in 1887 in the town of Avigliano of southern Italy. In 1890, his father emigrated to New York City. Leonard, his mother, and his two brothers, joined him in the East Harlem section of the city in 1896. He won a scholarship that enabled him to attend Columbia University. In 1913 he took a job as a teacher of French in DeWitt Clinton High School. A perceptive analyst of the Italian experience in America and an immigrant himself, he developed an approach to education based on his own experiences in New York City schools. Covello developed a strong commitment to cultural pluralism and to the importance of immigrant children becoming conscious and proud of their native cultures while learning to adapt to their new environment. Covello also succeeded in creating a new concept of education—the community-centered school—which provided a social and cultural context for the education of immigrant children.

Irene Impellizzeri is a teacher, researcher, administrator, psychologist and community worker. She was born in Brooklyn, the daughter of a teacher. Impellizzeri has worked in New York City's urban environs and carried on the tradition of education spawned by her mother. She got her B.S. from New York University in 1941, her M.A. from Columbia Teachers College in 1942 and her Ph.D. in Educational Psychology from Fordham University in 1958. She taught in elementary and secondary schools, then at Fordham University from 1951 to 1966. She became dean of the School of Education at Brooklyn College in 1971. First appointed to the New York City Board of Education in 1980, by 1986 she was unanimously elected its vice president and in 1987 she was made university dean for teacher education at CUNY.

No ivory-tower scholar, she has always thrown herself into the urgencies of education in America. She has involved herself with research into the learning patterns of children, with the gifted and the handicapped, with seminal research on auditory perception and learning achievement, and with performance-based and field-based teacher training. These and other breakthrough contributions she has made in education have brought her national attention.

Richard Bossone, university dean for instructional research at the City University of New York, is an outstanding professor, administrator and researcher. He got his B.A. from the University of California at Berkeley, his M.A. from San Francisco State University and his Ph.D. from the University of Southern California. He became a professor in the English department of CUNY in 1967 and rose to the position of dean and director of corporate development by 1979. As an educator, Bossone has made a major contribution in instructional programs, research, materials and projects to meet a broad array of educational needs. He lectures, writes and consults for many organizations, institutions and companies.

Bossone has also significantly advanced the cause of Italian Americans. He was one of the founders and presidents of the Italian American Faculty Association. His reports on discrimination against Italian Americans in the university resulted in legislative hearings that produced affirmative-action statutes for Italian Americans. He helped found the Italian American Institute. Bossone has won many awards for his distinguished achievements and contributions. His President's Medal lauds him for his "contribution to education," but Governor Cuomo's Certificate of Appreciation praises him for "his outstanding contributions to the Italian American educational community" and for "his commitment to social justice for all Italian Americans."

Giovanni Cecchetti, distinguished professor of Italian at U.C.L.A., has devoted almost forty years to the diffusion of the Italian language and culture throughout the American continent. A renowned literary critic and translator of Italian classics, he is also a distinguished poet. The Italian government has honored him with many awards, especially the rare Presidential Gold Medal for special artistic and cultural merit. He has published fifteen books and over one hundred and fifty articles on literary works from the time of Dante to present day.

At age twenty-four, Cecchetti was awarded a Doctor's Degree in literature by the University of Florence in 1947. A year later he joined the faculty of the University of California at Berkeley where he raised the Italian program to its highest possible level. In the mid–1950s, he went to Tulane University and founded a center of Italian studies while also helping to establish Italian programs in many other universities. He then created another advanced program of Italian studies at Stanford University and after four years moved to U.C.L.A. as chairman of the department of Italian. The U.C.L.A. Center of Italian Studies is considered the most significant outside Italy.

Robert J. DiPietro, born in 1932, got his B.A. from the State University of New York at Binghampton in 1954, his M.A. from Harvard University in 1955 and his Ph.D. from Cornell University in 1960. He is now professor of Linguistics at the University of Delaware and has devoted much of his academic work to establishing Italian courses as well as linguistic programs. He has written eight books and numerous articles on linguistics and English and Italian. DiPietro is vitally committed to the study of Italian as a language and to the Italian American cause of education. He is education chairman for the National Italian American Foundation.

Joseph Scelsa is an extremely well educated man with a page full of degrees, including an M.A. and Ed.D. from Columbia University. He joined the graduate faculty of CUNY's Herbert H. Lehman College in 1980 and is a professional counselor with a private practice in mental-health counseling. He has written numerous articles, served on many committees and has won an array of awards. Scelsa was appointed director of the Italian American Institute of the graduate center of CUNY in 1984. His dedicated efforts on behalf of Italian American students have been vitally successful in bettering the educational life of all Italian American students.

There have been many Italian Americans who have excelled in the world of education. Richard Gambino is a professor at Queens College and chaired the first program of Italian American studies in the country. Also a superb author of fiction and nonfiction, Gambino wrote *Blood of My Blood,* a classic of Italian American literature that is a deeply moving and profound depiction of the dilemma of Italian Americans. Philip Zimbardo is a psychologist at Stanford University and is renowned for his research on shyness, especially in children, and has written several classic books on the subject. Salvatore La Gumina is a noted professor of history at Nassau Community College and a respected writer, especially on Italian American history.

Larissa Bonfante, classics professor at New York University, is a leading scholar on the Etruscan era and has written several books that are considered the best on the subject. Mario Del Chiaro, professor of Art History at the University of California at Santa Barbara, is also an expert in Etruscan, Greek and Roman antiquities, and has carried out numerous archeological expeditions.

Gaetano Lanza, born in Boston in 1848, the son of a Sicilian immigrant and an American mother, became the very heart and soul of the department of Mechanical Engineering of the Massachusetts Institute of Technology for forty years beginning in 1871. Lanza entered the University of Virginia at age seventeen and distinguished himself in mathematics, graduating in 1870. He joined the MIT faculty the following year and became the head of the department in 1883. Through his efforts, MIT's department of Mechanical Engineering became the best in the country.

Franco Modigliani, born in Rome, first came to MIT in 1960 as a visiting professor in the Sloan School and was appointed professor in 1962. He became internationally known as an authority on monetary theory, capital markets, corporate finance, macroeconomics and econometrics. He has written many books and professional papers, and consults for the Federal Reserve Bank, the U.S. Treasury department and the Bank of Italy. In 1975, Modigliani gained national recognition when he called for a permanent tax cut of 30 to 40 billion dollars, to reduce inflation. He also proposed sweeping reforms in worldwide fiscal procedures in 1971 which were important to the United States economy. In 1985, Modigliani was awarded the Nobel Prize in Economics.

Anne Attura Paolucci, born in Rome, is a full professor and serves as chairperson of the English department at St. John's University. She is also an award-winning playwright and poet. She graduated from Barnard College in 1947 and got her M.A. from Columbia University in 1950 and her Ph.D. in 1963 in English and Comparative Literature. Paolucci has been awarded many prestigious awards, including President Reagan's New York Educators for Excellence award in 1984. She is founder and president of the Council on National

Literatures and editor of its prestigious worldwide series *Review of National Literatures*. She sits on the National Graduate Fellows Program Fellowship Board, a presidentially appointed body of the U.S. department of Education. Paolucci is also the firebrand behind the "Columbus: Countdown 1992" project to celebrate the five-hundredth anniversary of the discovery of America by Cristoforo Columbo.

Sister Margherita Marchione, born in 1922 in Little Ferry, New Jersey, received her B.A. from Georgia Court College and her M.A. and Ph.D. from Columbia University. She is president of Corfinio College in Italy and the American Institute of Italian Studies. She has received many awards and honors for her scholarship, especially for her extensive research and writings about Filippo Mazzei's contribution to the creation of the United States. Sister Marchione is professor emerita of Italian Language and Literature at Fairleigh Dickinson University. She was recently named honorary president of the Philip Mazzei International Association and the recipient of the Philip Mazzei award for selected writings and correspondence.

Silvio Bedini, born in 1917 in Ridgefield, Connecticut, went to Columbia University and graduated in 1942. From 1961 to 1965, he served as curator of the Division of Mechanical and Civil Engineering of the United States National Museum and in 1970 he got his LL.D. degree from the University of Bridgeport. From 1965 to 1973, he was assistant director of the Museum of History and Technology and from 1973 served as deputy director of the National Museum of History and Technology. In 1978, he became special assistant to the director of the Smithsonian Institution and Keeper of the Rare Books in Washington, D.C. Bedini, in addition to his considerable work, especially at the Smithsonian Institution, has written numerous books, articles and monographs on science and technology throughout history. He is a member of and affiliated with many scientific societies throughout the world.

Carlo Pedretti is a renowned scholar and has emerged clearly as the preeminent expert on Leonardo da Vinci. He now heads the Armand Hammer Center for Leonardo Studies at U.C.L.A. Peter Riccio, the learned director of Casa Italiana at Columbia University, preserves Italian culture and heritage in a beautiful haven of peace, refinement and glory.

Andrew Rolle of Occidental College in Los Angeles has written several important books on the Italian Americans. Roberto Vaglio-Laurin, professor of Aeronautics and Astronautics at New York University, is an engineer hailed as one of the world-class authorities in hypersonics. Rudolph Vecoli is director of the Immigration History Research Center of the University of Minnesota and has written many valuable books on the Italian American story. Francis X. Femminella is a leading expert in ethnicity as professor of Sociology and Education at the State University of New York at Albany.

Also, Philip Vairo is president of Worcester State College and has been an extremely active man in the field of education, as well as a passionately proud Italian American. He has fought behind the scenes for years to bring Italian Americans into the higher ranks of education. His work in education has been significant and extensive.

This conscious quest to know, to understand and to share what one knows is particularly vital to Italian Americans. This thirst for knowledge and its sharing with others in the teaching-learning experience reached great heights in the contributions of Italian Americans to education. And for Italian Americans, education was the key to open the golden doors of opportunity in America.

THE LAW

In the legal professions, many Italian Americans became national heroes and won accolades for their diligence, bravery, courage and commitment to enforcing the law, capturing criminals and putting them behind bars. These Italian American policemen, detectives and crime-fighters represent a proud legacy of adherence to an ethical, moral and legal set of values. In addition to the pursuit of justice and a passionate concern for maintaining law and order, these crime-busters also embody a particularly humanistic value system that incorporates a strict enforcement of the law with a liberal sense of "doing the right thing," not necessarily the legal thing, but the moral thing.

This heritage of humanistic law enforcement has deep roots. In fact, it was Angelo "Charlie" Siringo, the son of an Italian immigrant, who led the posse that captured Billy the Kid at Stinking Springs. He had herded cows since he was fourteen and chased rustlers into Mexico throughout his career as a cowboy. He also wrote a colorful book about this.

Charles Bonaparte is also a classical example of the Italian American commitment to the law. Bonaparte served as Secretary of the Navy under President Theodore Roosevelt in 1905, was appointed Attorney General by Roosevelt as well, and in 1908 founded the Federal Bureau of Investigation or the F.B.I.

There are literally multitudes of Italian Americans serving in law enforcement today and throughout our history, especially in police departments all across the country. Several stand out for their outstanding careers. Lieutenant Joseph Petrosino headed a special Italian squad of the New York police department to fight the Mafia's "Black Hand" criminal activity. On a trip to Sicily to investigate links between the Sicilian and New York Mafias, he was murdered by two unknown gunmen.

Congressman Mario Biaggi was the most decorated policeman in the United States when he served on the New York City police department from 1942 to 1965. Frank Rizzo became famous and controversial as police commissioner of Philadelphia. Frank Serpico exposed corruption in the New York City police department. David Toma was an outstanding narcotics detective. Sonny Grasso became famous for his huge drug bust as depicted in the highly publicized movie *The French Connection*. Ralph Salerno was a former New York City police detective in the organized crime unit who became chief rackets expert for the city.

Michael Spiotto excelled in the Chicago police department as did Joseph Di Leonardi, who commanded one of the most respected homicide divisions in the country, famous for closing 90 percent of its cases. Richard Pastorella, a detective with the New York City police department's bomb squad, was injured in 1982 by a terrorist bomb device and lost his eyesight. He formed a vital voluntary police self-support group to help police officers avoid injury and support them if they are hurt in the line of duty.

The remarkable heritage of accomplishments by Italian Americans as judges represents an outstanding continuance of a long tradition of bringing justice to the world. This heritage echoes the days of the Roman Senate and the Roman Empire's social commitment to rule by law rather than by men. The Emperor Justinian codified the laws governing the citizenry and this body of legal precepts, which has come to be known as Justinian law, provided the foundation for the legal system of western civilization. Ever since Italians came to this country, they have carried this exquisite legal tradition into their lives and the lives of all Americans.

In 1870, Carlo Rapallo, a lawyer from New York, was elected to the New York State Court of Appeals and dispensed justice for seventeen years till he died. In 1888, President Grover Cleveland appointed Andrew Houston Longino United States District Attorney for the Southern District of Mississippi. Ferdinand Pecora, born in 1882 in Sicily, served as legal counsel to the U.S. Committee on Banking and Currency during the 1930s. Also a politician, he became a justice of the Supreme Court of New York State. Edward Corsi came to America from Abruzzi at age ten and became a lawyer and writer. Corsi held posts as immigration commissioner at Ellis Island, U.S. commissioner of Immigration and Naturalization and industrial commissioner of New York State in the 1930s and 1940s. In 1955, he served as assistant to the U.S. Secretary of State. In 1936 Matthew Abbruzzo was appointed by President Franklin D. Roosevelt the first Italian American federal judge of the U.S. District Court serving in the Eastern District of New York.

Mario Procaccino, from the Bronx, graduated Fordham Law School in 1939, and served as comptroller of New York City, judge in the Civil and Municipal Courts and chief law assistant of the Supreme Court, Bronx. In 1956, he was appointed director of Mortgage, Banking and Housing for New York City when he established model government housing. Many remember him for his colorful race for the office of mayor of

New York City in 1969 when he lost this three-way split by a slim margin.

Michael Angelo Musmanno, born in 1897 near Pittsburgh, received his law degree at Georgetown University in Washington, D.C., and excelled as a lawyer, judge and author. Over his broad and multi-talented career, he was one of the team that defended Sacco and Vanzetti in 1927, was appointed by President Truman as one of the presiding judges at the International War Crimes Trials in Nuremberg in 1946. He served in World War II receiving many decorations and after the war was a member of a Navy team to determine if Hitler was actually dead. He was elected a justice on the Pennsylvania Supreme Court in 1951 and authored many books.

Mario Clinco, from New York City, was admitted to the New York bar in 1938 after receiving his law degree from Fordham University. He served in the Army as an intelligence agent and moved to California after the war. He was admitted to the California Bar in 1948 and became a presiding judge of the Superior Court of Santa Monica. Clinco was voted Trial Judge of the Year twice and his intense dedication endeared him to all who knew him. He was one of the founders, with Judge Rao, of the American Justinian Society of Jurists. A passionate and enthusiastic man who loved everything Italian American, Clinco truly personified our heritage at its best.

Edward Domenic Re became a lawyer and a law professor at St. John's University. From 1961 to 1968 he served as chairman of the Foreign Claims Settlement Commission of the United States and he also served on the Board of Higher Education of New York City from 1954 to 1969. He was appointed assistant Secretary of State for Educational and Cultural Affairs by President Johnson from 1968 to 1969. He was appointed judge of the United States Customs Court in 1969 and has written several major law school textbooks.

Paul Peter Rao also was appointed judge of the United States Custom Court in 1948 by President Truman and was one of the only Italian American judges to serve as chief justice of a federal court when he was promoted to chief judge of that court by President Johnson in 1965. Rao also served as assistant

Attorney General of the United States under Presidents Roosevelt and Truman from 1941 to 1948. He is the primary person responsible for the creation of the Customs Court Act of 1970. Rao is perhaps best known to Italian Americans as one of the co-founders of the American Justinian Society of Jurists in 1966. His brother, Charles Rao, founded the well-known private club for Italian Americans in New York, the *Tiro a Segno* on MacDougal Street in Greenwich Village. Rao's son, Paul, Jr., is a well-known and successful attorney in New York City. Rao was born in 1899 in Prizzi, Palermo, Italy, came to America in 1904, and got his law degree from Fordham University Law School and was admitted to the bar of New York State in 1924. His illustrious career in the law has brought him many awards and decorations.

Recently there has been a leap forward in the number of women in the field of law generally and on the benches of courts across America. Rose A. Caputo received her B.A. at Adelphi University in 1947, her J.D. at St. John's University in 1950 and her LL.M. from New York University in 1959. She was admitted to the New York bar in 1951 and worked for herself in the general practice of law until 1977. She moved to the bench when she was appointed Worker's Compensation Board law judge in 1974, then became senior law judge from 1983 to 1984 and then supervising law judge with responsibility for about sixty law judges, six district administrators and a huge support staff. Caputo's position encompasses a vast array of administrative and judicial matters, and she participates in many professional and civic organizations. She has won many honors and awards as an Italian American woman, and has written a critical piece entitled *Status of Women, A Review of Gender Bias in the Courts.*

Marie L. Garibaldi received her B.A. from Connecticut College in 1956, her LL.B. from Columbia Law School in 1959 and her LL.M. from New York University in 1963. She was admitted to the New Jersey, New York and District of Columbia bars, and she worked in the regional counsel's office of the Internal Revenue Service in New York from 1960 to 1966. She worked in two law firms from 1967 to 1969 and from 1969 to 1982 respectively. She was then appointed associate justice of the Supreme Court of New Jersey where she now serves. Garibaldi belongs to many professional and civic organizations, lectures extensively, serves as director or trustee of several schools and companies, writes many articles and has received an array of prestigious awards.

Angela Mazzarelli, judge of the Civil Court of New York City, was born in 1946 in Milford, Massachusetts, a predominantly Italian area near Boston. In a very exciting and surprising race in 1985, she became the first Italian American elected to this high judgeship position in the Civil Court of New York City. Mazzarelli received her B.A. from Brandeis University and became a teaching fellow at Columbia University where she earned her J.D. She served as staff attorney with the Bronx Legal Services and as a special investigator for the New York City Department of Consumer Affairs, as well as special assistant to the general counsel of the Housing and Development Administration. She served as law assistant to the Board of Justices of the New York Supreme Court and as law clerk to a New York State Supreme Court justice. She was a partner in the private law firm of Wresien & Mazzarelli and teaches law at Pace University. Mazzarelli credits her success as a woman, as a judge and as a legal mind to her Italian American background. She is known and respected for her honesty, fairness, integrity, good judgement and compassion.

Lisa A. Richette, born and raised in 1928 in Philadelphia, is a nationally recognized jurist as well as author, lecturer and activist for human rights. She graduated from the University of Pennsylvania Phi Beta Kappa in 1949. She attended Yale Law School and became the first Italian American woman to graduate in 1952. She was appointed one of the first female assistant district attorneys in Philadelphia and became chief of the Family Court Division, another first. Richette is now presiding judge of the Court of Common Pleas for Philadelphia. Richette has contributed significantly to law reform in the juvenile, mental health and prisoners' rights areas. Her pioneering book *The Throwaway Children* thrust her into national attention. Richette has won many honors, including the Pearl S. Buck award, the Alice B. Paul Woman-of-Courage award and the Medal of Honor of the National Sons and Daughters of the American Revolution.

Joan Marie Durante was born in 1933 in Forest Hills, New York. She got her bachelor's degree at the College of the City of New York and her law degree from St. John's University School of Law. In 1962, she was admitted to the New York State bar. Durante was appointed to the U.S. District Court, Eastern District and then Southern District, in 1964, and to the U.S. Supreme Court in 1967. She worked as law secretary to Albert H. Buschmaun, justice of the Supreme Court of New York State. She herself was appointed to this same position and presently serves in the borough of Queens. Among Durante's prestigious judicial, professional and community affiliations, she is now president of the American Justinian Society of Justices, the first woman to achieve such high prominence. She is considered one of the most talented and brilliant women now serving on the bench.

Though not a judge, Elizabeth F. Defeis plays a vital and significant role as lawyer, educator, writer and dean in the area of the law. She graduated *cum laude* from St. John's University in 1955, studied at St. John's University School of Law till 1958, went to the University of Milan from 1963 to 1964 and got her LL.M. from New York University School of Law in 1971. She was admitted to the New York, New Jersey, Southern and Eastern Districts of New York Federal Court and the U.S. Supreme Court bars. She began work in the Department of Justice, went to the U.S. Attorney's office for the Southern District of New York and worked for several firms and companies. In 1971, she became a professor of Law at Seton Hall Law Center. In 1983, she was named dean of the center, where she now serves. Defeis has written many articles on a variety of legal issues and has developed and directed a complete video course on *Women and the Law,* which is used extensively across the country. She has just been named by the governor to serve as one of five citizen directors of the New Jersey Urban Development Corporation Board of Directors.

John J. Sirica was born in 1904 in Waterbury, Connecticut, entered George Washington University Law School at age seventeen, dropped out after a month, and peddled newspapers for a year in downtown Washington, D.C., six blocks from the courthouse where he would one day preside as chief judge. After another failed attempt, he returned once again to George Washington and made good grades while supporting himself as a boxing coach. He graduated in 1926 and passed his bar exams. Sirica continued his boxing work, but his mother finally persuaded him to give up boxing and return to the practice of law in Washington, D.C.

In 1930, he joined the U.S. Attorney's office and became a skilled prosecutor and trial lawyer. In 1967, Sirica was sworn in as a federal judge; however, destiny intervened and catapulted this son of an Italian immigrant to national fame and prominence when he became the presiding judge of the infamous Watergate trials. Into this man's hands was placed the fate of America. Sirica rose to the occasion of this historic destiny, handled all aspects with firmness, courage, integrity, wisdom, humanity and, most of all, reverence for our U.S. constitution. Most legal scholars say that Sirica probably saved the constitution in this momentous historic moment.

Ironically, it fell to another Italian American, Congressman Peter Rodino, to resolve the issue when his House Judiciary Committee recommended the impeachment of Nixon as president. Nixon escaped his punishment by resigning his presidency in 1974 and by being pardoned by his successor Gerald Ford. It is a fascination of history to consider that the two key roles in the Watergate trials and investigations and the judiciary hearings and impeachment proceedings were carried out by two Italian Americans—Sirica and Rodino. And it was their Italian American values of integrity and humanistic ethics that won the day for Americans, the U.S. Constitution and our democracy.

The ultimate goal of a judge is to play one of the most revered and influential roles in judicial history by serving on the highest court in the nation, the United States Supreme Court. Italian Americans have yearned for such an appointment for years and their wishes came true in June 1986 when Antonin Scalia was nominated as a Supreme Court justice. Scalia, born in 1936 in Trenton, New Jersey, of immigrant parents, graduated at the top of his class from Georgetown University and went on to Harvard Law School where he served as a law-review editor. He was later appointed by President Gerald Ford to head his office of legal counsel and taught at the University of Chicago for six years. President Reagan then appointed him to the Federal Appellate Court in the District of Columbia. His appointment as Supreme Court justice is indeed a historic landmark for all Italian Americans.

Italian Americans are also found in the offices of the United States Attorney General all across America. Michael De Feo is known for his expertise on organized crime. Diane Giacalone in New York City is prosecuting organized crime figures. Joseph Russoniello of San Francisco is highly regarded in the U.S. Attorney General's offices. Reena Raggi was nominated by Senator Alphonse D'Amato for the Federal District bench.

Thomas Philip Puccio, an intense, shrewd, and tenacious attorney, was born in 1944 in Brooklyn. He majored in English at Fordham University and then went on to Fordham School of Law. Upon graduation in 1969, he was persuaded to join the U.S. Attorney's office in Brooklyn. At age twenty-seven, within three years, he became narcotics chief and convicted major drug dealers. In 1970, Puccio's talents and intense dedication got him appointed, at age thirty-two, as head of the federal Organized Crime Strike Force for the Eastern District.

Puccio devoted three years almost exclusively conducting the highly controversial Abscam investigations, which resulted in the corruption convictions of six U.S. congressmen and one U.S. senator. Puccio's reputation was established nationwide and after thirteen years with the U.S. Justice Department, he moved to private law practice in 1982. Puccio gained national attention as a brilliant defense lawyer for socialite Claus von Bulow in his celebrated retrial on charges of murdering his wife. His sharp and skillful defense won acquittal for von Bulow and fame for himself and put Puccio at the top of his profession.

E. Lawrence Barcella, Jr., born in 1945 and raised in Washington, D.C., is a true hero of the criminal-justice system and has prosecuted over one hundred jury trials in his brilliant law career. Barcella got his A.B. degree from Dartmouth

College in 1967 and his law degree from Vanderbilt University School of Law in 1970. He became assistant United States attorney for the District of Columbia in 1971 and remained there until 1986. In this office, he served as deputy chief of the Major Crimes Division from 1975 to 1983 and as senior litigation counsel from 1984 to 1986. He is now counsel to Finley, Kumble, a major law firm specializing in white-collar criminal litigation.

Barcella has prosecuted many famous cases, such as the Edwin Wilson spy case, the murder of the Chilean ambassador and the hijacking of the *Achille Lauro* ocean liner. His major investigations include bribery, political corruption, customs violations (including arms and munitions), fraud, narcotics, terrorism, murder, rape, armed robbery and kidnapping. Several of his cases were of national and international scope. Among many honors, he won the John Marshall award for Outstanding Achievement in Litigation, the highest award of the Department of Justice, in 1983.

Laura A. Brevetti, born in Bensonhurst, Brooklyn, graduated from Lafayette High School and received her B.A. from Barnard College of Columbia University in 1973 and her law degree from Georgetown University in 1976. She spent her childhood in the notorious Bath Beach section, a known center of operations for three Mafia families.

Brevetti became assistant district attorney for Brooklyn from 1976 to 1980, and in 1980 she joined the Organized Crime Strike Force of the U.S. Department of Justice. In 1983, she was appointed assistant attorney-in-charge, the deputy chief of a fifteen-person attorney staff. By 1978, she had become the first woman appointed to the trial division of the District Attorney's Rackets Bureau. In 1980, she was the only woman to prosecute an Abscam case and has tried the full range of state and federal criminal prosecutions.

In October 1986 Laura Brevetti won a celebrated six-month trial in Brooklyn in which she convicted eleven individuals of operating a racketeering enterprise consisting of the Bonanno Crime Family, one of the five Mafia families in New York, and Local 814 of the International Brotherhood of Teamsters. The case was a capstone victory against organized crime.

Every now and then, a law-enforcement figure comes along whose charisma and zeal in the fight against evil captures the imagination of the public and focuses everyone's attention on this one person, as if in a personal crusade against injustice. Somehow, the collective hopes, aspirations and efforts of the many become symbolized by one person. So it is with Rudolph William Giuliani, U.S. attorney for the Southern District of New York, who supervises one hundred and thirty assistant U.S. attorneys in what can only be described as a holy war on organized crime.

Giuliani was born in 1944 in Flatbush, Brooklyn, and grew up on Long Island, New York. His family was Italian, his neighborhood was mixed and his values were Italian. He got his B.A. from Manhattan College in 1965 and his J.D. from New York University School of Law in 1968. Giuliani first joined the Justice Department in 1970 as an assistant U.S. attorney in the Southern District of New York. He was appointed associate deputy attorney general in the Department of Justice from 1975 to 1977. He returned to private practice from 1978 to 1981, but in 1981, President Reagan appointed him associate attorney general of the United States.

On June 3, 1983, Rudy Giuliani took the oath of office as the U.S. attorney for the Southern District of New York. The Criminal Division covers organized crime, narcotics, public corruption, securities and commodities frauds, major crimes and general crimes units. This U.S. attorney's office is the premiere outpost of the Justice Department.

And Giuliani is the premiere prosecutor—his victories in court have been monumental. Giuliani's major areas of attack on crime include terrorism, public corruption, drugs, tax fraud, civil rights violations, environmental damage and insider trading. However, the burning issue for Giuliani and for all Italian Americans is his war on the Mafia. He is passionately committed to breaking the back of organized crime and believes that Italian Americans should face the "Italian" nature of the Mafia head-on for what it is and take an offensive position against it.

Giuliani's brilliant idea was to attack the board of directors who control and guide all of New York's Mafia families in contract murder, drug trafficking, labor racketeering and loan sharking. In a single trial at Manhattan's federal courthouse, Giuliani has prosecuted the presumed heads of the Genovese, Gambino, Lucchese, Colombo and Bonanno families. In the so-called "Pizza Connection Case," he handed down thirty-eight indictments.

Rudy Giuliani is a brilliant criminal prosecutor with a sharp, creative legal mind. His dedication to law, morality and ethics, and his war against the Mafia, as well as all other forms of organized crime, have made Giuliani a hero to Italian Americans who wish, more than others, to crush the Mafia. To Italian Americans, it is vitally important and meaningful that Giuliani, who leads the fight, is Italian American. This makes the taste of victory all the sweeter and the pride of Italian Americans all the greater.

Not as well known and a largely unsung leader was Silvio Mollo who served as the chief assistant U.S. attorney from 1939 to 1975 except for a leave of absence to serve in the Army during World War II. He received the prestigious U.S. Attorney General's Distinguished Service award and was an extraordinary public servant as a skilled prosecutor. His contributions to law enforcement were truly significant and as a teacher he passed his great knowledge of law onto a generation of lawyers interested in public service. Under the leadership of Congressman Mario Biaggi and Senator Alphonse D'Amato, the U.S. Attorney's Building in Washington, D.C. was named after Silvio Mollo.

Italian Americans have served in the office of State Attorney General also, such as Walter Alessandroni of Pennsylvania. District attorneys abound with Italian Americans such as the late Mario Merola of the Bronx and John Santucci of Queens.

Because of the unrelenting issue of the Mafia and organized crime that seems to haunt the Italian Americans, many feel that an Italian American should be appointed as U.S. Attorney General and this view has been put forth especially by Governor Mario Cuomo. Although Benjamin Civiletti served in this role in 1978, it is now that the Mafia issue has taken prominence and, perhaps more symbolic than real, an Italian American Attorney General would help solve this issue.

Italian Americans also dominate the legal profession as private practice lawyers. Many have moved from public service in attorney-general offices to judgeships to political appointments and back and forth between public service and private practice. Whatever the case, they have become spectacularly successful in each of these roles.

Charles Poletti, born in 1903 in Barre, Vermont, received his law degree from Harvard in 1928 and then studied in Italy at the University of Rome for his LL.D. He was admitted to the New York bar in 1930 and became a justice on the New York Supreme Court in 1937. He then served as lieutenant governor from 1939 to 1942 and became governor of New York State in 1942. Poletti's career in law, both as a public servant and private attorney, spanned a broad spectrum of community affairs, issues and concerns, and reflects a deep commitment to social justice.

Christopher Del Sesto, born in 1907 in Providence, Rhode Island, attended Boston University and then got his law degree at Georgetown University. He served on the staff of the U.S. Securities and Exchange Commission and became a special assistant to the Attorney General from 1938 to 1940. Del Sesto also served as governor of Rhode Island from 1958 to 1960.

Joseph Blasi, born in 1908 in Brooklyn, graduated from Loyola University in New Orleans, Louisiana, and began the practice of law in 1931. He served four terms as a member of the Louisiana House of Representatives and as judge of the Civil District Court for the parish of New Orleans in 1948. He has been in general practice as a lawyer most of his life.

Michael Di Salle, born in 1908 in New York City, went to Georgetown University, began practicing in Toledo, Ohio, where he grew up and became mayor. He was asked to head the Price Stabilization Office in 1950 and taught history at the University of Massachusetts. He served as governor of Ohio and then moved to Washington to join a private law firm.

Joseph Alioto, in addition to serving as mayor of San Francisco and probably one of our great potential presidents, is world famous in the field of international law and he hit the front page in the case of the Oakland Raiders' move to Los Angeles. Vincent Bugliosi of Los Angeles became prominent for his celebrated prosecution of the Charles Manson "family" and has become a best-selling author as well. Paul Caruso of Los Angeles is famous for his representation of the stars in Hollywood and for his skills as a defense attorney in murder trials. Lea D'Agostino prosecuted the Landis case in Los Angeles in which Vic Morrow and two child actors were killed while filming a scene for a movie. Michael A. Ferrara, Jr. is a trial lawyer in New Jersey renowned for his handling of personal-injury cases in which he uses charts, devices and props to win his famous product-liability cases against irresponsible manufacturers. James M. La Rossa is a famous defense lawyer and the well-known James A. Serritella is attorney for the archdiocese of Chicago.

Peter Tufo graduated from Beloit College and from Yale Law School in 1962. After serving in the United States Marine Corps, he joined the firm of Davis, Polk & Wardwell in New York City where he specialized in litigation and met his future partner John Zuccotti. In 1966, he served as counsel to the New York City Department of Investigation routing out corruption in city government. He was then appointed assistant to the mayor of New York. In 1972, Peter Tufo joined with John Zuccotti to realize their dream of owning their own law firm.

By 1985, Tufo & Zuccotti had become one of the classiest, most successful specialty law firms in the country as a real estate and land-use boutique with the best group of lawyers packed into any small firm anywhere. In 1986, the special success story of Tufo and Zuccotti became even more successful when they merged with the huge and prestigious Wall Street law firm of Brown, Wood, Ivey, Mitchell and Petty. This merger is in itself a symbol of how Italian Americans have progressed—since several decades ago, Peter Tufo or John Zuccotti probably could not have gotten a job at a prestigious Wall Street law firm. Now they own one. Tufo has also been creative in documentary filmmaking. In 1976, he hosted a television series *The Cost of Crime,* which won him an Emmy.

Melvin Belli, famous trial lawyer known internationally as the "King of Torts" and the "Father of Demonstrative Evidence," was born in 1907 in Sonora, California, the son of a pioneer family. Belli graduated from the University of

California's Boalt School of Law in 1933 and was admitted to the California bar the same year. He began his law career as the counsel for the Catholic priest of San Quentin Prison and took up the challenge of defending men already condemned to die.

Belli's cases have drawn national media attention and his list of clients is world famous. They include Jack Ruby in 1964 for the murder of Lee Harvey Oswald, the Korean jetliner disaster, the MGM Grand Hotel fire in Las Vegas, and the collapse of the Kansas City Hyatt walkway. He was the first attorney to file suit against Union Carbide on behalf of the Bhopal industrial disaster victims. While he has represented many stars and famous people, Belli is best known for defending the rights of victims of personal injury.

Belli has changed the nature of the courtroom with his innovations, which include the concept of adequate award, the development of the opening statement, the use of day-in-the-life-films to graphically show the life of a victim, aerial photography and the use of economist techniques. For these, he is called the "Father of Demonstrative Evidence."

He is the founder of the American Trial Lawyers Association and the International Academy of Trial Lawyers, and serves on many boards. He has written sixty-two books on civil- and criminal-trial procedures. Though the times and trials have changed, Melvin Belli still makes history and sets precedents in the courts. Few lawyers have had as profound an effect on our legal system as Belli.

When we look at the remarkable array of Italian Americans in the legal professions, including law enforcement, attorneys in public and private practice, district attorneys, attorney general offices, prosecutors and defense lawyers, and judges from the smallest court all the way to the Supreme Court, we see a dedicated commitment to government by law. The underlying strength of the powerful contributions of Italian Americans to the legal professions is rooted in the pursuit of justice, in enforcing the rule by law and in upholding the ideals of a democratic form of government. Citizens must answer not to other citizens but to the United States constitution. And, at the core of this strength is a value system steeped in humanism.

What a horrible and frustrating thing it is for Italian

Americans to be branded with the image of the Mafia when in fact, this criminal element represents such an insignificant number of its population and the proportion of Italian Americans in the legal profession is so high. This irony runs deep in the Italian American consciousness and is the source of much bitterness.

Most Italian Americans simply ignore the issue and refuse to dignify the slur with a response, letting their exemplary lives of moral rectitude speak for themselves, while others have chosen to form groups, organizations and associations to battle this straw dog. Whatever the case, the issue is painful, difficult to resolve and a dilemma haunting the Italian Americans. An Italian saying goes: "Those who slander us write in sand and those who praise us write in marble."

MEDICINE

Italian Americans have made remarkable contributions to the field of medicine, health, hospital care, and medical research. Italian Americans literally permeate the profession all across the country in private practices, hospital staffs, health care centers, health insurance companies and research facilities in clinics, hospitals and universities.

The tradition of the helping nature in medicine is a long, altruistic and humanistic one that spans all Italian and all Italian American history. In the 1800s, Dr. Felix Formento became president of the American Public Health Association. Dr. Giovanni Ceccarini, a renowned physician and surgeon, became the first chairman of the Sanitary Committee of the Department of Health of the City of New York. Most significant, perhaps, was the work of Mother Cabrini, the first American saint, and her Sisters of the Sacred Heart who founded hospitals as well as schools throughout America.

Dr. Tullio Verdi became personal physician to Secretary of State William Seward and other political leaders living in the capital. Verdi came to the United States with only five dollars to his name. He taught at Brown University and then turned to the study of medicine at Philadelphia's Hahnemann College, where he became the first native of Italy to graduate from an American medical school in 1856. It was Dr. Verdi's name that was used by the assassinators of President Lincoln to enter Seward's home.

Dr. Giovanni Arcieri, born in 1897 in Cosenza, Italy, came to America in 1923 with his Doctor of Medicine degree from the University of Rome. He served on the staffs of several hospitals both in the United States and Italy as a top specialist in chest diseases. He also was a faculty member of the New York Post Graduate Medical School and the University of Rome. Arcieri was not only a brilliant physician but an author of many medical books and articles, especially his Italian-English Medical Dictionary.

Dr. Charles Muzzicato, born in 1901 in Nicosia, Italy, received his education at Alfred University, St. Ignatius College and Loyola University, and became an expert in radiology and gastroenterology. He served on the staffs of several New York hospitals and on many boards of hospitals. He also became a member of the New York State Senate in 1941. Muzzicato won awards and citations from many schools, societies and hospitals.

In the area of overcoming a handicap or disability, the story of Henry Viscardi, Jr. is an inspiration symbolizing the victory of the human spirit. He was born in 1912 in New York City with stumps for legs and spent the first six years of his life in a hospital. Taunted in school for his deformity, he graduated and at a height of three feet and eight inches became manager of the basketball team at Newtown High School. He worked for three years putting himself through Fordham University and then became a clerk in a law firm.

In 1936, his life changed dramatically when George Dorsch crafted him a pair of artificial legs that others said could not be made. Viscardi, now two feet taller and able to walk, went on to great success in the field of rehabilitation and employment of the handicapped. In 1949, Viscardi was made executive director of JOB (Just One Break) to help the handicapped find employment and in 1952 he created Abilities, Inc. to train the handicapped to work in the electronics field. In 1955, he became president and chairman of the Human Resources

Foundation. Through this man's singular, courageous efforts, and in spite of unbelievable odds, numerous people with all kinds of disabilities found fulfilling lives of productive work and a sense of purpose in the world.

Adelio Joseph Montanari was born in 1917 in Winchedon Springs, Massachusetts. After a very difficult childhood he went to Antioch College in Yellow Springs, Ohio, in 1935. After three years of questioning what he was being taught, he was kicked out and traveled across the country for three years. When World War II began, Montanari fought in the Army, receiving the Purple Heart, Bronze Star and Good Conduct medal. In 1952, Montanari founded the Montanari Clinical School for emotionally disturbed children in Hialeah, Florida. He pioneered the field of education for disturbed kids who had been rejected elsewhere as hopeless, by the use of unusual, unorthodox and permissive techniques that were rooted in understanding, intuition and love. Though he got his college degree in 1955, it had no meaning to him. His philosophy detoured around the formal processes of traditional psychological precepts and headed straight to the children to help them. His motto was, "First reach them, then teach them."

Constance Urciolo Battle has emerged as a nationally and internationally known and respected physician, especially as the 1986 president of the American Medical Women's Association. She presently serves as the medical director and chief executive officer of the Hospital for Sick Children in Washington, D.C. Battle has devoted her extraordinary medical and pediatric skills to improving the lives of severely disabled children and their families. Also, her remarkable leadership qualities have turned her hospital around from a struggling institution to one recognized for excellence and compassion in the treatment of children with chronic illnesses or severe disabilities.

Battle, majoring in chemistry, graduated from Trinity College in 1963 and got her medical degree from George Washington University in 1967. She interned and was a resident of pediatrics at Strong Memorial Hospital in Rochester, New York. Battle has become world famous for her knowledge, expertise and skill in providing health care services to handicapped children and especially for her humanistic, psychosocial approach to their medical care and that of their families. She is also professor of Child Health and Development at George Washington University and visiting professor at Harvard University. In 1982, she received the American Academy of Pediatrics' citation for outstanding service.

Margaret J. Giannini, M.D., presently serves as the director of the Rehabilitation Research and Development Services with the Veterans Administration in Washington, D.C. She was appointed to the position by President Jimmy Carter in 1979, taking office in 1980. A pediatrician, she was the founder and director of the Mental Retardation Institute, the first and largest of its kind. Since 1950, Giannini has been a true pioneer in the creation of programs for the mentally retarded, developmentally disabled and handicapped. She is past president of the American Association on Mental Deficiency and past president of the American Association of University-Affiliated Programs. Her appointment to boards, chairs, committees, panels and consultancies, are numerous. Giannini is also involved with many community and professional organizations. She has received many awards in recognition of her professional and humanitarian services and achievements.

Giannini was born in 1921 in Camden, New Jersey, got her degrees at Boston University in 1939, at Temple University in 1917 and at Hahnemann Medical University in 1945. She interned at New York Medical College from 1945 to 1946, did her residency in pathology there from 1946 to 1947 and did another residency in pediatrics there from 1947 to 1948. Throughout her outstanding career, she has pioneered and created many programs that have had major impact on the medical world.

Anthony Fauci serves as director of the National Institutes of Health in Bethesda, Maryland; while she was not Italian American, Florence Nightingale, the founder of modern nursing, was born in Italy and named for the city of Florence. She dedicated her life to the care of the sick and war-wounded during the Crimean war in the mid-1800s. By the end of the war, she had become a legend. While her citizenship may have been English, her spirit was unquestionably Italian.

Perhaps the most significant achievement in modern medicine is that of Dr. Robert Gallo whose research work in the field of cancer and the currently fatal AIDS virus is considered the most important medical research going on in America today. Rita Levi-Montalcini, an Italian American biologist, won the Nobel Prize for Medicine in 1985. Her work also has contributed to the understanding of how cancer works in the cell structures of humans. Gallo and Levi-Montalcini are discussed in the Science Chapter.

Dominating the careers and accomplishments of Italian Americans in the field of medicine is a basic compassion for other human beings, a sincere desire to alleviate suffering and a passionate, humanistic caring for the health of all people. There seems to be an innate sense of love for others and a primal reverence and concern for human life. For Italian Americans, living is an art and they want to make sure we are all fit to enjoy it.

11

BUSINESS AND INDUSTRY

THE SPIRIT OF ENTREPRENEURSHIP

WE ARE living at a time driven by the spirit of entrepreneurship—everyone who can is starting his or her own
business whether at home in a kind of cottage industry linked
to the outside world by telephone or computer or out in the
wide world where every erstwhile entrepreneur is looking
for a "need to fill" or "an idea whose time has come." The
echoes of the "me generation" are being felt as individuals
strive for independence, their own sense of personhood,
their own self-fulfillment, their own self-realization and
self-actualization. Self-expression through entrepreneurial
endeavors is at an all-time high.

Throughout this section you will see from the lives of
those depicted certain values that reflect Italian and Italian
American culture, and you will see why these Italian Americans have achieved their success as entrepreneurs and business people.

Interestingly enough, it was Italian businessmen who were
the first, back in the Middle Ages and during the Renaissance, to develop some of the basic institutions from which
capitalism grew. The first European university chair in
economics was established in Italy in 1754. Italians have
actually been at the cutting edge of economic advance. After
all, they invented banking!

The Italian American immigrant situation was, of course, different since most of the immigrants came from poverty. Given the horrid conditions they left, their economic progress in America was decidedly fast. With instinctive business acumen, they started small businesses, many on pushcarts, and their hard work and perseverance paid off. From these humble origins, more enterprising businesses grew, such as restaurants, grocery stores and food businesses.

Since the whole family was needed to help the business succeed, education for Italian Americans in any major way was delayed until the end of World War II. The returning vets saw little future in their families' small ventures and they also had the G.I. bill to pay for their educations. They also began to fully understand that in America economic progress was linked to higher education. Those who chose not to go to school and not to begin their own businesses joined the masses of blue-collar workers just as many before them had done.

By the 1940s, Italian American blue-collar workers were substantially helped by their involvement with the unions, and their hard work was beginning to pay off. As they adapted to American life, their early hostility to unionization disappeared, and they became active and successful labor leaders.

Despite the prejudices and discriminations Italian Americans encountered, the same fight their forbears fought, these third and fourth generations did begin to make socio-economic progress in the post–World War II era. These later generations operated from better economic conditions —the result of a lot of hard work, sacrifice and bloody hands on the part of the older generations.

Over the last two or three decades, we have seen great successes in the socioeconomic dimensions of Italian American life. Family businesses have grown into huge corporate conglomerates, simple men and women have taken small dreams and built giant empires, and dynamic, well-educated, shrewd men and women have zoomed to top corporate power positions. The Italian Americans hooked themselves body, mind and soul into the American free-enterprise system and through their unique values and their creative spirit have made great successes of themselves.

Italians and Italian Americans have always been fiercely independent and individualistic, and the combination of these traits with a strong sense of pride, hard work, determination, industry and creativity makes for a perfect recipe for entrepreneurial success. The immigrants may not have had money, skills, education or understanding of American ways, but they had a fire burning within them that drove them to survive, to succeed and to do in life what they liked to do and could do best. They were devoted individualists passionately committed to individual opportunity, fortune and success. Even the most illiterate and poverty-stricken had a courageous spirit within their beings that yearned for the freedom to be themselves and for the opportunity to reach their potential.

The first Italian American millionaire was Generoso Pope, who worked as a laborer on a road gang as a young boy. He later published *Il Progresso Italo Americano* of New York, the first and only Italian-language daily newspaper. Pope was born in Arpaise, Benevento, in 1891 and came to America in 1904. He became successful with his Colonial Sand Company and made money running the Goodwin and Gallagher Sand and Gravel Corporation since 1932.

Fortune Pope, son of Generoso, born in 1918 in West New York, New Jersey, received his B.A. from Columbia University in 1939. He served in his father's company, Colonial Sand Company, as executive vice president, ran radio station WHOM as president and continued as publisher of *Il Progresso Italo Americano,* the largest Italian-language daily newspaper in the U.S. Fortune also became prominent in the Italian American community and served as president of the famous Columbus Citizens Committee of New York.

Generoso Pope, Jr., another son of Generoso Pope, also made a huge fortune in the world of publishing and is listed in *Forbes* magazine's list of the 400 Wealthiest People in America. Pope is the controversial publisher of the *National Enquirer* of Lantana, Florida, with the largest circulation of any newspaper in the world.

Pope graduated from MIT at age nineteen, and bought the *Enquirer* when he was twenty-five-years-old in 1952 for seventy-five-thousand dollars with a circulation of seventeen thousand. The newspaper now has a circulation of over 5.5 million and Pope is reputedly worth over 150 million dollars. Pope has created a monumentally successful publication, though he and his tabloid are perceived either one of two absolutely opposed ways. Some live by the *National Enquirer* as if it were their bible, while others see it as total trash. According to *Enquirer* writers, every story must be totally verified, checked, double-checked and triple-checked for accuracy. Some claim he is more accurate than *The New York Times*.

Pope is a self-admitted workaholic who loves his work, and he reviews about six hundred proposals a week and personally approves every story idea before publication. "Generosity Pope," as some call him, unquestionably has a gift for putting himself right into the shoes of the man on the street, and this has made him the number-one man in tabloid journalism. He also has a knack for making millions of dollars from knowing what the public wants to read.

As far back as the 1800s, Italians were clearly showing their entrepreneurial spirit. Giovanni Pertegnazza, who went by the name G. P. Morisini, was a Venetian who arrived here in 1851 and ultimately became a partner of the millionaire mogul Jay Gould in the Erie Railroad.

Fileno DiGregorio, born in 1885 in Bolograno, Pescara, Italy, came to America in 1912. In 1916, with five hundred dollars he created the United Lens Company, which became the largest independent manufacturer of lens blanks for the optical industry probably in the world. DiGregorio developed into a major industrialist and his superior lenses have been used in copy machines, cameras, projectors, microscopes, telescopes, rifle sights, binoculars and a variety of optical products for the space program.

Many Italian Americans went into the building and construction businesses, creating extremely successful enterprises. Since they had provided the raw labor to American industry, many naturally moved up the ladders of success to form their own companies.

Anthony Grace & Sons became a phenomenally successful construction business spanning three generations. Vittorio Greco, born in 1890 in Sicily, came to the United States at age fourteen, without money and speaking the Sicilian dialect. While quarantined at Ellis Island, he learned there was work on the railroad in Omaha, Nebraska, so he went there to lay tracks and spike rails. He studied mason building at night school and rose to railroad inspector. At age thirty, armed with his diploma in construction, he ventured to New York and became one of the most powerful contractors in the metropolitan area.

Vittorio's son, Anthony Grace, carried on his father's business both with his son Richard and with his partners, George and Charlie Forlini. Together they contract major projects for the Port Authority and constructed Kennedy, La Guardia and Newark airports.

Ross David Siragusa, born in 1906 in Buffalo, New York, went to high school in Chicago, worked for an electric company and in 1934 created the Continental Radio and Television Corporation by borrowing 3,400 dollars against his furniture. The company made radios under the brand name Clarion and in the first year grossed 250,000 dollars. During World War II, the company manufactured military products such as walkie-talkies. After the war, they became the largest makers of automatic record changers. The company became Admiral Corporation and it began to manufacture commercial televisions at a price consumers could afford and refrigerators. By 1974, Siragusa merged Admiral with North American Rockwell to the tune of 650 million dollars. Ross Siragusa, Jr., ran Admiral for a time and then left in 1976 to succeed in his own business by running GameTime in Alabama, which is the largest manufacturer of recreation, park and playground equipment in the world.

Giuseppe Bellanca, a Sicilian, was an inventor and pioneered the manufacturing of aircraft. The Bellanca two-seater plane is still a highly desired aircraft. Bernard Castro created the Castro convertible couch, became extremely wealthy and his company became the greatest company of its kind in America. Antonio Chichizola became a prominent merchant in the Bay Area and helped A. P. Giannini found the Bank of Italy. Pio

Crespi became the "Cotton King" of Waco, Texas. John Cuneo established the Cuneo Henneberry Company, later Cuneo Press, in 1924 in Chicago. This grew into one of the largest printing companies in the world.

Joseph J. Digange founded the First Los Angeles Bank with his partner Charles T. Manatt, lawyer and former chairman of the Democratic Party. The bank grew phenomenally and was bought by the Bank of San Paolo in Italy. Other banking entrepreneurs include Joseph Sabetta of First Pacific Bank, George Graziadio of Imperial Bank and Joseph Pinola of First Interstate Bank. Sebastiano Sterpa built Sterpa Realty into a huge success and sold it to Merrill Lynch Realty.

Amedeo Obici, born in 1877 in the town of Oderzo in the province of Triviso, came to America on a tramp steamer arriving at Bush terminal in Brooklyn in 1888 at age twelve. After grammar school, Obici worked for his uncle at his fruit stand and he noticed a passerby eating roasted peanuts. He followed the man, picking up the shells, and a brainstorm ignited in his head—he wanted to roast and sell peanuts in the fruit store. From this initial burst of an idea, the Planters Peanut Company came into existence in 1906 in Wilkes-Barre, Pennsylvania, and by 1947, when Obici died, there were thirty-six buildings and thirty-eight acres of land, one of the largest peanut companies in the world.

He was a man of great vision, an innovator of the industry and a remarkably intuitive businessman. Yet his primary values were hard work, simplicity, straightforwardness and approachability. Obici was one of the most colorful people in Italian-American history and one of the most entrepreneurially successful.

Amedeo Pietro Giannini, born in 1870 in San Jose, California, was unquestionably one of the most remarkable success stories of the twentieth century. His bank (originally called the Bank of Italy) was the Bank of America; it became the largest in the world. He founded a bank that simply met the needs of ordinary people and his philosophy expressed an interest in the lives of his customers and a genuine concern for serving others. As the "common people's banker," Giannini became the dominant personality and the single most significant innovator in banking. He created branch banking and dreamed of national and world banking. He simply invented modern banking.

Giannini was the consummate entrepreneur and he helped others themselves to succeed in businesses of their own. He cared about his customers and helped them in their financial needs, greatly improving their chances for success. His warm and friendly philosophy attracted more customers than any bank in the world. In 1936, he bought 6 million dollars in local bonds to fund the construction of the Golden Gate bridge. He funded small businesses, loaned people money not on their assets but on their character, helped customers with business advice and was aware of the unique needs of various industries. He helped the farmers and wine makers, and he funded the fledgling film business. He financed Walt Disney's *Snow White* and Samuel Goldwyn's *The Kid From Spain,* and he virtually invented the process by which films are funded.

By 1945, the Bank of America had became the biggest bank in the world with resources of 5 billion dollars. A. P. Giannini's dream had come true forty-one years after he started his outstanding career by creating his bank in 1906.

Vincent G. Marotta, born of Italian parents in this country, is a brilliant entrepreneur who, in the late 1960s, had an idea for a new kind of coffee brewing machine. He had recognized that coffee makers were the largest selling household item in the country and knew that he could invent and market a superior product. After two years of design, electrical engineering and refinement, Vincent Marotta invented the most popular coffee maker in the world—Mr. Coffee—and he created a worldwide mass market for automatic drip coffee. His first unit, the CM–1, hit retail shelves in 1972 and coffee making has not been the same since. Mr. Coffee is now the largest selling coffee maker in the world.

But this was not the first success of Mr. "Mr. Coffee." Marotta went to Mount Union College in Ohio where he excelled as a football player. He managed to play professional baseball for the St. Louis Cardinals, run first team track as a world-class sprinter and then play professional football for the Cleveland Browns in 1948.

After success in sports, Marotta became a dominant force in the real-estate development business where his business acumen, intense commitment to get ahead and friendly, natural ways with people quickly moved him ahead. He built and sold over five thousand homes, developed seven major shopping centers and owned and leased numerous buildings.

Though the invention of the Mr. Coffee automatic drip coffee maker was far afield from the gridiron and the construction sites, Marotta threw himself into his new business with enthusiasm and unshakable resolve. In 1972, the famous Mr. Coffee hit the market, and zoomed to an astounding success. By 1974, Mr. Coffee had become the leading seller of coffee makers in America and maintains an unrivaled worldwide 60-percent share of all coffee-maker sales. America fell in love with Vince's Mr. Coffee invention and with lots of hard work, the company quickly dominated the world market, and still does.

His awards and honors include the Horatio Alger award, the Outstanding Italian American Man of the Year in the United States, the Outstanding American award and the Humanitarian award from the National Italian American Foundation.

The Edward J. De Bartolo Corporation is the largest developer and manager of shopping malls in the country. The De Bartolo name is stamped indelibly on a variety of hotels, mixed-use projects, office towers, condominiums, industrial and executive parks, shopping centers, convenience and theme centers, thoroughbred race tracks and sports facilities. Throughout the country and around the world, the De Bartolo name is recognized as a dominant leader and master planner.

Edward J. De Bartolo attributes his success to "little more than his adherence to the work ethic and his belief in the 'American Dream.'" De Bartolo graduated from Notre Dame University as a registered civil engineer. After serving as an officer in the U.S. Army Corps of Engineers, De Bartolo returned to Youngstown, Ohio, his hometown, where he reorganized his stepfather's small paving business into a real-estate development firm. In 1949, the first De Bartolo shopping center was opened in Youngstown. During the past four decades, De Bartolo has developed over 68 million square feet of prime retail space in fifteen states and actually helped change the way America shops.

The De Bartolo Corporation is also a family operation. While Edward, Sr., serves as chairman and chief executive officer, his son, Edward J. De Bartolo, Jr., serves as president and chief administrative officer and his daughter, Marie Denise De Bartolo York, serves as executive vice president of personnel and public relations. Edward, Jr., began working with his father as a teenager. In 1968, he graduated from Notre Dame University and joined the firm's executive training program. He worked in every department to gain a complete understanding of the corporation's master plan. He held several executive positions and took over his present position in 1979. Marie graduated from St. Mary's College at Notre Dame and joined the company as its first director of personnel. Her expertise in sociology and community relations are valuable assets to the corporation. After serving four years as a vice president, in 1979 she achieved her present position.

The De Bartolo family is also a leading investor in sports enterprises. Three thoroughbred horse-racing facilities are operated by De Bartolo, including Balmoral Park in Chicago, Louisiana Downs in Bossier City, and Thistledown in Cleveland. A fourth is under construction in Oklahoma City called Remington Park. Edward, Jr., an avid sports enthusiast, bought the San Francisco 49ers in 1077 and his faith in and support of them were rewarded with Super Bowl championships in 1982 and 1985. They own the Pittsburgh Penguins of the National Hockey League and they operate the Civic Arena in Pittsburgh.

Francesco Galesi is a dynamic entrepreneur, a successful real-estate developer and a brilliant venture capitalist all rolled into one creative Italian American, the son of Italian immigrant parents. A true child of the Depression, Galesi was born in 1930 in New Jersey, the third of five brothers and one sister. His father had come to America in 1918 and struggled in the real-estate brokerage and investment business. He did well enough to put Francesco through college at Princeton, where he graduated in 1953 and joined his father's firm and his two older brothers.

Galesi discovered that the family had a real knack for putting together shopping-mall deals and soon could take credit for twenty-three shopping centers in the Northeast. After his brother Vincent died in 1968, Galesi took time for himself, leaving the business in the hands of his eldest brother, John. When he returned, he bought two huge army depots in upstate New York with 4 million dollars of mostly borrowed money. He refurbished the buildings for another 6 million dollars and leased them to many Fortune 500 companies, and made a ton of money.

Galesi then ventured into a broad array of businesses, which he parlayed into a fortune worth about 275 million dollars. Galesi seems to be a one-man corporate whirlwind around whom so many major, multimillion dollar deals appear, take form and are nurtured into creation as successful businesses by this visionary entrepreneur. Yet he is such a unique individualist that he has created an entrepreneurial empire yet retained his own original management style of operating it. While he has managed, through a mixture of sheer instinct, passionate energy, intense drive and remarkable business acumen, to organize a vast network of corporations, holdings and projects, he himself is the antithesis of an organization man.

Angelo R. Mozilo was born in the Bronx, New York, in 1938, the oldest of five children. He graduated Fordham University with his B.S. in 1960 and went to New York University for his graduate studies in real-estate law. From 1964 through 1968, he worked for United Mortgage Servicing Corporation and rose to vice president.

In 1968, Mozilo cofounded Countrywide Credit Industries, a financial-services company financing single-family homes that went public in 1969. While the company originally functioned as a traditional mortgage-banking operation originating and servicing mostly FHA-VA loans, Mozilo began expanding operations in southern California and by 1974 had built the company into thirteen branches. Mozilo went nationwide and made Countrywide into a unique mortgage-banking company that is the largest in the country and is publicly traded on the New York Stock Exchange.

Countrywide's branch network is unique and distinct from

those of other mortgage bankers. Countrywide's branches are small, generally consisting of two to four employees and it does not employ loan officers, but instead hires experienced loan processors, paid on a noncommission basis, to staff its branches. These workers do not solicit business, but accept and approve loan applications based on standardized formulas. Countrywide's low cost of originating a mortgage allows the company to price loans competitively and this allows more people to buy and own their own homes. Countrywide grew to one hundred branches in twenty-eight states by 1984 and went public in 1985 with a newly created company specializing in mortgage investments in loans generated by Countrywide. The 1986 *Fortune* magazine list of 100 Best Stocks defined Countrywide as the thirty-seventh largest gainer versus all public companies in America. Angelo Mozilo's company now services 4.4 billion dollars worth of mortgages and generates on its own 3.2 billion dollars worth of mortgage loans on single-family residences. Not bad for a kid from the Bronx!

Arthur Julius Decio, born in 1930 in Elkhart, Indiana, was a millionaire at age thirty-five. Decio grew up on the wrong side of the tracks as the son of an Italian immigrant father who worked as a grocer. In 1951, Decio's father took his savings and invested it in mobile homes, but he did badly. Decio had attended De Paul University from 1949 to 1950 and was working as a steel salesman when his father begged him to try either to rescue the small company or liquidate it. Decio recruited three friends, put up $3,200 of his own money and went to work in his garage.

Decio recognized early in the history of the mobile-home business that there was a need for low-cost mobile homes. The mobile-home industry was experiencing a major explosion and Decio exploited this good luck with brilliant financial skills. Decio created a 20-foot, smaller-than-usual new model that was cheaper and easier to transport than all its competitors. This unique model was a success and Skyline was on its way to the top. Decio got another bright idea—to imitate the automakers' methods of frequent model changes and national distribution. He created new designs and styles of mobile homes, which eventually became wholly different lines, each competing with the others. And he started building a national network of dealers. Decio's ideas paid off and he became one of the biggest producers of mobile homes in the country.

So, you wanted to know who the genius entrepreneur is behind C & C Cola, the first soft drink marketed in cans and once the third largest selling cola in markets where it was distributed. It is Charles P. Ferro, known in the business as "C & C Charlie," the man who drives Coca Cola and Pepsi Cola crazy.

Charles Ferro, originally from Brooklyn, only finished high school and immediately after serving in the U.S. Army started driving a truck as a beer distributor under the name of Ferro Beverages in Queens, New York. In 1964, Ferro pioneered a brand new concept to the beverage industry called "Thrifty Beverage Centers" which soon became successful.

In 1968, Ferro purchased a bankrupt, broken-down soda plant in Garfield, New Jersey, called C & C Cola. From 1969 to 1971, he manufactured private label soft drinks for several supermarket chains, and then decided to reintroduce C & C Cola as a new product. Ferro had John Ritchie as his flavor technologist, who is credited with the Pepsi-Cola formulation. By 1976, C & C Cola became a major contender in the cola wars. Ferro sold the company to I.T.T. and remained as CEO until 1979.

In 1980, Ferro resigned from I.T.T. and created a brand new Italian spaghetti sauce called Francesco-Rinaldi, which became the number three sauce in sales in the New York marketing area. In 1981, he purchased the failing Yoo-Hoo Chocolate Beverage Corporation and made money the very first month of his new ownership. He turned the presidency of Yoo-Hoo over to his son Patrick and today the company is worth many millions of dollars. He also sold Francesco-Rinaldi to Cantisano Foods of the Cantisano family, who are the original owners of Ragu.

In 1984, C & C Charlie earned back his nickname by repurchasing the C & C Cola Company, which had gone into great decline. Ferro is back on the cola warpath and has been going after Coke and Pepsi with enthusiasm ever since. Ferro's theme to do battle with the giants? "C & C. The next greatest cola in America. Move over (Bleep) Coke and (Bleep) Pepsi!"

Dominic Longo of the Los Angeles area opened a Toyota agency on St. Patrick's Day of 1967 and built it into the largest single point dealership in the world selling one make of car. The Japanese worshipped Longo and over the years would send delegations of businessmen, car executives and Toyota representatives to see his operation in order to figure out how this man could do what he did.

Dom Longo was a gifted entrepreneur steeped in Italian American values. At the core of his unique sales system was a singular devotion to service. When he insisted on keeping the service department open until late in the evening, everyone told him it was a mistake and a loser, and it was, but it created a psychology that the agency cared. It sold cars and that's what the car business is all about. For nineteen years, Longo Toyota outstripped every other Toyota agency in the world.

Dom Longo worked hard from 7 A.M. when they opened until 11 P.M. when they closed, and he loved his work. He totally revolutionized the way cars were sold and made numerous innovations. Salesmen had no desks, could not wear sunglasses, did not use "closing booths" and were forbidden to lie. The customer absolutely came first and because of this caring attitude he had more customers than anyone else. A demanding taskmaster but a marvelously humorous man, Longo changed the car business in his own unique way.

The wonderfully wacky world of female and movie-star impersonators known worldwide as *La Cage Aux Folles* actually began with a nightclub created by an extraordinary Italian American, Lou Paciocco.

One of six children of divorced parents, Paciocco saw work as an absolute necessity. His first job at five years old was shining shoes. Lou soon graduated to polishing fruit, then teaching dance at nineteen. At the age of twenty-three, he found himself in the U.S. Army. At age twenty-five, he began a successful career in real estate and within six years he owned his own company in the Bronx. The lure of politics captured his interest, and from age thirty to forty Lou was vice-chairman of the Republican Party at the state senatorial level in New York, as well as a member of Governor Rockefeller's Revenue-Sharing Committee.

Fortunately, at the age of 45, Lou Paciocco ignored the advice of well-meaning friends who told him that nightclubs were difficult ventures. He created the Los Angeles *La Cage Aux Folles* in 1981 and it became such a great attraction that he opened other clubs. Sensing that people throughout the country would frequent clubs where they could dine and be entertained as well, Lou opened La Cage Aux Folles next in Atlantic City, Las Vegas, Miami, Toronto, and now in Orlando, Florida.

John L. "Rick" Ricciardelli was born in 1922 in Ridgely, West Virginia, the son of a ditchdigger and a plumber's helper who came here from Italy. He could not afford to go to college, but this did not deter him from becoming a major success in the insurance business. Rick graduated from Westinghouse High School in Pittsburgh, Pennsylvania. From 1940 to 1945, he served in World War II as a staff sergeant in the United States Marine Corps.

Ricciardelli has become an eminent leader in his field. In 1947, he moved to Miami, Florida, and served as a casualty insurance agent from 1948 to 1961. From the beginning, Rick manifested a fierce desire to succeed, working fourteen-hour days. In 1962, Rick opened his own office as president and chairman of the Board of Specialty Insurance Underwriters, Inc., starting in a nine-by-seventeen-foot office in a downtown Miami building. He and his secretary, Debbie Wilkerson, used a door placed on two wooden sawhorses as a desk. While Rick convinced insurance agents to sell his policies, Debbie handled the telephones and managed what they called an office.

A great deal has changed since those early frenzied days of starting his insurance company. Debbie Wilkerson became his wife and now manages their two multimillion-dollar companies, which serve more than seven hundred agents in the state, and her phone on her workhorse desk has been replaced by a car phone. Their small office is now a twenty-two-thousand-square-foot building near Miami International Airport, and

Rick and Debbie run their business through a computer linkup to their agents throughout the state.

Underwriters Financial of Florida and Specialty Insurance Underwriters made history when they were both listed in *Inc. Magazine*'s fastest-growing private companies. This was the first time a husband and wife team had had two companies on the list.

Rick and Debbie Ricciardelli continue their successful business, and Rick carries on his strong commitment to community service and public life. He serves on a multitude of boards and positions of power. He is also a member of Local No. 655 of the Miami Musicians' Union. He plays jazz guitar. Florida Secretary of State George Firestone called Rick "one of the modern pioneers" of his business.

Arthur E. Imperatore—*Inc. Magazine* called him "The King of Productivity" in their cover story on him, *New York Magazine* called him "The New Emperor of the West Bank" (of New Jersey) and his employees call him "Mr. Arthur." Imperatore was born in 1925 in West New York, New Jersey, spent his childhood there and graduated from Memorial High School. He did not attend college.

Imperatore was the second-youngest child in a family of ten children headed by Italian immigrants. He was a child of the Depression, and it was tough for his father, who ran a produce business, to keep food on the table for such a large family, but somehow they survived. Since age seven, he had worked very hard and claimed, at age ten, he'd be a millionaire. In high school he worked as a Western Union messenger.

Imperatore fought in World War II as a navigator and afterward four of his brothers bought two army surplus trucks. They emblazoned "Imperatore Brothers" on the sides of the trucks and went into business. At age twenty-two, Imperatore came home from a day's work as a Fuller Brush salesman and found his brothers loafing. He went into a rage and demanded that they either take his name off the truck or get to work. He then decreed that he would not only join the trucking firm but would run it. And he did. Within a month they bought out a trucker named A&P Trucking. The A&P food chain forced them to change the name, so they made it A.P.A. Some say this was to stand for "Always Please Arthur." A.P.A. Transport became the most successful trucking business in the nation.

The force behind this impressive achievement has always been Arthur Imperatore's values and his personal standards of efficiency, accountability and concern for the welfare of his people. As he says: "The basic ingredient of success—and our most important asset—is people. We exercise care in the selection of our employees, we motivate them, and we consider them part of the A.P.A. family."

In addition to his family-style environment, Imperatore has led the way in managerial innovations long before corporations began to develop human-resource programs. His care of employees is expressed by the state-of-the-art recreational facility, the weight clinic, the Smokenders clinics, the fresh flowers on the desks of all the secretaries, the chartered cruises, the parties on his personal yacht, christened "Imperator," and the close personal, first-name relationships he has with his workers and colleagues. His values are solidly rooted in communal and personal loyalty. Everyone is expected to give and Imperatore prides himself on his fair, just and generous treatment of his employees.

Imperatore's methods have made the company a huge success, have won him the prestigious Horatio Alger award and have made him a fortune. But, the story of Arthur Imperatore does not stop here. That little kid who gazed across the Hudson River from the New Jersey Palisades toward the New York skyline is now creating a whole, self-contained city on 367 acres of land stretching two miles along the New Jersey Hudson river front, roughly opposite midtown Manhattan from 35th to 74th streets. Imperatore formed ARCORP Properties after he bought this deserted and desolate land for 7.75 million dollars. Thus began Arthur Imperatore's most imperious dream—to build a European-like city with a plaza like St. Mark's in Venice and water taxis like those of Venice. Projected cost: 10 billion dollars.

After hiring Cesar Pelli, recently retired dean of Yale's School of Architecture, Imperatore has truly embarked upon a glorious venture that will span three generations of his family over thirty to forty years. The ARCORP program, a rebirth of the waterfront area, will be a center for business, housing, shopping, the arts, entertainment and recreation. Since New York is the financial capital of the world, he plans a comprehensive transportation network to serve the city and link it to existing transportation centers in the area.

Arthur Imperatore has also directed his energies into a virtual galaxy of social causes, many of them Italian American. He has been honored by a vast array of civic and charitable organizations. In 1984, Arthur Imperatore became the nation's first recipient of the United States Senate Productivity award, a most prestigious honor for this brilliant son of Italian immigrants who sailed poverty-stricken into a harbor on which their son is now building a city to echo their Italian heritage.

The cover of *Fortune Magazine* on September 1, 1986 called the Gallo brothers "Marketing Marvels" and said: "Starting with $5,900, these sons of immigrants today sell $1,000,000,000 worth of wine a year. Julio makes it, Ernest markets it. They're a study in how to crush the competition." Their family-owned winery produces a remarkable 25 percent of all the wine drunk in the United States. They buy and produce one out of every four bottles of wine sold in the United States. While Julio pursues his search for the perfect grape, Ernest has become the pre-eminent king of wine marketing.

And those two old, lovable geezers, Frank Bartles and Ed Jaymes, who tout Bartles and Jaymes wine coolers from their porch and other unusual settings are really fictional characters who humbly "thank us for our support." And the real men behind those actors are two of the most brilliant, gifted, shrewdest, aggressive, secretive, feared and successful men in America—Ernest and Julio Gallo. And "our support" has made Bartles & Jaymes the number-one wine cooler in the market and has made Ernest and Julio two of the wealthiest men in the world.

It started when their father, Joseph Gallo, immigrated to California from the Piedmont region of northwest Italy and became a small-time grape grower in Modesto, California. While Prohibition in the 1920s put many grape growers out of business, Joseph survived by making wine for medicinal and religious use, as permitted by law. Unfortunately, tragedy struck in 1933 when he shot his wife and himself to death, apparently because of a business setback.

In 1933, the same year their father died, the twenty-first amendment to the constitution repealed Prohibition, and Ernest and Julio, now in their early twenties, decided to make the jump from growing grapes to producing wine. However, Ernest and Julio didn't know a damn thing about making wine, so off they went, with $5,900.23 in their pockets, to the Modesto Public Library where they checked out two thin instruction pamphlets on how to make wine.

The task of making the wine fell to Julio, while the job of finding customers and selling them fell to Ernest. Since the wine and liquor business exploded with the repeal of Prohibition, the Gallos burst on the scene with unlimited enthusiasm and confidence. They sold wine in bulk for years and in 1938 began to bottle their own wine under the Gallo label, since it yielded more profits. Sales and profits grew.

The Gallos now dominate the wine industry. Gallo is the most vertically integrated company in the industry. They are aggressive innovators in pursuit of perfection and excellence. Julio is still a hands-on manager who troops through their vineyards daily and scans their acreage by helicopter. He constantly seeks to grow a better grape and make a better wine. Equally demanding is Ernest in the marketing of Gallo products. He insists on absolute loyalty and pushes distributors to sell his wines exclusively. A Gallo salesman must read and live by his three hundred page training manual, which describes and diagrams every conceivable aspect of the wine business.

The pursuit of perfection in the creation of high-quality and mass-consumed wine products has driven the Gallos to worldwide recognition as the number-one company in the world. The Gallo Company is entrenched in the hands of Julio and Ernest's families. Julio's son, Robert, and son-in-law, James Coleman, oversee day-to-day production while Ernest's sons, David and Joseph, work in marketing.

Robert Charles Joseph Edward Sabatini Guccione, chairman of the Board of Penthouse International, is universally recognized as a brilliant entrepreneur who has the rare talent of combining the vision and sensitivity of the artist with the entrepreneurial savvy and commercial instinct of the gifted businessman. He has an unerring sense of the public's appetite for change, a sense that has earned him a top position in *Forbes* magazine's list of the 400 Wealthiest People in America. He is the creative genius behind *Penthouse* and *Omni,* two of several magazines that have each, in its own way, revolutionized the publishing industry.

Bob Guccione was born in Flatbush, Brooklyn, in 1932 and in 1948, after winning several scholarships to various colleges, including Princeton, he had to choose between two loves— painting and science—and between school or no school. Guccione chose painting and no school. Guccione spent a year in Los Angeles living "on the bum," trying to get work. Here in Los Angeles he met his first wife, Lillyan, and they moved to Rome. Guccione acted in five Italian feature films, actually landing a starring role in *The Oarsmen of Amalfi.*

Guccione wandered to Tangiers where he met Muriel, who would become his second wife and bear him four children. In Paris, he survived by sketching pencil portraits and as a writer for an ad agency. Bob and Muriel wound up in England going stone-cold broke. Guccione got a drycleaning job and quickly rose to managing director of the company. He took a freelance job doing cartoons and articles for the *London American* newspaper. Soon he was editor-in-chief and managing director of the newspaper, and quit the drycleaning business in the early 1960s.

One day Guccione was standing at a newsstand and noticed that *Playboy* magazine sold very well in England, but there were no other competitors. Thus Bob Guccione got the creative flash to create the magazine that would become *Penthouse* and make him a multimillionaire.

It took Guccione three years to launch his new magazine and he did it with no money, no advertisers, entirely on credit, six months behind in the rent, totally broke, against the law (technically), under surveillance by the London police department who were waiting to serve him a summons, and engaged in an all-out war with the British House of Commons. And, he was fighting bigotry since he was perceived as criminal because he was Italian and, more to his disadvantage, Sicilian. This compounded the problems he already had with the obscenity issue.

When the magazine hit the stands in 1965, it caused a great furor all over England, but it sold out. Guccione was on his way to success, while his second marriage broke up. He wound up hiring Kathy Keeton, an actress about whom *Penthouse* made fun when she starred in *The Spy That Came In From The Cold.* A year later, he and Kathy dated socially, and they have been together ever since. With this initial success, Guccione and a very small staff took an empty office, tore the bathroom door off its hinges, stole six milk cartons to make a desk with the door on them, and Guccione and *Penthouse* began their destiny together.

Guccione became world renowned for creating the natural look in photography. He sought to present women in a romantic spirit that conveyed their innocence and eroticism. Already a very talented artist, he applied his knowledge and experience in art to the photographing of women, and in the process developed a new genre of nude photography. He also initiated a new sensibility in fine-art illustration and pursued an attack style of journalism.

Guccione brought *Penthouse* magazine to the United States in 1969 where it immediately caused a sensation. The first issue sold 235,000 copies and by 1979, the circulation had reached over 4.5 million. *Penthouse* had become and would remain the number-one-selling men's magazine in the world.

In 1978, Guccione founded *Omni* magazine, the futuristic magazine that pioneered a bold new concept in scientific journalism by presenting science, technology and the future in a unique editorial format. This multi-award-winning magazine was the first to recognize and communicate the wonder and excitement of science. And this too became a huge success.

Guccione also publishes *Forum, Variations, Penthouse Letters, The Girls of Penthouse,* in a special edition, *Nuclear, Biological and Chemical Defense* and *Technology International,* a new magazine that began publishing in April 1986, *Four Wheeler,* which he acquired in June 1986, and *Longevity.* His company also includes book publishing, licensing and products divisions.

Guccione's interest in films inspired him to make his first

independent feature film, a 17.5-million-dollar-controversial spectacular called *Caligula,* which depicted the decadence and depravity of ancient Rome. His next film was *Moll Flanders,* an adaptation of Daniel DeFoe's classic tale, and he has plans to make other films. In 1985, Guccione launched Penthouse Video, an innovative line of video programming created to capture the spirit and popularity of *Penthouse* magazine. He also created and produced the award-winning science/ entertainment television series, *Omni, The New Frontier,* inspired by the extraordinary success of *Omni* magazine. The series received rave reviews from critics, two Emmy nominations and won the prestigious Clarion award.

Guccione's deep and intense commitment to his work keeps him totally involved with all aspects of the company's business. However, he still devotes free time to his passion for art. His magnificent private collection of great art has an international reputation. He is respected as one of the world's top collectors and his collection runs from Botticelli to Modigliani.

Guccione and Kathy Keeton have just bought a sixty-five-acre Hudson River estate on which they plan to build an Italian villa. They have already bought three container loads of Renaissance furniture from Venice and Verona. Guccione has always been close to his Italian background. Whenever he speaks of his heritage, which he values highly, he stresses that his lineage goes back to Sicilian roots. And this is definitely a wonderful way to stay in touch with your Italian heritage—just buy it and bring it home to America!

Ettore Paolucci was a sulphur miner in Bellisio Solfare in Pesaro, Italy, and when the sulphur ran out, he took his wife Michelina to America. The *padroni* had told of jobs in the Minnesota iron mines, and they journeyed to America, passed through Ellis Island and were taken by train to Minnesota, where they settled in Aurora in a clapboard house with an iron pit for a front yard provided by the mining company. Luigino Francesco Paolucci was born here in 1918, the second of two children, and he became Jeno F. Paulucci, one of the most dynamic entrepreneurs in America.

Jeno's childhood was extremely difficult. His father worked six days a week and thirteen hours a day for a daily amount of

$4.25. The family struggled for survival and they set up a grocery storefront in their home, now in Hibbing. At age sixteen, Jeno hawked fruit at an open-air fruit stand in Duluth for David Persha, a man who would later become his partner in his first business. When he was stuck with a batch of soiled bananas, he pitched them as "special Argentine bananas" and sold them for four cents extra per bushel, and a gifted natural salesman hit the world. He toyed with being a lawyer, but realized a salesman could make a hell of a lot more, so he hit the road selling wholesale groceries. Soon he was making more than the president of the company.

One day, while in Minneapolis, he discovered a group of Japanese immigrants making an oriental delicacy with the sprout of the mung bean grown in hydroponic gardens. He bought a bushel, rushed home to call on his old employer, David Persha, to form a partnership, got a $2,500 loan from a food broker, Antonio Papa, began canning bean sprouts, then created Chinese food using his Italian mother's soup recipes, studied a map of China, picked the name Chungking, crossed out the "g," called his product Chun King. So here was this Italian, barred from the homes of childhood friends because he was a "dirty little wop," who created Chinese food with Italian recipes and Japanese bean sprouts in a company of Lithuanians, Finns and Swedes to make millions of American dollars. He built an enormously successful business and sold it to R. J. Reynolds for 63 million dollars in 1966.

After Chun King, he created Jeno's Inc. to produce frozen pizza, which he built into a huge success and sold to Pillsbury for a fortune. Now he is developing a billion-dollar self-contained community named Heathrow located near Orlando, Florida, and after Disney, he is the largest landowner in the central part of the state. He also has immense political power and he uses it.

Jeno feels he owes so much to his being Italian American and in recognition of his own experiences as an Italian American and the debt he feels obligated to pay, he has become founding chairman of the National Italian American Foundation, begun in 1976. He also founded *Attenzione* magazine in the late 1970s with Leda Sanford, a brilliant editor and publisher, and together they created the best national magazine for Italian Americans in the country.

Jeno Paulucci, the recipient of the Horatio Alger award, an outstanding businessman, an admitted workaholic and a generous philanthropist, represents a magic combination of hard work, creativity, passion, enthusiasm, instinct, salesmanship, dedication, individuality and eccentricity that has, in totality, made him a truly gifted entrepreneur. Life may be a relay race to this unusual and mercurial man but when it comes to responsibility, Jeno says: "You plant, you harvest, you plow a little back in for the next crop." And, "Dammit, we are our brother's keepers. We've got a responsibility, and we've got to live up to it." And so he does, in so many ways.

Italian Americans seem to be emerging as dominant leaders of the entire wave of entrepreneurial spirit gripping America. We even have an entrepreneur of entrepreneurship in the person of Joseph R. Mancuso who is the founder and president of the Center for Entrepreneurial Management in New York City. This is the largest nonprofit membership association of entrepreneurs. He also founded the Chief Executive Officers Club, an elite organization of CEOs. Mancuso is also a respected educator and author of more than fifteen books on entrepreneurship and small-business management. His books have become the bibles for thousands of entrepreneurs, along with his tapes, lectures, seminars and national media appearances. Mancuso received his B.S. from Worcester Polytechnic Institute, his M.B.A. from Harvard Business School and his Doctorate in Education from Boston University. Mancuso represents the very best in the creative business community, a true Renaissance man of entrepreneurship, an entrepreneur's entrepreneur. And in true Italian American tradition, he is sharing his valuable knowledge—for profit and for the personal satisfaction of helping others to succeed as well.

Entrepreneurship seems to be in the blood of Italian Americans, whether it is expressed in a small family business or within the ranks of corporate life. The compulsion for individualism, the pride of personal expression, the strong drive for ego satisfaction (sometimes big ego satisfaction), the desire to own your own business and home, and the instinctive impulse to create something with your own name on it, with your personal touch, your unique stamp, are all part of a complex motivation for entrepreneurial adventure and success.

Italian Americans seem to insist upon doing their own thing, their own way and to their own satisfaction. And the rest of the world will benefit, because somehow Italian Americans seem utterly dedicated to creations that make the world a better place. Perhaps the core drive is really creativity and what is more creative than building a monument to yourself and the world by creating a thriving business enterprise? What better "work of art" to leave the world and your family than your own profit-making company?

THE SPIRIT OF INTRAPRENEURSHIP

The spirit of entrepreneurship that is gripping American society and that is involving more Italian Americans is also a part of corporate life. The term being used for entrepreneurship within a corporate culture is "intrapreneurship" and we are now seeing a giant wave of emerging Italian American corporate leaders. These men and women, products mainly of the post-World War II education influx, are coming to dominate the national business consciousness and are taking over very powerful corporate positions.

Many Italian Americans committed themselves to the race for success as part of a corporate environment because they saw this as a fast track to success. Many simply opted for the security of weekly paychecks since they had Depression parents who insisted their children get educated and get jobs. These second-generation Italian American parents, who had suffered the pain of poverty and who chose the safety and security of jobs in corporations, in the civil service and in government work, simply could not understand how their children could go off and do anything that was not a "real job."

While the Italian family may have been a nurturing, loving environment, it was not materialistic in its training of its children for the rough, tough business world. This is not to say that those who were products of this kind of upbringing would not become shrewd, accomplished business people, but it did mean that the Italian family did not revolve around dinner-table talk about "how business was."

The values of hard work, honesty, integrity, diligence, love, loyalty, honor and pride that Italian Americans prided themselves on sometimes did not gibe with the realities of the American market place. The world outside the family, the school and the neighborhood was simply operating on a different set of norms and resolving this clash of values has caused many an Italian American great conflict. Fortunately, the penetration of Italian Americans into the professions is changing this situation really fast. What is fascinating is that we are really witnessing a success of value systems when we see the emerging Italian American leaders who, more and more, are arriving at the forefront of American corporate life. In the main, while they may have struggled hard within their souls to get there, they have not sold themselves out on their values. Oddly enough, it is these very values that have put them at the top of their careers and at the cutting edge of corporate American business life.

Of course, many family-run businesses that became giant corporate operations have combined the entrepreneurial skills of starting a business, building it into a successful company and then developing it into a major corporation. Many second- and third-generation inheritors of thriving businesses went to college and came back to run their parents' business with all their newly acquired Harvard-Business-School knowledge. In some cases, while this may have meant greater profits, the pain of family dissension and the clash of old and new values made the price of a richer bottom line very high to pay. The transitions from Mom-and-Pop operation to big company to giant corporation represent monumental achievements for their Italian American founders.

Joseph P. Viviano is an interesting example of the crossover from entrepreneurship in a family company to intrapreneurship in a major corporation. Viviano's father, Joseph T. Viviano, came to the United States from Palermo, Sicily, in 1899, and in 1928 founded the Kentucky Macaroni Company in Louisville. In 1946, the firm adopted the name

Delmonico Foods, Inc., after the famous New York restaurant. In 1966, Hershey Foods Corp. acquired Delmonico Foods, and thus acquired Joseph Viviano.

Viviano, born in 1938 in Louisville, got his college degree at Xavier University in Cincinnati. He began his career in 1960, when he joined his family pasta business and learned everything he could about the production of pasta. In 1968, after Hershey Foods had acquired Delmonico, Viviano was named vice president of operations and promoted to president in 1972. When Delmonico was merged with San Giorgio Macaroni, Inc. in 1975, he was appointed president of the combined companies. In 1980, he became president of the newly formed San Giorgio-Skinner Co. In 1984, Viviano was promoted to senior vice president of Hershey Foods Corp. and in 1985 he became president of the Hershey Chocolate Company, the largest division of Hershey Foods Corporation. He also sits on the corporation's board of directors.

Mike Bongiovanni, born in 1920 in Hoboken, New Jersey, went to public schools and graduated from Rutgers University with a B.S. in Pharmacy in 1941. He spent four years in World War II as a captain in the Air Force, winning many medals. He then joined E. R. Squibb & Sons in 1946 and started as a sales representative from 1946 to 1951 and became division manager from 1951 to 1958, and rose to several vice presidencies at Squibb through the early 1970s. From 1972 to 1981 he served as president of U.S. Pharmaceutical Company and by 1981 had become president and chief executive officer of Squibb Specialty Health Products Group and a member of the board and vice president of Squibb Corporation. In 1984, he was made chairman of Squibb Medical Products Group. He retired in 1985 and is now a consultant to the Office of the Chief Executive of Squibb. Bongiovanni won the Horatio Alger award in 1979. Throughout his successful career, Bongovianni set the very highest personal standards of hard work, responsibility, dignity and self-respect within the corporate structure.

Domenick G. Scaglione was born in 1933 the last of seven children in Partinico, Palermo, Italy. When his father died in 1936, Scaglione was sent to live in an orphanage in 1938 where he spent most of his childhood. In 1951, he joined his mother and her family in Ozone Park, New York. Scaglione became one of the most brilliant financial men in banking and rose to the position of vice president of the Chase Manhattan Bank in New York City.

He first worked in a sweatshop as a sewing-machine operator making dresses while he attended evening courses at Jefferson High School and Drake Business School. He served in the U.S. Army and joined First National Bank in 1954 as a "Rack Clerk" while studying full time in The Collegiate Business Institute. By 1964 he was responsible for the operation of the banks' branch at the New York World's Fair.

In 1964, he joined Commercial Bank of North America and succeeded in several high positions. In 1970, he joined the Chase Manhattan Bank as a vice president. He is now senior marketing officer for all of Europe. Scaglione is now responsible for huge financial dealings with major money and power brokers all over the world.

Scaglione is a member of numerous civic organizations, especially those that are Italian American. He has been honored with awards by many institutions and associations. Perhaps the most significant was the Ellis Island Medal of Honor award by the United States government on October 27, 1986.

Roger Enrico, the man responsible for keeping "the taste of a whole new generation" bubbling deliciously and devotedly down the gullets of zillions of faithful Pepsi-Cola drinkers worldwide, was born in 1944 in Chisolm, Minnesota, the son of Italian parents. Enrico's first job was with a small independent bottling plant near his home, where he performed every task from labeling to washing bottles. He worked as a stock boy in a small grocery store and later sold pots and pans in Minneapolis.

Enrico graduated from Babson College in Wellesley, Massachusetts, in 1965 with a degree in finance. He returned to Minnesota and went right to work for General Mills in the employee-relations department. He joined the Navy after fifteen months and then returned to General Mills four years later as assistant brand manager on Wheaties. After two years he began to thirst for an entrepreneurial challenge, but within the corporate environment.

Then Enrico discovered Frito-Lay, a subsidiary of PepsiCo, Inc. in Dallas, and came aboard as associate manager in 1971. By 1974 he was promoted to marketing director for all the company's corn snacks. Over the years from 1975 to 1983, he held several international posts in the Pepsi Empire and became executive vice president of PepsiCola USA. Enrico was tapped to assume the mantle of president in 1983. He is now president and chief executive officer of PepsiCo's Pepsi-Cola Company and oversees all key elements of the corporation's domestic and international business. Total revenues for the empire are 4 billion dollars.

Today Roger Enrico claims victory in the dramatic "Cola Wars." But to Enrico, the war is serious business, not to be taken lightly, for there are billions of dollars at stake in whether our population really joins the "Pepsi Generation" or decides it wants the "Real Thing." Actually, the story is fun, interesting and exciting, and anyone interested can read it in Enrico's book *The Other Guy Blinked: How Pepsi Won the Cola Wars.*

Enrico, the royal allied commander of the PepsiCo forces, is truly brilliant. He is the man who convinced Burger King to switch to Pepsi and he added Slice, a juice-based lemon-lime drink designed to take on 7-UP. When Coca Cola brought out their New Coke, he turned this into an ingenious victory for Pepsi. Enrico knew that Coke really blew it on their new product and had to retreat to their Classic Coke. Thus, "the other guy blinked" and Pepsi claimed victory for now being number one in colas.

Roger Enrico is an inspired executive who knows how to succeed in a huge corporate environment, but his very personal style is almost antibureaucratic. No matter how busy, he always takes time for his family. He believes that companies should always define themselves in human terms. His values are rooted in a highly humanistic philosophy. His rule for top managers is: "Don't do anything in writing that you can do on the telephone, and don't do anything on the phone that you can do in person." He delegates authority and has confidence in his workers, but makes sure he has top quality people around him. And he stays in touch with them.

Enrico has publicly acknowledged his debt to an Italian heritage and his life itself is a tribute to that heritage. At one point in the frenzy for creative advertising he had Lee Iacocca, Geraldine Ferraro, Dan Marino and Joe Montana signed aboard to do ads. When asked by an associate, "What are you trying to do, Roger—help your brothers and sisters get work?" he replied, realizing for the first time they were all Italian, "It's a complete coincidence. But now that I think about it, it's because Italians are doing all the important things today."

Dante Carl Fabiani, born in 1917 in Waterbury, Connecticut, was the son of Italian immigrants from Atrodoco, near Rome. He grew up in Waterbury and went to Tri-State University in Indiana, getting his B.S. in 1938. Fabiani's first job was with the Auburn Rubber Corp. in Indiana in 1938 and he obtained a degree in Industrial Engineering at Purdue University in 1942 while working at the General Electric Company. He worked his way through various positions and arrived at McDonnell Aircraft Corp. as vice president of finance in 1960. He then was appointed executive vice president of Crane Company.

Fabiani moved up the corporate ranks quickly and his brilliant business acumen has put him on the boards of directors of many top corporations. He was the dynamic president of Crane for almost twenty years from 1961 to 1980. Crane is a billion-dollar-plus conglomerate doing millions of dollars of business in aerospace and industrial and defense products. His gifted stewardship has guided the company to huge profits.

Fabiani attributes his successful leadership to choosing the right people and motivating them to achieve. He is a hands-on manager and totally people-oriented in his work. His commitment to hard, diligent work is based upon a solid foundation in pride of accomplishment. Family also is the source of great pride and love for his motivation and guiding principles. Fabiani spends his time with his wife Virginia and his beloved family in Westport, Connecticut. He is proud of his Italian ethnic background and credits it with much of his accomplishments.

For millions of Italian Americans, and for millions of Americans, Lido Anthony "Lee" Iacocca is the personification of the corporate success climb to power, wealth and fame. Lee was born in 1924, the son of Italian immigrants who arrived here in 1902, poor, alone and scared, from their home town of Benevento, Italy. Iacocca grew up in Allentown, Pennsylvania and his uncanny instinct for marketing began with his father who by this time owned movie houses and was himself a great promoter.

Like many others, the Iacocca family lost all its money during the Depression, but their strong familial ties carried them through this and many other crises. Iacocca studied engineering at Lehigh University and at Princeton. In 1946, he arrived in Detroit aboard the Red Arrow train with thirty dollars in his pocket. He began working at the Ford Motor Company as a student engineer. World War II had just ended and Lee found himself in the promised land of frenzied opportunity as the auto companies were scrambling to reorganize, manufacture and sell cars to an anxious, waiting public on the verge of a whole new era. Iacocca worked his way up the ladder of corporate success at Ford, piling achievement upon achievement. He was responsible for the creative design of several cars, the most famous of which became a classic—the Mustang. His success with the Mustang helped earn him the top position of Ford Motor's presidency in 1970. He successfully ran the company for eight years but his disputes with Henry Ford, the owner, grew worse and he was finally ousted in 1978 by Ford. This was a devastating experience for Lee Iacocca, but his will to prevail overcame his defeat.

Iacocca then took over the financially disastrous Chrysler Corporation and performed a miracle. Chrysler was simply in total financial ruin and Iacocca raised it from the ashes and turned it into a great success, catapulting himself to the status of national folk hero. He described his amazing achievement at Chrysler to *U.S. News & World Report:* "The first requisite in running a major corporation is the ability to pick good people, because you can't do anything alone."

Iacocca also spent four years as chairman of the Statue of

Liberty-Ellis Island Foundation, a private sector group of sponsors, and of the Federal Advisory Commission on the Statue of Liberty. His herculean efforts made the fabulous events of the 1986 centennial celebration possible.

His success at Ford, then at Chrysler, his trials and tribulations, his winning victories in the world of high finance and in the corporate jungle, his rising above the pain of discrimination, his hard work, diligence and determination, his love of family and his Italian heritage, and his unselfish work on the Statue of Liberty and Ellis Island celebrations have all made Iacocca a folk hero to Americas all across the country. He is a legend and an inspiration to all Italian Americans.

BUSINESS—WOMEN

While we have an overabundance of information on Italian American men who have succeeded in business, we have found it extremely difficult to obtain material on Italian American women who are making it. In looking at the huge successes of people on a broad basis in the entrepreneurial arena, we were hard pressed to come up with more than a small group of women in the highest reaches of big success. Helen Franzolin Boehm stands out, as do several others, but in comparison to the men, there's absolutely no balance.

Two of the most successful and entrepreneurial Italian American women wielded their wooden spatulas to great fortunes. So much for the aversion some women have to the kitchen. And, happy to say, *mie care,* these women are far from the stereotype Italian American women. Remember, stereotypes are also rooted in truth, and if succeeding in business means giving up the cooking, what a tragedy that would be. Interestingly enough, some of the men owe their fortunes in some measure to the Italian kitchen and to their Italian mothers' recipes which they took to create huge business successes.

The problem of finding successful Italian American women was also true for the corporate world. It may be that Italian

American women have been acculturated not to "go public" with their accomplishments because the man is supposed to be the successful one whose success is touted publicly.

Throughout all the other dimensions of contributions we see great entrepreneurial and intrapreneurial skill at work, whether by men or women, in many careers, jobs and professions.

Letitia Baldridge, the daughter of a Congressman and social secretary to Jacqueline Kennedy, remarked of Helen Franzolin Boehm of Edward Marshall Boehm,Inc.: "When a woman of humble parentage has five heads of state concurrently addressing her as "Helen," there must be some magic in her life. Perhaps it's a powerful dose of luck, talent, ambition, timing or chutzpah, or a combination of all."

Boehm works of art are collected worldwide, sit in honored places at Buckingham Palace, Élysée Palace, the White House, the Great Hall in Peking and the Vatican, and are on view in almost one hundred museums and institutions around the world.

In 1911, Pietro and Francesca Franzolin sailed from Genoa, Italy to America and debarked at Ellis Island from a crowded ship, each carrying a child, Helen's older brother and sister. Helen, born in Brooklyn in a clapboard house in Bensonhurst, was the daughter of a northern Italian father with artistic Florentine blood and of a southern Italian mother with hot, hearty, solid Sicilian blood, a marvelous combination indeed! Her baptismal name was Elena Francesca Stefania Franzolin.

When her father died tragically from injuries gained from working in a furniture plant, Helen, age thirteen, joined her other six brothers and sisters to work and support the family. She was raised in a strict Italian and Catholic way, yet her family was the strongest support system in the world, helping her to overcome all tragedies. Helen attended New Utrecht High School in Brooklyn. She learned to sew from her mother, who was a tough taskmaster. Mom's philosophy was that perfection was the only thing to strive for, and this required perseverance.

Helen met Edward Marshall Boehm at the Air Force Convalescent Center in Pawling, New York during World War II. This handsome man was showing wounded men how to model figures in clay. Helen watched his deftness and surgeon-like skill spellbound as he created his works of art. She was smitten for life.

Helen and Ed married just before the end of World War II. While Helen worked to support them, Ed studied, researched and learned the treasured secrets of making hard-paste porcelain. In 1950, Edward and Helen Boehm started a basement studio in Trenton, New Jersey, Neither had much experience or training, but they had the spirit to succeed and the intense desire to excel—and they were the perfect complement to each other. Ed had the shy, creative nature with the raw, innate artistic genius, while Helen had the ebullient, dynamic and energetic talent with the entrepreneurial spirit and aggressive saleswomanship.

Ed Boehm became the first American maker of priceless hard-paste porcelain of world-class quality and was a genius of the art. Fortunately for the world, when he died in 1969, he had already shared his knowledge and expertise with the artists and craftsmen who joined him. His talent catapulted America to the number-one leader of the world in this historically revered art.

However, it was Helen Boehm's entrepreneurial spirit that waged the battle on the business front and brought the Edward Marshall Boehm Company to world prominence. She continues the tradition by energizing, motivating and orchestrating the future of this preeminent firm. Not only has she received the Horatio Alger award, but she is the first woman board member of that prestigious award group. When given the Canova Medal of the Vatican Museums as the first American ever to receive this prestigious award, Helen Boehm began by saying: "Tonight, receiving this medal is significant coming from the land of my parents . . .."

Celeste Lizio, founder of Celeste's pizza and better known as "Mama Celeste," started learning to cook from her mother when she was seven years of age. In 1930, Celeste and her husband Tony, newly married, came to the United States and settled in Chicago. They opened a grocery store on the city's west side. As a child, Celeste had always helped her mother in the kitchen, where she learned the secrets of old family recipes for Italian food.

Seven years later, Celeste, age twenty-eight, and Tony opened their own restaurant in Chicago and called it the "Vedazie Beer Garden." This was later changed to "Celeste's." Celeste and Tony cooked together, featuring homemade pizza and other fine Italian specialties. They welcomed friends and neighbors to their restaurant and gladly gave any leftover food to those in need. The Lizios raised four children who helped them in the restaurant as they grew. Demand for Celeste's delicious foods increased so dramatically that other restaurants and institutions added several Celeste products to their own menus. This fortuitous growth and unexpected desire for their foodstuffs prompted the Lizios to close their restaurant in 1960 and sell their ravioli solely to restaurants and institutions. They relocated their headquarters to Celeste's first plant in Stickney, Illinois, where they continued to produce all their products manually. Soon restaurants and institutions throughout Chicago were serving Celeste ravioli.

In 1969, the company was incorporated and moved to modern facilities in Rosemont, Illinois, where a full line of frozen Italian foods, including pizza, ravioli, manicotti, lasagna, fettucine noodles, cavatelli and sauce, is produced for both retail and institutional sale. Later that same year, Quaker Oats acquired Celeste Italian Foods Company and brought their considerable marketing expertise and financial strength to the line of quality Celeste frozen products.

The Lizio family still remains actively involved with many aspects of this rapidly growing business and continues to create recipes for new products. Celeste Lizio can't seem to get out of the kitchen even though she's a proud grandmother of eleven and great grandmother of two. Her husband and partner, Tony, passed away in 1969. Celeste's mother did one fantastic job on teaching her *bella figliuola!*

Rose Totino was one of seven children of Italian immigrants who immigrated from Scopoli, a small village in northern rural Italy, in 1910 to the Minneapolis area. Among entrepreneurs she is now a superstar as the founder of Totino's Frozen Pizza, the largest frozen pizza company in the world with sales over a billion dollars a year.

Born Rose Cruciani, she learned Italian cooking in the family kitchen, especially how to make pizza with a crisp crust. She left school to work as a housecleaner for $2.50 a day to help meet the family expenses. Her brothers were allowed to stay in school, a classic bias toward the Italian male, while she had to work. Jim Totino, who left school in the ninth grade, became her husband in 1925. Following her mother's recipes, Totino made and served her delicious pizza to friends and family, who all kept telling her that her pizza was good enough to sell publicly.

In 1952, Rose Totino and her husband Jim decided to cast their lot into the entrepreneurial world of risk and sought a loan of $1,500 from a local bank in Minneapolis. The banker, like many of the people in the area, did not even know what pizza was, so she marched in with a freshly baked sample, gave him a slice, and marched out with her loan. Jim continued in his job as a baker while they opened "Totino's Italian Kitchen" with a large neon sign in the window saying "PIZZA." Customers had to be educated to what this Italian delicacy was; someone actually walked in and asked for "Mr. or Mrs. Pizza."

The whole family helped out in the business and it boomed. Jim quit his job, Rose made her pizza, they all worked eighteen to twenty hours a day and Rose's pizza became a success.

In 1962, the Totinos withdrew their fifty-thousand-dollar savings and, ventured into the frozen-food business. They started with frozen Italian entrees, but lost their shirts. Just when they were about to call it quits, they heard of a prebaked pizza crust that had become available and with a fifty-thousand-dollar Small Business Administration loan they went into the frozen-pizza business. By 1963, they began an operation at a plant in St. Louis Park. In 1970, they borrowed 2.5 million dollars to build a plant in Fridlay, where they could make their own pizza crust. By 1971, the Totino Finer Foods company was doing ten million dollars annually and in 1975 the Totinos sold their business for thirty-five million dollars to the Pillsbury Co. By 1978, the newly developed "Totino's Crisp Crust Pizza" was the top frozen-pizza seller under the creation and guidance of Rose Totino, the first woman vice president at Pillsbury.

Rose Totino's success was due to persistence, courage and stamina. She never gave up hope, got along on what they had, and worked hard. She recognizes the value of people and builds on their strengths. She is a fiery motivator, who continues to command respect as a creative executive though she has not left her kitchen. She is admired for her business sense, her sincerity and her hard work.

Rose Totino has been awarded many honors in her professional and personal life. She values highly her Italian roots and travels to her home town in Italy often. She shares her Italian heritage by rewarding her most successful salesmen with trips to Italy.

Leda (Marie Therese Giovannetti) Sanford (Gordon) was born in a small Tuscan hill town near Lucca, Italy, the daughter of an American mother and an Italian father. With her family, she came to America in 1939 at age five and a half to escape the ravages of World War II. She spoke no English and grew up mainly in the Bronx in an Italian neighborhood. After the war, her father was unhappy in America and moved the family to the Italian Riviera and sent Leda off to a convent school where she learned the lessons befitting a young lady, like embroidery, art, the Italian language and the social graces. But she was very unhappy, and her mother realized this and moved back to America with Leda and her sister.

Sanford's life in those early years was close-knit, family-oriented and typically bound very tightly within this Italian neighborhood. She attended Our Lady of Solace parochial school and graduated from Christopher Columbus High School at age sixteen.

Upon graduating, Leda wanted to be a journalist. Leda's dream was to be the editor of a magazine, live in a Manhattan penthouse, be a strong, successful woman, though glamorous and romantic. She enrolled at The Fashion Institute of Technology in New York City and graduated at age nineteen. Her life took a whole new turn when she met Howard Sanford, a Presbyterian engineer from Tennessee. She married, moved to Westchester county, bought a house, became a housewife, had babies, taught Sunday school and turned into the epitome of a nice suburban lady. In her attempt to become part of homogenized America, she lost her identity. After twelve years of matronly duty, she realized her mistake, divorced Howard Sanford, moved out of her suburban "Father-Knows-Best" home and moved into a cramped apartment over a Pelham deli with her two sons.

In 1966 at age thirty-three with two children at home, she landed her first job as an assistant on *Teens and Boys*. She learned fast, did well and impressed her bosses as she worked her way up from editorial assistant to fashion editor to editor. Then she moved to *Menswear* magazine, a Fairchild publication, where she eventually became editor in chief.

The big leap for Leda came when she won the publisher's position at *American Home* magazine in 1975. What she brought to this publication with 2.25 million readers was her extensive knowledge in cooking, housekeeping, fashion, marriage and publishing. Sanford changed the direction of the magazine into a more sophisticated lifestyle publication geared to the "groping, emerging woman," the contemporary liberated woman who works, striving for fulfillment, and who also functions as a mother, maintaining family values. In short, she herself was the prototype of the "new woman" the magazine sought to reach. At the time, she was the only woman publisher of a major magazine with a circulation over 1 million, and was editor in chief. Sanford saved *American Home* from bankruptcy, revitalized sales, increased advertising revenue and relaunched the new magazine specifically targeting the "new woman." This she did while caring for her two children as well.

The eventual demise of *American Home* in 1977 was like a death in the family for Sanford. She served for a year as publisher for *Chief Executive* magazine until she met Jeno Paulucci, entrepreneur, who had wanted to establish a national magazine to serve the pressing needs of the emerging Italian Americans. Paulucci was impressed and installed Sanford as founding publisher and editor in chief of *Attenzione* magazine in 1979, the first national publication of its kind.

For Leda, the exciting challenge of *Attenzione* was like coming home. It fulfilled her professional goals as a small publisher and editor while it satisfied her heart and soul as an Italian American woman. The magazine was aimed at the Italian Americans who were becoming newly conscious of their identity and at all non-Italians who share a love of things Italian. The magazine was a splendid hit and won the ASME award for design excellence in 1981. Leda's creative energy made *Attenzione* into the best national Italian American magazine in the country.

Sanford left *Attenzione* in 1982 to accept a position as vice president of Knapp Communications and publisher of *Bon Appetit* magazine with a circulation of 1.3 million readers. She left Knapp in 1983 to work as president of her own company, Total Magazine Services, in which she consults for the magazine publishing industry. She is also the United States publisher of *FMR*, the beautiful Italian periodical owned by Franco Maria Ricci.

Leda Sanford has become a top executive and industry leader who is recognized for her expertise in magazine publishing. She has succeeded in spite of many obstacles while maintaining her cherished values of an Italian heritage. Leda Sanford has shown what women can accomplish with talent, brains and the will to succeed.

Jackie Lewis, sister of Bob Guccione, was born in 1934 in Englewood, New Jersey, and graduated from Marymount Academy, a high school for girls in Tarrytown, New York. After a brief enrollment at Bucknell University, she got married to an Air Force man and lived in numerous places, including occupied Germany. After her divorce she returned to school getting her B.A. in sociology in 1970 at the University of Evansville and got married again. She got her Masters degree in sociology in 1972 at the University of Connecticut, divorced for the second time and went to work for *Penthouse* magazine from 1972 to 1975. After marrying for the third time she left *Penthouse* and began freelance writing and became executive director for *Impact* magazine.

From this varied background, Lewis became a major publisher, now running no fewer than ten magazines. Knowing that sex magazines sell as much for the letters in them as for the nude girls, Lewis hit on the successful idea of *Letters* magazine in 1979 and from the first day this was a hit. Working out of her home for two years, she scored another hit magazine in 1980 called *Family Affairs.* In 1980, she published *First Hand* magazine, and in 1984, Lewis and her twin sister, Jeri Guccione Winston, started *Espionage* magazine, also a success.

By the time Jackie Lewis was done, she has had four children, three husbands, one grandchild and ten magazines. She became a consummate editor/publisher and a successful business woman, even though she was working as a woman in a male-dominated business and she maintained a home with four kids after three divorces while doing all this.

Rosemarie Greco, born in South Philadelphia, the youngest of five children whose father was an Italian immigrant, started as a secretary and rose to be the first woman to head one of the nation's one hundred largest banks at age forty. Greco is the president of Fidelity Bank, the largest commercial bank in Philadelphia with 129 branches.

Greco's father had hoped to send her to college because she dreamed of becoming a teacher, but he died when she was age sixteen. With no money, she joined a convent to pursue her teaching. She left the convent at age twenty-one before taking her vows, because she felt the church was not changing fast enough for her. Still wanting to teach, she enrolled in night classes at St. Joseph's University and took a job as secretary at Fidelity Bank.

Greco worked hard and excelled at her new job, studied bank procedures, soon began training new employees and became personnel director. By age twenty-nine, she graduated *magna cum laude* from St. Joseph's and was an officer in the bank. Her skills at organization, picking people for the right job, getting them motivated and getting the job done impressed the chairman and in 1981, she was put in charge of the bank's 67 branches. Greco's guiding spirit expanded the bank to its present 129 branches and in 1987 she was made its president.

Beyond Greco's personal success in attaining a high corporate position, she is also dedicated to community service and civic duty. Mayor William J. Green appointed her to a two-year term on the city's first mayor's Commission for Women. In

1983, she was appointed by the mayor as the first chairperson of the Women's Commission. Mayor Goode then appointed her in 1984 to serve on the City Planning Commission, which she did until she was named to the Philadelphia Board of Education in 1985. In addition to several other appointments, Greco is also a published writer and a featured speaker for many special events, conferences and seminars.

Greco never became a teacher, but she sees her management role as educational in that it leads people through a process of acquiring skill. She got to the top through a commitment to hard work—she just decided she'd be the best branch secretary the bank ever had. Her diligence, perseverance and hard work won her success in achieving her aspirations. Nor has Greco, now a talented, powerful executive, forgotten her roots—she lives near the Italian market just a couple of blocks from where her mother was born and raised. Being president of a major bank in her home town is the source of special pride to this Italian American woman.

Can a woman from Potsdam, New York, raised by her Italian grandmother, married at age twenty and the mother of three children, find success as the president of a major construction firm? Well, yes, if she is Delores Y. Critelli, who helped found Power Line Constructors and who has led the company to major financial growth and success as its dynamic president.

Critelli was born in Utica, New York, and has lived all her life there in the Upper Mohawk Valley country. Her mother passed away when Delores was three and her upbringing was assumed by her grandmother. She married at age twenty and moved to Potsdam, New York, with her husband, who attended and later graduated from Clarkson University. She had three children but heard the siren's call of fulfillment outside the home in 1963.

Critelli helped found Power Line Constructors with her partner Elmer Wahl. They entered the business of constructing and maintaining high-voltage electrical systems with four employees at an office on Main Street in Utica, and it grew rapidly. The company became a necessary link in bringing surplus energy from the Power Grid of the gigantic Quebec Hydroelectric Facilities in Canada to customers in the New

York State and Vermont area. As the demand for more power grew in the area, so did the company. Officials and business people found that they performed high-quality work and met time schedules. The company was awarded major contracts, including the lighting of Route 81 south of Syracuse and the steel erection work on the 765-KV substation for the N.Y. State Power Authority. Large corporations, such as General Electric, came to rely on the company so much that by 1972 they built their own building in Clinton, New York.

Critelli took over as president when her partner Wahl retired in 1976 and she runs the whole operation herself with her son David as vice president. The company is now a major power in the power-construction business. She serves on the Business Council of New York State's Construction Industry Council and is on the board of the Mohawk Valley Workshop for the Handicapped and the Children's Hospital and Rehabilitation Center of Utica.

Meanwhile this mother of three and successful president of a company was chosen to be included in New York State's Office of General Services fiscal calendar to represent a particular month. She keeps busy following her own slogan above her desk: "Keep pedaling—the only direction you can coast is downhill."

Joan P. Orazio is executive vice president of Gary Goldberg & Company, Inc., a financial-planning and investment firm with more than four thousand corporate and individual clients throughout the United States. She is an expert in the field of financial planning for individuals and families in transition, such as those nearing retirement, as well as those in education, corporate and independent business. She is a recognized authority in helping single women and their families plan their financial lives. She also has taught college courses in personal money management and conducts workshops and seminars for numerous civic and corporate organizations across America.

After receiving her B.S., *summa cum laude,* from Mercy College with emphasis in accounting and finance, Orazio graduated from the College of Financial Planning in Denver, Colorado. She became a certified financial planner and worked in several positions as an independent consultant for a national financial-services organization. She joined Gary Goldberg & Company in 1977 and became both executive vice president of Gary Goldberg & Company and a major force in her industry. She has received many awards, such as "Woman of Achievement" and "Woman of the Year," and she is an active member of her community. She participates in a variety of civic affairs and has been a trustee and treasurer for the Rockland Community College since 1984.

This woman, now listed in many *Who's Who*s and a highly successful business executive and financial expert, is also a successful mother. Orazio had returned to school after raising four children. As she said, "I guess I'm a classic 're-entry' person. I successfully had both a family and a career, and any woman that has been in the work force knows that it's hard to do." Orazio is an inspiring role model for Italian American women and she participates actively in Italian American events, especially for women.

Janice Zarro, vice president of federal affairs for Avon Products, Inc., received her B.A. from Rutgers University and her J.D. from Chicago-Kent College of Law. As an attorney, she served as counsel to the Judiciary Committee of the U.S. House of Representatives and as counsel to the U.S. Senate Committee on Labor and Human Resources. In 1980, she joined Avon Products in the general counsel, government affairs department in New York.

In 1982, Zarro organized and established a Washington government-affairs office for Avon Products, which she now heads. Her responsibilities include lobbying, fund-raising, communicating to senior management, monitoring and formulating policy on federal legislative efforts and serving as an advisor to the Avon Fund for Responsible Government. She also functions as a liaison for the corporation with federal agencies, trade associations and numerous Washington organizations that Avon may support.

Beyond her corporate duties, Zarro also serves on many civic and governmental delegations and panels. She was selected as one of the ten members of a U.S. businesswomen's delegation to study the problem of women in small businesses in Central America and to encourage economic development. This trip, coordinated by OEF International and funded by the United States Information Agency, included visits to Honduras, Costa Rica and Panama to meet with top-level government leaders and Central American businesswomen.

Zarro is committed to furthering the cause of women and is a member of the Women's Forum and Women in Government Relations. She holds the national chair of the Women in Business Committee of OEF International. She serves on many other powerful boards and has been honored with many awards and citations. She received a leadership award for professional achievement from the National Women's Economic Alliance Foundation. Zarro is also an active member of the National Organization of Italian American Women.

Eleanor Cutri Smeal was born in 1939 in Ashtabula, Ohio, as the first daughter and fourth child of Peter Cutri from Calabria and Josephine Agresti Cutri, also from an Italian immigrant family. She was brought up in Erie, Pennsylvania, as a Catholic but attended public schools because her mother wanted her to meet people of varied backgrounds.

Eleanor Cutri got her B.A. in 1961 from Duke University in North Carolina and her M.A. from the University of Florida in 1963 in political science and public administration. Here she met Charles Smeal, a student in metallurgical engineering, and they married in 1963. She began work on a doctoral thesis into the attitudes of women toward woman political candidates.

Later in 1969, having moved to the Pittsburgh area, Smeal wanted to complete her Ph.D. and found there was no child-care service available for her son Tod and daughter Lori. Also suffering from a confining back ailment, it was during this time that Smeal became painfully aware of disability insurance for wives and mothers. She read everything she could on the suffragists and the growing women's movement. She and her husband became confirmed radical feminists and joined the National Organization for Women in 1970.

Eleanor Smeal began in 1971 as convener and first president of a NOW chapter in South Hills, a suburb of Pittsburgh, and stayed there until 1973. From 1972 to 1975, Smeal served as president of Pennsylvania NOW. She made educational injustice a target and fought for equal opportunity for girls in school sports and physical-education programs. By 1977 Smeal was voted in as president of NOW by an alliance of local chapters and small communities. Her victory symbolized a major philosophical shift away from the dominance of elitist, large-city and centralized structure toward a grass-roots, decentralized and local community-oriented organization. Smeal wanted NOW to be accessible to women from all walks of life, including housewives, and she won the support mostly of housewives she organized. She asserted the vital need for the economic security of homemakers and designated the passage of the Equal Rights Amendment as the most important goal of NOW for all women.

Within two years, Smeal enlarged the appeal of NOW and doubled the membership to one hundred thousand, making it the world's largest feminist organization in 1979. She has been at the forefront of every important women's conference and national committee in the country and her leadership has made NOW a major political force in the nation. The 1978 *World Almanac* listed her as one of the twenty-five most influential women in the United States. *Time* magazine chose her as one of thirteen women among those chosen for its cover story "50 Faces in America's Future."

Two Italian American women are at the forefront of the new corporate-training programs that seek to increase productivity through the creative use of human resources. Arleen La Bella and Dolores Leach cofounded Professional Resources, Inc. and the Center for Career Enrichment in the Washington, D.C. area with offices in Reston, Virginia.

La Bella received her master's from the University of Buffalo and her doctorate in applied behavioral sciences from the University of Massachusetts. Her experience as a seminar leader, consultant and author spans fourteen years developing programs for private consultation and public seminars all across the country. Her creative training systems and specially designed materials are used by many Fortune 500 corporations, including AT&T, Exxon and Kodak. She also teaches as adjunct professor at the University of Buffalo and has presented seminars at many colleges and universities. La Bella conducts human resource training programs for several government agencies, such as the U.S. Department of Defense Communications and the IRS.

Dolores Leach also has fourteen years of experience as a workshop trainer, and has developed programs and seminars throughout the country. She has conducted human resources training programs for several government agencies, such as the U.S. Department of Transportation. She has taught at the University of Buffalo and the University of Colorado's Center for Business, Industry and Government. She received her M.S. from the University of Buffalo.

Together La Bella and Leach co-authored the book *Personal Power: Today's Guide for the Working Woman,* a very hot book in the women's movement and they cofounded Professional Resources, Inc., a very successful human resources management training and consulting firm.

Catherine Bartoletta, one of eighteen children, was married before age fifteen, was the mother of two children before she was seventeen and became a grandmother before she was forty. In 1928, Bartoletta was earning a poor living for her family by working as an Italian language interpreter for attorneys and answering phone calls for a small local hauling firm. This gave her an idea and with five hundred dollars and no experience Bartoletta bought two Brockway trucks and entered the freight trucking business. As president of North Braddock Line, Inc., she now operates a huge fleet of trucks serving the northeast United States. As far as can be determined, Bartoletta was the first woman in the country to operate a trucking company.

Letizia Buitoni became a top executive in charge of international relations for the vast Buitoni Italian food enterprises. At an early age, she showed a flair for music and at age sixteen she made a brilliant operatic debut in Milan. She studied voice training with her father, a famous maestro di canto called Antonio Cairone. While Buitoni spends her time coordinating the firm's worldwide activities, she also works diligently in projects to discover and encourage new talent, particularly in the field of opera.

Angela Forenza came from Larchmont, New York, and studied industrial design at Pratt Institute on scholarship and at Columbia University. She entered the advertising and public-relations field and then joined the world-renowned jewelry firm of Van Cleef and Arpels. Throughout the 1950s, she was manager in charge of advertising and public relations and rose from that to become a top executive in the industry.

Betty Ossola became executive vice president and general manager of the fifty-year-old J. Ossola Company founded by her father. She was responsible for introducing many of the continental varieties of food items her company produces to the American market.

Laura Picchietti was born in 1910, the second of five children, and came to America from Turin, Italy, at age three. She and her husband, John Picchietti, worked at their local grocery store until 1940 when they opened the Deerfield Bowling Academy in Deerfield, Illinois. This business venture led to the birth of DBA Products Company with the development of the company's first chemical product. Laura learned very fast about every facet of the business, and in 1945 she created her own advertising agency, the Deerfield Advertising Agency, to handle the promotional work of DBA Products. In 1950, DBA Products began to grow and started international importing and exporting, eventually selling their products throughout the world. Laura quit the advertising business to run DBA Products and when her husband died in 1959, she took over the entire operation, making the company a huge success.

Angela Maria Piergrossi, born in Abruzzi in 1920, moved to Massachusetts at age five and graduated from Quincy High School. She studied business and foreign languages at night, while working at her uncle's company, the Hub Folding Box Company in Boston. Angela rose to the top level of management in this business, which she helped make into one of the largest and most modern multimillion-dollar manufacturer of boxes in America.

Adele Graceffa Malone came to America at age three and married Charles Malone, who encouraged her to get involved in his trucking business and handle its public relations. When her husband died, she became president of the company and ran it with great success. She was appointed by President Nixon to the U.S. Small Business Administration. Adele involved the company with many charitable causes and around the late 1940s, she became vitally involved with politics. She successfully ran several electoral campaigns, such as that of John Volpe's successful run for the governorship of Massachusetts.

Louise Caputo, one of five children, born in Brooklyn, New York, studied premed at New York University and worked at Coty, Inc. as one of its youngest sales managers in charge of the company's metropolitan New York sales division. While working there, she was discovered by Fabergé who hired her as executive assistant to the vice president in charge of marketing and sales. She worked very hard and was appointed to the position of Vice President and Director of Creative Marketing, responsible for coordinating the creation and marketing of all new packages, products and promotions for Fabergé. She was responsible for the entire creation of Organdi, including its name.

Lilyan H. Affinito, born in Monongahela, Pennsylvania, got her B.S. from Cornell University in 1953 and an M.L. from the University of Pittsburgh. She became a certified public accountant and joined Price Waterhouse in Pittsburgh in 1956 and moved to New York City in 1962. She joined Simplicity Pattern Company, a huge corporation traded on the New York Stock Exchange, as controller. By 1976, she was appointed chief operation officer with the titles of president and treasurer. Simplicity sells and manufactures paper patterns for home sewing and is believed to be the largest pattern company in the world.

Eve Amigone Nelson, the youngest of seventeen children, graduated from the University of Buffalo School of Journalism and joined a department store in her native Buffalo as a junior copywriter. She went through the executive training course, worked for R.H. Macy's in New York, worked as vice president of a ten-unit chain of department stores in Houston and in 1959 became advertising and promotion director of E.J. Korvette, Inc., one of the fastest growing chains of department stores in the country at the time. She supervised the opening of many new stores and also served as the creative head of a chain of luxury beauty salons, owned and operated by Korvette's. A fine line of cosmetics bears her name.

Rose Miele Spagnola came to the United States from Italy and went to public school in Newark, New Jersey. She went to work after graduation for the Prudential Life Insurance Company, married Carl Albano and had three children. A few years later, in 1952, tragedy struck and Carl died unexpectedly, leaving Rose to run his business, Central Wrecking Company, though she had no experience or knowledge of this industry. She ran the company with amazing success and is probably the only woman head of a demolition and wrecking company.

We have attempted to present a cross spectrum of success stories on Italian American women, representing both the spirit of entrepreneurship in the creation and formation of a thriving business and the spirit of intrapreneurship in the climb to the top echelons of corporate suites. Some of these women started their own businesses, some took over family businesses and some succeeded within the structured framework of corporate life, despite the fact that many start at the absolute bottom of the ladder.

Whatever the case, it is interesting to see how enterprising, hardworking, diligent, proud and creative these women actually have been in their successful evolutions, each in her own way. While the number of successful Italian American women is exceeded by that of Italian American men, what is provocative is the quality of the success enjoyed by these women. The roles they chose to play were vital ones in the society, and their individual successes have been so vibrant and joyful, almost as if it were that much more worth it because it was that much more difficult.

Also, there is a tendency to cover only those Italian American women who have emerged over the past ten or twenty years, since they stick particularly in our memories, which have grown short in any case. Many of the successful women we covered were successful quite some time ago, when it was so much harder for a woman, much less an Italian American one, to get ahead and move to the top. Their successes are even more noteworthy for the time in which they were achieved. In this sense, they were truly ahead of their time and therefore all-the-more inspiring for their individual successes.

12

SCIENCE AND
ENGINEERING

GALILEO GALILEI fathered the modern scientific age and was
almost put to death for his "heretical" thoughts. It is
perhaps impossible to imagine a time when most people
really thought the sun revolved around the earth, but when
Galileo sought to bring the news that, no, the earth revolved
around the sun, he was arrested and sentenced to death for
heresy. He simply changed the way we understand the world
and invented something called modern science. How much
we owe this Italian genius!

At the core of the creative work of Italian Americans is a
similar driving, passionate thirst for knowledge, an uncon-
trollable excitement for the thrill of discovery and a relent-
less pursuit of what makes the world go round. This deep-
seated quest for reaching out into the world, playing with it
experimentally, discovering its nature, drawing conclusions
and then sharing the joy of unearthing some truth or
observation seems an especially Italian trait. The same
impulses that drove Galileo and Columbus to explore the
world, intellectually and physically, would also drive their
descendants to new shores of exploration.

By World War II, with a solid foundation of education,
with discrimination on the wane, with a strong dose of
American assimilation coursing through them and with

economic success within their grasp, the second- and third-generation Italian Americans were flooding the professions. The war required scientists as well as warriors. The scientific tradition that reached its eminence in the Renaissance would once again rise to the occasions of history and meet the needs of a modern world.

However, Italian Americans made many scientific advances well before the war. The early missionaries were expert in agricultural sciences as well as experimenters and scientific investigators. The 1876 International Centennial Exposition in Philadelphia brought together many Italian and American scientists. Father Joseph Neri pursued investigation into electricity by using large batteries, magneto machines and dynamos. By 1869, he had developed an electrical-lighting system in which he used carbon electric lights. Father Benedict Sestini was an astronomer and mathematician who created a series of drawings of the sun's surface that were engraved and published. He also wrote two books, one entitled *Analytical Geometry* in 1852 and *Elements of Geometry and Trigonometry* in 1860. In 1878, he made a complete observation of a total eclipse from Denver, Colorado.

E. O. Fenzi was a horticulturist who came to Santa Barbara, California, to work on soil cultivating. He experimented with many foreign and exotic plants in the 1890s and succeeded in creating a very attractive and prolific area out of the barren, dry land. His book, *Santa Barbara Exotic Flora,* is considered one of the most valuable on California horticulture. He was awarded the Meyer Memorial medal by the Council of the American Genetic Association for horticulture in 1922.

Frederick Rossini, born in 1899 in Monogahela, Pennsylvania, received his education at the Carnegie Institute of Technology and the University of California. He was trained as a scientist in physical chemistry and became head of the thermochemistry and hydrocarbons sections of the National Bureau of Standards until 1950. He served as head of Carnegie Tech's Department of Chemistry and directed the American Petroleum Institute Research Laboratory there. Rossini became president of the Commission on Thermo-Chemistry and served as editor, secretary and president of the prestigious

Washington Academy of Sciences. He has won numerous awards and has written many books and scientific papers.

George Speri Sperti, born in 1900 in Covington, Kentucky, received his B.S. in electrical engineering from the University of Cincinnati in 1928, his Ph.D. in 1934 from the University of Dayton and another doctorate from Duquesne University in 1936. As a research professor and director of research, he was one of six scientists inducted as a member of the Pontifical Academy of Sciences by Pope Pius XI in 1936. Sperti is credited with the invention of the K-Va meter, the light-treatment process, a famous healing ointment known as "Sperti's Biodyne" and the Sperti sun lamp.

Pascal Pirone is a famous plant pathologist who invented the Rutgers Aero Plant Propagator. He serves as senior plant pathologist and senior curator of education for the famous New York Botanical Garden. He has taught plant pathology at Rutgers and Cornell Universities. Pirone is also well known as the author of several books on horticulture, including *Diseases and Pests of Ornamental Plants*.

In California, Paola Silvestri Timiras, born in 1923 in Rome, became a professor in the Department of Physiology at the University of California at Berkeley in 1967. She served as a consultant to the Atomic Energy Commission in the Division of Biology and Medicine. Her research is mainly devoted to the physiology of development and aging, and to the hormonal and environmental factors affecting the brain.

Oreste Piccioni, born in Italy, became a professor of physics at the University of California in San Diego. He studied under the tutelage of Enrico Fermi and worked in physics doing research into the discovery of antiprotons and into the existence of antimatter. In fact, in 1972, Piccioni filed a lawsuit against Emilio Segre and his colleague Owen Chamberlain who had both won the Nobel Prize in Physics in 1959. His lawsuit alleged that Segre and Chamberlain had not duly acknowledged his contribution to the work on antiprotons.

Giuseppe Bellanca, born in 1886 in Sciacca, Agrigento, Italy, was a pioneer in aviation. From 1908 to 1909, just several years after the historic flight of Orville and Wilbur Wright, he designed and built a "pusher-type" twin-propeller plane and began his aviation career in 1906. From 1908 to 1911, he designed and built the first tractor biplane with vee landing gear struts. He graduated from the Royal Technical Institute in Milan in 1910 and came to America in 1911. Bellanca taught himself to fly in a "Bellanca parasol monoplane" in 1912 and for many years was associated with various aircraft companies as a consultant. His *Columbia* was actually the first cabin aircraft to cross the Atlantic. One of his planes flew the only nonstop crossing from Japan to the U.S. in 1931. The Bellanca two-seater airplane is still popular among aviation enthusiasts.

Salvador Luria was born in 1912 in Turin, Italy and received his M.D., *summa cum laude,* from the University of Turin in 1935 in biology. He went on to become a specialist in radiology at the University of Rome, but when the political situation before World War II worsened, Luria went to Paris in 1938 to become a research fellow at the Institut du Radium. He then emigrated to the United States in 1940, as many other Italians did, in response to fascism and performed research at Columbia University until 1942. He was also awarded a Guggenheim fellowship allowing him to work at Vanderbilt and Princeton Universities.

Luria then taught at Indiana University from 1943 to 1950. He lectured in biophysics at the University of Colorado, was a Jesup lecturer in zoology at Columbia University and joined the faculty of the University of Illinois as professor of bacteriology in 1950. He was a Nieuwland lecturer in biology at Notre Dame University in 1959. Luria then went to the Massachusetts Institute of Technology to organize a new teaching and research program in microbiology for their Department of Biology in 1959. In 1972 he became director of the Center for Cancer Research.

Luria is one of the leading pioneers of molecular biology and is internationally known for his research in the fields of virology and genetic engineering. He was the first to discover mutations in viruses that permit them to overcome immunological barriers. In 1969, along with Max Delbruck and Alfred D. Hershey, he was awarded the Nobel Prize. Their significant basic research on viruses is regarded by many as being primarily responsible for modern advances in the control of viral diseases and for advances in molecular biology.

Their discovery that viruses mutate and change their characteristics from generation to generation was an amazing breakthrough that not only contributed immeasurably to the war on viral diseases but created the foundation of the success of James Watson, who worked for his doctorate under Luria, and Francis Crick, who identified the elusive DNA molecule. It was because of this pioneering work by Luria and his two teammates that we understand today the process of DNA replication, DNA synthesis and protein synthesis, which are all life-sustaining mechanisms for all types of cells.

In short, the very essence of life could be understood.

Luria is a member of numerous academies and has received many honorary degrees. In 1974, he won the National Book Award in the sciences for his first nonacademic book, called, *Life: The Unfinished Experiment.* Luria is active in the peace movement and various organizations to keep science humanistic. He has taught a class in world literature to graduate students to insure their involvements in matters outside science. He believes that scientists must inform political leaders and the public of the work they are doing and what it means. Since he is greatly responsible for releasing the genetic-engineering genie from the bottle, he cautions scientists to be mindful of the impact of their work. Luria is also interested in the arts and sculpts as a hobby. He is a scientist, an artist and a humanist in the tradition of the Renaissance.

Renato Dulbecco had also collaborated with Salvador Luria and also won the Nobel Prize in 1975 for his work with James Watson in the "discovery" of DNA. Dulbecco was born in Catanzaro, Italy, and originally studied applied medicine at the University of Torino. He then specialized in research, biology and physics. Dulbecco emigrated to the United States after World War II and settled first in Bloomington, Indiana, where he had worked in research with Luria and Watson. He moved to California to teach at the California Institute of Technology from 1949 through 1962 and then went to the Salk Institute until 1972. In 1975, Dulbecco received the Nobel Prize for his advanced work on the relationship between oncogenic DNA viruses and cancer. He continued to pursue his great research in the fight against cancer at the Imperial Cancer Research Fund laboratories in London.

Rita Levi-Montalcini, 1986 cowinner of the Nobel Prize in Medicine, is a scientific genius whose creative experiments in cell biology have opened up a promising and important new area of cancer research. She is one of only seven women to ever win a Nobel Prize in the sciences. Levi-Montalcini was born a twin in 1909 in Turin, Italy, a major intellectual center from the time of Italy's unification. Turin became a center of political resistance to fascism in the 1920s and 1930s and had a strong, cultured, prosperous and influential middle-class Jewish population. Levi-Montalcini is Jewish and traces her family's roots back to Israelites who lived in Italy during the Roman Empire.

Levi-Montalcini grew up in the exciting and intellectually stimulating environment of Turin, in a close family of free-thinkers headed by a strong, authoritarian father, and in a progressive, creative and humanistic atmosphere. She became a strong, spirited but stubborn young lady who decided early in her life to be a doctor and never to marry. In 1938, anti-Jewish racial laws were enacted by Mussolini and she was barred from practicing as a doctor and was forced to leave the University of Turin in 1939. She left for Brussels to work as a research biologist, but when the Nazis took over Belgium, she sought refuge with her mother and sister on a farm in the Piedmont countryside. It was here in her tiny bedroom that served as a makeshift laboratory that Levi-Montalcini's experiments on chicken embryos developed into the work for which she won the Nobel Prize.

In 1943, Nazi troops marched through northern Italy and Levi-Montalcini fled to Florence with her family. She put her surgically skilled hands to work forging identity papers for refugees and partisans. The family survived in fear but with courage and determination, living underground.

With the war at an end, Levi-Montalcini returned to Turin University, but in 1947 she accepted an offer to work at Washington University in St. Louis for six months. She stayed thirty years, became a U.S. citizen and was later made a full professor. Continuing her initial experiments with chicken embryos begun in her bedroom, she followed up her original neurological hypotheses and made a breakthrough in 1952. In a thrilling great moment of discovery, Levi-Montalcini discovered the substance that serves as a messenger between the body's cells and the nervous system. Subsequent experiments with Stanley Cohen, the biochemist with whom she shared the Nobel Prize, identified the "nerve-growth factor" and isolated the protein that allows developing cells to grow by stimulating the surrounding nerve tissue. Levi-Montalcini and Stanley Cohen followed up this discovery to reveal the dynamics of the nervous system at the molecular level.

This new knowledge about how a specific protein governs cell growth is a big breakthrough for cancer research. The application of this knowledge is of great value in the search for a cure for cancer, Alzheimer's, Parkinson's and other degenerative diseases. Unquestionably, Rita Levi-Montalcini's scientific discovery was a valuable insight into the workings of the central nervous system and brain cells.

Another Nobel Prize winner was Emilio Segre, born in 1905 in Tivoli, Rome. Segre actually studied with and received his doctorate degree under the personal sponsorship of Enrico Fermi, with whom he later collaborated on the exciting new research into neutrons. From 1036 to 1938, he served as the director of the Physics Laboratory of the University of Palermo in Sicily. As did many others who left Italy during the difficult years before and during World War II, he emigrated to America and first worked in Berkeley at the University of California.

Segre then joined the Los Alamos Laboratory as a group leader in the famous and then-secret Manhattan Project to invent the atomic bomb. After working in this momentous research from 1943 to 1946, he returned to Berkeley in 1946 as a professor of physics. His work in atomic physics and nuclear physics won him the Nobel Prize in 1959, which he shared with Owen Chamberlain, for their breakthrough discovery of the antiproton.

The man who sought the secret of the neutron was Enrico

Fermi, perhaps one of the most brilliant intellects of our century and a man endowed with the most extraordinary and highest human abilities as a scientist. He was the father of the Nuclear Age, the leading expert in atomic energy and the creator of the first self-sustaining chain reaction, essential to the development of the atomic bomb. He was the greatest living expert on neutrons of his time and won the Nobel Prize in 1938 for his experiments in radioactivity.

Enrico Fermi was born in 1901 in Rome where his family had moved from Piacenza, a town in northern Italy. He grew up in Rome, attended the Liceo and enrolled as a fellow at age seventeen in the University of Pisa. He was immediately recognized as possessing an amazingly analytical mind. Within a year, Fermi was zealously committed to the new theoretical physics introduced recently by Albert Einstein, which presented the theory of relativity and the quantum theory on the absorption or radiation of energy by matter. In 1922, Fermi received his doctorate *magna cum laude* in the specialized field of nuclear physics.

After a couple of years working abroad, in Germany and Holland, especially with the famous German physicist, Max Born, Fermi returned to Italy, obtained his "Libera Docenza" at the University of Rome and taught mechanics and mathematical physics at the University of Florence in 1925. Here he discovered the statistical laws governing particles that are now called "fermions." In 1926, he won the newly established chair of theoretical physics at the University of Rome. With the advent of quantum mechanics, he and his team moved from atomic physics to nuclear physics, and this shift led to Fermi's breakthrough work on the neutron.

Fermi pursued his research from the 1920s through the 1930s, and one day he heard the chatter of the Geiger counter after he had exposed fluorine to his neutron gun. This showed he had created radioactive material. He intensified his efforts and succeeded in changing the original element into related, neighboring elements on the periodic table of elements. The dream of a lifetime and the goal of alchemists of all time had been achieved. Fermi had discovered element number 93 and made world headlines. The Atomic Age had begun.

In 1938, Enrico Fermi won the Nobel Prize in Physics for his nuclear discoveries. The day Fermi was informed of his Nobel Prize was a major turning point for him, his family and the world. Since his wife was Jewish, the Italian government had revoked his passport, but after pleading with top fascist officials he retrieved it, since he had to travel to Stockholm to accept his prize. Several months later, in December 1938, the Fermis came to New York.

Fermi went to work as professor of physics at Columbia University in 1939. Niels Bohr, the famous Danish physicist, also arrived in America and informed Fermi that German scientists had proved that the uranium atom could be split apart with neutron bombardment, thus shattering the myth about not being able to split the atom. Fermi had actually first split the atom in Rome in 1934, but did not realize it, one of the greatest oversights in history. However, had Fermi recognized his accomplishment, he surely would have made his discovery public, and then German scientists would have unquestionably developed the atomic bomb before anyone else.

Fermi, shocked by this news, dropped everything and focused his creative energy on neutrons again. He began intense work on his "atomic pile" and tried to persuade government officials of the value of one atomic bomb over millions of Hitler's conventional bombs. He enlisted his close friend Albert Einstein to write on his behalf to President Roosevelt to explain the urgency because the Germans were pursuing the same research at a faster rate and with unlimited funding from Hitler.

Roosevelt appointed a committee to investigate, while the War Department gave some funds to keep Fermi and his group still experimenting. One week after Pearl Harbor in 1941, Roosevelt appointed Arthur Compton as head of the Uranium Project, with unlimited government funding. In 1942, Fermi moved his work to the University of Chicago and within a month, achieved the first self-sustaining chain reaction, thereby creating the first controlled release of nuclear energy. On December 2, 1942, Fermi's atomic pile caused the first nuclear-chain reaction. The news was kept totally secret, and when James Conant told Roosevelt of this momentous event he had just witnessed, he said, "You'll be interested to know that the Italian navigator had just landed in the New World."

President Roosevelt immediately gave the go-ahead for further uranium research and the development of the atomic bomb, code-named the "Manhattan District Project." During this time Fermi worked closely with J. Robert Oppenheimer in Los Alamos and many other great scientific minds in a mad, mad rush to beat the Germans in creating the atomic bomb. On July 16, 1945 in the desert, code-named "Trinity," the first atomic-bomb test was conducted and, code-named "Fat Man," the first plutonium bomb was exploded. The detonation stunned those who saw it; the first explosion equaled twenty-thousand tons of TNT. Three weeks later, the first atomic bomb was dropped on Hiroshima, victory in Europe having already been won. The Japanese refused to surrender, however, and a second bomb leveled Nagasaki. World War II came to an abrupt end. Fermi was presented the Congressional Medal of Merit from the U.S. government, the highest award given to civilians.

Fermi continued his work after the war and lectured extensively throughout America at many universities. Other scientists walking in his path continued further experiments in nuclear energy and when they discovered element 100, they named it "Fermium" in honor of Fermi. In 1952, Fermi died of cancer, a disease afflicting many of those who worked closely with radioactive materials.

Guglielmo Marconi, born in 1874 in Italy, grew up in a villa near Bologna, and is credited as the father of radio. He was always intensely fascinated with the nature of the world around him and avidly read every scientific book and journal he could find. He revered those scientists who had experimented with electricity, including Augusto Righi, Nikola Tesla and Benjamin Franklin. He also was receiving an excellent education through tutors.

At age twenty, Marconi took a trip to the Italian Alps with his half-brother Luigi and here he discovered a magazine article that would change his life and ultimately the world. At the time, the scientists all over the world were experimenting with Hertzian waves, which were demonstrated by Heinrich Hertz of Germany. Through this magazine Marconi learned, to his excitement and joy, about these Hertzian waves, and he became obsessed with the notion of transmitting sound waves through the air.

He rushed home to his villa and locked himself away in his room, which now served as his workshop. Though everyone, including his family, thought he was nuts, he persisted diligently with his ideas and in time he succeeded in ringing a bell downstairs through the use of Hertzian waves. He then put a Morse-code key into his device to transmit dots and dashes. By 1895, with an antenna, groundings, and a receiver, he successfully sent his first signal across a field near his home.

The Italian Minister of Post and Telegraph gave Marconi a flat-out refusal of interest in his invention. So he and his mother set out for England, where the British Navy had a possible interest. However, when going through customs, Marconi's strange black box with funny wires, dials and batteries aroused suspicion, so the British officials destroyed it.

Marconi rebuilt his precious invention and got in contact with Sir William Preece, the chief engineer of telegraphs in the British post office system, who had also achieved some success in his own wireless experiments. Marconi and Preece conducted tests together in 1896 and first sent messages of one hundred yards, a mile, then nine miles. On July 2, 1897, Marconi obtained a patent for his wireless transmitter. His company became the Marconi's Wireless Telegraph Company, Ltd. and at age twenty-three, Marconi owned half the company's stock.

Marconi generated worldwide interest and excitement in his invention when he communicated through rain and fog with a ship eighteen miles out at sea. People came from everywhere to see this experiment, especially naval and military observers who had heard of this fascinating invention. In 1898, wireless equipment was ordered for several lighthouses, and Marconi's company began to generate income. By 1899, Marconi was installing his device on three large British battleships, and already they were being used for naval maneuvers. However, other countries and their scientists joined the experimental race to perfect Marconi's invention and to patent their own versions of his invention. Marconi had to really move fast.

In 1899, Marconi came to New York City after approaching

the United States armed forces with the purpose of demonstrating his wireless for them. While the U.S. Navy carried out tests on Marconi's invention, Marconi incorporated the Marconi Wireless Company of America in New Jersey on November 22, 1899. This company would become the Radio Corporation of America or RCA twenty years later.

The first intercontinental, trans-Atlantic radio message was sent on January 19, 1903 when President Theodore Roosevelt sent a noisy greeting in dots and dashes to King Edward VII of England via a Marconi station at South Wellfleet on Cape Cod. When the anxious reply was received, history was made. Marconi then spent many years fiercely battling with rival communications giants such as Bell Telephone and AT&T, as well as with government bureaucracies.

Marconi lived the rest of his life constantly researching and bringing his wireless communication system to the whole world. He was honored many times and had great financial success in spite of the battles he waged. Certainly there were many amateurs, inventors and scientists who were also working on wireless transmission at the same time, but it is basically accurate to say that Marconi is the actual inventor of radio. Marconi took the available knowledge a quantum leap forward to the actual successful wireless transmission of sound.

Marconi's creative genius spawned a revolution in communications worldwide, thus linking the human race in a network of radio waves. However defined, as inventor of the radio or father of radio, Marconi took the first human step onto the threshold of something new. Marconi ushered in the Media Age to the twentieth century.

Carlo Rubbia, described as "an ebullient yet irascible Italian, whom fellow physicists love to hate," was born in 1934 in the small town of Gorizia in northern Italy, the oldest son of an electrical engineer. From an early age, he loved science, and when the ravages of World War II destroyed his home, Rubbia collected and experimented with abandoned communications equipment. This led to a deep understanding of electronics that became one of his strengths as a physicist. He moved to Pisa with his family and received his degree in physics from the University of Pisa in 1958.

From 1958 to 1959, Rubbia worked at Columbia University,

then the center of high-energy physics research, as a research fellow. To go from the countryside of Italy to the city of New York was a shock for Rubbia. In 1960, he joined the faculty of the University of Rome and in 1961, he became a physicist for the European Organization for Nuclear Research or CERN. His initial project was the building of a particle accelerator, a fundamental tool in high-energy particle-physics research.

The Holy Grail of physics has always been a "unified-field theory," which would confirm that the four fundamental forces of nature—gravity, electromagnetism, the "weak force" of radioactive decay and the "strong force" that holds protons, neutrons and subatomic particles together in a nucleus—are really four different manifestations of one basic force and thus subject to a single set of laws. What Rubbia did was to make a quantum leap in the movement toward this unified-field theory.

The race between Fermilab and CERN was hotly run, and Rubbia was in the middle. In 1969, he joined Fermilab, and by 1973 he had constructed the most powerful "particle accelerator," a fundamental tool for high-energy particle-physics research, in the world. CERN led first in their discovery of "neutral currents" in 1973, just as Rubbia's group at Fermilab made the same discovery. Unfortunately, Rubbia's visa expired and he had to leave, and in his absence, Fermilab published a flawed experiment that hurt Rubbia's reputation. In 1976, Rubbia conceived a brilliant, but seemingly farfetched, plan to modify an existing accelerator to solve the problems of creating "weak-force quanta." Fermilab rejected the idea, but CERN committed 100 million dollars to Rubbia for his crazy project, which would hurl beams of protons and antiprotons against each other to completely destroy each other and be converted to pure energy.

The experiment, against much skepticism, was conducted, and this proved to be the most exciting moment in Rubbia's life, and it won him the Nobel Prize for Physics in 1984. Rubbia confirmed the existence of the three weak-force quanta now known as W-, W+ and Z particles. This victorious verification was hailed as the most important achievement of the century in physics. In 1984, Rubbia and his team announced another dazzling discovery—the detection of the sixth "quark."

Quarks are the basic, indivisible constituents of matter, and the sixth quark, also called "top" or "truth" quark, was the last to be found. These are produced only at extremely high energies such as those that occurred during the "big bang."

The "Alitalia scientist" made a significant step toward the confirmation of the unified-field theory and brought us closer to understanding the creation of the universe! Carlo Rubbia has brought the precious Holy Grail of physics within human reach.

In addition to his search for the secret of the universe, Rubbia has tried to disprove the long-standing belief that matter is stable by searching for evidence of this in an abandoned silver mine in Utah, is looking for the hypothetical "magnetic monopole," which has one pole or electric charge instead of the usual two, searching for evidence of this in an abandoned iron smelter in Wisconsin, is searching for antimatter throughout the universe and hopes to use the space shuttle to detect cosmic rays!

Robert Charles Gallo, research scientist and virologist at the National Cancer Institute in Bethesda, Maryland, is responsible for making a quantum leap forward in finding a cure for the epidemic disease Acquired Immune Deficiency Syndrome or AIDS. Gallo was born in 1937 in Waterbury, Connecticut. When he was thirteen years old, his younger sister contracted leukemia and ultimately died from this disease. This painful experience motivated Gallo toward a career in medical research and turned him away from regular patient care. Gallo entered Jefferson Medical College in Philadelphia, obtaining his degree in 1963. He interned and did his residency at the University of Chicago from 1963 to 1965. The National Cancer Institute hired him as a clinical associate in 1965 and by 1968, he was appointed to the post of senior investigator.

Gallo became intrigued by the new theory linking viruses to the cause of cancer. By 1975, he had isolated a human leukemia virus, but this turned out to be a virus associated with leukemia in monkeys. After this perplexing experience, Gallo and his team set out to create a "growth factor" to sustain malignant human "T-cells," which direct the body's immune system. Gallo isolated the unknown virus from the blood of a leukemia patient and from the T-cells cultivated in his laboratory. He named the virus "human T-cell leukemia virus," and its two variants are now called HTLV–I and HTLV–II.

With the virus now identified, Gallo began research into its precise character. He compiled an international dossier of leukemia cases from all over the world and noticed that HTLV-related leukemia was rare in the United States but common in Africa, the Caribbean and Japan. He also found out that it was passed from person to person by intimate contact or through blood transfusions. Thus, the HTLV virus was confirmed as a carcinogen and as a "retrovirus" that inverts the DNA-RNA cell-reproduction process. This means the actual cell becomes a factory for new viral genetic particles that go unrecognized by the body's immune system.

In 1981, this monumental work by Gallo on viruses became significant when the inexplicable and fatal new disease, AIDS, began killing an alarming number of patients, primarily homosexuals and intravenous drug users. Gallo immediately noticed the geographic distribution of HTLV. In 1982, he proposed that AIDS might be caused by an HTLV-related virus and suspected that the AIDS virus "wiped out its own tracks" by killing the cells it infected. Gallo and his team were able to identify the AIDS virus and although different from HTLV–I and HTLV–II, it bore such close resemblance to these, he named it HTLV–III or "Human T-cell Lymphotropic Virus, Type Three." Along the way, Gallo and his research group discovered a new herpes-like virus called "human B-lymphotropic virus" or HBLV. This discovery has opened up a whole new field of virology.

Gallo is now searching for a treatment for AIDS victims and a vaccine that halts its transmission. Robert Gallo has earned many prestigious awards, including two Lasker awards, usually a prelude to a Nobel Prize. While the cure for AIDS remains an enigma, Robert Gallo's greatest reward may be knowing he could be the one to save the rest of humanity from the tragic and fatal consequences of the AIDS epidemic.

Unbeknowest to most, Federico Faggin is the man responsible for the creation and development of "silicon gate technology" and the microprocessor, the key element in computer technology. A microprocessor is the integrated circuit that interprets and executes instructions from a computer program. When combined with other integrated circuits that provide storage for data and programs, often on a single semiconductor base to form a chip, the microprocessor functions as the heart of a small computer or microcomputer. The creation of the microprocessor made possible such modern inventions as the hand-held electronic calculator, the digital wristwatch and the electronic game. It is also used in a myriad of consumer appliances and computerized devices of every conceivable use. While computers had already been invented, and everyone in the computer technology field was talking about such a device, it was Faggin who actually did it. The microprocessor was an idea whose time had come, and Faggin was the one to create it.

Federico Faggin, from Vicenza, Italy, studied physics at the University of Padua from 1961 to 1965 and received his doctorate *summa cum laude*. He came to America in early 1968 to join the Fairchild Semiconductor Company in the Silicon Valley section of northern California. Faggin developed the original silicon gate technology for the fabrication of high-performance integrated circuits, which make possible memories and microprocessors. This basic, valuable, breakthrough work opened the way for many computer advances in 1968.

Just after Faggin's work here was completed, his boss and several others left Fairchild Semiconductor to form Intel, based precisely on Faggin's research and development. In early 1970, Faggin joined Intel to be the one to create and develop the first microprocessor for them. A Japanese company commissioned Intel and put up the money to develop the microprocessor. The firm wanted to manufacture electronic calculators and Intel proposed the development of the microprocessor and the memory chips to do the job. Intel got the contract, but needed Faggin to create what they had been proposing.

Faggin created the first microprocessor for Intel, and, as a result, the first actual manufactured pieces off the assembly line of the microprocessor, the Intel #4004, bore the initials "FF" for Federico Faggin. However, Faggin was disturbed after he had invented this wondrous technology that Intel had signed with the Japanese company on an exclusive basis. He felt the application of the technology should be industry-wide, so he proposed that the deal be renegotiated to drop the exclusivity proviso in exchange for a lower price. This done, Faggin then hit the road to promote, publicize and market the many applications of the "FF microprocessor" and he succeeded. Intel became a huge corporation, but Faggin and Ralph Ungerman, who worked for him at Intel, left to form their own company called Zilog, Inc. in 1975.

Faggin got Exxon Enterprises to fund Zilog, Inc. as a venture capitalist, and the company made money from its inception, using the technology he developed at Intel and thus becoming its competitor. He left Zilog in 1980 and in 1982 he founded Cygnet Technology, which specialized in voice and data work, and he sold it in 1986.

Federico Faggin then created his new company called Synaptics, Inc., which is doing very progressive and farsighted work in "neurosystems" and "nontraditional artificial intelligence." He is investigating the functionality and application of neural (brain) tissue to the solutions of "intelligent machines." He is breaking new ground in the field of artificial intelligence by using the brain, rather than the traditional concept of the computer, as a paradigm for a system.

Rocco A. Petrone, born in 1926 in Amsterdam, New York, studied at the Massachusetts Institute of Technology and received his degree in mechanical engineering in 1952. Upon graduation, he became totally involved with the American space program, and it was his voice that guided Neil Armstrong to the famous first step on the moon in July 1969. It was Petrone's job as Apollo program director of NASA to get those astronauts to the moon and back home to Earth safely.

Petrone first worked on the Redstone Missile Development Project in Huntsville, Alabama from 1952 to 1955. He served as a member of the U.S. Army general staff in Washington, D.C., from 1956 to 1960, and then became the manager of the Apollo Program at Kennedy Space Center from 1960 to 1966. He worked as director of launch operations from 1966 to 1969. He then was promoted to director of the Apollo Program, and thus directed the first landing of a man on the moon.

Petrone continued his brilliant career in the NASA Space Program and then joined private industry. He became president of Rockwell International, one of the prime manufacturers and contract suppliers to the program. It is particularly relevant that the name *Columbia* is used on the spaceships that hurtle human beings beyond the known world, just as Columbus did in his three tiny ships.

John R. Casani, the brilliant director of a magnificent dream—the fantastic Galileo Project to send a spacecraft to Jupiter, was born in 1932 in Philadelphia. He graduated from the University of Pennsylvania in 1955 with a bachelor's degree in electrical engineering and joined the Jet Propulsion Laboratory in 1956 to design inertial guidance systems for guided missiles. He has played key engineering roles in the most important space projects of our country, if not the world, including *Explorer I*, the *Pioneer, Ranger,* and *Mariner* rockets and the first probes of the Moon and other planets. In 1974, Casani was honored with NASA's Outstanding Leadership Medal for his "leadership as Spacecraft System Manager of the Mariner Venus-Mercury 1973 Project." In 1981, he won the National Space Club's Astronautics Engineer award for his "outstanding direction of the Voyager Project."

Casani is now director of the Galileo Project, so-named for the four moons of Jupiter that Galileo observed with his telescope and which convinced him that Copernicus was correct in arguing that the Earth went around the Sun, not the other way around. It is fitting that the Galileo mission, which may tell us what the "stuff of the universe" may be and something about the creation of the cosmos, be named in Galileo's honor. It is also a fitting tribute to the creative energy of Italian American science and engineering that John Casani is the guiding spirit and force behind this project.

From Galileo to the Galileo Mission, Italian Americans are carrying on the torch of fire ignited by the man who founded modern science. Italians are still seeking to discover, understand and know the world, and sharing the joy with all others for the benefit of all mankind.

13

RELIGION

ORGANIZED RELIGION has always been an ambivalent, complex and ambiguous affair for Italian Americans, even though as a group they are highly spiritual. Because Christianity and Roman Catholicism were created, developed and evolved as essentially Italian phenomena, it is not surprising that the Italian missionaries who came after the discovery of the New World played a key role in the history of America's spiritual and, especially, educational life. Nor is it surprising to those who know Italian history that those Italian immigrants who came later were more ambivalent about the church, having experienced centuries of disasters that had, to a great extent, been caused by the Catholic Church and the Papal States. The Risorgimento and its aftermath would change the religious life of Italians significantly.

Before the Italians, other Catholics had immigrated to the United States, but the way Italians expressed their faith set them apart from other Catholic immigrants. The southern Italian peasants who immigrated to America in the late 1800s and early 1900s considered their version of Catholicism to be separate from the church hierarchy. These southern immigrants saw the Roman Catholic Church as more of a political entity than a religious one. They viewed their religious practices as separate from the political affiliations of the leaders of the Roman Catholic hierarchy. As a result, many other ethnic groups suspected the Italians' loyalty to the church's leaders because of their politics.

These schisms were deep-rooted and had developed over many centuries. The roots of contemporary Italian religious traditions, customs and rituals date back to early times. The ascension of Christianity took place in the transition from ancient times to medieval times and paralleled the decline of the Roman Empire. By the fourth century, Christianity had taken hold as a majority religion, replacing traditional paganism, Mithraism, Stoicism and Manicheism. In 325, the Emperor Constantine convened the First Council of Nicaea to squelch the Arian heresy. This council rejected Arianism, but also reinterpreted the mystical teachings of Christ and adapted them to the political needs of the papacy at the time.

With the fall of the Roman Empire, ironically caused in part by the rise of Christianity, it was Christianity itself, as a religion and philosophy, that maintained a unifying force keeping Italians together as a people. The church was centered in Rome and had become strongly impregnated with Roman values, customs and traditions, many of them pagan in origin. Thus, Catholicism evolved and remained for many centuries an especially Italian phenomenon. And Rome was the center of what became a worldwide, universal and truly catholic world-state. As a religious philosophy and as an institution, Catholicism has survived intact with significant changes in the eleventh, sixteenth and twentieth centuries.

Saint Augustine, the brilliant Christian theologian, had immense influence on Christianity in the early fourth century, and all Christian theologians, Roman Catholic and Protestant, revere him as the founder of theology. His *City of God* is a monumental defense of Christianity against paganism and we owe our concept of sin and redemption to Augustine. However, it was Saint Gregory the Great who enunciated the theological distinctiveness of Catholicism in the last half of the sixth century. He established the supremacy of the pope and his temporal power on Earth, and the present-day Catholic liturgy comes from him.

It is also to Saint Gregory that contemporary Italian Catholics owe many of their religious practices and beliefs. Gregory freely and allegorically interpreted the Bible and put forth his ideas in many writings. He believed in a Christianity that was oriented to praying to the Blessed Virgin and the various saints as intermediaries between people and God. Care of departed souls in the afterlife was paramount and the afterlife was inhabited by a hierarchy of angels and demons who have influence here on Earth. This truly appealed to Italians, who had for centuries honored the souls of their ancestors and worshipped many deities. Ironically, it was Saint Gregory who was most responsible for impregnating Christianity with pagan elements that would continue to present day.

The formulation of rationalist Catholic philosophy owes its heritage to Augustine and Gregory primarily. Catholicism became different from all other religions because it added the rational process to its belief system. To the intuitional grasping of a religious belief as an act of faith was added the intellectual process of explanation and justification for religious truth. Catholicism shaped the destiny of mankind as a religion but also, unintentionally, saved the use of reason from extinction during the Dark Ages. This would come back to haunt Catholicism during the Age of Science.

Political conflicts in the church hierarchy always played an important role in world history, aside from theological battles. In 1054, a dispute over a theological question split the Christian Church into the Roman Catholic Church and the Greek Orthodox Church, creating two separate church hierarchies— one in Rome and the other in Greece. Two different civilizations evolved around these hierarchies. Later, disagreements between the popes and other European political leaders instigated the great upheaval of the Protestant Reformation initiated by Martin Luther. This created the Protestant Churches and led to battles between Catholics and Protestants in much of Europe.

During the Middle Ages, the popes took advantage of their political authority and the wealth it brought them to rebuild Rome, which had fallen into decline after the split in 1054 that had divided the church as well as the Roman Empire. During the time of great artistic renewal, the Renaissance, the popes and wealthy noble families, such as the Medicis, sponsored artists and artisans throughout the world. Once again, Rome became the center of commerce as well as the center of Christianity. In addition, the papacy virtually controlled artistic commissions and the content of all artistic projects. So, as interest in Greek and Roman art increased, the power of the papacy was strengthened.

Eventually, the Roman Catholic popes ruled the area surrounding Rome, called the Papal States. Until the newly unified nation of Italy took away most of its property in 1873, the church was the largest single landowner in Italy. Because of the political power of the church hierarchy, Italian peasants regarded parish priests as noblemen who often sided with the rich landowners against them. As a result of these factors, the Italians' attitude toward the church as an institution became sometimes distrustful and anticlerical. Italian Catholics wound up putting more faith in the power of individual saints than in the clergy, whom they saw as agents of the rich and cruel landowners.

Because the southern Italians' heritage developed from many different cultures and influences, Catholicism became an unusual Italian mix of ancient values, concepts and symbols. Italian Catholicism developed into a unique philosophy that helped the Italian peasants cope with life's problems. They prayed to the saints for help with these problems and found escape by celebrating their faith with festive parades, in which they carried statues pinned with money through the streets while musicians played and vendors sold Italian food. These joyful and jubilant *festas* were held on holy days and the feast days of saints.

When the Italians arrived in America in the late 1880s, the Catholic clergy were, like their congregations, predominantly Irish. The Italians' dramatic and enigmatic rituals, religious expression and forms of worship seemed outrageous, flamboyant and pagan to the somber Roman Catholics, especially the Irish. The festive street parades, wildly colorful spectacles and almost circus-like competitions, such as "climbing the greasepole," stunned the pious, dignified and reverential Irish Catholic laity and priests.

Nor could the Italians understand the somber, serious and fire-and-brimstone ways of the Irish. The Irish thought the flamboyant Italian religious customs attracted too much attention and opened Catholics to ridicule. Tensions grew, and many priests prohibited Italians from attending regular church services. Many times the Italians were relegated to hearing mass in the church basements. The Irish priests pressured the Italians to abandon public shows of religious fervor and discouraged the mysticism of Italian Catholicism. What a fabulous irony—the Roman Catholic Church, an essentially Italian creation, was now rejecting its original inventors!

With a history in Italy of resentment toward the church, with a language problem, with an unwillingness to support the parishes through weekly contributions (better to send money home to Italy), and with rejection and hostility from the Irish prelates, Italian immigrants were left to worship in their own way. And, during this time, they often kept their children away from the Catholic schools because the clergy encouraged them to give up Italian traditions and customs.

The Italian immigrants responded to all this effrontery by pressuring the Church to establish separate Italian parishes. The bishops at first refused, but finally allowed national parishes with no geographic or neighborhood boundaries. Italian immigrants joined together to create these parishes. They raised money, donated labor and built churches throughout America.

Despite their reluctant welcome into the American Catholic Church, the Italian immigrants held firmly to their beliefs. They continued their customs, traditions and rituals because they were a focal point of family life. Their religion set the tone for numerous family experiences—baptisms, first communions, confirmations, weddings, funerals, feast days and even Sunday after-mass dinners. And although many second-generation Italian Americans married outside their ethnic group, they usually married other Catholics.

While Italians were finding little acceptance from the clergy, Protestant ministers stepped in to meet the spiritual and physical needs of the immigrants. During the early twentieth century, the Protestant evangelical movement opened soup kitchens and recreation and education centers in Italian neighborhoods. The Protestant churches' involvement with the Italian Catholics finally spurred the Catholic Church to begin helping Italian immigrants. In 1891, the Irish Archbishop Michael Corrigan organized the Society of Saint Raphael to aid Italian immigrants and established a temporary shelter in New York City for women and children. The Catholic clergy began to involve Italian Americans in activities associated with holy days and feast days of saints, as well as social organizations.

During this period, the Protestant missionaries continued to have an effect on the Italian population. By 1910, more than three hundred Protestant missionaries were working fulltime in Italian American communities. Help from the Protestant clergy combined with the prevailing anti-Catholic sentiment created a small fervor for conversion—by 1916, fifty thousand Italians had joined American Protestant churches. Many saw this as a way to "become more American." On the other hand, however, many Italians felt compelled to stay Catholic, as painful as this may have been, for it represented staying Italian or maintaining their *Italianità*.

Monsignor Geno Baroni, founding president of the National Italian American Foundation, says the Church taught the immigrants "how to be Americans by running away from our cultural heritage, our accents, our language, our food." But, the Italians did not learn these lessons well.

There is a bitter irony to this Catholic Italian American experience in that there were many significant contributions by the early missionary fathers and by many other Italians before the mass migrations. The Jesuits in particular made great achievements in education. Here and there throughout America, Italian American clergy made their impact felt. Father Charles Constantine Pise was the first priest born in America of Italian descent, in 1801 in Maryland. He became the first Catholic chaplain of the U.S. Congress in 1832 and wrote the first Catholic novel, *Father Rowland, A North American Tale*. Father Joseph Rosati was the first bishop of the new diocese of St. Louis, Missouri, in 1827 and built the first hospital and orphanage in the midwest. His school for deaf-mutes was the first of its sort in the United States. In 1870, Ignazio Persico became the bishop of the diocese of Savannah, Georgia. Benedict Aestini was a well-known priest of the nineteenth century.

The immigrant experience, however, was a mass phenomenon quite different from any previous religious participation in America. Faced with the desperate needs of the millions of Italian Americans, the church hierarchies in Italy and America sought ways to meet the spiritual needs of the immigrants. Various religious orders were called upon, such as the Franciscans, Jesuits, Pallotines and Salesians, to help by establishing schools, churches, missions and social centers in Italian communities. For example, in 1859, the Franciscans founded St. Anthony of Padua on Sullivan Street in New York City to serve the Italian immigrants. It continues to do so. Churches like this were established all across America.

Eventually, the church in Rome sent priests and nuns who spoke both English and Italian to teach and preach in America. Italian Americans gradually began sending their children to the Catholic schools. A significant step was taken when Pope Leo XIII, with Bishop Giovanni Battista Scalabrini as its founder, established the Apostolic College of Priests in Piacenza, Italy, in 1887 to prepare priests for Italian American parishes.

Scalabrini became known as the "Father of the Immigrants" and his Scalabrinians created many missions, parishes, schools and social centers in Italian American communities across the country. The Scalabrini fathers fought to set up national parishes and helped establish the tradition of the colorful street festas in honor of patron saints. The music, processions, dancing, food, drink, fun and fireworks attracted numerous crowds, and the money made from these festas was used to support the churches and schools in the communities. The Scalabrinians, along with all the other orders, helped in major ways to bring together the Italian Catholic immigrants and the American Catholic Church.

Perhaps the most significant religious contribution to America was made when Mother Francesca Xavier Cabrini was enlisted by Pope Leo XIII in 1889 to come to America with her Missionary Sisters of the Sacred Heart to help serve the spiritual needs of the Italian immigrants.

St. Frances Xavier Cabrini, born in 1850 in Sant Angelo of Lodi on the plains of Lombardy, Italy, was raised in a modest Christian home and became enthralled by tales of foreign missionaries. When she was a child she felt sure that God had called her. During her teens, an old servant became ill and Francesca cared for her in all her basic needs. From then on, her mission of caring for the sick and needy became clear for her life. In 1880, at age thirty, Cabrini was granted permission to use an old Franciscan monastery in Godono with seven young women to live and work with her. While renovating the chapel, she could not fit a statue into a niche on the alter, so she substituted a picture of the Sacred Heart, which became the symbol for her newly born order, the Missionary Sisters of the Sacred Heart of Jesus, and which was approved in 1888 by Pope Leo XIII.

Cabrini first wanted to venture into China as a foreign missionary, but Pope Leo urged her to go instead to America where she could be of greater service to the Italians who were moving there in droves. With a group of dedicated nuns, Cabrini went off to New York City, where she found herself, along with many other poor immigrants, in the most slovenly quarters and poorest living conditions. These first Italian immigrants could not speak English well enough to get any "social aid," were poor and unable to afford doctors or hospitals and found themselves unfairly characterized as criminals and lowlifes. It was Cabrini who sought to help these poor immigrants by providing for all their basic needs. Also, she played a pivotal role between Italians and Americans by interpreting each to the other.

Mother Cabrini, though she suffered through the rampant anticlericism of the Italian immigrants, was looked upon as an angel of mercy descended from heaven when she went about door-to-door bringing food, medicine and clothing to the poor Italians. She and her dedicated sisters, despite many heartbreaking experiences and terrible frustrations, persevered in their noble ministry. Cabrini's vision created elementary and secondary schools, hospitals and orphanages, colleges and training schools for nurses, and educated young people in music, art, dancing, sewing, typewriting and cooking. Her work took her to such diverse places as Chicago, Illinois, Pennsylvania, Colorado, Seattle, Washington, California, New Orleans, Louisiana, South America and Europe. She crossed mountains and oceans to fulfill her mission, and by the time she was done, her rich heritage included sixty-seven flourishing foundations for charitable work, of which thirty-seven were in America.

Mother Cabrini finally succumbed to overwork and a bout with malaria and died in 1917. One thousand devoted sisters carried on her visionary caring work in service to others. She became known as the Patron Saint of the Immigrants and countless Italians were relieved of their misery and able to make a rich contribution to their adopted land because of her work. She was mourned deeply by many people in many countries who had been helped by her and inspired by her loving and giving nature.

Mother Frances Xavier Cabrini was canonized on July 7, 1946 as the first and only American Roman Catholic saint. Her feast day is November 13.

"In the beginning was the Word and the Word was with God and the Word was God," and the Word was with the Eternal Word Television Network founded by a most amazing woman, Mother Mary Angelica, in 1981. Through her zealous and devoted efforts, the Word is broadcast on the world's first Catholic cable television network to 10.8 million homes by 331 cable systems in 36 states and 3 broadcast systems. We've had the "singing nun," the "flying nun" and now, the "broadcasting nun."

This remarkable woman, Mother Mary Angelica, was born in 1923 in Canton, Ohio, as Rita Francis and grew up in a spiritually enriched Italian neighborhood where her local parish church played a key role in her life. Here she attended mass, went to school, enjoyed herself at dances and thrilled to the joy of Italian street festas. She grew up in an Italian family with a father who came from Calabria and a mother whose parents immigrated here from Naples. This warm, rich and joyful religious background would set the stage for the making of this most creative spiritual woman of God.

In 1944, Rita Francis entered religious life as Sister Mary Angelica by joining the Franciscan Nuns of the Most Blessed Sacrament in Cleveland, Ohio. She toiled in her religious life from 1946 at the Santa Clara Monastery in Canton, Ohio, and in 1962 took on the enormous task of founding Our Lady of the Angels Monastery in Birmingham, Alabama. By 1973, she had created and initiated a book apostolate of 15 million books in distribution throughout the world to thirty-eight countries. And she has authored fifty-seven books on the spiritual life, including among her titles *Dawn on the Mountain, Ad Lib with the Lord* and *Knowing God's Will.* In addition to this monumental creative and spiritual output, Mother Angelica began making television shows for nationwide broadcast on the Christian Broadcasting Network and herein lies a tale.

In 1980, Mother Angelica complained to the manager of the television station, for whom she was a good customer doing shows, about a movie she felt mocked Jesus Christ. The manager refused her request, so she stormed out of the studio, announcing her intention to strike out on her own. "I don't need you," she told the startled manager, "I only need God. I'll buy my own cameras and build my own studio." She arrived back at the monastery to find a construction crew working on a foundation for a new garage and she immediately told the foreman to make the building 10 feet wider and 10 feet longer. She proclaimed to everyone's surprise, "We're going to build a television studio!"

One year later, on August 15, 1981, with a motto of "Your Spiritual Growth Network," the Eternal Word Television Network went on the air for the first time at 6:00 P.M. and became the fastest growing basic cable network in the country, now boasting over 10 million viewers.

This remarkable enterprise was the dream of a determined woman of God, a nun with little money, a handful of supporters and a big idea. In spite of many skeptics, E.W.T.N. reached high success through the devout determination of a single-minded, awe-inspiring woman. Yet Mother Angelica may disagree, for as she says, "Any number of times I've turned to the Lord and said 'O my God, what have I done?' But He has provided everything we need. When we need a certain kind of equipment or a repair to some of our equipment, God takes care of it. He really wants this network to succeed. . . . This network has not succeeded because of me. It is God's doing."

Bishop Francis J. Mugavero was born in Brooklyn, the son of Sicilian immigrants who came here as children from two small towns (Caltavuturo and Collesano) near Palermo. His father was a barber and he grew up in a very close-knit family of three boys and three girls in a poor section. Pushed to study hard, he went to parochial school and then decided to attend Cathedral High School in preparation for life as a priest. By 1968, Mugavero was ordained bishop of the diocese of Brooklyn, thus becoming the first Italian American to attain this high position in the largest diocese in the United States. Brooklyn has become known as the diocese of immigrants and Bishop Mugavero has been highly successful in addressing the specific needs of immigrants both old and new. Mass is celebrated in seventeen languages across his diocese.

Joseph Cardinal Bernardin, born and raised in Columbia, South Carolina, became head of the archdiocese of the Catholic Church in Chicago, the second largest diocese in the nation. His father and six brothers had immigrated to America from the small town of Tonadico in the Primiero valley of Trent in northern Italy in the 1920s, first coming to Vermont and then to Columbia in the South. In 1927, his father returned to Italy to marry his mother and he was born in 1928 in Columbia.

Bernardin's story is somewhat unique in that there were very few Italians in South Carolina or in the South generally. These few stuck together and knew each other well. He went to St. Peter's School and grew up in a devoutly religious environment. With his one sister, they were the only Italian Catholic kids in the neighborhood and they strove to become American. He enrolled at the University of South Carolina with an interest in medicine, but decided to become a priest after one year. His decision was based on a commitment to be of service to people, and he then enrolled at St. Mary's College in Kentucky. He graduated St. Mary's Seminary in Baltimore with a degree in philosophy and studied theology at Catholic University in Washington, D.C., and got his master's in education. He was ordained a priest in 1952.

Bernardin served the church as a priest in the diocese of Charleston, as auxiliary bishop of Atlanta, and now oversees the diocese of Chicago as the first and only Italian American cardinal since 1983. He has brought a richness to the Catholic Church through a passionate commitment to cultural diversity on the one hand and to a basic solidarity of all Catholics united by one faith on the other hand. He has become nationally known and controversial for his opposition to the nuclear arms race and his struggle for world peace as chairman of the Bishop's Committee.

14

THE ARTS

ITALIANS HAVE always had a flair for the arts, for drama, for spectacle, for music, for writing, for storytelling, for the visual, for aesthetics, for design and for beauty. Anyone who has grown up in an Italian family surely understands what grand opera is all about. This is unquestionably rooted in a sense of making life, with all its joys and sorrows, into art. And what better way to live? What higher form of art is there than the art of living? It is as if art and life are inseparable for the Italian American, and the expression of self is an absolute essential to life, as vital as breathing and eating. Italians take everything and make an art of it!

If anything characterizes the Italian American nature, it is a powerful creative drive. There is a kind of artistic ethos and aesthetic sensibility that makes Italians unique, and this goes back as far as the Etruscans.

Etruscan objects of art, especially jewelry, were truly timeless in their aesthetic beauty. The Romans continued this tradition of exceptional art and design, examples of which can *still* be seen throughout Europe. The Renaissance then produced the largest single explosion of creativity and art in the history of the world. Its effect on Western civilization was monumental. That creativity crossed every spectrum of the human experience and brought us the opening of the new world, the dawn of modern civilization and the very creation of modern science. This rich heritage and culture, in one form or

271

another, has been carried forward in the spirit of Italians and Italian Americans.

It is easy to see the legacy of an illustrious artistic past evidenced in the activities of those Italians who came to America. Whether fixing shoes, sewing clothing, cooking pasta, or, indeed, engaging in any other kind of labor, craft or artisanship, Italian immigrants evidenced a strong pride of creative expression.

To some extent this creativity may be due to the fact that Italian immigrants came from a country that had spent its whole history in the violent clutches of constant change. Between eras of greatness and demise, there had been invaders from within and outside its borders. Many came to "visit" and many came to stay, but whatever the case, each influenced the culture and the civilization. And Italians survived; some were the better for it and some were worse off, but one thing was sure—the Italians became a very creative people in the process of adapting to these changing worlds.

Perhaps the sense of constant change made them want to freeze life in time and space so it would stay the same, impermeable, eternal—so it could be understood and dealt with. But isn't that what art does anyway? Pluck emotional, intellectual and spiritual realities from eternity, freeze joys, fears and anxieties in time and space, and help us live our lives? Does it not provide us with a way of dealing with the human experience, positive or negative, with life itself, in a meaningful way?

Whatever the case, the truth of the matter is clear enough. Italian Americans have contributed so much to the creative arts, it is just impossible to cover everyone! So, while we hope to create, in our own artistic way, a general picture of artistic contribution, we have chosen an array of representative people to cover in some detail in each category. We apologize to the other millions of Italian American artists we may have inadvertently omitted.

OPERA

Acting is in the blood of every Italian. Emotion, drama, humor, virtuosity, passion, spectacle, gesture, adornment and embellishment are vital. Symbols and appearance

are everything. Life must be lived artfully and displayed
dramatically. The expression is the thing expressed. Form
and substance are one. Feast the eyes! Swell the heart! The
show's the thing! Which brings us to opera, grand and otherwise.

Opera began in Florence and was quintessentially an Italian
invention. While Giulio Caccini and Iacopo Peri wrote
Eurydice, considered the first opera, Claudio Monteverdi is
considered the creator of opera. The first opera house, Teatro
San Cassiano, opened in Venice with Manelli's *Andromedie.*
Giuseppe Verdi united Italians with his music before they were
united politically.

From 1805, Lorenzo Da Ponte popularized opera in Ameri-
ca and zealously promoted opera and the building of opera
houses. The first Italian American opera singer was Eliza
Ostinelli, the daughter of the famous conductor Louis
Ostinelli. At one time, if an aspiring opera star did not have an
Italian name, there was no chance of success.

Soprano Rosa Ponselle, born in 1897 in Meriden, Connecticut, was discovered by the impresario William Thorner when
he heard her sing in a vaudeville act with her sister Carmela,
billed as the Ponzillo sisters. Thorner got an audition for her at
the Metropolitan Opera Company and she captivated the great
Enrico Caruso with whom she soon debuted in 1918 as
Leonora in *La Forza del Destino.* After an instant success,
Ponselle went on to a triumphant operatic career until 1936
when she retired from opera after marrying Carle A. Jackson,
a wealthy industrialist.

Soprano Licia Albanese, born in 1913 in Bari, Italy, studied
at the Bari Conservatory, then with Giuseppina Baldassare-
Tedeschi and debuted as Mimi in *La Boheme* in 1934. She sang
at La Scala many times together with Beniamino Gigli. Her
lyrical and musical soprano voice was perfect for Verdi and
Puccini roles. In 1940, she came to America to begin a
twenty-year tenure at the Met and in 1942 she reached a
supreme height in a triumphant performance as Violetta in *La
Traviata.*

Anna Moffo, born in 1933 in Wayne, Pennsylvania, studied
at the Curtis Institute of Music and then at the Academia di
Santa Cecilia in Rome. She debuted in 1955 at the Rome

Opera and went on to many other opera houses, including La Scala. In 1959, she had her debut at the Met as Violetta in *La Traviata* and continued to give moving performances there.

Renata Tebaldi, one of the greatest sopranos of her time, was born in 1922 in Pesaro, Italy. As a child, she was stricken with polio, but her warm, loving Italian mother cared for her and nursed her through this illness to health. She studied singing at the Boito Conservatory in Parma and made her debut in Rovigo as Elena in *Mefistofele* in 1943. After the war, Arturo Toscanini signed her for La Scala. A series of worldwide tours brought her great critical acclaim, and she made her debut at the Met as Desdemona in 1955. She went on to become a brilliant soprano and her dazzling performances have stirred audiences around the world.

One of the best tenors ever, Mario Del Monaco was born in Florence in 1915 and studied at the Conservatory of Pesaro where he also learned painting and sculpture. He won a prize in a singing contest and made his debut at the Teatro Puccini while on leave from the army in World War II. He played several sensational performances and went on tour with the Teatro San Carlo in 1948, which made him internationally known. After performing in several opera houses, he debuted at the Met and became one of its members in 1951. Acclaimed worldwide, he possesses a powerful vocal expression and vibrant high register that have made him famous for his singing of Verdi and Puccini roles.

Loretta Di Franco, a lyric coloratura at the Metropolitan Opera, was born in 1942 in Brooklyn and studied at Juilliard School of Music and Hunter College. She won the first prize of the Metropolitan Opera National Auditions and joined the Met as a member of the chorus, becoming a soloist there in 1965 when she debuted in *Pique Dame*. Di Franco has also performed in concerts, choruses, festivals and on radio and television, winning many awards for her bright, lyrical operatic singing.

Gian-Carlo Menotti, born in Cadegliano in 1911, came to the United States in 1928 and became a composer, librettist, playwright, scriptwriter and director. He has accumulated an impressive array of creative achievements with *Amelia Goes to the Ball, The Old Maid and the Thief, Sebastian* and *Amahl and the Night Visitors* among them. *The Consul* in 1950 and *The Saint of Bleecker Street* in 1954 both won Menotti the Pulitzer Prize. He also studied at the Curtis Institute of Music in Philadelphia and taught composition there from 1948 to 1955. He created the Festival of Two Worlds at Spoleto, Italy, and Charleston, South Carolina, which brings old and new world music together. Menotti is a gifted, original and unique composer who has reached the top of the opera world as the preeminent master of the musical-drama form. He is the dean of Italian American composers with over twenty operas to his credit.

Beni Montresor has become an award-winning stage and scenic designer. His creative work was honored in 1981 with a twenty-year retrospective show at the Lincoln Center Library for the Performing Arts in New York City. He has created set designs and scenery for over thirty operas at the Metropolitan Opera, The New York City Opera, the Festival of Two Worlds and many other opera houses. Montresor is regarded as one of the most artistic, creative and best stage designers in the art.

Carl Princi, well-known opera host, narrator and actor, began his career in a New England stock company and entered broadcasting in Boston. He has made many albums and has appeared in over forty movies and television productions. In 1953, Princi joined KFAC in Los Angeles and became vice president of programming and community involvement, serving until 1987. His opera programs were popular across the West as the original host of "World of Opera" and "Opera House." He has done more than anyone else to promote opera through his lectures, courses, radio and television shows, and recordings. With his wife, Althea, he hosts the popular "World of Opera" Tours all around the world. The winner of many awards for his achievements in the cause of opera and the arts, Princi is considered the nation's top opera authority.

Opera impresario Alfredo Salmaggi came to New York in

1905 and devoted sixty years to popularizing opera. He staged performances for large crowds and charged only a quarter for admission. His productions were grandly presented at stadiums and at Madison Square Garden for all to enjoy. Vincent La Selva, born and raised in Cleveland, Ohio, the son of immigrants, continues the tradition of bringing opera to the people through his New York Grand Opera Company. His productions are performed for large crowds in Central Park.

The Metropolitan Opera House is the absolute pinnacle point of success for opera stars. When it opened for its first season, in 1882–83, the conductor chosen was Augusto Vianesi who assembled an orchestra of fifty musicians who were mainly Italian. The golden age of the Met started in 1908 when Giulio Gatti-Casazza came from La Scala of Milan to be its reigning general manager for twenty-seven glorious years until 1935. Arturo Toscanini, the greatest conductor of all time, became the Met's chief conductor and his baton was a magic wand that truly made this era golden. The entire history of a hundred years of the Met saw the greatest performances by Italians from its beginning. By far, the most frequently performed operas at the Met have been Italian.

There have been many, many Italian opera stars, but there was only one Enrico Caruso—The Great Caruso—the most-popular and best-loved tenor in America and Italy, if not the world. Born of a peasant family in 1873 in Naples, Caruso always knew the precious gift of his voice. The beauty, range and vibrant power of it made him one of the greatest of all singers. He was used to living like a king in Italy, so when he moved to New York City, he took a fourteen-bedroom suite at the Hotel Knickerbocker overlooking Broadway in Times Square. Both in person and through his phonograph recordings, he enraptured audiences all over the world. A gifted performer, he was hailed as the greatest tenor in the world.

A man of passionate humanity, deep faith in people and warm humor, Caruso epitomized the very essence of an opera star. With a passion for perfection, he worked on his voice as his instrument. He took a naturally good voice and made it a great one through perseverance and hard work. He also knew that the source of his power and genius was uniquely within his own being as a self-sustaining fire. He loved people for what they were inside and never failed to help anyone in need. He had a deep-seated love for America and America loved him back, with great devotion.

Caruso pushed himself beyond human endurance, and one night in 1920, not knowing he had bronchial pneumonia, he felt blood in his mouth as he sang. His condition worsened, but he refused to stop performing. Towel after towel was passed to him as the blood gushed from his throat. He still continued to sing the aria, to the horror of the audience that began shouting and screaming "Stop him! Stop him!" For the first time ever, Caruso finally relented and stopped but he finished the aria. He died in 1921 at the age of forty-eight and the world mourned the passing of this magnificent artist. Fortunately, The Great Caruso lives on in his recordings.

DANCE

Since the Civil War, Italian Americans have contributed to the dance and ballet of America. Three ballerinas from La Scala danced at Nibla's Garden in New York. Maria Bonfanti and Rita Sangelli danced the principal roles in *The Black Crook*, the longest-running musical of the time. Bonfanti became the *prima ballerina* at the Met from 1888 to 1894 and opened a dance school in New York City. Giuseppina Morlacchi performed in *The Devil's Auction*. She married an Indian scout and toured with him and Buffalo Bill across the West. These three ballerinas helped lay the foundation for the Americanization of ballet.

Today New York City is the dance capital of the world and Italian Americans play a major role in the art of ballet. Gerald Peter Arpino, born in 1928 in Staten Island the son of an immigrant, enlisted in the Coast Guard in 1945 where he met Robert Joffrey, a dance student, while stationed in Seattle. He studied dance and became a member of the Ballet Russe in 1951. He performed on television and in Broadway musicals and joined the original Robert Joffrey Ballet when it was created, in 1953, as one of six dancers. Arpino became the choreographer of the Joffrey.

Peter Gennaro, born in 1924 in New Orleans, became a great dancer and choreographer and has made many appearances on television. He has also performed on Broadway and is a major force in the dance world. Kay Mazzo, born in 1947 in Chicago, joined the New York City Ballet company at age fifteen. A successful and brilliant performer as a ballerina, she became the company's youngest principal dancer at age twenty-two. Mazzo's success has brought her to work with Balanchine and Jerome Robbins.

Louis Falco, born in 1942 in New York City, is a dancer and choreographer who gained an international reputation for his talent. He now directs his own Louis Falco Dance Company. Edward Villela, born in Long Island in 1936, became a principal dancer of the New York City Ballet and choreographer for the New Jersey Ballet. His brilliant dancing and creative choreography have won him worldwide recognition.

Elba Augusta Agata Colomba Farabegoli was born in 1909 in New York City, the only child of Italian immigrants. She studied with Leonard Covello at New York University, who taught her how to use Italian history and cultural materials in community-centered schools. In 1931, she helped found the Folk Festival Council of New York; since then, she has become recognized as the leading advocate of preserving folk traditions. She is known by Italian folk groups nationwide as the founder and moving force behind the Italian Folk Arts Federation of America.

Ann Corio, born in Hartford, Connecticut, won a dance contest at age fifteen and joined a burlesque troupe. Corio was the very personification of the art of stripping and saved burlesque from oblivion with her off-Broadway revue *This Was Burlesque*. No Harvard man could graduate without seeing Ann Corio perform her act.

José Greco, the leading "Spanish dancer" all over the world, was born at Montorio nei Frentani, Campobasso, Italy, in 1918. He came to America in 1928 and studied at Leonardo da Vinci Art School in New York City. He has performed in the United

States, Europe and Latin America as a great Spanish flamenco
dancer.

MUSIC

Music also was essentially Italian—Italians gave music its
orderly seven-tone scale and much of its terminology, such as
basso, falsetto, opera, coloratura, soprano, oratorio, solo, libretto, tempo, piano, viola, piccolo, trombone, timpani, and
many others, including finale. The Italian contribution to the
world of music is overwhelming, but that of the Italian
American is equally significant.

Music seems to be in the blood of Italians—the language
itself is musical and that is why opera is quintessentially Italian.
Anyone who has had an argument with an Italian must think
they're all conductors of orchestras. Italian music is the most
emotionally stirring and primal of all—it reaches into your
soul, it captures your heart, it captivates your mind and carries
you away on an odyssey into the sublime.

We have seen the early contributions in music of Italian
Americans, and the great tradition of these pioneers was
carried on after them by the immigrants who came here in the
late 1800s. Vittorio Giannini, born in 1903 in Philadelphia,
composed many operas, several symphonies, concertos and
choral and chamber works. He was the son of tenor Erruccio
Giannini who founded Verdi Hall and brother of famous
soprano Dusolina Giannini.

Thomas Pasatieri, born in 1945 in New York City, graduated
from Juilliard School of Music, composed sixteen operas and
wrote over five hundred songs. Dominick Argento, born in
York, Pennsylvania, went to the Peabody Institute and the
Eastman School of Music and has composed numerous operas,
choral and orchestral works. Giuseppe Bamboschek, born in
Trieste, came to the U.S. in 1913 and became a conductor,
opera coach and composer. He conducted for the Met from
1913 to 1930 and was musical director of the Philadelphia La
Scala Opera Co. from 1939 to 1946. He conducted his first
concert at age sixteen. Michele Corino, born in 1918 in Cuneo,

Italy, played the accordion professionally at age ten, made over fifty records in Italy and formed his own orchestra in 1940. He came to America in 1947 where he excelled as a composer and orchestra leader.

Vincent Persichetti, born in Philadelphia in 1915, studied at the Philadelphia Conservatory and the Curtis Institute of Music. He has chaired the Composition Department of the Juilliard School of Music since 1963 and is a composer, pianist, conductor, teacher and critic. Walter Piston (Pistone) was born in 1894 in Belmont, Massachusetts, went to Harvard and taught there from 1926 to 1959. He composed eight symphonies and won a Pulitzer Prize for one of them.

David Del Tredici, born in California in 1937, went to the University of California at Berkeley, then got his M.F.A. at Princeton. His compositions have been performed by symphony orchestras around the country, including *Final Alice* which was commissioned for the U.S. Bicentennial of 1976. He is a gifted composer, recital and symphony pianist, as well as a Harvard teacher. Peter Mennin (Mennini), born in 1923 in Erie, Pennsylvania, studied at Oberlin Conservatory and the Eastman School of Music. He composed many symphonies, concertos, and chamber and choral music. He served as president of Juilliard for twenty years. Donald Martino, born in 1931 in New Jersey, is a composer and teacher, and was chairman of the Composition Department at the New England Conservatory. In 1974, he won a Pulitzer Prize for his *Notturno*.

Norman Dello Joio is one of the country's most respected composers and was born in 1913 in New York City. He studied at Juilliard and Yale, and has five honorary doctorates in music to his credit. He was the third generation of Italian organists in his family and his godfather, with whom he studied, was the organist at Saint Patrick's Cathedral. At age fourteen, he became an organist and choir director for a church in City Island, New York. In 1957, he received a Pulitzer Prize for music. His compositions for ballet, opera, symphony and choral groups express his church influence.

But no one can compare with the maestro, Arturo Toscanini. Toscanini, hailed as "the greatest operatic and orchestral conductor of the twentieth century," was born in 1867 in Parma, Italy. Ever since he was a child, Toscanini had an uncanny ear for music. He studied music in Parma and graduated with honors. Working as a cellist in an opera company, he was called upon to conduct when the regular conductor walked off. While the audience was stunned when this inexperienced youth appeared, they were equally stunned when his baton produced an enraptured, perfect performance. He got a standing ovation.

Toscanini performed all over the world, became director of the Teatro alla Scala in 1898 in Milan and came to America in 1908 when he took over the New York City Metropolitan Opera Company. His years at the Met are called the golden era and his concerts at Carnegie Hall were always sold out. In 1937, NBC created an orchestra for him and RCA Victor Company recorded his concerts for broadcast.

Toscanini was an effusive and furious taskmaster. He pursued the perfect symphony with a passionate vengeance and a dynamic energy. His commitment to great music was unrelenting. His mark on the art and craft of conducting is indelible. Toscanini died in New York on January 16, 1957. The whole world mourned the passing of its greatest musician.

Italian Americans are also totally involved in the creative life of popular music, jazz and rock and roll, up to and including rock videos. Many of today's performers share a musical heritage with the greats of classical music. Ponselle, Caruso and Toscanini may be far off from Madonna, Springsteen and Mangione, but they are linked by a common creative sensibility.

The tradition of musical bands goes back to the halls and piazzas of small villages back in Italy. The Italians had a tradition of gathering for festas and celebrations for holidays, weddings, birthdays and for any other conceivable reason for having a good time. Music played an integral part in all these festive occasions. Also, on really special public occasions and national holidays, musical bands were always formed to play in public squares and parks for the whole community. This tradition crossed the Atlantic with the immigrants and blossomed here, so much so that many Americans had their first musical experiences through Italian bands and the free concerts they gave across the country. In 1836, the first band to tour the United States, called "The Comet," was Italian.

Italian Americans dominated the large popular bands across the country. Giuseppe Creatore was one of the most well known masters of the big bandleaders. Carmen Cavallaro, born in New York City, joined the Rudy Vallee orchestra and zoomed to great popularity when he released his album *Dancing In The Dark*. He was famous for his classical adaptations.

The greatest ballroom bandleader was Guy Lombardo, who led his Royal Canadians for forty-eight years, from 1929 to 1977, playing the "sweetest music this side of heaven." New Year's Eve simply was not complete without Lombardo and his band playing at the Grill Room of the Roosevelt Hotel, while millions of people crowded Times Square and millions crowded at home, all across America, to hear or watch the "ball" descend to mark the new year. Guy Lombardo's music is indelibly linked with this experience.

Henry Mancini, born in 1924 in Cleveland, Ohio, played the piccolo at age eight, took up flute and by twelve added the piano. By high school, he knew every Glenn Miller tune by heart. He studied at the Music School of Carnegie Institute of Technology in Pittsburgh and at Juilliard in New York City. After the army, he played with Glenn Miller's band and studied composing. In 1952, he worked on the composing staff of Universal International Pictures and scored many films. In 1958, he had a lucky break when he scored "Peter Gunn," the mystery television series. This success brought him "Mr. Lucky" to score. Mancini became an international success in film scores that won him many Oscars, Grammies and Gold Records. Mancini, a composer, performer and conductor, loves jazz and expresses himself musically in a unique, bold and original instrumentation. Some of his haunting melodies are unforgettable, such as "Moon River" from *Breakfast at Tiffany's* and the theme from *Days of Wine and Roses*. He is the preeminent composer of scores for movies and a great jazz musician.

Giorgio Moroder, born in the Dolomite Mountains of

northern Italy, is a gifted musician/composer/producer hailed as the man who created the sound of the 1980s. Yet he can't read music that well and doesn't know how a Moog works. He left school at age nineteen to play music and began composing. His first hit was "Son of My Father" but his big break came with Donna Summer when together they did "Love to Love You Baby" in 1973, which brought him international recognition. He scored *Midnight Express* in 1978 and won an Oscar for his creative effort on the synthesizer. His other hits include "Flashdance," platinum Donna Summer albums, Blondie's single "Call Me," David Bowie's "Cat People," "Never Ending Story," "Danger Zone" by Kenny Loggins and "Take My Breath Away" by Terry Nunn and Berlin, both from the film *Top Gun*. Moroder moved to Beverly Hills in 1979 and has won several Oscars and Golden Globes. He is considered the top music producer in Hollywood now.

Surprising as it may seem, Italian Americans have greatly contributed to the art of jazz from its beginnings as an originally American form of musical expression, growing out of New Orleans. Nick La Rocca, born in New Orleans the son of Sicilian immigrants, played cornet and trumpet, composed and conducted and became one of the best jazz musicians in America. He made history as the bandleader of the Original Dixieland Jazz Band when they moved from New Orleans to Chicago then to New York. His jazz compositions became classics, and he produced the first recorded jazz.

Joe Venuti, born in 1904, became a jazz violinist when he moved to New Orleans at age twelve and played with Eddie Lang the jazz guitarist whose real name was Salvatore Massaro, born in 1902. The duo became famous in New Orleans and went on to play with the Paul Whiteman Orchestra in New York. Venuti carried on as a soloist when Lang died young. In 1944, he went to Hollywood, appeared in many films, led his own band and cut many records. Venuti is still playing and is respected as the greatest jazz violinist in the history of the art.

Peter Duchin, son of Eddy Duchin the great pianist, was born in 1937 and began to play at age five against his wishes. Nevertheless he became a prominent jazz musician, has recorded several albums, and now composes and writes Broadway musicals. Chick Corea, born in 1914 in Chelsea, Massachusetts, became a pianist, composer and bandleader whose talents cross over from classical to jazz. His many records and albums have all sold in the millions and have brought him national fame.

Charles Frank Mangione, known as Chuck, was born in 1940 and graduated from the Eastman School of Music. He taught here and then began composing jazz and pop music and playing flügelhorn with his quartet. His brilliant jazz and classical quality of performance have thrilled audiences, and his remarkable, unique talent has won him many Grammy Awards and honors.

SINGERS AND ENTERTAINERS

Integrally related to opera and music is, of course, popular singing and the whole world of entertainment. Again, Italian Americans seem to have a monopoly on popular singers and entertainers. Whether vocal or instrumental, Italian American performers have achieved the height of excellence in their art and craft, and they have won the hearts of Americans all across the country. The Italian language is so mellifluous, it just seems to lend itself so well to song.

Many opera stars also sang outside the opera houses and in popular settings. Mario Lanza, one of the greatest tenors of all time, was born in 1921 in Philadelphia, Pennsylvania. He studied at the Berkshire School of Music, performed for Victor Recordings and became successful as a singer through concert tours, radio, opera, recordings and movies. He was the first vocalist to sell 2.5 million albums in history and the first to receive a golden disc for his record company with "Be My Love." Lanza portrayed the life of Enrico Caruso in the movie *The Great Caruso,* and just like Caruso, he became a famous tenor very quickly in a short life. Lanza died in 1959 at only thirty-eight-years old. His early and sudden death came as a shock to all who loved him.

Louis Prima, born in 1912 in New Orleans, became a jazz singer and trumpet player in Los Angeles and then formed his own band, which toured the country. His brother Leon played trumpet and his sister Mary played piano. He became a favorite in the hot clubs of Las Vegas, Lake Tahoe and Reno. Along with his wife, Keely Smith, Sam Butera and the Witnesses, Prima made music throughout the swing era and the 1950s that filled nightclubs and thrilled audiences. Some of his famous compositions are "Brooklyn Boogie," "Oh Babe" and "Sunday Kind of Love."

Frankie Laine (Frank Paul Lo Vecchio) was born in 1913 in Chicago and spent years singing his heart out in restaurants for dinner patrons as a waiter. A record-company executive heard him sing and Laine recorded "That's My Desire," which sold 2 million copies. He followed this hit with many others that sold over a million records each, among them being "Mule Train" in 1949, "Jezebel" in 1951 and "I Believe" in 1952. Laine has performed in every type of entertainment and became famous for a style of singing characterized as loud and full of gyrations.

Johnny Desmond, born in 1921 as Giovanni Alfredo de Simone in Detroit, studied at the Conservatory of Music and went to work with the drummer Gene Krupa later. Glenn Miller discovered Desmond during an airforce tour and helped him to take off. He became a popular, loved entertainer on the nightclub circuit and starred in *Say Darling*, the musical, in 1958. He excelled in classical ballads.

Connie Francis (Concetta Franconero) was born in Newark in 1938 and spent years singing at social functions, weddings and local celebrations. George Scheck put her on his television variety show "Startime" in 1950. She won Arthur Godfrey's "Talent Scouts" first prize, and she sang on the cocktail-lounge circuit. In 1955 she contracted with MGM records. She recorded ten singles and they all flopped. Prepared to give up her career, she enrolled in Rutgers University, but her father recommended she record "Who's Sorry Now" to finish the last record on her contract. The cut was a huge hit, selling a million copies in six months. Now a huge success, she followed up with such classics as "Lipstick on Your Collar" and "My Happiness," and others. She starred in films and sang the lead song for her first film *Where The Boys Are*. Connie Francis became a world-wide star.

Vic Damone (Vito Farinola), born in 1928 in Brooklyn, sang

"There Must Be a Way" to Perry Como as they rode together in an elevator. Como urged him to sing on Arthur Godfrey's "Talent Scouts," and he won a tie for first place. Milton Berle booked him and by twenty years of age, he was making five thousand dollars a week. Though he had a volatile up-and-down life, mostly due to success at an early age, Damone is a superb entertainer who performs to captivated audiences.

Kaye Ballard (Catherine Gloria Balotta) was born in 1926 in Cleveland, Ohio, and persevered to become an actress, comedienne and singer against her family's wishes. She wasn't "pretty enough" for drama class in high school, so she turned to comedy. She went right into burlesque after graduation and soon was on the road with her own show. She toured with Spike Jones's band of musical madmen in 1945 and got a small Broadway part in *Three To Make Ready* in 1946. She had her own television series, "The Mother-in-Laws," with Eve Arden from 1967 to 1969. She is a consummate performer, great comedienne and terrific singer.

Perry Como (Pierino Rolando Como), born in Cannonsburg, Pennsylvania, the seventh son of a seventh son, grew up poor, but by age fourteen, he owned a three-chair barber shop. In 1934, he gave up cutting hair and went on tour with the Ted Weems Band making twenty-eight dollars a week with a wife, a car and a baby. The tour brought Como to Hollywood, where he worked in several movies. He shot to stardom and signed a 25-million-dollar contract with NBC for a weekly television show. This show became memorable for the relaxed and casual Mr. Como sang his way to America's hearts. He has six kids of his own.

Liza Minnelli, dynamic actress and performer, was born in 1946 in Hollywood, California, the daughter of Judy Garland and Vincente Minnelli, a film director from Italy. Minnelli grew up in the movie colony along with the children of many other famous stars. After studying and working in summer stock and off Broadway, Minnelli got the lead role in the Broadway musical *Flora, the Red Menace* in 1965 and she won an Antoinette Perry Award for her performance. For some time, she had to evolve out of her role as Judy Garland's daughter and prove her own talent. In 1968 she was nominated for an Oscar for her role in *The Sterile Cuckoo,* and this convinced the world she was brilliant on her own merits. Since she was also a critical success in the Broadway show *Cabaret,* Minnelli has performed and acted in film, television, on Broadway and in nightclubs and amphitheaters everywhere. Minnelli's explosive talent is exciting and thrilling to experience.

Liberace (Wladziu Valentino Liberace) was born in 1919 in Menasha, Wisconsin, to an Italian father and a Polish mother. His father Salvatore was a musician and taught him and his older brother George to play. Lee and George began in show business with Lee on piano and George on violin. They went on the road with bands and orchestras, and Lee became a master showman by adding glitz, corn, ham and humor to his performances. In 1952, Lee won his own television show and put George in as conductor and violinist. The Liberace show took off like a rocket and shot Lee to international fame. Through the 1950s, he was a top-paid entertainer and a favorite in Las Vegas. Liberace became notorious for his outrageous sequined clothes, his candelabrum on his grand piano, his effeminate voice and his mother or "Mama," who made frequent guest appearances. Though his act was ridiculed, especially by the press and music critics, he was the sweetheart of millions of women over forty, and he made millions of dollars. Sadly, Lee was stricken by AIDS and died in 1987. He was one of the greatest showmen who ever lived.

Dean Martin (Dino Crocetti) was born in 1917 in Steubenville, Ohio, the son of a barber from Italy and a woman just out of the convent in America. Martin quit school to work as a shoe-shine boy and a gas-station attendant. He worked as a boxer, steelworker, cigar-store clerk and a croupier, while singing in cafes as Dino Martini. He learned to sing by watching Bing Crosby movies and couldn't read a note of music. In 1946, while working clubs in New York City and New Jersey, he was on the same bill with Jerry Lewis, who was lip-synching to records as an act. They started kidding around with each other's acts and that's how their own act got started. Martin and Lewis shot to fame. They made sixteen movies for Paramount, including *The Caddy, Jumping Jacks* and *Pardners.*

They broke up in 1956 and made national headlines. Martin ignored the bad press and vindicated his decision by signing a record 34-million-dollar contract with NBC for a weekly television show, which became a popular success. He proved his true talent to the world as an actor, great entertainer, hot nightclub performer and major recording star.

Tony Bennett (Anthony Dominick Benedetto) was born in 1926 in Long Island City and was discovered in 1949 by Bob Hope, who changed his name. He served in the army for two years during World War II and then studied at the American Wing Theatre. Bennett is a remarkable talent who is able to enthrall audiences with the power of his performance and the phrasing of his singing. His direct, sincere presentation is especially suited to live audiences, and as a nightclub performer, he is always a sellout, particularly in Las Vegas. He is one of a dwindling group of classic pop singers. His fidelity to his craft has made him a supreme singing artist and he is also a gifted painter. His most memorable image for the world may be his most requested song "San Francisco," where he left his Italian heart.

Frank Sinatra (Francis Albert Sinatra), known as "the voice" and later as "Chairman of the Board," was born in 1915 in Hoboken, New Jersey. He was the son of a Sicilian, Martin, and his wife, Natalie, who had immigrated to America from Italy. His father was a boilermaker who had also boxed as a bantamweight under the name "Marty O'Brien." Natalie, or "Dolly," was very involved in local politics and community events and wanted Frank to go to college, while his father wanted him to be a fighter.

Sinatra and his girlfriend heard Bing Crosby sing at the Loew's Journal Square Theatre in Jersey City in 1933, and he vowed to become a singer. He first sang in a group called The Hoboken Four and he won a Major Bowes amateur contest. Harry James heard him sing at the Rustic Canyon near Alpine, New Jersey, and signed him for his band. Tommy Dorsey made him a better offer to join his band, and it was here that Sinatra learned how to control and use his voice like an instrument. He learned how to sing like a professional.

Sinatra hit the country like a bomb after his first smash hit record, "I'll Never Smile Again" in 1940. By 1942, audiences, mainly adoring women, began to scream, swoon and faint over "old blue eyes." Thus began one of America's great love affairs. His piercing blue eyes had a certain hypnotic quality, and his voice had a tonal beauty, but somehow each member of the audience felt that he was sharing a deep, dark secret with them alone. This love, by both women and men, has persisted throughout Sinatra's records, performances, films, concerts and television shows. Though he has had a career of many ups and downs, and his "Sicilian temper" may have alienated the press and others, the record will show that the man who "did it his way" is a consummate artist, a magnificent performer and perhaps one of the greatest entertainers of the twentieth century.

ROCK AND ROLL

Italian Americans swell the ranks of rock and roll, though some are hardly known as being Italian American.

Paul Anka, born in Ottawa, Canada, in 1941, came to New York in 1956 and was thrown out of every studio and record company. At age fifteen, he performed his own composition of "Diana." People loved it and he was on his way to perform in the same theaters that threw him out. By age sixteen, Paul had three gold records and made a million dollars on his composition of "It Doesn't Matter Anymore" sung by Buddy Holly. By age twenty-one, he was an international star with hundreds of award-winning songs.

Frankie Avalon (Avalone), born in 1940 in Philadelphia, played trumpet as a prodigy, had a teenage nightclub at age fifteen and became a star with his hits "Dee Dee Dinah" and "Teacher's Pet." At age seventeen, he recorded "Venus," which was number one on the charts for five weeks and sold millions of records. In the 1960s, he teamed up with Annette Funicello, another Italian American, in a series of beach movies that enthralled the youth of America. Avalon has emerged today from the new wave of rock as a serious performer.

Fabian (Fabian Forte), also from Philadelphia, was born in

1943 and attracted the attention of a talent scout who took him to Hollywood in 1958. By age eighteen, he was a millionaire. His handsome face slightly resembled that of Elvis Presley, but his voice was not the best. Somehow the music promoters made Fabian into a huge phenomenon through promotion and advertising. He performed in several movies such as *Hound Dog Man* and *Bus Stop*. Whatever the case for his talent, Fabian created a sensation across the country for a time.

Bobby Darin (Walden Robert Cassotto) was born in 1936 in the Italian neighborhood of East Harlem. Though unable to attend elementary school because of illness, he went to Bronx High School of Science, but his flashy dress and drum playing made life for him difficult. After dropping out of Hunter College and working odd jobs, he took the name "Darin" from a phone book and with Don Kirshner got the money to cut two demos by singing radio ads. In 1956, he won a Decca Records contract and a spot on Tommy Dorsey's television show. He finally made it with his "Splish Splash," then "Dream Lover" and "Mack the Knife," which sold 2 million copies. He began doing films, met Sandra Dee and they married. He became a successful entertainer with national appeal.

Sonny Salvatore Bono, born in 1940 in Detroit, became a major rock star and composer with many hits. His fame became worldwide when he teamed with Cher as Sonny and Cher, and their television show in the 1970s was a huge success. Their records were hits from the 1960s on and they are remembered most for "I Got You, Babe."

Frank Zappa, born in 1940 in Baltimore, perhaps most famous for his rock group of the late 1960s, the Mothers of Invention, began in a high-school band in California. When it was not yet in fashion to be "freaky" and outrageous on stage, Zappa had "freaky" groups called Captain Glasspack and the Magic Mufflers, who were bizarre and shocking. Trained in classical music, Zappa created an original and unusual style that borrowed imaginatively from all other musical forms to produce not just music but social and political satire. Zappa satirized just about everything in unique and clever ways and became a legend. The Mothers of Invention broke up in the late 1960s, but Zappa continued a very productive life as lyricist, composer, performer, record producer and actor in his own films.

The "Boss" Bruce Springsteen, super rock star and cult hero, was born in 1949 in Freehold, New Jersey, of Dutch and Neapolitan Italian descent. His father drifted from job to job, and his mother was a secretary in this working-class town. As a child, Springsteen found music his only solace and source of enjoyment in life. After seeing an Elvis Presley performance on television, he scraped together eighteen dollars to buy a secondhand guitar. He taught himself to play the guitar, the harmonica and piano. By age fourteen, he played in local bands. He dropped out of a local community college and then spent all his free time playing and writing music.

He started several hard-rock bands and soon began to develop a following in New Jersey. In the 1960s, he joined the hippie migration to San Francisco and played in a group called Child. His break came in 1972 when he was contracted by Columbia Records. He soon zoomed to international stardom and is famous for songs like "Born in the U.S.A." His strong appeal to alienated youth and the middle class has catapulted the very talented Springsteen to superstar status.

Madonna Louise Veronica Ciccone, famous rock star, was born in 1958 in Bay City, Michigan, the third child in a family of three girls and three boys. Her father, a second-generation Italian American worked for Chrysler/General Dynamics, and her mother was French Canadian. In junior high school, Madonna acted and danced in plays, and dancing became her adolescent passion. Her dance teacher, impressed by her dedication and discipline, took a personal interest in furthering her career and introduced her to the glamour and sophistication of Detroit nightlife.

Madonna won a dance scholarship to the University of Michigan but dropped out after two years to seek her fortune in New York. She studied with various dance groups but then became drummer-vocalist for a rock group called Breakfast Club. Her brief appearance in the film *Vision Quest* in 1984 brought her some attention, but her album *Like a Virgin* and her music videos transformed her into a pop-culture symbol and a star. "The Material Girl" married film star Sean Penn in 1985 and continues to make a major impact in the entertainment business.

SCULPTURE

The great tradition of Italian sculpture saw its emergence in America in the work of many artists and ranges from the absolutely unbelievable to the sublime.

Mark di Suvero, born in 1938, is perhaps the best known contemporary sculptor. The Whitney Museum, along with the City of New York, presented an exhibit of di Suvero's many works in 1975 to 1976. The show exhibited sixty-five works, both inside the museum and scattered throughout the parks and streets of the city. These works ranged from table tops to steel structures standing five stories high.

Joseph Coletti, born in 1898 in San Donato, Italy, came here at age two and studied painting with John Singer Sargent. He studied at the Massachusetts Art School from 1915 to 1917 and graduated from Harvard University in 1923. He became a world-recognized sculptor with major works in church and historical sculpture for fifty years.

Italo Scanga, born in 1932 in Lago, Calabria, came to the United States in 1947. As a sculptor he has had many one-man exhibitions, and his work is part of the permanent collections of the Museum of Modern Art, the Metropolitan Museum of Art, the Los Angeles County Museum of Art and others.

Frank Gasparro was chief sculptor-engraver for the United States Mint in Philadelphia, his hometown. He has designed many coins and medals, especially the bicentennial medal and the Mint's presidential medals from Johnson to Carter. Caesar Rufo was a sculptor-engraver who worked as senior sculptor for the famous Franklin Mint. He created the Metropolitan Opera's Centennial Medallion.

Patrick Morelli, born in 1945 in Syracuse, New York, began working fulltime as a sculptor and architectural designer around 1977, based in New York City. Morelli's art combines the strength and humanity of the realistic tradition and the subtle and elusive expressiveness of the abstract tradition of modern art. Among his many prize-winning sculptures is a ten-foot, bonded-bronze monument entitled *Roots* at the King Center in Atlanta.

S. Paolo Abbate sculpted memorials in New York and Connecticut. Beniamino Bufano, from San Francisco, created the beautiful *Statue of Peace* at the entrance to San Francisco International Airport. His *St. Francis* overlooks the city's beautiful waterfront. The Piccirilli family of five artist brothers created the statue of Lincoln for the Lincoln Memorial, which is nineteen feet high and made of twenty-eight blocks of marble carefully fitted together. Vince Palumbo, a fifth-generation stonecarver, has kept this lost art alive and has worked at Washington's National Cathedral over twenty-five years.

Jimilu Mason, noted Alexandria, Virginia, sculptress, was born in 1930 in Las Cruces, New Mexico. She received her B.A. from George Washington University and has been a professional artist since 1955. Mason has exhibited widely, including in such places as the Smithsonian Institution, Corcoran Gallery, Pennsylvania Academy of Fine Art and the Detroit Museum of Fine Art. Mason's works reside in many permanent collections, and in 1966 she was selected to sculpt the official marble bust of President Johnson in the Senate wing of the Capitol. Mason, whose mother is Italian, sculpted the famous Brumidi bust of Carrara marble in Pietrasanta, Italy.

Simon Rodia is truly bizarre. In 1921, with no building permit, Rodia began building those bizarre towers in Watts, Los Angeles, out of bits of glass bottles, tile and junk. The three towers stand ninety-nine, ninety-seven and fifty-five feet tall. As his towers got taller and taller, disputes with city officials got hotter and hotter. People thought the guy was whacko as they watched him swinging along his towers on a window-washer's lift singing Italian arias. The constant bickering over safety finally got to Rodia, so he stopped his work. In the 1950s, the city government tested the strength of the towers and they were declared a historical monument. Now Los Angeles proudly touts the towers to tourists.

PAINTING

Italian Americans began contributing through painting early in our history, beginning with the works of the great fresco painter, Constantino Brumidi. After him came many other artists. Joseph Stella, born in 1877 in Muro Lucano, Lucania, came to America and used his immigrant experience as the subject of his art. His early sketches captured the anxious moods of foreigners from every country as they left Ellis Island and began life in America. For over twenty years, Stella was respected as a key figure among progressive painters in the United States. He was part of the famous Armory Show of 1913 in New York and is known for his *Battle of Lights, Coney Island* and his six versions of the Brooklyn Bridge.

Gregorio Prestopino, born in 1907 in New York City in Little Italy, studied at the National Academy of Design. He suffered through the Great Depression, and this became thematic material for his paintings. He liked to paint the common people and catch their expressions at work and play. He worked usually in water color with clean, simple lines and lively color. His *Portsmouth Street* captured the plight of the common man's unemployment. He became a successful painter whose works hang in the Whitney and Hirshhorn museums and others.

Alfred D. Crimi was born in 1900 in San Frantello, Sicily, the son of a Sicilian stonemason, and came to America in 1910. He painted to express his rich though sometimes painful odyssey coming from a quasimedieval Sicilian town to the urban, industrial American city of New York, then across the country. His multidimensional creations express the joy of life in America and the new dimensions of the Italian American ethos born from a synergy of two great cultures. He was also president of the Audubon Society.

Frank Stella, born in 1936 in Malden, Massachusetts, the son of a Sicilian doctor, studied with abstract painter Patrick

Morgan at Phillips Academy in 1950, got his B.A. from Princeton in 1958, moved to a storefront studio on the Lower East Side of New York City, and became a master of minimal art painting and one of the world's greatest artists.

Stella supported himself as a housepainter while he created his "black" paintings, which impressed the art world for their stark simplicity and austere aesthetic. He was discovered by the art dealer Leo Castelli and by age twenty-three, he was the youngest artist in the Museum of Modern Art's *Sixteen Americans* exhibition. His "aluminum" series came next, consisting of simple stripe patterns, and when some of the stripes wouldn't fit the corners of the canvas, he just chopped them off, and thereby created the first modern "shaped canvases." His "copper" series were radically shaped canvases, and his "Benjamin Moore" series was named for the brand of paint he used right out of the can. His "purple" series were all polygons.

In 1970, at age thirty-three, Stella became the youngest painter ever given a retrospective by the Museum of Modern Art in New York. Stella's creations are sold and housed in museums worldwide, not bad for a former housepainter. He is hailed a genius in his field and a breakthrough artist in modern art.

Leo Castelli, one of the most influential patrons of the arts and art dealers of the twentieth century, was born in 1907 in Trieste. Castelli grew up in an enriched environment, the middle child of wealthy and socially prominent parents. He was committed to learning, especially language and art and wanted to be the perfect Renaissance man.

Castelli gained his law degree in 1924 from the University of Milan and started a job with an insurance company. In 1932 in Bucharest he met and married Ileana Schapira, and he acquired his first artwork. In 1939 he opened a gallery in Paris with Rene Drouin and their first exhibition on surrealism was a smash success. The war brought the Castellis to New York, and after serving in the army, Castelli realized his true passion was collecting modern art.

Castelli began to visit galleries, artists' studios and museums, and educated himself in his life's pursuit. In 1957 the Castellis opened a small gallery in the living room of their apartment on

East 77th Street, dealing first in established painters. However Castelli always had an instinctive passion for original work, which he felt would chart a new course in contemporary art. In 1958, Jasper Johns' exhibition of his representational paintings at the Castelli Gallery and of the Robert Rauschenberg show three months later hit the art world like a bomb. These two artists influenced pop artists of the 1960s significantly, and Leo Castelli instantly became famous for spotting new talent. In 1959 he discovered Frank Stella. Castelli offered Stella financial support, which allowed him to devote himself to his art full time. In one year, Stella was hailed as the most important young New York painter to emerge since Johns and Rauschenberg.

Since this time, Castelli has taken on artists such as Roy Lichtenstein, James Rosenquist and Andy Warhol, the art world's first superstar of modern times. By the mid-1960s, the Castelli Gallery was unquestionably the preeminent gallery for new artists.

Leo Castelli is now unsurpassed in his power to sell and promote artists' work on an international scale. His generosity in supporting artists, especially experimental work, has made him an eminent patron of the arts. An elegant, sophisticated and brilliant man, Castelli has truly achieved his dream of becoming a Renaissance man, not as a Michelangelo perhaps, but as a Lorenzo de'Medici.

PHOTOGRAPHERS

Francesco Scavullo, born in 1929 in Great Hills, Staten Island, moved to Manhattan when he was eight. His grandparents all came from Potenza, Italy. He grew up in an extremely enriched environment, since his father was a rich and successful self-made man. His mother took him to galleries, museums, the ballet and the opera. Educated by Jesuits at Xavier High School, he worked as a teenager for Horst, a famous photographer known for his chiaroscuro portraits of moody Hollywood stars. Scavullo began his career as a professional photographer in 1948 and for the past four decades has photographed nearly every celebrated man and woman in America, if not the world. He photographs the fashion collections of major designers and works for all the top magazines. His photos hang in permanent collections at the Metropolitan Museum of Art, and he is respected as the dominant photographic influence on American beauty and fashion.

Tom Vano, born in Long Island in 1926, is one of America's highly respected photographers. His first photographic subject, taken when he was thirteen years old with a Kodak Brownie, was his father's grocery store in Astoria, Queens. He worked in photo shops learning about photography. He enrolled at the New York School of Modern Photography, but World War II took his art into the U.S. Army, from which he emerged highly decorated and highly accomplished as a photographer. He fell in love with San Francisco, a photographer's paradise, in 1948. He moved there and opened his own studio, which quickly became the best in the city. His works express a "quality of surprise" both in subject and treatment. He has a unique talent for communicating a mood and achieving that delicate balance between photographic technique and aesthetic integrity. He is a very special photographer, and his client list is full of top corporations. His studio, now run with his son Jon, produces some of the best and most creative photographic art in America. Vano's artistic works are widely published and are exhibited in major museums and galleries, including the Museum of Modern Art.

THEATRE

Albert Innaurato, born in Philadelphia in 1948, graduated from the Yale School of Drama in 1974 and by 1977 three of his plays were running simultaneously on New York stages. His play *Gemini* started off Broadway in 1977 and then moved to Broadway, where it became one of the longest-running plays in theatre history. Six of his plays were published with the title *Bizarre Behavior*. Innaurato works in residence at New York's

Public Theatre and the Circle Repertory Company. He is the recipient of prestigious Guggenheim and Rockefeller grants.

Julie Bovasso, born in 1930 in Brooklyn, became a playwright, actress for stage, screen and television, and a director. She has received Obie awards for best actress, best experimental theatre and for her work in bringing Theatre of the Absurd to the United States. She won a Triple Obie Award for acting, writing and directing *Gloria and Esperanza* in 1969. She also wrote, directed and acted in *The Moon Dreamers* in 1969. Her other works include *Standard Safety, The Nothing Kid, Shubert's Last Serenade* and many others. Bovasso has become a major creative talent and a vital artistic participant in the theatre.

Mario Fratti, born in 1927 in Italy, arrived in New York in 1963 as a drama critic for Italian newspapers. He has been writing and producing plays at the rate of two or more per year. He also writes and publishes his work in Italian and became a teacher of playwriting at Hunter College in 1967. He won the Eugene O'Neill Competition for Composers and Librettists in 1979 for his Broadway musical success *Nine,* which is an adaptation of Fellini's *8½.* Fratti, a brilliant playwright, also won the Richard Rogers Award for this libretto.

Italian Americans have also contributed to musical theatre, a seemingly natural place for them to create and produce.

Harry Warren (Salvatore Guaragna), born in 1893 in Brooklyn, wrote the original musical *42nd Street* in 1933 on which the contemporary hit is based. Warren also wrote the hit Broadway musicals *Sweet and Low,* and *Crazy Quilt* for Billy Rose and *Laugh Parade* for Ed Wynn. He moved to Hollywood to write *42nd Street* and spent almost sixty years composing almost four hundred songs for more than fifty movies. He won three Academy Awards for *Lullabye of Broadway, You'll Never Know* and *On the Atchison Topeka and Santa Fe.*

Michael Bennett (Di Figlia), born in 1943 in Buffalo, created two major award-winning musicals—*A Chorus Line* and *Dream Girls.* Frank Corsaro, born in 1924, went to Yale School of Drama and became a top director of theater and opera. The hits he directed include *A Hatful of Rain, The Night of the Iguana, Treemonisha, Whoopy, Knockout* and others. He has directed over thirty operas for the New York City Opera and more than fifty others in the U.S., Canada and England.

Donna de Matteo was born in 1941 in New York City and she began her creative-writing career with the artistic fabrication of reports on books that did not exist for the nuns at Marymount. She has since become a successful playwright in Manhattan with her first play *Barbecue Pit* being produced off Broadway. Her play *Sister Fox* was based on the interaction of three generations of Italian American women, not surprisingly modeled on herself, her mother and her grandmother. Her ten plays to date have been produced in Manhattan theatres and in many cities outside New York. She helped found the Forum of Italian American Playwrights and the National Organization of Italian American Women. As a gifted creative talent, de Matteo is on a path of great success as a playwright.

Jo Ann Tedesco, an actress/playwright who grew up in Syracuse, New York, says she learned how to make sauce from her grandmother and how to think from the Jesuits. After a B.A. in English literature, several jobs as teacher, caseworker and probation officer, two children, and a tour as an actress/ lecturer, Tedesco had her first play *Sacramento* produced at the Public Theatre and the H B Playwrights Foundation. Three of her one-act plays were featured off off Broadway, and she too is coming up as a creative and talented playwright.

ARCHITECTURE

The Italian tradition of architecture goes back as far as the Etruscans and the Roman Empire. The dictum that "all roads lead to Rome" refers to a time when the Mediterranean Sea was the waterway nexus of every culture that played a part in the birth, growth and spread of Western culture while also functioning as a connecting network to the enriching influences of the Eastern cultures. Rome was the heartbeat of the center of this Mediterranean cosmopolis both by land and sea, both north to Europe and south to Sicily and Greece, and both east to the Orient and west to the New World. The meaning of the dictum is also literal as well as figurative because the

Romans really did build roads, and many other structures, bridges, buildings, etc., all throughout the vast empire.

The Romans had a genius for spreading their achievements throughout the world, and this was particularly true of architecture. Granted they took the best of many contributing cultures like that of the Greeks and the Etruscans, but their embellishments, improvements and the role they played in disseminating their works through a wide and efficient organization were unique to the Romans. The idea of vast enclosed space, like the Pantheon, was uniquely Roman.

The monuments to Roman architecture, city planning and building forms not only are still visible in the modern world, but are sources of value for contemporary inspiration in our modern cities. The rectilinear grid of Roman encampments and towns was rooted in the Roman sense of formal patterns laid out for practical purposes. American cities take their lessons from the Romans here. Roman piazzas, which were circumscribed by beautiful buildings and colonnades, serve as models for American civic centers. The Romans ensconced their villages in hilltop nests to leave land for farming, and contemporary city planners use this as a model for modern complexes. The great architectural engineering inventions, such as the arch, the barrel vault, the dome, the viaducts, the aqueducts and the first use of concrete, still remain essential for engineering science. Many actual buildings and structures in America are inspired by and styled on Roman creations, such as Pennsylvania Railroad Station, which was based on the Roman Baths at Caracalla.

The further influence of Italian architectural and engineering inspiration came from the Renaissance, in a sense a rebirth of Roman traditions, and especially from the most influential architect of all time, Andrea Palladio. The quintessential architectural artist, Palladio affected all of modern architecture and especially that of colonial America. Jefferson's Monticello was Palladian in realization, as have been many other architectural works since the time of Palladio.

Many Italian American architects carry the tradition of Rome into their architectural creations. Pier Luigi Nervi engineered St. Mary's Cathedral in San Francisco. Mario Ciampi designed the Berkeley Museum and redesigned Market Street in San Francisco.

Vincent Russoniello, born in 1890 in St. Andrea de Conza, Avellino, Italy, came to Scranton, Pennsylvania in 1905 with his family. He worked in a stone quarry and then a stone yard where he learned to cut blocks to specification and set them in place at building sites. Around 1908, Russoniello took correspondence courses in architecture and got a job with a local architect. He soon struck out on his own and by the mid-1920s, he had launched a profitable career as an architect.

Working with A. N. Russo, an Italian sculptor who imported Italian marbles, he quickly became adept at designing unique and imposing churches, such as St. Patrick's Roman Catholic Church in Wilkes-Barre. Russo supervised the quarrying and cutting of each stone at Carrara, Italy, then shipped them to New York and Scranton. Italian immigrant stonecutters, masons and laborers then assembled the building like a giant puzzle around the structural steel that Russoniello designed for the job. Russoniello became a major designer of beautiful buildings and, especially, churches, some twenty of which he built during the 1920s, 1930s and 1940s.

Pietro Belluschi, born in 1900 in Ancona, Italy, came to America at age twenty-five. Working in an "international" style, he became nationally known as one of America's most respected architects. He served as design consultant to San Francisco's Performing Arts Center and to the architects of the Bank of America's International Headquarters. He designed the Juilliard School of Music at Lincoln Center and the Art Museum in Portland, Oregon. He has designed over a thousand buildings in this country. He also served as dean of Architecture at the Massachusetts Institute of Technology from 1951 to 1965.

Paolo Soleri, born in 1919 in Torino, journeyed to America with the wonderful opportunity to serve as apprentice to Frank Lloyd Wright in 1947, but returned to Italy two years after due to personality clashes and philosophical disagreement over architectural theory. In Italy he built the Solimene ceramics factory, which shows the influence of Wright. Soleri moved to Scottsdale, Arizona, where he has been designing a whole city, Arcosanti, in which he designs his "earth houses" using only natural materials out of the environment. His genius stunned viewers when he created an exhibit on urban planning at the Corcoran Gallery in Washington, D.C. in 1970. Soleri is a unique visionary who could emerge as the most influential city designer in architecture.

Robert Charles Venturi, born in 1925 in Philadelphia, has been hailed as the "Father of Postmodernism" for his brilliant architectural creative vision. From childhood, Venturi aspired to become an architect. In 1947, Venturi graduated from Princeton University in architecture and in 1950 he received his M.F.A. He worked for several architects, but in Rome in the 1950s he evolved his own original philosophy of architecture. He observed Rome's pedestrian scale, its piazzas and the complex interweaving of great architecture with the common, everyday landscape of Italy.

Returning home to Philadelphia, Venturi worked with Louis I. Kahn, and fused a love of the past with an appreciation of contemporary values and techniques. He was inspired by Kahn, but set off on his own divergent and original path, adding social concerns and analyses into his architectural designs.

In 1966 he published his *Complexity and Contradiction in Architecture*, a manifesto of his design philosophy. He rejected the utopian objectives of orthodox modern architecture, and, among other bold breaks from modernism, declared, "It is perhaps from the everyday landscape, vulgar and disdained, that we can draw the complex and contradictory order that is valid and vital for our architecture as a whole." In other words, we have a lot to learn from the commonplace.

Venturi has significantly influenced and inspired many architects everywhere. The mention of his name throws some architects into shock or rage, but his novel, innovative and provocative creativity has made him a cult hero. When he designs a building he seeks to be sure it does not violate the setting but instead melds with the neighboring buildings and contextual environment. The role of Rome in inspiring Ventu-

ri in forming his particular and unique creative vision symbo-
lizes the amazing power of the Italian tradition.

DRAMATIC ARTS

The Italian American contribution to the dramatic arts—on
stage, on the silver screen, on the television screen and in video
production—has truly become monumental, especially over
the last several decades. The very essence of Italian life, and its
values and traditions, seem perfectly created and designed for
dramatic presentation. If you want to understand what real
drama or comedy is like, just live with an Italian family. In
short, the makings of Italian life are the makings of dramatic
and comedic art. Gestures, animation, (over) dramatization,
emotional display, spectacle, showmanship, musicality, orna-
mentation, grand opera, movement, symbol making and facial
expressions make up the sum and substance of theater arts.
Perhaps the natural propensity Italians have for living life to its
fullest translates to the world as "dramatic," and all the Italian
American artists are doing is transferring this from living room
to stage.

America is a giant stage onto which Italian Americans have
stepped, made their debut and won their laurels. If there was
ever an abundance of success and achievement, it is here. We
have sought to give a hearty representation here of the
wondrous delights that have been achieved. We apologize to all
of you Italian dramatists, on and off the stage, whom we may
have not included.

ACTING

Acting is in the blood of every Italian—just watch the
endearing antics of an Italian mother with her bambino while
she knows she is being watched—and you will know what we
mean. There seems to be in the Italian genes a natural
inclination to stage a drama, invent a comedy, act out a

character, arrange a spectacle and, to assure that the energy is not wasted, be sure there is an appreciative audience.

There is a propensity to live life at very high or very low frequencies on the emotional scale—the joys are sublime but the sorrows are absolutely tragic. Italians may be living one quantum dimension above everyone else, and what passes for normal behavior for Italians may be perceived as extraordinary to others. But Italians are just being their own dramatic or comedic selves. While the world may see them as overemotional, excitable, full of gestures, even melodramatic, they're really just busy living life to the fullest.

Marlon Brando once told a stage actor who was having terrible difficulty in a scene, "Look, your face is the stage—it all happens in your facial expressions on the screen." This, of course, is no surprise to an Italian. For Italians this comes naturally, for on their faces one can read every expression and any emotion humanly possible.

Rudolph Valentino was born in 1895 in Castellaneta, Italy, as Rodolfo Alfonzo Raffaelo Pierre Filibert Guglielmi di Valentina d'Antonguolla. His father was a cavalryman, and he received his schooling in a military academy. In 1913 at age eighteen, he arrived in New York City and found his way to California, where he did some bit parts from 1917 to 1920. Metro produced *The Four Horsemen of the Apocalypse* with Valentino in the lead role and with the premiere of this movie came the birth of the "Latin Lover" on the Hollywood screen. The American female population fell in love with this Italian man. He was a romantic Apollo who treated women with courtesy and deference, but whose eyes promised much more, which would be revealed behind the bedroom door.

Valentino was pure cinematic magic, sexual magnetism personified, the Italian lover incarnate. He made *The Sheik* and millions of women swooned as his menacing eyes penetrated Agnes Ayres preparing for the clinch. Valentino went on to many other successes, including *Blood and Sand,* which is considered his best and which was directed by Fred Niblo, another Italian American. While in New York, at the height of his success, he was seized with a gallstone attack and died from peritonitis. His funeral caused mass riots at Saint Patrick's

Cathedral as millions of women, who had dreamt of being carried away on Valentino's white Arabian steed, mourned his untimely death.

Elissa Landi, born in 1904 in Venice, made her debut in London and moved to the New York stage to star in *A Farewell to Arms*. This beautiful actress received several film offers, and she left for Hollywood to become a movie star through the 1930s for Paramount. Among many films, she starred in *Enter Madame* with Cary Grant and in the Cecil B. De Mille spectacular *The Sign of the Cross* with Fredrick March, Charles Laughton and Claudette Colbert. Landi also became a successful writer and poet.

Don Ameche or Dominic Felix Ameche, born in 1908 in Kenosha, Wisconsin, started acting at the University of Wisconsin, toured in vaudeville acts and appeared regularly on radio serials like "The First Nighter." His distinctive voice attracted millions of listeners, especially women. Then Hollywood discovered the tall, dark, handsome man behind the voice and Ameche has not stopped making successful movies since the 1930s. Along the way he starred on Broadway and television. Most people think Ameche invented the telephone because he played the life of Alexander Graham Bell! Ameche is still performing and his last hit was the movie *Cocoon*.

Ida Lupino, one of the great actresses of Hollywood, was born in 1918 in London. Her father, Stanley Lupino, was one of England's most popular and versatile comedians. The Lupino family had a great history of performance in the theatre. Ida Lupino acted from childhood on and studied at the Royal Academy of Dramatic Art. Her first lead in a film was at age fifteen, when she starred in *Her First Affair* in 1932. In 1933, she left England to go to America where she was offered a contract with Paramount Pictures. Lupino has starred in many films since then, and her dynamic, vivid and passionate portrayals have earned her fame throughout the entertainment industry. Lupino won the New York Film Critics award as best actress in 1943. She played a key role in the making of Hollywood from the 1930s on and went on to win acclaim in many performances. She also became one of the first and few woman directors in Hollywood.

Ernest Borgnine (Ermes Effron Borgnino), born in 1915 in Hamden, Connecticut, spent ten years in the U.S. Navy and studied drama on the G.I. bill. He went into film acting and after several films gave a stunning performance as a sadistic sergeant in *From Here to Eternity*. This typecast him as a "heavy" and he made many films as such, like *Bad Day at Black Rock*. However, Borgnine gave a brilliant, sensitive portrayal of a fat, lonely Bronx butcher in *Marty*, which won him an Academy Award. Who could forget the memorable lines from that movie? "What do you want to do tonight, Marty?" "I don't know, Angelo, what do you want to do?" After *Marty*, Borgnine no longer had a typecasting problem and went on to become a major success in film and television. Many remember his long-running television series "McHale's Navy."

Anne Bancroft, award-winning actress, was born Anne Marie Italiano in 1931 in the Bronx, New York, the daughter of immigrants from Italy. As a child, Bancroft knew she wanted to be an entertainer. She studied acting in New York and began her career in films in Hollywood. For six years, however, she was typed as a B-film actress, and she decided instead to return to New York to make herself a success on the stage. She performed in *Two for the Seesaw* to terrific response and then in *The Miracle Worker,* where she played Annie Sullivan, Helen Keller's teacher, she won every dramatic award possible, including an Oscar in 1962 for the film version. In 1964, Bancroft married comic genius Mel Brooks. Some of her movies include *The Pumpkin Eater* and *The Graduate,* the latter bringing her more awards and some notoriety for her portrayal of the older-woman lover of the character portrayed by Dustin Hoffman. Bancroft directed, acted in and also wrote *Fatso,* a movie about an Italian American, played by Dom De Luise, who can't stop eating. And Bancroft can't stop giving great performances in films, television and theatre.

Robert De Niro grew up in the Little Italy section of New York's Greenwich Village and was described by *Newsweek* magazine's cover story on him as "the natural successor to Brando and Dean." His parents are both artists, his father being a sculptor, painter and poet. De Niro is a natural film actor, and his gifted mastery of emotional expression shows in every role. He becomes every character he plays, whether it be the angry violent boxer he played in *Raging Bull*, the dim-witted baseball catcher dying of Hodgkin's disease in *Bang the Drum Slowly*, a Hollywood producer in *The Last Tycoon*, the psychopathic New York cabdriver in *Taxi Driver* or the young Sicilian immigrant who establishes a mafia dynasty in *The Godfather*. De Niro has a fabulous talent as an actor. There is a protean dimension to his acting, and he has an instinctive insight into behavior that makes him the most expressive actor in the art. Perhaps it's ancestral as well as instinctive.

Sylvester "Sly" Stallone was born in 1946 in Hell's Kitchen and grew up on the streets of New York. He was an unknown actor with a few credits to his name—*The Lords of Flatbush*, *Capone* and *Deathrace 2000*—until *Rocky* made him one of the biggest stars in film and immensely wealthy. On the verge of disaster, out of work, with his wife pregnant and only one hundred dollars in the bank, he wrote the script for *Rocky*, as the legend goes, in three and a half days. When its value as a hot property became known, offers from top actors poured in to his agent's office, but he refused them all and held out to play the role himself. Persistence and belief in self paid off—the *Rocky* films made box-office history, and since then Stallone has become a giant in the industry as an actor, writer and director.

Talia Shire, younger sister of Francis Ford Coppola and a star of *Rocky*, began her acting career in Roger Corman films such as *The Dunwich Horror*. She played in her brother's film, *The Godfather*. She was nominated for an Academy Award for this performance. She starred in the television show "Rich Man, Poor Man" and then became a huge star in *Rocky*. She is a superb actress and has formed her own production company to make the films she wants to.

Alan Alda, actor, writer and director, is a phenomenon unto himself and has consistently been number one on America's list of favorite television personalities. He is perhaps most famous for his amazing career as star of the highly praised series "M*A*S*H." Alda was born in New York City in 1936 and got his B.S. from Fordham University in 1956. His Broadway performance in *The Apple Tree* won him a Tony-award nomination and *Fair Games for Lovers* won him the Theatre World award. He appeared in *Paper Lion, Jenny, The Mephisto Waltz, California Suite* and *Same Time Next Year*. He wrote, directed and starred in *The Four Seasons* and *Sweet Liberty,* and wrote and starred in *The Seduction of Joe Tynan*. Alda is a gifted talent whose creativity has left its special mark on many films, plays and television shows. "M*A*S*H" has become an American institution not just for its entertainment and comedy, but for its profoundly sensitive and humanistic messages. The world has honored Alda for his contributions and achievements with Emmy awards, Golden Globe awards and the Humanitas award, among many others.

Daniel John Travanti, top-rated star of television's hit show "Hill Street Blues," was born in Kenosha, Wisconsin, and got his B.A. at the University of Wisconsin and his M.A. at Loyola Marymount in Los Angeles. His television appearances include "Kojak," "The F.B.I.," "The Mod Squad," "Barnaby Jones," "Hart to Hart," "Knots Landing" and the TV movie *Adam*. Travanti won an Emmy and a Golden Globe award for his profound and sensitive portrayal of Capt. Frank Furillo on "Hill Street Blues." His talent in this role has kept him at the top of the list of America's favorite television performers and has gained him great prominence as a hero to Italian Americans, who praise him for projecting such a positive media image.

Susan Lucci, one of the hottest actresses on television, was born in Westchester, New York, studied at Marymount College and became the star of "All My Children" starting in 1970. By 1986, she was awarded a contract for 1 million dollars, making her the highest paid soap star in television history. She has also appeared in "Fantasy Island," "The Love Boat" and the TV movie *Invitation to Hell*. Lucci's talents have won her many awards and several Emmy nominations as best actress in a daytime drama series.

Armand Assante is a handsome native New Yorker, who spent twelve years on legitimate theatre stages across the country and in New York performing the works of Shakespeare, Shaw and O'Neill before coming to national prominence in television and film. He is an alumnus of the American

Academy of Dramatic Arts in New York. Assante has won a reputation for versatility: his film roles have included Goldie Hawn's French lover in *Private Benjamin,* an amorous violinist in *Unfaithfully Yours* and Mickey Spillane's legendary tough-guy detective Mike Hammer in *I, The Jury.* Assante starred in the films *Little Darlings, Paradise Alley, The Prophecy, Love and Money, Belizaire* and, *Animal Behavior.* Television audiences best know Assante from his key roles in several hit miniseries, such as "Rage of Angels" and "Napoleon and Josephine." He's been seen in three important Broadway productions: *Boccaccio, Comedians* and the Circle in the Square production of *Romeo and Juliet.* When not before a camera, Assante lives with his family on a farm he bought several years ago in upstate New York.

Joseph Bologna, gifted actor and talented writer was born in Brooklyn in 1938, studied at Brown University and served in the U.S. Marine Corps. Drawing brilliantly on his Italian background, he and his wife, Renee Taylor, wrote the stage play and film script of *Lovers and Other Strangers,* in which he also starred. They also wrote "Acts of Love and Other Comedies," "Paradise" and "Calucci's Department" for television. Some of Bologna's major accomplishments as an actor are his feature films *My Favorite Year, Woman in Red, Blame It On Rio* and the TV movie *Honor Thy Father.* Bologna's multiple talents as actor and writer have made him a big star and won him many awards. He has a gift for capturing the Italian essence brilliantly in his art, and this pays homage to his beautiful family, which plays such a vital role in his life.

Al (Alfred) Pacino, consummate actor, was born in 1940 in New York City, attended the High School of Performing Arts and honed his acting skills at the Actors Studio from 1966 on. He served his apprenticeship as an actor, director and comedy writer in many off-off-Broadway theatres, such as the Cafe La Mama, the Living Theatre and the New Theatre Workshop. His first appearance off Broadway in *The Indian Wants the Bronx* won him an Obie award in 1968. His Broadway debut in *Does A Tiger Wear A Necktie?* won him a Tony award in 1969 and he was named by a *Variety* poll as "most promising new Broadway actor." Pacino has truly fulfilled this promise—he has become a huge success in theater and feature films. He made his film debut in 1969 in *Me, Natalie* and his major hit movies include *Scarecrow, Serpico, Dog Day Afternoon, Bobby Deerfield, And Justice For All, Cruising, Author! Author!, Scarface, Revolution* and *The Godfather* (Parts I and II). Pacino is a serious, gifted artist whose creative acting achievements have gained him awards, praise and great honors.

COMEDY

In comedy, Italian Americans have been making it in clubs, on stage, in films and on television throughout the country. The natural propensity for drama is equally balanced with a natural bent for comedy in the Italian American personality.

Henry Armetta, born in Palermo, Sicily, stowed away at age fourteen on a ship headed for America and was discovered in Boston. John Armato took him from the police and gave him a home and work. While working as a pants presser, Armetta attracted the attention, because of his jovial disposition, of Raymond Hitchcock, and he wound up in a stage play. In 1923, he came to Hollywood and starred as an Italian character comedian in films. Armetta's talents went from comedy to drama. In *Night Life of the Gods* he demonstrated some of the weirdest characterizations ever performed on a set. Yet in *A Bell for Adano* he showed the finest dramatic expertise.

Lou Costello, the dumpy, roly-poly, zanier half of the Abbott and Costello comedy team, was born in 1908 as Louis Francis Cristello in Paterson, New Jersey. Schooling and Lou never agreed with each other, and night after night he stayed after school writing on the blackboard, "I'm a bad boy." This later became his tag line. He quit school and ended up on the back lots of Hollywood as a studio stunt man. Doubling for stars gave him the idea of becoming an actor, so Costello set out for New York to take voice lessons. On the way he was stranded in St. Joseph, Missouri and answered an ad for a "Dutch" comedian in a show. He got the job, changed his name to Costello and never left the burlesque or vaudeville stage.

In 1929 Costello was playing the Empire Theatre in Brooklyn and his straight man fell ill. He was approached by Bud Abbott, who was working in the box office. They were perfect for each other, and thus was born one of the funniest comedy teams in history. The public adored their crazy, noisy, fast-and-foolish antics and wonderful loud-talking acts. They played the burlesque and vaudeville circuits, and their first break came in 1938 when they performed at the Loew's State in New York. Ted Collins, Kate Smith's radio impresario, discovered them there and gave them a guest appearance on her radio program. They were a hit and became regulars. From then on, Abbott and Costello starred on Broadway and in many Hollywood films. They also starred in many television shows and brought joy and laughter to millions of kids of all ages for decades. Who could forget their famous "who's-on-first" skit or Costello's wide-eyed yell, "Hey Abbott!" Costello endeared himself to the American public and became a success amassing great wealth. Not bad for "a bad boy" who couldn't resist dunking girls' pigtails in inkwells.

Jimmy Durante, born in New York City in 1893, had his nose—his "schnozzola," as he called it—insured with Lloyd's of London for a million dollars. During his long career, Durante worked on stage and screen and everything in between. While a speakeasy owner in New York in the 1920s, Durante appeared in Ziegfeld shows on Broadway before going to Hollywood to make such films as *Irene and Mary, The Passionate Plumber,* and *Get Rich Wallingford.* His radio performances were characterized by his mangling of the English language, and his television sign-off phrase, "Good night, Mrs. Calabash, wherever you are" became his trademark. Told once by John Barrymore that he ought to play Hamlet, Jimmy replied, "To hell with them small towns. New York is the only place for me." Inka-dinka-doo, Jimmy.

Joseph Piscopo, terrific actor and outrageous comedian, was born in Passaic, New Jersey, in 1951 and got his B.S. from Jones College in 1973. He has performed in numerous regional theater productions and toured the dinner-club circuit as a stand-up comedian and improvisation artist. Piscopo achieved national acclaim for his brilliant comedy work as a repertory player on "Saturday Night Live" from 1980 to 1984. He has also worked as a sportscaster and radio personality, and starred in several feature films, including *Johnny Dangerously* and *Wise Guys*. His hilarious antics now appear in television commercials and he has authored *The Piscopo Tapes*. If you want to know how great his imitations of famous people are, ask Frank Sinatra, fellow Italian American.

MEDIA ARTS

Italian Americans permeate the ranks of the media from advertising to newspapers to magazines to book publishers to television and radio. And it is a strange irony that the most pressing and disturbing issue for Italian Americans is the negative image generally presented in the media of Italian Americans. As more Italian Americans fill positions of power in media, surely this problem will wane.

FILM AND TELEVISION DIRECTORS

The director is the controlling creative force in the making of a movie. His or her artistic vision as it reflects the content and purpose of the script and his or her creativity in inspiring the performances of actors shape the destiny of a film. Each director, of course, has his or her own personal style. So too with Italian American directors who have risen so successfully over the last several decades as with those who have been around from the beginning. Each director has developed a personal, original and unique style.

Frank Capra, born in Bisaquino, Sicily, in 1903, celebrated his sixth birthday in the *Germania*'s black steerage hold, crammed in with other retching, praying, terrorized immigrants. The trip to America for Capra was a horror. He arrived in Los Angeles after thirteen days of cramped hardship in an overcrowded train. Capra worked his way through high school and then the California Institute of Technology, majoring in engineering. After years of various jobs, he met a producer, Walter Montague, and through him made his first film, *Fultah Fisher's Boarding House*. He was hooked, and thus was born one of America's greatest directors.

Capra's career encompasses a whole spectrum of movie greats; *American Madness* in 1932 about an idealistic banker who lends money based on character rather than collateral (based on A. P. Giannini); *It Happened One Night* in 1934 with Clark Gable and Claudette Colbert started an era of "screwball comedies"; *Mr. Deeds Goes to Town* in 1936 pits Gary Cooper as a small-town poet against the hucksters of the big city; *Lost Horizon* in 1937 preached a love-thy-neighbor philosophy; *Mr. Smith Goes to Washington* in 1939 starred Jimmy Stewart as a duped, idealistic senator who upholds justice; and, his classic, *It's a Wonderful Life* in 1946 demonstrated the value of a good life, again starring Jimmy Stewart.

To all appearances, Capra's films express the values of democracy, capitalism and individualism, but, perhaps unwittingly, his images are reflected on the screen through a filter of Italian values: love, pride, hard work, simple honesty, common sense, humility, idealism, individualism, suspicion of authority, courage in the face of adversity and, most of all, a deep sense of humanism. Paradoxically, Capra shows a view of life as American as apple pie, but the result has a definitely Italian quality. Capra is unquestionably a pre-eminent movie director and creative film genius.

Francis Ford Coppola, born in 1939, is one of the most creative directors now making films. His father Carmine was first flutist for Arturo Toscanini and is a composer for films. Francis directed his first film *Dementia 13* for Roger Corman, patron saint of young filmmakers. His first major-studio release *You're a Big Boy Now* received excellent notices but his next films went unacclaimed. He then won an Oscar for writing *Patton* and he produced *American Graffiti*, revealing himself to be multitalented. He established his own studio, the American Zoetrope in San Francisco, but found this was fraught with difficulties. Coppola then directed the dazzling movie *The*

Godfather, which established him as a gifted director. He followed this with *Godfather II and III*, which surpassed *I* in artistic achievement.

Coppola continued a brilliant career as a director and has always tried to reach beyond the bounds of traditional filmmaking through experimentation, such as with his production of *One From The Heart*. *Apocalypse Now* is an awesome film, and Coppola keeps getting better at what is already a truly gifted talent for cinematic expression.

Martin Scorsese, born in 1942 in Flushing, Queens, grew up from age eight in New York's Little Italy, and for him, the movies were a great escape from the mean streets that were filled with violence. After giving up the pursuit of a religious vocation when he failed the exam for Fordham University's divinity program, he enrolled at New York University, where he discovered the film department. Here he found his true vocation as a filmmaker.

In the 1960s, Scorsese won awards for his student films and in 1968 made his first feature film, *Who's That Knocking At My Door?* In 1970, he was supervising editor on *Woodstock* and associate producer of *Medicine Ball Caravan*. In 1972, he directed *Boxcar Bertha* for Roger Corman. *Mean Streets* won him widespread acclaim and starred the then-unknown Robert De Niro, but was not a box-office success. However, Warner Brothers did fund his *Alice Doesn't Live Here Anymore* in 1975, which won Ellen Burstyn an Oscar. Then came *Taxi Driver, New York, New York, The Last Waltz, Raging Bull, The King of Comedy, After Hours* and *The Color of Money*.

Scorsese has forged an intensely individualistic, deeply personal and somewhat controversial style of filmmaking. He leans heavily on a kind of subjective realism, which runs on an undercurrent of pervasive violence. He experiments with cinematic devices outside traditional form and mixes a quasidocumentary idiom with unusual originality. The results are always creative, provocative and unique.

Lewis John Carlino, born in 1932 in New York City, became a well-known movie director as well as playwright. In the early 1960s he specialized in one-act plays and won the Vernon Rice

and Obie awards for three simultaneously running plays—
Cages, Telemachus Clay and *Doubletalk* on New York stages. He
also writes his own screenplays for the films he directs, such as
The Great Santini and *Resurrection*. Carlino is now a distinguished director in the industry.

FILM AND TV PRODUCERS

E. Duke Vincent, or Eduard Michel Earl Joseph Ventimiglia,
born in New Jersey in 1932, is responsible for delivering to
your living rooms, for your enjoyment, "Dynasty," "Hotel"
and "The Colbys." He also brought you many hit television
shows, such as "Gomer Pyle," "The Jim Nabors Hour" and
"Arnie." Vincent had his own production company from 1968
to 1977, which he merged with Aaron Spelling Productions in
1979. He serves as executive supervising producer or supervising producer on all television shows produced by Spelling and
is senior vice president of the company. He was also a jet pilot
in the "Blue Angels" squadron, and when he started making
television shows, his name was too long for the credit box, so he
made it "E. Duke Vincent."

Garry Marshall, or Gary Marscharelli, was born in the Bronx
and became a millionaire by taking a composite of three
high-school dropouts he knew from his De Witt Clinton High
School days and creating "Arthur Fonzarelli" alias "The Fonz"
of his hit television series "Happy Days." Marshall began as a
copywriter for the *New York Daily News* at fifty dollars per week
after getting his B.A. from Northwestern University in journalism. He played drums in a combo, did a stint in the Army,
created one-liners with Woody Allen, wrote for Phil Foster,
Joey Bishop, Jack Paar and teamed with Jerry Belson on over
one hundred sitcoms, including "I Love Lucy," the "Dick Van
Dyke Show," "The Odd Couple" and a couple of movies. It
took two and a half years to get "Happy Days" on the air
because no one else believed in it, but since then, Marshall has
become one of the most successful film and television writer-
producers in Hollywood, bringing more hits like "Laverne and

Shirley" to the air. "Happy Days" became a national monument to American life of that era. Marshall is a brilliant comedy writer who has a genius for finding the common denominators for comedic situations. He is now a top producer.

Renee Valente, from the Bronx and a graduate of Evander Childs High School, is a most remarkable Italian American woman producer. Her "QB VII" was the first miniseries on television, and she brought Burt Reynolds to national attention in her film *Hawk* in the mid 1960s. Valente began her producing career in the 1950s with shows like "Kraft Theatre" and won an Emmy for her "Art Carney Specials." She became head of production for Talent Associations from 1960 to 1962, producing many series and specials. She produced through the 1960s and became vice president of talent for Columbia from 1968 to 1975. She then worked two years as executive producer and vice president of movies for television for Columbia, producing movies like the *Caryl Chessman Story* with Alan Alda and *Contract on Cherry Street* with Frank Sinatra. In 1978, she formed Renee Valente Productions and has been producing major features, movies of the week and television miniseries ever since.

John Furia, Jr., is a major producer in the film and television business with his own production company formed in 1984. He developed the series and wrote the pilot for "Hotel" for Aaron Spelling Productions. His top shows include "The Sun Also Rises," "My Mother's Secret," "Life with Paul Sorvino," "Rage of Angels," with Armand Assante and others. Furia has produced many movies of the week such as *The Blue Knight* and many television series like *Kung Fu.* He also has written many shows, such as *The Name of the Game, Twilight Zone, The Waltons* and *The Singing Nun.* His awards are many and his talent is brilliant, but he is also very well respected for his intelligent and sophisticated taste in his creative projects. In a business that can be very dehumanizing, Furia is known as a warm, caring man with highly humanistic values. He is a prince of the industry.

Ever wonder who's behind *Tom and Jerry, Huckleberry Hound, Yogi Bear, The Flintstones, Scooby-Doo, Top Cat, The Jetsons,*

Magilla Gorilla, Herculoids, Super-friends and *The Smurfs*? Well, wonder no more, it's Joe Barbera, born on Delancy Street in 1911 in New York, the son of Sicilian immigrants. He grew up in Brooklyn and always loved to draw. Barbera worked at a bank to support his classes at Pratt Institute and the Art Students League and hustled his cartoons to magazines like *Colliers*. Around 1930 he tried to connect with Disney, but instead broke into animation at three legendary East Coast studios: Max Fleisher *(Popeye)*, Van Beuren *(Toonerville Trolley)* and Paul Terry *(Terrytoons)*. At MGM in the late 1930s, he met Bill Hanna who had a gift for comedy, story and characters. They created *Puss Gets the Boots* which was nominated for an Oscar and "Tom" and "Jerry" were born. For two decades they made *Tom and Jerry* cartoons until MGM closed down the animation studio. Barbera and Hanna decided to start their own animation studio and they gambled on the growing television market. They won. Hanna-Barbera has developed many hit shows and somewhere in the world now, every hour of the day or night, some child or grown-up is watching their cartoons. Joe Barbera is now the preeminent animation artist in the world and "the world's number-one babysitter." *Sixty Minutes* dubbed him "The Sultan of Saturday Morning Programs," Smarter than your average Barbera, that Joe.

FILM AND TV EXECUTIVES

Salvatore J. Iannucci, born in 1927 in Brooklyn, lived with his grandparents in Little Italy of New York City. Iannucci fought his way out of a poor neighborhood by getting his B. A. at New York University in 1949 and his law degree from Harvard Law School in 1952. His distinguished career in entertainment began with staff attorney positions at RCA and ABC from 1952 to 1954; in 1954 he joined CBS as an executive in the business affairs department. By 1964 he was Vice President of Business Affairs of CBS Television, the first Italian American in such a position. He served as president of Capitol Records, president of Playboy Entertainment Group, president of Filmways Entertainment, executive vice president of Embassy Communications and senior vice president for Aaron Spelling Productions. He now heads the entertainment law division of Bushkin, Gaines, Gaimes & Jonas. He is now a partner in the worldwide firm of Korn-Ferry International, the preeminent executive search firm. He is also on the boards of UCLA and the Hollywood Radio and Television Society. Iannucci has gained a top reputation as a consummate television executive, a master deal-maker; he has worked devotedly for Italian American causes, especially in the media.

John J. Agoglia, also a native of Brooklyn, attended Brooklyn College. He spent 14 years with CBS Entertainment, serving as vice president of business affairs in New York, taking over the same position held by Iannucci. He joined NBC in 1979 as vice president of program and talent negotiations. In 1980, he was named senior vice president of business affairs and in 1984 he was given added responsibility as executive vice president of NBC Productions, a newly created position. Agoglia's extensive experience and knowledge of broadcasting, and his distinguished talent as a strong, creative executive have brought him great success, NBC great profits and the entertainment industry great programming.

Anthony Cassara, born in 1944 in the Bronx, got his B.S. degree from New York University in marketing and promptly joined the U.S. Navy as an air intelligence officer. He began his broadcasting career in New York at Metro Television Sales, then Telerep and The Petry Company. Cassara joined KTLA in 1973 and by 1977 was vice president and general manager. He made KTLA the number one independent television station in Los Angeles. His innovations in programming were copied nationwide, and in 1979 he was named president of the Television Division of Golden West Broadcasters. In 1982, he structured a mega-deal sale of this division to Golden West Television, a new television entertainment conglomerate, and became its president and CEO. In 1984, he was named president and CEO of Wometco Broadcasting Company. Cassara is a bright and gifted television executive with a complete knowledge of the business. His creative and innovative management has brought his companies to the height of success in the entertainment industry.

Carol Altieri, born and raised in Queens, majored in Music, Speech and Drama at Ithaca College, spent a year at Claremont Business School, and joined CBS in 1969 as a secretary in the Press Information Department. In five years she was program practices editor and was transferred to Los Angeles in 1979 as senior editor. By 1984, she was appointed West Coast Vice President for Program Practices and oversees the clearance of all shows at CBS originating on the West Coast. Altieri is an extremely bright and successful television executive who puts her considerable knowledge to work in the name of creating better television programming.

Angela Petillo was born in 1949 and raised in Asbury Park, New Jersey. She received her B.A. in English at Montclair State College in 1971 and then worked a year in the inner-city school system near New York City. From 1972 to 1976, she travelled in Western Europe, North Africa, the Mid-East and Russia. She lived for a while in Rome, where she taught at the Vatican and Notre Dame International School, and she also worked as a model and photographer on the *Achille Lauro*. In 1976, Petillo moved to Los Angeles as an assistant to producer Alex De Benedetti at the De Laurentiis Corp. She studied law at night and got her J.D. degree from Loyola Law School in 1980. She joined ABC as a lawyer until 1985 when Creative Artists Agency hired her as a business affairs negotiator in their television department. Petillo is now one of the powerhouse deal makers in the land of Hollywood.

As President of the Motion Picture Association of America, Jack Valenti is unquestionably the preeminent ambassador to the world for the entertainment industry. Born in 1921 in Houston, Texas, Valenti graduated from high school at age 15 and studied at the University of Houston. His life was interrupted by World War II where he flew 51 bomber missions. He came back and graduated with a degree in business, then got his Master's degree from Harvard Graduate School of Business Administration. After one career in advertising, and another career in government as President Lyndon Johnson's troubleshooter, chief aide and righthand man, Valenti left the White House in 1966 to become president of the M.P.A.A. Under his dynamic and innovative leadership the association has made many progressive advances for the entire entertainment industry.

TELEVISION

John Scali, born in 1918 in Canton, Ohio, received his B.S. degree from Boston University in Journalism in 1942. He became a war correspondent for the Associated Press in 1944 in Europe and worked for A.P. until 1961. He joined ABC Television and Radio in 1961 and through his talented and expert reporting of the highest quality proceeded to win every award in the profession and to become the dean of electronic-media journalists in America. Expressive of Scali's impact, the American Federation of Television and Radio Artists created in his honor the "John Scali Award" which is given to television reporting approaching Scalie's degree of excellence.

Richard Valeriani, a native of Camden, New Jersey, graduated from Yale University in 1953, studied at the University of Pavia in Italy and the University of Barcelona in Spain, and served in the U.S. Army. He began his journalism career with *The Trentonian* in 1956 and joined NBC News in 1961 as bureau chief at Havana. After the Bay of Pigs fiasco, he spent several years covering riots, rebellions, wars and crises, including the civil war in the Dominican Republic which won him an Overseas Press Club Award. He joined the Washington bureau in 1965 and spent 15 years covering the activities of Presidents and Secretaries of State. His book *Travels With Henry* (Kissinger) won critical acclaim. Now NBC's national correspondent in New York, Valeriani has covered many national and world events from all 50 states and 90 countries. He is recognized as an award-winning, eminent television journalist.

MAGAZINES

For some reason, Italian Americans have made their inroads into magazine publishing on the business, management and advertising side rather than the editorial. An old, respected magazine, though not a mainstream one, is the *Messenger of the Sacred Heart* founded by Father Benedict Sestini in 1866; this Catholic magazine has worldwide circulation. *Il Carroccio* was co-founded by Father Nicola Fusco with Agostino De Biasi in 1915 and lived till 1935 as a bilingual cultural magazine for Italian Americans on social and political problems.

In more commercial publishing, the most successful publisher of a national magazine was Bob Guccione first with *Penthouse* and then with *Omni* magazines. His mark on the magazine publishing world is unmistakable. He defies categorization and is in a league all by himself. He is first an entrepreneur and second a publisher, but he is more of a real publisher than most. He does *not sell* ad space—he directs, orchestrates and envisions the use of his magazine as an advertising medium. He is totally involved editorially and artistically.

Carlo Vitterini published *Redbook* magazine in the 1970s and now *Parade* magazine. He was one of the first Italian Americans to get to the top. Leda Sanford made history for women and Italian Americans when she became publisher and editor of *American Home* magazine in 1975. She was the first woman publisher of a national magazine with a circulation of over one million. She also was founding publisher with Jeno Paulucci of *Attenzione* magazine, the first Italian American national magazine in America. Grace Mirabella, editor of *Vogue* magazine is another top person. John Boni, one of Vittorini's managers at *Redbook*, is now publisher of *Parents* magazine and head of Gruner and Jahr.

Pamela Fiori began her career in publishing in 1968 at *Holiday* magazine and joined *Travel & Leisure* of American Express Publishing Corporation as associate editor in 1971. She became editor-in-chief in 1975 and through her leadership and creative direction, *Travel & Leisure* has developed into an elegant lifestyle magazine. With more than one million subscribers, it is considered the leading travel magazine in the United States and has been nominated four times for general excellence by National Magazine Awards. Fiori has received many awards personally in recognition of her achievements.

In another class by himself, is Peter Callahan who, mind you, had an Italian mother and is married to a Sicilian wife.

Callahan is owner-president of MacFadden Holding, Inc., a $35 million publishing company he founded in 1975. Macfadden sells more than 35 million magazines annually. Callahan was born in 1942 in New York, got his undergraduate degree from St. Francis College and his M.B.A. from Columbia University. Among his many magazine publications are *True Story, True Confessions, Modern Romance, Teen Beat, Chief Executive, Us* and *Cheri* magazines. Callahan, the son of a truck driver, identifies with the blue-collar men and women who read his magazines and prides himself on the loyalty of the people who work for him. He should—his magazines in 1980 were bringing in $20 million a year.

Rose Ann Adolfi is vice president of circulation and editor of four magazines for Harle Publications. She also manages the subscription department. Thirteen years previous to this, she worked part time as a mail clerk in Harle's subscription department for their puzzle magazines. Adolfi was born and raised in Brooklyn, and began her career only after working as a housewife for 13 years. Her successful rise in publishing as an Italian American woman is admirable.

There is a veritable Guccione Dynasty in publishing now. Jackie Guccione Lewis, sister of Bob, began her own business and publishes *Letters* and *Dear Penelope* magazines. Joseph Michael Lewis, son of Jackie, is editor of *Dear Penelope*. Jeri Guccione Winston, Jackie's twin sister and sister to Bob, is vice president at *Penthouse*. Tonina Guccione Biggs, daughter of Bob, runs the *Penthouse* record division in Los Angeles. Anthony Guccione, son of Bob, is being groomed to be president of *Penthouse*. And, Anthony Guccione, father of Bob, is treasurer of *Penthouse*—his starting salary in 1966 was $75 per week.

BOOK PUBLISHING

In book publishing, there are also many Italian Americans contributing to the literary world. Alberto Vitale is president and chief executive officer of The Bantam, Doubleday, Dell Publishing Group. Nick Accifento is with Crown Books, as is

Carl Apollonio. Louis Boccardi is executive vice president of Farrar, Straus & Giroux. Joseph Consolino was president of Arno. Joseph Consolino, Jr. is with Random House. Tom Consolino is at William Morrow. Robert Diforio is chairman of New American Library. George De Lacorte was chairman of the board of Dell Publishing Co., Dell Books, Laurel Books, De Lacorte Press and 25 magazines. He is the largest publisher of comic books in the U.S. and at one time owned over 200 magazines. The Delacorte Theatre is named after him. John Cuneo founded Cuneo Press, which became one of the most successful publishing businesses in America.

Michael di Capua is a literary editor. Jonathan Galassi is an award-winning editor now at Farrar, Straus & Giroux. Robert Ginna, Jr. is editor at Little Brown. Joseph Guadagno is vice president of finance for Random House. Leonard Riggio pioneered discount books and owns B. Dalton and Barnes & Noble. Angelo Rizzoli is the head of a huge communications empire. Joseph Vergarna is an editor, as well as an author, at Harper & Row.

Vic Cavallaro heads his own company, Madison Street Productions. Lisa Amoroso is a designer for G.P. Putnam's Sons and a top freelance illustrator. Candida Donadio is a power-house agent with clients like Mario Puzo. Adele Leone is an agent. Toni Lopopolo is an outstanding editor at St. Martin's Press. Ann Spinelli is art director for G.P. Putnam's Sons.

Joseph Papaleo, also an outstanding writer, has just founded Delphinium Press, a new publishing company with the specific goal of publishing novels that have great artistic merit, with special attention to Italian American writers. Bravo, Giuseppe!

ADVERTISING

There are many Italian Americans in advertising and it seems a natural place for their creativity to take form. Many of the best agencies were started by Italian Americans.

Jerry Della Femina, born in 1936 in Brooklyn, started his career in advertising as a copywriter and by 1967 was running his own company. He was named Advertising Executive of the Year in 1970 and wrote a classic book on his profession, *From Those Wonderful Folks Who Gave You Pearl Harbor*. He also wrote a book about growing up Italian. His agency, Della Femina, Travisano & Partners, Inc. is one of the most creative and successful in advertising.

Robert Giraldi, born in 1939 in Peterson, New Jersey, got his B.F.A. from Pratt Institute in 1960 and began his creative career in New York City as associate creative director and at Young & Rubicam from 1960 to 1971. He joined Della Feminia, Travisano & Partners and became vice president and head of the creative department from 1971 to 1973. By 1974, he was president of his own company, Bob Giraldi Productions, and has become famous for his creative talents. He has written and directed commercials, films, videos and stage plays. Giraldi has been heaped with honors for excellence as an artist, including many Clio awards, Gold awards, Andy awards, One Show awards and Cannes Film Festival Awards.

P.S. That fast-talking guy for Federal Express, remember him? He's John Moschitta.

WRITERS

In the *beginning*, was the word . . .

Italian Americans have particularly excelled in creative writing and especially in fiction. Clearly there is an active fantasy life at work in the Italian American psyche, and we are sure that everybody reading this book feels that he or she has a novel rumbling around inside just waiting to burst forth in great splendor upon an expectant audience.

As with all writing, the trick is to put on paper, in black and white, those fantasies, ideas, feelings, stories, dramas and comedies that are burning within you seeking expression. Then you have to get published. (And then you pray and wait for royalties.)

Many Italian American writers have written about the Italian American experience and many have taken the experience as the background for their work. More and more Italian American writers are emerging in magazines, books, films, television shows and poetry. The Italian American experience itself has become a hot subject these days, a direct outgrowth of the coming of age of Italian Americans, the increased number of powerful, visible Italian Americans such as Cuomo, Iacocca and Ferraro, and the general and overwhelming interest shown in Italian Americans by non-Italian Americans.

The increase of Italian American *writing* may also be an expression on the part of Italian Americans to genuinely share their experiences, perceptions, thoughts and feelings, not just because they are of value to others, but because the stories are so rich in content, theme and substance . . . and, of course, so dramatic and funny. There is also a yearning to "set the record straight" about the Italian American and to present a true picture of who and what we really are as opposed to the negative stereotypical image often presented in the media.

It is wonderful to report that there are *so many* Italian American writers and we can only hope to give a delicious sampling of who they are . . .

Pietro di Donato, born in 1911, is preeminent among those who wrote of their Italian American experience. Also a bricklayer, playwright, biographer and short story writer, this novelist's classic work of art was his *Christ in Concrete* in 1938. He depicted the squalid world of Italians and the construction worker during the 1920s and 1930s as told through the son of the family, Paulie. In his struggle, Paulie's Italian family values clash with those of American society. In 1960, he wrote *Three Circles of Light*, and his brilliant piece on Aldo Moro in *Penthouse* magazine won him the Overseas Press Club Award in 1978.

Jerre Mangione, born in 1909 in Rochester, graduated Syracuse University, wrote for *Time* magazine and became book editor for McBride & Company from 1934 to 1937. He was the national coordinating editor of the Federal Writers' Project from 1937 to 1939 and special assistant to the U.S. commissioner of immigration and naturalization from 1942 to 1948. He wrote several novels, especially *Mount Allegro* in 1943, which tells of a son who returns to Sicily where he feels a mystical sense of being at home. The book is a masterpiece on the subject. Among others, he wrote *Reunion* in Sicily in 1950, *A Passion for Sicilians* in 1968 and *America Is Also Italian* in 1969. Mangione teaches and directs the writer's program at the University of Pennsylvania.

John Fante, born in 1909 in Denver, is a novelist and screen writer who has spent decades writing on the Italian experience. His first novel, *Wait Until Spring, Bandini* in 1938 told of Italian family life in his native Colorado. His film *Full of Life* about an immigrant father determined to build his children a fireplace, won him an Academy nomination in 1957. His *Dago Red* is a collection of family sketches and is one of his best works. He also wrote *The Brotherhood of the Grape*.

Andrew F. Rolle, professor of American history at Occidental College in Los Angeles, got his M.A. and Ph.D. degrees from UCLA and has written many books, including several on the Italian American experience, especially *The American Italians* and *The Immigrant Upraised*. This last is a seminal work depicting a very different picture of the immigrant experience. Instead of the "uprooted, defenseless pawns adrift in a sea of confusion and despair" ghetto image, he shows how the Italians west of the Mississippi experienced an "upraised" and more rewarding life as highly accepted members of society.

Richard Gambino, born of Sicilian parentage in Brooklyn, may be in a category all of his own. A professor at Queens College, New York, he pioneered a program of Italian studies that was the first in the country and has promoted Italian American causes with great success for decades. His book, *Blood of My Blood: The Dilemma of the Italian Americans* in 1974 is a supreme achievement in presenting the Italian American experience in America. His novels include *Vendetta* in 1977, which depicts the tragic lynching of Italians in New Orleans, and *Bread and Roses* in 1981 which is a multi-generational saga about an Italian family dynasty that made the world its own.

Anthony Di Franco, born in 1945 in New York City, went to Xavier High School and graduated from Fordham University in 1966. He earned his Masters degree in 1969. He also got his Secondary School Administration degree, taught high school and joined the faculty of Suffolk Community College. In 1983 he published his first book of nonfiction *Italy Balanced on the*

Edge of Time followed in 1984 by a biography of Pope John Paul II. In 1984, he published his first novel, *The Streets of Paradise*, set against the mass migrations at the turn of the 19th century. His short story in 1984, *The Garden of Redemption*, was chosen to be in the O. Henry Prize Collection. His novel *Ardent Spring* is a love story taking place against the rise of Fascism between the World Wars. Di Franco directs his powerful creative talent toward true and positive portrayals of the Italian American experience.

Italian American women, in addition to coming into their own generally, have especially been writing about their experiences and Italian backgrounds. They too have been drawing upon their lives as Italian Americans for themes, subjects and stories.

Lucia Chiavola Birnbaum, born in 1924 in Kansas City, spent several years at the University of Kansas City from 1940 to 1943, but dropped out. She wound up in Berkeley, California, getting her B.A., M.A. and Ph.D. by 1964 at the University of California. Birnbaum, a brilliant political activist and feminist, has written *Liberazione della Donna*, a fascinating and comprehensive account of the Italian feminist movement— from long-time communists to Catholic nuns and Sicilian housewives. This intriguing, yet disturbing, book tells the dramatic story of the victorious struggle of Italian women who claim "Io sono mia" (I am my own person). The presentation of this uniquely rich feminist vision by an Italian American woman has had profound meaning for and major impact on other Italian American women and *all* feminists.

Helen Barolini, born in 1925 in Syracuse, New York, is a poet, essayist and novelist who got her B.A. degree in 1947 from Syracuse University and her M.L.S. degree from Columbia University in 1959. She has been a teacher, librarian, associate editor and writer since the 1940s. Her novel *Umbertina*, which examines the ethnic experience of Italian American women, established Barolini in 1979 as a passionate and articulate spokeswoman of the Italian American experience in literature and won many top honors. In 1985, she published *The Dream Book*, and already this has become a landmark in American letters. It collects, for the first time, Italian American women authors who are creating in various literary genres and presents them as a group. In addition to an abundance of stories, essays and poems, Barolini has just published another book *Love in the Middle Ages* (of life, not world history).

Linda Brandi Cateura published her highly successful collection of interviews called *Growing Up Italian* in 1986. This is an honest, warm look at how being brought up as an Italian American shaped the lives, characters and careers of 24 well-known Italian Americans such as Mario Cuomo, Tony Bennett, Geraldine Ferraro and Francis Ford Coppola. The *good* things they remembered were food, culture and family closeness, and the *bad* things were discrimination and bigotry. Cateura was a literary editor at *Harper's Bazaar*, an editor at *Family Circle* and *Woman's Day*, and a press associate for Mario Cuomo when he was New York State Secretary of State.

Frances Winwar or Francesca Vinciguerra, born in 1900 in Taormina, Sicily, came to America at age seven and became the dean of American biographers, a superb novelist, a brilliant translator and an excellent literary critic. She was educated at Hunter College and Columbia University, and co-founded the Leonardo da Vince Art School in New York City. Over four decades she wrote seven novels and in 1933 published her first of 13 biographies, *Poor Splendid Wings*, winning the non-fiction prize from *The Atlantic Monthly*. Her translation of Boccaccio's *Decameron* is considered the absolute best, and she translated librettos of Verdi for the Metropolitan Opera. Winwar also wrote historical works and juvenile books.

Laura Archera Huxley, widow of Aldous Huxley, is a successful psychotherapist and author who wrote *Between Heaven and Earth* and *This Timeless Moment*. Her most famous book was *You Are Not the Target* in 1963 which was a forerunner of the new-age, positive-thinking, self-help books so prevalent today. Her book was a "positive plan for self-discovery" and presented her "life-enhancing secrets." Interesting enough, the book really was ahead of its time.

Rose Basile Green is a prolific and distinguished poet as well as an accomplished prose writer, critic, translator and lecturer. She grew up on a 120 acre farm in Harwinton, Connecticut, earned her B.A. from the College of New Rochelle in 1935 with an English major, and won her M.A. from Columbia University. Her thesis for a Ph.D. at Pennsylvania State in 1962 was "The Italian American Novel" and this became her first book. She examined 70 novels by writers of Italian descent and demonstrated their aethestic value and social implications. Since then she has been quite prolific and her work has won her many honors. She helped create Cabrini College from 1957 to 1962 and is professor emeritus from the English Department she headed. From a one-room schoolhouse, Green became director of a college and one of the best Italian American women writers.

Deanna Paoli Gumina, born in 1944 in San Francisco, got her B.A. and M.A. from the University of San Francisco. She has written many articles on a whole array of Italian American themes and subjects, including the California fishing industry, the San Francisco earthquake, the wineries, immigration, churches, the Italians of North Beach, Italian American women; she also wrote a history of Italians in San Francisco. Her works are penetrating and profound on these subjects. Gumina is a talented writer who has gone outside her ethnic writing to broader concerns and subjects. She represents a significant perspective on the Italian American woman.

Patricia Lobosco was born in Bensonhurst, Brooklyn, got her B.A. in 1972 and her M.A. later in 1982 from Brooklyn College, both in English literature. She began her career teaching English in a secondary school, a career she continues while also working as a writer and contributing editor to *The Brooklyn Via* newspaper. This paper, published in a monthly magazine format, services the predominantly Italian communities of Brooklyn, an area to which many new Italian immigrants still come. Lobosco has just started a bright career as a writer.

Francesca Stanfill was born in Oxford, England, and grew up in New York and Los Angeles. She graduated from Yale University and worked as a journalist for the *New York Times*, where her articles appeared in the *Times Magazine*, and for *Women's Wear Daily*. Her first novel *Shadows and Light* was the story of a young woman's initiation into love and erotic passion set in New York, Venice, Crete, Instanbul and St. Moritz. Stanfill is now writing her second novel, *Wakefield Hall*.

Maureen Mole, was born in Brooklyn, New York, in 1950 and earned a B. A. in English in 1971 at St. John's University. After graduation, she taught language arts in elementary school and did freelance modeling in fashion shows. Moving to Bridgewood, New Jersey, in 1973 to be close to her parents, she became involved in community affairs and specialized in coordinating social events. All Mole's prior experiences culminated in a career, began in 1977, as a professional lecturer on the topic of entertaining. In 1980, Simon & Schuster published her successful how-to book, *The Book of Entertaining At Home.*

MYSTERY

In the field of mass-production mystery writers, there are two Italian Americans who are giants.

Evan Hunter or Salvatore Lombino, born in 1926 in New York City, received his B.A. from Hunter College in 1950 and became certainly one of the most creative and prolific writers in America. Under the name of Evan Hunter, he has written some 20 novels: one of the most famous is *Blackboard Jungle*, written in 1954 and later made into a classic film. He wrote *Strangers When We Meet, Last Summer, Mothers and Daughters* and *Streets of Gold*, which is set in the East Harlem Italian neighborhood. Under the name Ed McBain, he wrote 37 mystery novels in his "87th Precinct Series." Under the names Hunt Collins and Richard Marsten, he wrote other mysteries. His plays, movie scripts and television scripts for "The Chisholms" at CBS were written as Evan Hunter.

Michael Angelo Avallone, Jr., born in 1924 in New York City, is by far the most published Italian American and possibly the most prolific writer in the country, if not the world! His parents were equally prolific—he was one of 17 children. In the three decades from 1953 to 1983, Avallone wrote more than one thousand works under his own name and 16 pseudonyms. There are over 40 million copies of his 186 novels still in print. His awesome, creative talent encompassed mysteries, science fiction, occult, sex and juvenile novels, and novelizations of movies and television shows. His character Ed Noon, created for his first novel *The Tall Dolores*, was so liked that it lasted into 38 novels.

POETRY

In poetry, the first Italian American to achieve national stature and recognition was Arturo Giovannitti, born in 1884 in Campobasso, Abruzzi, who moved to Canada in 1900 and studied at McGill University. He came to New York, attended Columbia University, worked as a coal miner in Pennsylvania, and returned to New York where he became a socialist and edited *Il Proletario*. He was arrested in 1912 with labor organizer Joseph Ettor at the famous Lawrence, Massachusetts, textile strike by the IWW. His poems of his experiences were published in 1914 as *Arrows in the Gale*. This, along with *The Walker*, his masterpiece, made Giovannitti the most the most important Italian American poet of his time.

Giovanni Cecchetti, Distinguished Professor at UCLA, aside from his remarkable work in creating and organizing top university Italian departments, has written 15 books and 150 articles dealing with literary works which are widely known in Europe and America. He is a renowned literary critic, translator and a poet as well. One of his books won an international literary prize in Italy and the Italian Government honored him with the very rare Presidential Gold Medal for special artistic and cultural merits. He may be the most renowned writer of Italian poetry living outside of Italy.

John Ciardi, born in 1916 in Boston, graduated from Tufts and the University of Michigan. He taught English at the University of Kansas City, Harvard and Rutgers, and is considered the dean of Italian American poets, translators and literary critics. He wrote 14 volumes of poetry from 1940 to 1979, plus an array of essays, anthologies and textbooks. His translation of Dante's *Divine Comedy* is world renowned and his 14 volumes of juvenile poetry written in honor of his three children are brilliant. Ciardi was once called "An elephant with a nightingale's voice."

Gregory Nunzio Corso, born in 1930 in New York, became

the poet-spokesman for the "beat generation." After a troubled childhood with five different foster parents, dropping out of grammar school, three years in prison and many different jobs, he began writing and reciting his poetry around this country and in Mexico and Europe during the 1950s. He published 10 volumes of poems, 2 novels, 2 plays and several screenplays. Corso's first book was *The Vestal Lady on Brattle and other Poems*.

Lawrence Ferlinghetti, born in 1920 in Yonkers, studied at the University of North Carolina for his B.A., Columbia University for his M.A. and the Sorbonne for his doctorate, and is perhaps the most famous Italian American poet. In 1953, he founded the City Lights Bookshop in San Francisco and his own publishing house, City Lights in 1955. This became a mecca for artists and writers of the beat generation and Ferlinghetti, also a painter, book designer and graphic artist, became the poet laureate of a whole movement. From 1955 to 1981, he wrote hundreds of poems and became famous for his public poetry readings and his battles over obscenity issues. He put out a dozen poetry volumes, a surrealist novel, many experimental plays and many articles. He is most known for his *A Coney Island of the Mind*.

SCIENCE FICTION, CHILDREN'S BOOKS, ILLUSTRATORS

Frank Frazetta, preeminent illustrator/artist, born in 1928 in Brooklyn, sold his first crayon drawings to his grandmother for a penny at age three. By age five his teachers were astounded that he could draw better than ten-year-olds. In school, he made comic books and at age eight enrolled in the Brooklyn Academy of Fine Arts with classical Italian artist Michael Falanga who, on seeing Frank's test drawing, proclaimed, "Mama Mia! We have a genius here!" By 16, he was a professional working as an assistant to science fiction cartoonist John Giunta. In 1944, his career in comic books began, and by 1950 he had his own comic called *Thun'da, King of the Congo*. Frazetta became a brilliant illustrator turning out magnificent art on book covers, movie posters and all graphic forms. His most famous are the *Buck Rogers* covers, *The Johnny Comet* strip, Edgar Rice Burroughs illustrations and *Lord of the Rings, Kubla Kahn* and *Women of the Ages* portfolios. According to legend, the Buck Rogers covers inspired George Lucas for his *Star Wars* saga.

NOVELISTS

Dom De Lillo, born in the Bronx in 1936, graduated from Fordham University in 1958 with a degree in Communication Arts, worked at an advertising agency and became a full-time writer. From 1971 to 1982, he wrote seven novels, which have developed a huge following and gained him great acclaim. An unusually original writer, some of his titles are *End Zone, Great Jones Street, Ratner's Star, Running Dog* and *White Noise.*

JOURNALISTS–NOVELISTS

In journalism, there are a multitude of Italian Americans writing for newspapers, magazines and periodicals across the nation. Some have worked in the ethnic press, many in mainstream publishing and several have become huge smash-hit writers of books, scripts and television shows.

Philip Caputo, born in 1941 in Chicago, served in the U.S. Marines in Vietnam from 1965 to 1967, and became a Pulitzer Prize-winning reporter for *The Chicago Tribune.* His personal experience of the war as a soldier and journalist made his 1977 book *A Rumor of War* a bestseller. He now devotes full time to writing novels.

Paul Gallico, born in 1897 in New York City, became a most successful journalist-writer-editor. He wrote sports columns, short stories, books and screenplays. From 1922 to 1936, he worked for the *Daily News;* he left to devote himself to the creation of 41 books, 200 short stories, nine screenplays and two television spectaculars, encompassing fiction, children's literature, fables, ghost stories and biographies. Remember *The*

Poseidon Adventure and *Pride of the Yankees*? They're his.

Gay Talese, born in 1932 in Ocean City, New Jersey, started his career as a writer by becoming a copy boy at *The New York Times* after graduating from the University of Alabama in 1953. He then worked as a reporter for *The Times* until 1965 and wrote his first book *New York: A Serendipiter's Journey* in 1961 which brought critical acclaim but very little financial reward. His creative talent as a human-interest writer gained notice with a piece called *Then and Now* about Nita Naldi, the famous movie star then living in obscurity. In 1965, he left *The Times* and in 1969 published his bestselling history of *The Times* called *The Kingdom and The Power*. In 1971, he published another hit *Honor Thy Father* which made him a ton of money. Talese is highly regarded as one of the pioneers of the new journalism along with Tom Wolfe, Norman Mailer and Truman Capote. His latest bestseller was *Thy Neighbor's Wife*. Talese is diligently writing his own book on the Italian American experience.

Nicholas Pileggi, born in 1933 in Brooklyn, went to P.S. 26 and New Utrecht High School in Bensonhurst, and graduated from Long Island University in 1955. Coincidentally, Nick Pileggi and Gay Talese are cousins and their careers ran somewhat parallel. During college, Pileggi worked nights at Associated Press as a copy boy and became a reporter for A.P. upon graduation. After his years writing at A.P., he joined *New York* magazine in 1968 writing non-fiction and is now contributing editor there. An excellent writer, Pileggi has become famous for his extremely creative pieces on politics, corruption, crime and urban affairs and has always drawn upon his Italian American experience for his creativity. His first novel, *Wise Guy*, was number one on *The New York Times* bestseller list of March 8, 1987. Pileggi now joins a prestigious group of Italian Americans who have been there too.

PHENOMENA

Leo Buscaglia is known internationally for one small word with the biggest of all possible meanings—LOVE. Buscaglia is a professor of education at the University of Southern California and his very popular course which enrolls literally hundreds of students is simply called LOVE. In 1973, he published his first book consisting of his lectures and entitled *Love*. Already a very well-known lecturer, Buscaglia skyrocketed to fame when book sales really took off. Over the ensuing years, he wrote many books, including *Because I Am Human, Personhood* and *Living, Loving & Learning*, among others.

Buscaglia is unquestionably a publishing phenomenon—at one time four of his seven books were on *The New York Times* bestseller lists. His books sell in the millions of copies and anyone who has had the love-filled joy of experiencing Leo Buscaglia can understand why. He hypnotizes people with his loving words about human love; audiences, after his presentations, walk as in a trance toward his outstretched arms for a loving embrace. His television shows also attract multitudes.

But, Buscaglia is more than an educator, lecturer and writer—he is a phenomenon as the embodiment of one simple word, LOVE, and this phenomenon is quintessentially Italian American. Isn't it interesting that Leo Buscaglia, the "Love Doctor," embraces and expresses values that are so Italian in origin? And isn't it interesting how starved our population seems to be for that one simple thing—LOVE—? This is what Leo teaches, lovingly. Leo is the supreme artist of the high art of living, loving and learning.

Mario Puzo, born in 1920 in New York City the son of illiterate Italian immigrants, became one of the most significant writers of the 20th century and created some of the best fiction ever written. Puzo and his four brothers and two sisters were raised by his mother after his father, a trackman for the New York City Railroad, deserted the family when Puzo was 12. His mother was a strong, autocratic "family chief" and they lived in Hell's Kitchen on Manhattan's West Side, then a predominantly Italian neighborhood.

Puzo spent a lot of time reading at the library and by age 16 had decided to become a writer. After serving in World War II, he worked as a civil servant during the late 1940s into the 1950s. He studied literature and creative writing at Columbia University and the New School for Social Research. In 1950, he published his first short story *The Last Christmas* and in 1955, his first book *Dark Arena*, about the dehumanizing effects of war on winner as well as loser. The novel was hailed for its direct, naturalistic style as one of the best of the postwar era. He wrote *The Fortunate Pilgrim* in 1965 after a stint editing men's magazines and writing short stories and articles. This book may be the best ever written about Italian immigrants in America for its beautiful merging of social history with fiction. In 1966, he published *The Runaway Summer of David Shaw*, a picturesque and acclaimed children's book.

By the mid-1960s, now in his mid-forties, with great critical esteem but very few royalty checks, Puzo set out to write a bestseller. He wrote *The Godfather*, but his publisher, Atheneum, rejected his ten-page plot summary. He took it to G.P. Putnam's Sons who gave him a $5,000 advance. In 1969, *The Godfather* shot to the top of *The New York Times* bestseller list where it stayed for twenty-two weeks—and the Italian American, in a way, came of age in America. Again Puzo had merged social and cultural history into a compelling and fascinating story. Puzo sold the film rights to Paramount for $85,000 and when the movie was directed by the gifted Francis Ford Coppola, it became a phenomenal hit in 1972, grossing more than $60 million and winning three Academy Awards. Puzo and Coppola collaborated on the script for *The Godfather, Part II*, and in 1974 that was also a hit movie. In 1974, Puzo co-wrote the script to *Earthquake*, the book *Las Vegas* in 1977, *Fools Die* in 1978, co-wrote the script to *Superman* in 1978 and *The Sicilian* in 1984. Writers out there struggling might note that Puzo was in his late forties when he made it big. Remember this in your moments of deep despair over your lack of creative success.

The Godfather is an insightful and penetrating look into the real nature of ethics and morality. It says something very disturbing about the values and traits of character needed to survive in a world that seems moral on the outside but is corrupt on the inside. If *The Godfather* is a "true" fiction depicting violent personal power without moral consequences, then *society* is in trouble, not the *artist*. He's only bringing us the bad news.

Puzo had the talent, and good fortune, to create a popular central character that was powerfully and genuinely *mythic* as an *American* phenomenon posed in an Italian American setting, history and ethos. The power of "Don Corleone" is transcendant of *all* other powers, whether human, legal or judicial, and it yields true justice above and beyond that which is moral on the outside but corrupt on the inside. This is pretty powerful stuff. To the dismay of Italian Americans however, this powerful myth is merged totally with the fascination our society has for evil and the Mafia.

Puzo succeeded in creating a phenomenon and, unwittingly, in creating a dilemma for Italian Americans. On the one hand, Italian Americans admire and respect his awesome creative and artistic power as a writer. Yet they are disturbed by the *romanticizing* of the Mafia, by the strong symbolic power of the *myth* and by the perpetuation of a *negative stereotype*. And the characters are so compellingly attractive! Of course, all Mario Puzo wanted to do was write a bestseller and tell a good story. Along the way he may have unexpectedly tapped into *the* phenomenon of the 20th century and *the* moral dilemma of our time.

By way of ending this chapter, we have especially discussed two quite remarkable phenomenons that transcend all boundaries, whether ethnic or otherwise. In the case of Mario Puzo, we have the phenomenon of power and corruption in America vis à vis the Mafia, and with Leo Buscaglia, we have the phenomenon of LOVE, Italian style. Each in his own way expresses a universalism and a primary humanism so quintessentially Italian American. Each has spread his message through the powerful use of words.

In the *end* was the word . . .

P.S.

Giovanni Schiavo was, unquestionably, the most diligent, devoted and dedicated writer, researcher, historian and publisher of the Italian American world. The man was truly remarkable for his tireless efforts in acquiring and disseminating knowledge and information on the Italian experience in America. Everyone who has written about the Italian American finds him or herself swallowed by his awesome sources of information. We have all benefitted from the toil of this man, and in his lifetime he was not properly recognized for his superb achievements. *Tante grazie*, Giovanni.